The history and description of
SYDNEY HARBOUR

The history and description of

SYDNEY HARBOUR

P. R. STEPHENSEN, BRIAN KENNEDY

REED

First published 1966
This edition 1980

A.H. & A.W. REED PTY LTD
53 Myoora Road, Terry Hills, Sydney
68-74 Kingsford-Smith Street, Wellington 3
11 Southampton Row, London
also at
Auckland and Christchurch

National Library of Australia
Cataloguing-in-Publication data:
Stephensen, Percy Reginald, 1901-1965.
 The history and description of Sydney Harbour.
 Rev.ed.
 Index
 ISBN 0 589 50243 3
 1. Sydney Region - History. 2. Sydney Harbour, New
 South Wales - History. I. Kennedy, Brian, joint author.
 II. Title.
994.4'1

Set by Davella Typesetters
Printed and bound by Kyodo-Shing Loong, Singapore

AUTHOR'S NOTE

THIS IS THE FIRST FULL-LENGTH BOOK ON SYDNEY HARBOUR THAT has ever been published. Many articles on special aspects of the Harbour have been printed in journals of learned societies, in professional and trade periodicals, and in popular magazines and newspapers; there have been references to the Harbour in many books of Australian history, biography, travel, and reminiscences; but, except for one short work, of tourist-guide scope, published ephemerally in the 1890s, there has been no attempt to offer to the public, in one handy volume, a comprehensive history and description of a Harbour that is acknowledged to be one of the best and most beautiful havens for ships anywhere in the world.

Authors and publishers of books, deterred perhaps by the extent of the task, and aware that there are critics who pounce too avidly on minor errors in factual writings, have avoided a responsibility which, in its achievement, may be considered by idealists or carping critics, to be inadequate. The present volume, then, is not claimed to be better than it should be, as a pioneering effort in its field. The fate of pioneers is to be surpassed: anyone who in the future may decide to write a better book on Sydney Harbour than this one will at least find the channels lit and buoyed.

The intention here is to offer, for general rather than for specialist information, a synoptic view of Sydney Harbour as a living entity with many aspects, each seen in its proportion to the whole; but, within the limits of the practicable, it is not feasible to describe in detail every minor topographical feature in 152 miles of shoreline, or to mention everything that has happened in 177 years of civilized settlement along those shores. Selection implies rejection, and, with it, decisions of emphasis. The author of a descriptive text may strive for the effects of a landscape painter rather than of a photographer. A camera may record everything within its range, but the human eye and mind select what is conceptually significant.

A complete history and description of Sydney Harbour, presented solely as factual documentation, in the manner of a gazetteer or a directory, would be at least ten times bigger than the present work, so immense is the amount of historical and descriptive material available; but the method of discourse adopted here, though systematic, is not that of a catalogue. Instead—on the suggestion of the publishers—the book has a narrative flow. The text tells of an inshore excursion around the Harbour, from the South Head along the southern shore to Parramatta, returning along the northern shore to the North Head, mentioning, in that narrative sequence, the most noticeable or otherwise important topographical features, landmarks, seamarks, and installations on the foreshores of that bright waterway, which, with its panoramas of sunlit headlands, coves, bays, islands, and channels, gleaming in its blendings of green and gold, flecked with tints of red, beneath a brilliant blue sky, has enchanted millions, yes millions, of visitors to, and residents of, Sydney, where civilized settlement in Australia began. (Bright scenes! William Vincent Wallace, composer of the operatic aria, "Scenes that are Brightest," lived in Sydney for two years, 1836-8, as a young man. . . .)

To assert, as some critics do, that factual writing, being "un-imaginative," is therefore "uncreative" and "non-literary," is merely to repeat an outworn dogma that has no valid place in the modern and pragmatic world. A street-directory is, in the literary sense, not a book, but "a thing in book's clothing"; but that is because it lacks style, rather than because it lacks "imagination."

In Australia, particularly, much of the best writing has been in deliberately local characterization of persons and places, based on facts, or on interpretations or even on the embroidering of facts, rather than on "pure imagination." A work that is chiefly descriptive or delineative in intention may nevertheless be classed as literary if it not only imparts information but also expresses ideas, or if it is written with some distinction of style, to give pleasure as art, or at least as entertainment.

The production of "factual literature"—not a contradiction in terms—has largely increased, and there are many signs that readers of books in the modern world expect to "learn something" from a book, and not merely to escape from the world of reality into a world of imagination, or of chimera. In this sense, regional descriptions and histories of Australian localities contribute to the building up of a national consciousness based on a continent that has many variations of climate and of scene, with a territorial range virtually from the Tropics to the Pole.

The Continent of Australia, far too big to be poured into the mould of one book, requires that its composite image should be presented in many books. In that aggregate, cumulatively build-ing the totality of the literature of Australia, imaginative and factual, each locality will have its due emphasis, based on its distinctive history and characteristics, as seen in the perspective of the whole. Not only the similarities, but also the differences, between Darwin and Hobart, Adelaide and Cooktown, Melbourne and the Ord, Sydney and Esperance, Perth and Wagga Wagga, Brisbane and Alice Springs, make up the Australian totality. Every place has its *spirit*, as the Ancient Greeks understood that term; and each place is different from every other place. The validity of enduring art is in the depiction of particulars, not of abstractions, provided that the particulars are selected and arranged in a convincing or pleasing design. If that is achieved, a factual book on Sydney Harbour, or on any other distinctive Australian vicinity, would belong integrally to the literature of Australia.

The story, if it may fairly be called such, of Sydney Harbour, as told in these pages, has been written, not as a thesis for a doctorate, but to be offered for sale for general information and for the preservation of lore. Its publication has not been subsi-dized by any governmental, academic, institutional, or commercial interest; it is only the enterprise of its publishers that has produced a vendible commodity for which there is a need, and therefore a demand, in the book market. To criticize it beyond that, or to find fault with it for not being what it does not pretend to be, would be unrealistic.

Whatever defects may be found in it by critics who expect perfection, this volume, while it remains the only one on its subject, must be considered as the standard work: and that is a heavy responsibility for the author, as an individual, to bear. Much of the lore of Sydney Harbour is traditional, and some is conjectural; in some aspects authorities differ; and much that has happened has been imperfectly recorded, or cannot be readily ascertained. Though care has been taken to make this volume accurate in its details, and proportioned in its parts to the whole, it must, as a pioneering effort, have its shortcomings. Any suggestions from kindly readers for improvements in the text will be carefully considered for inclusion in future editions.

P. R. Stephensen

P. R. Stephensen died suddenly on 28th May, 1965, before this book, which he considered to be his greatest literary achievement,was completed. Chapters 14 and 15 and Part II were supplied by Brian Kennedy, who would like to make the following acknowledgments.

A number of people have generously contributed information to this supplement. Among them are landscape architect and harbour enthusiast Allan Correy, whose wife, Jane, by coincidence, edited the original manuscript of Stephensen's book. Mrs E. Graham of the North Sydney Historical Society has also been of enormous help. Special thanks to Mrs Deborah Alexander for typing the manuscript, and also to Mrs Dorothy Norry.

Thanks also to Errol Lea Scarlett, archivist, St Ignatius College; D.C. Miller, Secretary, Geographical Names Board; J.A. Wierzbick, Marketing Services Manager, Public Transport Commission of New South Wales; Ray Hide, Assistant Manager, Manly Marineland; J. Ragan, Town Clerk, Leichhardt Council; Deputy Town Clerk, Ashfield; John Cookson, DJ's Properties, Drummoyne; Mrs Walters, Sydney City Librarian; T. Barratt, Superintendent, Sydney Harbour National Park; J.L. Gale, Secretary-Manager, Royal Prince Alfred Yacht Club; Michel Le Bars, General Manager, Cruising Yacht Club of Australia; Robert Bruce, Australian Heritage Commission; L.A.S. Johnson, Royal Botanic Gardens, Sydney; David Hooker, Water Wings; M.G. Park, Town Clerk, Mosman; David Brown, Publicity Manager, Sydney Opera House Trust; W. Phipson, Town Clerk, Hunters Hill; John Death, Public Relations Officer, Department of Transport, New South Wales; W.H. Robertson, Government Astronomer; D.A.W. Marshall, Homebush Abattoir Corporation; The New South Wales 18-ft Sailing Club; T.F. Gibson, General Manager, Ferry Services; Mrs Stephensen, Sydney Maritime Museum; Mrs Alice Doyle; Jack Kenny and the library staff at Australian Consolidated Press; Geoffrey Lee Martin, Public Relations Consultant, the Australian Gaslight Company; Mr Carter of Manly Fun Pier and Shark Aquarium; G.M. Kirby, Secretary of the Australian Sail Training Association; E. Moroney, Honorary Archivist, Hunters Hill Historical Society; Mary Kaye, Publications Officer, Taronga Zoo; L.P. Carter, Town Clerk, City of Sydney; Mrs Deidre Newton, Willoughby Library; the staff of the Stanton library; Jim Oliff, State Pollution Control Commission; "Macquarie University Student Project Environment Studies Program: Dobroyd Head Environment, June 1977"; M. Thistlethwayte; Alice Oppen, President, Sydney Harbour and Foreshores Committee; Owen Magee, Director, Sydney Cove Redevelopment Authority; John R. Pola, Consultant to Sydney Cove Redevelopment Authority; Valerie Lhuede; T. Desmond Dove, Deputy Town Clerk, Drummoyne; Town Clerk, Lane Cove; Brian Hughes, Maritime Services Board; Gwen Gordon and Jeanne McGlynn of the Manly-Warringah and Pittwater Historical Society; Mrs Hunt, Mosman Historical Society; Lane Cove 18-ft Sailing Skiff Club; Mrs Lorna Crowle; R.W. Mullins; Manly Yacht Club; A.S. Onorato, Royal Volunteer Coastal Patrol; Ian Hutchison, Manly 16-ft Sailing Club Ltd; Barrie N. Smart, Command Public Relations Officer, Navy Public Relations; Commanding Office, HMAS *Watson*; John Stapleton, Sydney Harbour National Park; Mrs Maisy Stapleton, Curator, Elizabeth Bay House.

CONTENTS

Part I Up to 1966.

I

THE GENERAL VIEW   SEE ALSO PART II

SYDNEY HARBOUR, ONE OF THE WORLD'S BIGGEST AND MOST RENOWNED
seaports, is an inlet of the Pacific Ocean, on the eastern coast of
the island continent of Australia. Situated in Lat. 33° 52′ S.,
Long. 151° 12′ E., and therefore within the temperate zone of the
Southern Hemisphere, it has a climate similar to that of the
Mediterranean or of Southern California. Except at its entrance
— nearly one mile wide between bold headlands — the Harbour
is landlocked, free of ocean swell, and protected by low sandstone
ridges from the malign force of gales. It seems almost perfectly
designed by Nature as a secure haven for vessels large and small.
Its expanse of sheltered tidal water is twenty-one square miles,
but it has so many indented inner bays and coves, separated from
one another by promontories, that its foreshores measure 152
miles within an east-to-west scope of fifteen miles.

The Harbour — officially named Port Jackson — has three
estuarine arms, which converge to meet in a Sound of deep water
immediately inside the ocean entrance at the Heads. Of these
three arms, North Harbour (in the lee of North Head), and
Middle Harbour (facing the entrance) are not used by large
ocean-going vessels. The Main Harbour is the southern arm, in
the lee of South Head, extending on an east-west stretch of fifteen
miles from Watson's Bay to Parramatta. This is a tidally flooded
valley formed originally by the confluence of two small freshwater streams, the Parramatta and Lane Cove Rivers. Whether
by volcanic subsidence in ancient times, or by the scouring of the
sandstone terrain for millenniums by tides and freshwater floods,
the result is a fjord-like basin — surrounded not by steep cliffs
but by the low wooded ridges and valleys of the Sydney
peneplain, which lies between the Blue Mountains (50 miles
inland) and the ocean shore.

The average width of the Main Harbour, between the promontories of its northern and southern shores, is one mile, allowing
ample sea-room at its entrance for two channels of navigation.
There is depth of water in these channels to accommodate
vessels of the largest size, as also at many anchorages, moorings,
and wharves on the reaches westwards for ten miles in from the
Heads. Navigation for smaller vessels extends for five miles
farther upstream than that, and also within the many secluded
coves along both shores of the Main Harbour and its arms.

In more than half the total area of the Harbour, there is a
depth of at least thirty feet at low tide. In most of the coves
there is navigable depth almost to the water's edge. The run of
the tides is moderate, having an average rise and fall of five feet. 11

The depth between the Heads at the ocean entrance is 80 feet, and, in the two approach channels within the Main Harbour, the depths are 42 feet and 40 feet respectively at low water. In the bays in which large vessels may anchor, or berth at moorings, or tie up at wharves, deep water extends close to the shore, which has enabled a large number of wharves and docks to be constructed without excessive costs for dredging or need for jetty-building. At most of the berths used by ocean-going vessels there is a minimum depth of 36 feet. The greatest depth within the Harbour is 155 feet.

Around the shores, fissured by this large expanse of sheltered water, are spread the city and suburban municipalities of Sydney, the oldest civilized settlement in Australia and capital of the State of New South Wales, with a population (in 1965) of 2⅓ million, widely scattered over a total municipal area of 670 square miles. Sydney is·an emporium and industrial city and mercantile seaport, the largest in Australia, visited on an average by 4,000 ocean-going mercantile vessels annually. It is also the biggest Naval Base in the Southern Hemisphere, and is the main fleet and support base of the Royal Australian Navy.

In the first twenty years of civilized settlement at Sydney (1788 to 1808), the Governors of New South Wales — Phillip, Hunter, King, and Bligh in succession — were all naval officers, and to that extent the foundation of Sydney was a naval operation, which preceded the mercantile development of the port. Ever since that time, and continuing to the present day, the character of Sydney Harbour as a naval base has been sustained, with large developments in modern times. Merchant shipping, which also had its origin in the earliest years of the port's history, has grown to a prodigious extent.

The populating of Australia by Europeans was, until the modern development of ocean-crossing air transport, entirely a maritime achievement. This was the biggest and longest-sustained migration of a folk over such great ocean distances ever known in history. Australia is 13,000 miles by sea from Europe by the route for sailing-vessels, in which, for the first hundred years, most of the passengers, mails, and cargo to and from Australia were carried. In those voyages the Port of Sydney was, as it remains to a considerable extent today, Australia's Front Door, and is likely to be even more greatly developed as such in future years, as seaborne trade increases between Australia and the many and populous other lands fringing and within the vast expanse of the Pacific Ocean.

The Main Harbour, spanned by the Sydney Harbour Bridge, five miles in from the Heads, is divided by that prominent landmark into the Upper Harbour (westward of the Bridge) and the Lower Harbour (eastward of the Bridge).

On the southern shore, in the vicinity of the Bridge, are the principal mercantile wharves and docks of the Port of Sydney, but these also extend upstream on both shores in the Upper Harbour at intervals over a stretch of another five miles. The western part of the Harbour and its arms are crossed by several bridges for road and rail traffic, which were in use long before the big Harbour Bridge was opened in 1932.

The naval installations, with the large naval dockyard at Garden Island, and various other naval establishments, are situated principally on the Lower Harbour, to the eastward of the Bridge, but there are some naval establishments also in the Upper Harbour, where shipbuilding yards, and other industrial manufacturing activities on the waterfront, are chiefly developed.

The commercial trading centres of the twin cities of Sydney and North Sydney are concentrated near the principal wharves and docks in the vicinity of the Harbour Bridge. The residential suburbs extend along both shores of the Lower Harbour, Middle Harbour, and North Harbour, to the external ocean beaches, but there are also populous Western Suburbs along the Upper Harbour, including those on the shores of the Parramatta and Lane Cove Rivers.

Within both the Lower and Upper Harbours are some islands, of comparatively small area, but there are no reefs or banks in the Main Harbour presenting any serious obstruction to navigation. The Sow and Pigs Reef, near the entrance to the Main Harbour, is the only shoal in the Harbour's navigational reaches for large vessels. It is well marked and well lit.

Very little silt is deposited in the Harbour by its freshwater tributaries, which are few and small. The main run off from the Blue Mountains and from the coastal peneplain is carried to the ocean by the Hawkesbury River, which debouches at Broken Bay, sixteen miles to the north of Sydney Heads, and thus serves, as though designed by Nature, to divert silt from Sydney Harbour. There was originally a sandbar, with 20 feet clearance, the detritus of aeons, inside the entrance to Sydney Harbour, but this has long ago been dredged, and does not build up to any perceptible extent. There is in the Port of Sydney virtually no navigational problem of the shifting sandbanks or mudbanks or shoalwater which occur in ports at the mouths of large freshwater rivers, or in shallow estuarine basins.

Several of the headlands, and other parts of the Harbour shores, are naval or military or public recreational reserves — some covered with trees and shrubs preserving the character of the original landscape, and some developed as parks with grassy swards and exotic and native trees. These reserves and parks make striking contrast with the "built-on" parts of the shore. Among them are Bradley's Head and the Taronga Park Zoological Gardens on the northern shore of the lower Harbour, and the Botanic Gardens and Domain at Farm Cove on the southern shore.

Characteristic of the life of the Harbour is the busy coming and going of ferry-steamers, conveying passengers to and from the northern suburbs and the ferry-terminal at Sydney Cove. Another feature of the brilliant scene on the sparkling sunlit waters, in the clear weather that prevails at Sydney in most months of the year, is the large number of yachts which picturesquely spread their sails, especially on Lower Harbour and on

Middle Harbour.

Small power-driven vessels, too, are prominent in the ever-moving pageant of the Harbour's life. These include naval launches, customs and police launches, pilot-vessels, and tugs, besides pleasure-cruisers, fishing-vessels, lighters, and barges. Sydney's temperate climate, with many "blue-and-gold" days, a long summer and a mild winter — in which snow, frost, and ice are unknown, and gales are few and of short duration — provides the incomparable setting for harbour scenes that are world renowned for their beauty and variety.

The plan of this book is to describe the Harbour systematically, beginning at the South Head, and proceeding westwards along the southern shore to the head of navigation near Parramatta; thence returning eastwards along the northern shore to Middle Harbour, North Harbour, and North Head. In that progress along 152 miles of indented shoreline, the headlands, bays, and islands will be described in sequence, with their chief historical associations and present-day aspects.

The name "Sydney Harbour," in common usage, refers to all the waters inside the Heads, and is accordingly so used in the title and text of this book; but the official designation of those waters is "Port Jackson." Definitions in the Admiralty Sailing Directions are as follows:

"Port Jackson is the name given to all the whole of the waters within an imaginary line drawn from Outer North Head to Inner South Head.

"Sydney Harbour is the name given to all Port Jackson except North and Middle Harbour.

"The limits of the Port of Sydney are defined as all the area westward of an imaginary line joining Inner South Head and Middle Head."

In this present volume, the name "Sydney Harbour" covers "Port Jackson" as defined in the Admiralty Sailing Directions. The term "Main Harbour" is here applied, for purposes of description only, to the limited area defined in the Admiralty Sailing Directions as "the Port of Sydney."

The illustrations and the index may enable the reader more readily to follow the unfolding story of this grand waterway on the shores of which civilization in Australia began, and has matured.

2

SOUTH HEAD

THE SOUTH HEAD IS A GENERAL TERM FOR A PROMONTORY, THREE miles long, terminating in a peninsula named Inner South Head, which marks the southern side of the ocean entrance to Sydney Harbour. This promontory is a sandstone ridge, averaging 200 feet above sea-level, and varying in width from one mile at its base to a quarter of a mile at the peninsula. Its eastern shore, facing the ocean, is an escarpment of sandstone cliffs, which receives at its foot the battering of the breakers rolling in from the wide Pacific. This scarp rises sheer out of deep water, with soundings of from ten to twenty fathoms close inshore.

Here the ocean abruptly meets the land, with no shelf of shallows to reduce the impact of the surf. The cliffs are grandly beautiful as sighted from seaward, especially so to the home-coming sailor. They are a landmark for vessels on courses from the southward or eastward, bearing up for the entrance.

In contrast, on the western shore of the South Head promontory, within the Harbour, the ridge slopes to placid bays with sandy beaches. These bays, named in succession southwards from Inner South Head, are Lady Bay, Camp Cove, Watson's Bay, Parsley Bay, Vaucluse Bay, Shark Bay, Hermit Bay, and Rose Bay. In the offing of Camp Cove, within the Harbour, dividing the approach to the port into two channels, is the Sow and Pigs Reef, and between the headlands of Rose Bay is Shark Island, clear of the main channel.

The South Head promontory is a massive breakwater in Nature's design of the Port of Sydney. It breaks the force of the ocean's seas and of the ocean's swell, and of easterly gales, to shelter the Main Harbour. A vessel entering the port, on a westerly course between the Heads, rounds Inner South Head on reaching the Sound, where she alters course and proceeds to the southward for two and a half miles, passing immediately into the lee of the land, in waters free of ocean swell and steep seas. She again alters course, to proceed upstream westward, by rounding Bradley's Head, with the massive bulk of the South Head promontory astern. The transit from open ocean to sheltered water, on this course with two turns, each of approximately 90 degrees, is sudden and spectacular, revealing the vistas of the large land-locked haven.

The South Head promontory is not only the southern bulwark of Sydney Harbour against the fury of the ocean's tempests, but is also one of its bastions of naval and military defence. The Macquarie Lighthouse, on the summit of the cliff near Outer South Head, and the Hornby Light, at the peninsular tip of the

15

promontory on Inner South Head, give mariners their bearings for the entrance at night. The naval and military installations on Inner South Head, in conjunction with other artillery garrison posts on Middle Head and North Head, have provided a strong coastal defence against prospective enemy raids or intrusions.

On Outer South Head — a protuberance of the cliff a mile to the southward of Inner South Head — is the Signal Station, from which, in the earlier years of Sydney's history, flag and semaphore signals announced the arrival of vessels. From there, nowadays, maritime movements are observed and reported by radio and telephone signals to the port authorities.

Midway between Outer South Head and Inner South Head, on the seaward side, the cliff face is fissured at The Gap, where the peninsula narrows to less than a quarter of a mile, as though the ocean had almost succeeded here in its attempt to breach the land's ramparts with a large bite. The views from the cliff-top at The Gap are superb: eastwards to the horizon of the open ocean; westwards to the spread panorama of the Main Harbour; northwards across the water to the bold bluff of North Head; and southwards along the cliffs for three miles to Ben Buckler, one of the two crescent horns of Bondi Bay and Beach.

Though the cliffy headlands are a plain landmark at the entrance to Sydney Harbour, there have been mishaps in making port, here, as at other ports, especially in the days of sail, when vessels, under no other propulsion than that of the winds, approached the shore. During a storm the full-rigged sailing ship *Dunbar* ran ashore and was wrecked at The Gap, with heavy loss of life, in 1857. She was bearing up for the Harbour entrance — so near and yet so far — after a passage from England. This tragedy gave The Gap a sinister reputation; and gradually it became almost a tradition at Sydney for persons intending to commit suicide to leap over the edge of the cliff there. Deeds of heroism have been performed by the men of the Police Cliff Rescue Squad who have saved many lives.

Pilotage of merchant vessels entering, leaving, or moving within Sydney Harbour is compulsory. The Maritime Services Board of New South Wales maintains a pilot station at Watson's Bay, in the shelter of Inner South Head.

THE NAMING OF PORT JACKSON

On 1st April, 1770, H.M. Barque *Endeavour*, 368 tons burthen, 22 guns, commanded by Lieutenant James Cook, R.N., with a ship's company of 94, including the scientists Joseph Banks and Daniel Solander, shaped course from Cape Farewell in New Zealand, with the intention, as Cook noted, "to steer to the westward until we fall in with the E. coast of New Holland, and then to proceed along that shore to its northern extremity."

Cook did not "discover Australia," as is sometimes asserted, but he was certainly the first European navigator to make a running chart of our continent's previously uncharted and unexplored eastern coast. He crossed the Tasman Sea in nineteen days, and sighted land at Point Hicks (near the present-day border of New South Wales and Victoria). Then, coasting to the northward, he entered on 29th April and anchored for eight days in a large bay which he named Stingray Harbour. This name he subsequently altered to Botany Bay, because of "the great quantity of new plants etc. Mr Banks and Dr Solander collected in this place."

On Sunday, 6th May, 1770, Cook's journal continued: "Having seen everything this place [Botany Bay] afforded, we at daylight in the morning weighed [anchor] with a light breeze at N.W. and put to sea, and the wind soon after coming to the southward, we steered along shore N.N.E. At noon we were by observation in the Latitude of 30° 50′ S., about 2 or 3 miles from the land and abreast of a Bay or Harbour wherein there appeared to be safe anchorage which I called *Port Jackson*. It lies 3 leagues to the northward of Botany Bay."

In that nonchalant manner, the sturdy Yorkshire seaman and great navigator recorded the first sighting by Europeans of Sydney Harbour. He did not enter it. From seaward, "2 or 3 miles from the land," he could have sighted only the entrance between North and South Heads, and the opening to Middle Harbour beyond. His observation of the Latitude was at fault, but that was not surprising, as his instruments — judged by present-day standards — were primitive.

Running before a southerly breeze, the *Endeavour* was evidently a slow sailer, or the breeze was very light, as it took her six hours to sail approximately ten miles from Botany Bay to Port Jackson. His estimate of the distance ("3 leagues") was accurate, a "league" being approximately three miles. He wisely stood well offshore, clear of the cliffs.

Cook had little more than a glimpse of the entrance to Port Jackson, but his remarkable nautical knowledge and intuition enabled him to judge that it appeared to offer a "safe anchorage" — so much so that he conferred upon it the name of Sir George Jackson, one of the Secretaries of the Admiralty, who could not have known until many years later what a great honour that would prove to be. He lived to the grand old age of ninety-three years.

Having thus passed by, Cook sailed along the shore to the northwards, and in the afternoon passed and named Broken Bay (the mouth of the Hawkesbury River). He did not know the magnitude of the discovery that he had made at "Port Jackson," but that terse entry, in his journal of 6th May, 1770, was to have a sequel, nearly eighteen years later, in the full discovery and exploration of the port.

CAPTAIN PHILLIP'S DISCOVERY

Britain's loss of the American colonies in 1776 was the chief reason for the decision taken by the British Government in 1786 to form a colony in New South Wales — the somewhat incongruous name that had been given, in published narratives of Cook's voyage, to the eastern shore of the island continent which Dutch navigators in the previous century had named "New Holland." It was decided that the colony to be formed in New South Wales should be a place of exile for convicts, who could no longer be sent, as previously, to the American colonies.

In August 1786, Britain's Secretary of State for Home Affairs and the Colonies, Lord Sydney, asked the Admiralty to provide escort for a fleet of transports to convey prisoners of the Crown to Botany Bay, and naval guard for a settlement to be formed in that vicinity. The command of this expedition was given to Captain Arthur Phillip, R.N., who was also appointed as Governor Designate of the intended Colony of New South Wales. His second-in-command was Captain John Hunter, R.N.

The "First Fleet" — as it is known in Australian history — assembled off the Isle of Wight, and put to sea on 12th May, 1787. It consisted of nine chartered merchant vessels conveying convicts and stores, escorted by two naval vessels, H.M.S. *Sirius* (520 tons) and H.M.S. *Supply* (an armed tender, 170 tons).

The passage to Botany Bay, a distance of 15,000 miles by the route sailed, with calls at Tenerife, Rio de Janeiro, and Capetown, and rounding the South Cape of Van Diemen's Land (Tasmania), took eight months. All the eleven vessels lay safely at anchor in Botany Bay on 19th January, 1788.

Captain Phillip quickly decided that Botany Bay was an unsuitable place for a settlement. The official account of his voyage, published in London in 1789, stated: "The openness of this bay and the dampness of the soil, by which the people would probably be rendered unhealthy, had already determined the Governor to seek another situation. He resolved therefore to examine Port Jackson, a bay mentioned by Captain Cook as immediately to the north of this. There he hoped to find, not only a better harbour, but a fitter place for the establishment of his new government."

Speed was essential in determining where the people should be disembarked, as many of them were in poor health after the long passage. Phillip therefore decided to explore Port Jackson without delay, and for that purpose to make a trip there with an exploring party in three pinnaces (open boats with sails and oars), accompanied by Captain Hunter and by the Sailing-Masters (navigating officers) of *Sirius* and *Supply*, James Keltie and David Blackburn, with a party of seamen to man the boats, and a guard of Royal Marines under command of a Captain of Marines, David Collins, who was to preside over the Law Courts in the colony. The reason for taking three boats was to complete the survey quickly "by examining several parts of the harbour at once."

The official narrative continues: "On the 21st of January, they set out [from Botany Bay] upon this expedition and early in the afternoon arrived at Port Jackson, which is distant about three leagues. Here all regret arising from the former disappointment [at Botany Bay] was at once obliterated, and Governor Phillip had the satisfaction to find one of the finest harbours in the world, in which a thousand sail of the line might ride in perfect security."

Those three naval pinnaces were the first European vessels to enter Sydney Harbour. They rounded Inner South Head, and were beached in its lee in a bay to which the name of Camp Cove was given, because the party made camp there for two nights as a base for the boat explorations within the Harbour.

The official report stated: "The different coves of the harbour were examined with all possible expedition, and the preference [as site for a settlement] was given to one which had the finest spring of [fresh] water, and in which ships can anchor so close to the shore that at very small expense quays may be constructed where the largest vessels may unload. . . . In honour of Lord Sydney, the Governor distinguished it by the name of *Sydney Cove.*"

That decision taken, "On the 24th January, Governor Phillip, having sufficiently explored Port Jackson and found it in all respects highly calculated to receive such a settlement as he was appointed to establish, returned to Botany Bay. . . . It was impossible after this to hesitate concerning the choice of a situation. Orders were accordingly given for the removal [of the fleet from Botany Bay to Sydney Cove]."

On the very next day, 25th January, Phillip sailed from Botany Bay in the naval tender, H.M.S. *Supply* (commanded by Lieutenant Ball, R.N.), and anchored overnight at Sydney Cove, to await the arrival of the other vessels of the fleet. This naval sloop was the first ocean-crossing decked vessel to enter Sydney Harbour — a notable event in nautical history. "The rest of the fleet, under convoy of the *Sirius*, was ordered to follow . . . On the 26th, the transports and store ships, attended by the *Sirius*, finally evacuated Botany Bay, and in a very short time they were all assembled in Sydney Cove, the place now destined for their port, and for the reception of the new settlement."

Aboard the *Sirius* was Surgeon John White, R.N., Surgeon-General to the fleet and to the settlement, who, in his *Journal of a Voyage to New South Wales,* published in London in 1790, stated his impressions of the Harbour: "Port Jackson, I believe to be, without exception, the finest and most extensive harbour in the Universe, and at the same time the most secure, being safe from all the winds that blow." He added that the Harbour "would afford sufficient anchorage for all the navies of Europe."

Captain Collins of the Marines, in his *Account of the English Colony in New South Wales,* published in London in 1798, referred to "this noble and capacious harbour, equal if not superior to any yet known in the world." Another officer of the Marines, Captain Watkin Tench, in his *Narrative of the Expedition to Botany Bay,* published in London in 1789, described the Harbour as "a port superior, in extent and excellency, to all we had seen before."

These superlatives from officers of the First Fleet were all the more remarkable as the Fleet had called at the famed harbour of

Rio de Janeiro on the passage out. Some allowance may be made for enthusiasm at the end of a long and tedious passage, but these officers of the Navy and of the Marines were men of wide nautical experience, who had been in many ports, and had no reason to exaggerate in statements which they allowed to be printed and published. The conclusion must be that they believed what they said, and had good reasons for their enthusiasm.

Within a few days after the settlers had landed at Sydney Cove, Captain Hunter, accompanied by Lieutenant Bradley, R.N., and Sailing-Master Keltie, with a boat party, began the systematic charting and sounding of the Harbour, and prepared sailing-directions for entering it. It appears that it was Hunter who conferred the name of the Sow and Pigs on the partly submerged rocky shoal, near the entrance, which was the only serious hazard to navigation.

In those days when steam propulsion had not been invented, a vessel entering a harbour had to proceed under sail to her anchorage or berth, perhaps making tacks or beating to windward — always a difficulty in narrow waters, and especially inside ports. The soundings taken by Hunter in the Harbour revealed that it gave ample room to sailing-vessels for manoeuvre. This was one of the advantages which, to men trained in sail, made this Harbour seem superior to any other in the world. There was room and depth within it for working even the largest sailing-vessels of the time easily to a safe anchorage in any weather.

In his terse and matter-of-fact style, Hunter's praise of the Harbour was strictly practical. He stated: "After passing the Sow and Pigs, you may take what part of the channel you please, and anchor where you like." Very few other harbours in the world could offer sea-captains that invitation.

SEE ALSO PART II   THE SIGNAL STATION

After the pioneer settlers had been landed at Sydney Cove, the nine chartered transports sailed away, three of them bound for China, and the others to return to England. The two warships remained on the station. Both were used subsequently to convey parties to establish a sub-colony on Norfolk Island. The *Sirius* in October 1788 went to Capetown for provisions, returning to Sydney in May 1789. She was wrecked at Norfolk Island in March 1790.

Approximately one thousand people had been landed at Sydney Cove — men, women, and children, including the officials, the Marine guard, and the convicts, together with stores and some livestock. When the transports had departed, the pioneer settlers, suffering from a shortage of provisions, were isolated "at the uttermost extremity of the Globe." Eagerly they awaited the vessels bringing more provisions, and "news from Home."

A "Second Fleet" was expected, but it did not arrive until June 1790, nearly two and a half years after the arrival of the First Fleet. At an early stage, Governor Phillip must have realized that it would be an advantage to have a lookout stationed on South Head, to signal the arrival of vessels, but he was faced with so many difficulties in establishing the settlement at Sydney Cove that it was not until January 1790 that a signal station was set up at the Harbour's ocean entrance. Then a flagstaff was erected on South Head, and huts were built for a naval party from H.M.S. *Sirius*. After a few weeks, this station was left in charge of Daniel Southwell, Master's Mate of the *Sirius*, and a gunner. The flagstaff was visible from the Observatory that had been constructed on the rocky ridge at Dawes Point, on the western side of Sydney Cove.

The signallers had a lonely life, scanning the ocean in vain, day after day, for sight of a sail. They were supplied and relieved at intervals by a boat from the settlement, five miles distant by water, until, at a date not ascertained, a foot-track was opened for communication by land on the route later to be cleared for the Old South Head Road, a distance of eight miles.

The flag signal was hoisted for the first time on 10th February, 1790 — but this was only to announce the return of the sloop *Supply* from Norfolk Island.

Day after day went by with no further signal. Then, at last, as Watkin Tench records, "On the evening of the 3rd June, 1790, the joyful cry of 'the flag's up' resounded in every direction. . . . I instantly ran to a hill and seized a telescope in the Observatory. A brother officer was with me: but we could not speak; we wrung each other by the hand, with eyes and hearts overflowing."

That signal announced the arrival of the transport *Lady Juliana*, the vanguard of the five vessels of the Second Fleet, the others of which arrived on 20th, 26th, and 28th June, bringing provisions and mails and approximately one thousand additional convicts, male and female, many of them seriously ill from scurvy due to malnutrition. Such were the "teething troubles" of the infant settlement of Sydney, but stout hearts and the bounty of Australia enabled that infant to grow to sturdy maturity.

After the arrival of the Second Fleet, the number of ships visiting Sydney steadily increased. These included naval vessels, convict transports and storeships, mercantile trading vessels, and whaling and sealing vessels, British and American. The first foreign-owned trading vessel to enter Sydney Harbour was the American brigantine *Philadelphia*, on 1st November, 1792.

The Signal Station at South Head has been continually manned from January 1790, to the present day. At some date not ascertained it ceased to be a naval responsibility and was taken over by the civilian authorities, probably in connection with pilotage.

Semaphore replaced flag-signalling in the 1840s, when the building at present in use was erected, but the outstanding development occurred on 26th January, 1858, when the 70th anniversary of settlement was marked by the opening of the first electric telegraph line in New South Wales, connecting the Signal Station at South Head with the Royal Exchange, at Bridge Street in the city.

Since 1936, the Signal Station has been controlled by the Maritime Services Board of New South Wales, which was constituted in that year as successor to the Sydney Harbour Trust and the New South Wales Department of Navigation. The control of shipping within the Harbour is the responsibility of the State and not of the Federal Government.

At the head offices of the Maritime Services Board, on the western shore of Sydney Cove, a modern communications centre operates by radio-telephone, and by the normal telephone network, in contact with the Signal Station and with the pilot vessels, tugs, and other vessels and services attending to the arrival, departure, berthing, and movements of shipping. By this medium, the pilotage and other services are integrated with the work of the Signal Master and his staff at South Head. As all sea-going vessels on long-distance routes are equipped with radio, the expected time of arrival of a vessel inward bound is known at the Signal Station long before she comes into sight; but visual observation remains essential for checking and reporting her actual arrival in the offing, and other incidents within the horizon outside the Heads, which occasionally include visual distress signals from small craft such as yachts, launches, and fishing-boats not equipped with radio.

THE OLD SOUTH HEAD ROAD

Major-General Lachlan Macquarie — he was promoted to that rank in 1811 — was Governor of New South Wales for nearly twelve years, from 1st January, 1810 to 1st December, 1821. During his term of office the population of the Colony was trebled, increasing from 10,000 to 30,000. Land settlement was extended far to the westward beyond the Blue Mountains and southward to the Murrumbidgee River. In this period of expansion, the Port of Sydney developed its character as an emporium, exporting chiefly wool, tallow, hides, and timber, and importing manufactured goods. Sydney Town was enhanced by the erection of many fine public and mercantile buildings; its streets were formed and extended; and roads for wheeled vehicles were constructed far into the interior of the Colony, enabling produce and merchandise to be transported in drays and wagons to and from the port.

The first road built to the order of "Macquarie the Builder" was from Sydney Town to South Head. This road was made, not by convicts, but by twenty-one soldiers of the 73rd Regiment (the Highlanders) of which Macquarie was commander-in-chief. They were garrison troops, stationed at Sydney. The expense of building the road was met not from public funds but by subscription of the merchants and other citizens of Sydney.

By enlarging a previously used foot track or bridle path, the road was formed for horse-drawn vehicles along the crests of ridges, avoiding the swamps near the foreshores of the Harbour. This is the route nowadays known as the Old South Head Road, eight miles long from Hyde Park in the city to Watson's Bay. A monument at its terminus at Watson's Bay states that the road was "compleated in ten weeks from 25 March, 1811."

The chief reason for building the Old South Head Road was to enable official and commercial messengers, newspaper reporters, and other people from Sydney to drive or ride out to meet incoming vessels, which usually anchored in Watson's Bay for inspection of papers and to await berths alongside city wharves, or favourable breezes, before sailing up the Harbour. This practice enabled mails to be landed there, and information of a vessel's passengers and cargo to reach Sydney a few hours, sometimes a few days, before the vessel berthed at the city wharves.

Even a few hours gained was important to people who were eagerly awaiting news from England, or consignments of merchandise, or perhaps the arrival of relatives or friends. Whenever the signal flag was raised at South Head, indicating that an incoming vessel was in the offing, a procession of horseback riders, gigs, and carriages set out from the city, as fast as the horses could go, most of them arriving at Watson's Bay in time to greet the vessel when she anchored. The news that she brought from "Home" (England) was at least four months old, since only the speediest sailing-vessels of that period could make the outward passage in that time, and many of them took five or six months. Nevertheless, that news of bygone events was mental nourishment for the colonists, one of whom, Barron Field, declared, in a little book of verse published at Sydney in 1819: "A ship's the only poetry we see."

The thronging of the Old South Head Road by cavalcades of welcome to ships continued to be a feature of Sydney life at least until 1858, when the opening of intercolonial overland telegraph lines enabled news brought by ships to be flashed electrically from Adelaide or Melbourne to Sydney a week or more earlier than it could have reached Sydney by sea. Not until 1872 was Australia linked by undersea electric cable with Europe, thus enabling the news of the world, and commercial and personal messages, to overtake the time-lag that had been characteristic of Australian life in the first eighty-four years of colonial settlement.

As steam gradually replaced sail in the ocean conveyance of passengers and mails — especially after the opening of the Suez Canal in 1869 — the Old South Head Road ceased to be Sydney's news-route. Steamers usually proceeded up-harbour to berths, without anchoring in Watson's Bay. Today the Old South Head Road, and the New South Head Road (constructed along the foreshores in the 1840s), serve as arteries of traffic for the residential suburbs of the Municipality of Woollahra, which includes the South Head promontory. The two roads converge at Watson's Bay, eight miles from Sydney by the Old South Head Road, and seven miles by the New South Head Road.

THE MACQUARIE LIGHT

The first known reference to a light at South Head is a remark by Collins, dated 15th January, 1793, that the arrival of a ship after dark was signalled by the lighting of a large fire. This would serve not only as a signal of the vessel's approach, but also as a beacon to enable the shipmaster to take bearings of the land. Masters of sailing-vessels arriving off a port at night-time would usually remain in the offing until dawn before attempting to enter.

In 1794, an iron basket was erected on a tripod at South Head, and a fire lit in it every night. This would be sighted by shipmasters and recognized as a beacon, and not as an accidental blaze or campfire. That system of lighting the South Head by a bonfire beacon continued until the Macquarie Tower was built.

Governor Macquarie in 1816 instructed the convict architect, Francis Greenway, to draw the plans of what was to be the first lighthouse in Australia. A strikingly beautiful but simple and classical design was produced by Greenway. A brass plate that is still preserved records: "The Foundation Stone of this Building, destined to the double purpose of a LIGHT and GUARDHOUSE, was laid by His Excellency, Govr Macquarie on the 11 day of July 1816."

The site was near the edge of the cliff, adjacent to the Signal Station at Outer South Head, one mile from the tip of the peninsula at Inner South Head. This site is the highest point on the South Head ridge, 277 feet above sea-level. The tower was 76 feet high, and the lamp was visible 24 miles to seaward. At the base of the tower were two wings surmounted by domes which gave the whole structure its appearance of beautifully balanced design. Macquarie was evidently expecting adverse criticism of his expenditure on a light-tower adorned in that way, when he insisted that the building was intended for the double purpose of a lighthouse and military guardhouse.

The work of construction was completed within seventeen months. On 16th December, 1817, Macquarie and his wife, with a party of friends, drove out at dawn, "to view this noble, magnificent edifice," (as the Governor noted in his diary) and to take breakfast there. The Governor noted further: "This being an auspicious day, I presented the Government Architect, Mr Greenway, his emancipation [pardon] this day, it being delivered to him at Macquarie Tower this morning before breakfast."

The architect could then take his seat at the table with the vice-regal party, a free man — and he had well earned his freedom and his breakfast. A brass plate affixed to the west wall stated: "This building, intended for the double purpose of a lighthouse and barrack, is named Macquarie Tower, in honour of the founder. The work was commenced in 1816 and completed in 1817. L. Macquarie Esq., Governor."

The oil-lamp and lens were installed in 1818. To pay the expenses of maintaining the light, all vessels entering the Harbour (other than those locally registered) were charged dues at the rate of twopence per ton of their gross tonnage.

The first Lightkeeper was Robert Watson, who had arrived in the colony thirty years previously as quartermaster in H.M.S. *Sirius*, escort vessel of the First Fleet. He had been appointed Harbourmaster in 1811, and Watson's Bay was named in his honour, but he had been dismissed from that position in November 1816, for "stealing a quantity of canvas."

Evidently Governor Macquarie took pity on the elderly ex-Harbourmaster when he appointed him the Lightkeeper, but Watson died after holding that position for only a year.

The original lighthouse stood for 65 years. In 1880, as its stonework was deteriorating, the Government decided to build a new lighthouse alongside it, of the same design, but 85 feet high instead of 76 feet, and equipped with electric light. This work was begun on 1st March, 1880, when the Premier, Sir Henry Parkes, laid the foundation stone and delivered an oration. He pointed out that shipping in Sydney Harbour had increased from 34,000 tons in 1816 to 2½ million tons in 1879. Referring to the Government's decision to build the new lighthouse, Parkes declared, "We set an example of enlightened enterprise in this, as in every other walk of life," and went on to quote Longfellow's poem, *The Lighthouse*:

> *Steadfast, serene, immovable, the same*
> *Year after year, through all the silent night,*
> *Burns on for evermore that quenchless flame,*
> *Shines on that inextinguishable light.*

The original lighthouse continued in service until the new lighthouse was opened on 1st June, 1883, and the old one was then demolished. The electric light proved unsatisfactory, and for a time a kerosene light was used. The modern electric-lighting plant was installed in 1933, and its character has not been changed since then.

The lighthouse, which stands in five acres of grounds, has been maintained since 1915 by the Australian Federal Government, which is responsible for coastal lighting and navigation outside harbours: there are 21 coastal lights in New South Wales, controlled by the Marine Branch of the Department of Shipping and Transport. As most of the operation of a modern lighthouse is mechanically automatic, the maintenance of the Macquarie Light is the responsibility of an officer of the lighthouse mechanical staff.

The light is of 1,140,000 candlepower. At a focal height of 344 feet above sea-level, it has a geographical range of 25 miles in clear weather. The lens is of the Fourth Order Fresnel, 250 mm. focal radius. The lantern is equipped with two 1,000-watt bulbs (one in use and one in reserve), with electric current from the public supply. In the event of failure of that supply, there is a standby diesel electric generator, and a further standby of acetylene gas installation. Mechanical defects of any kind cause an alarm-bell to ring in the lightkeeper's quarters. The light is manually switched on a quarter of an hour before sunset and switched off a quarter of an hour after sunrise.

The lantern revolves, powered by a small electric motor. It is a group flashing light, giving two flashes every ten seconds, in the sequence .3 seconds flash then 1.7 seconds dark then .3 seconds flash then 7.7 seconds dark.

The light is visible at its full candlepower from 204° through westward to 359°, covering all the ocean approaches to Port Jackson, and with a greatly reduced candlepower within the port. The occultation and the reduced beam are effected by steel shutters in the curved plateglass surround of the lantern.

A spiral stairway of 100 fretted cast-iron steps inside the tower leads to the lantern-room, which has also an external balcony. Visitors are restricted to Wednesday afternoons, with permits obtainable on application to the Marine Branch of the Department of Shipping and Transport. The signatures of all visitors since 1880 are preserved in the Visitors' Books, kept with other historical material in a room at the base of the tower.

Many lighthouses are difficult of access, standing on lonely headlands or islands; but this one is alongside a main road within the boundaries of a great city. In the beauty and effectiveness of its site, and its graceful architectural design, the Macquarie Light is one of the world's most notable beacons, and worthy of the Harbour that it irradiates.

THE PILOTS

In May, 1792, Collins noted: "A fishery was established at the South Head, under the direction of one Barton, who had formerly been a pilot, and was to board all ships coming into the harbour and pilot them to the settlement."

From this it may be assumed that Barton and a boat's crew camped — probably at Camp Cove — and occupied their time in fishing from a boat in or near the entrance to the Harbour, in readiness to go outside and meet incoming vessels on signals from the Signal Station. The pilotage fee was a matter of bargaining between the pilot and the shipmaster, as a private enterprise and not for government revenue.

According to another tradition, the first pilot at Port Jackson was Henry Hacking, who had arrived as a quartermaster in H.M.S. *Sirius* with the First Fleet in 1788. He had made a minor reputation as an inland explorer on game-shooting expeditions, and had discovered a sea-inlet south of Botany Bay which was named, in his honour, Port Hacking. In a letter written to Governor King in 1803, David Collins, who had left Sydney in 1796, mentioned Hacking's "to me, well-known abilities as a pilot."

Hacking was convicted at Sydney in 1803 of stealing running-gear from H.M.S. *Investigator*, the vessel in which Commander Matthew Flinders, R.N., had in the previous year discovered the shore of South Australia and had charted the Gulf of Carpentaria. She had been condemned as unseaworthy, and was lying at moorings. Hacking was sent to Van Diemen's Land, where Collins appointed him as the first pilot of the port of Hobart.

In September, 1800, Captain P.G. King, R.N., took office as Governor of New South Wales, in succession to Captain John Hunter, R.N. One of Governor King's first edicts, on 10th October, 1800, was to establish harbour dues, for the purpose of raising funds to maintain an orphanage in a house at the corner of George and Bridge Streets (site of the present-day Anchor House). This was the beginning of a stricter governmental control of ships entering the harbour.

A notice in the *Sydney Gazette*, 29th May, 1803, announced the appointment of William Bowen as Harbour Pilot. He had been First Mate in H.M.S. *Lady Nelson* on the discovery of Port Phillip in January 1802, and on that occasion had been in charge of the boat that explored ahead of the *Lady Nelson* to take soundings at the entrance to that previously uncharted port. Bowen continued to act as pilot at Sydney for seven years, until his death in 1810, when an announcement in the *Sydney Gazette* stated that his successor was Alexander Mason, formerly Mate of the ship *Speke*.

In August, 1811, Governor Macquarie appointed Robert Watson as Harbourmaster, at a salary of £50 per annum. Watson acted also as a pilot. A notice in the *Gazette* of 10th December, 1814, stated, "The Governor has been pleased to appoint Mr Robert Murray to be Pilot in Port Jackson, in the room of Mr Robert Watson who has resigned that situation."

All these pilots of the early period in the Harbour's history lived in huts at Camp Cove or Watson's Bay. They maintained their own boats and crews, and charged whatever they could get by bargaining with shipmasters, who had the option of "sailing up" without a pilot if they considered the fee excessive.

In September, 1813, rates of pilotage were gazetted for the first time. The charges allowed were £4 for vessels under seven feet draught, thence progressively to £14 for vessels of twenty feet draught, and £15 for vessels exceeding twenty feet draught. Non-British vessels were charged one-quarter more. These fees allowed for the pilot to be aboard for up to three days, after which he could charge eight shillings per day detention money. That proviso indicated a procedure of bringing vessels to a first anchorage at Watson's Bay — for official inspection, and to discharge mails, disembark some passengers, and transact some business with merchants, before they proceeded up-harbour to unload and load cargo.

Governor Macquarie's fixing of pilotage rates protected shipmasters from extortionate charges, but the engagement of pilots remained optional until 1833, when for the first time it was made compulsory. Pilots' licences were then issued for the first time, and exemption certificates were granted to some shipmasters — usually of coastal or intercolonial vessels, or of whaling or sealing vessels registered at Sydney.

Though the rates of pilotage were fixed, the pilots pocketed the fees. They maintained their own boats and crews, and were in competition with one another to be the first to lie alongside any vessel making the signal for a pilot. This led to keenly-contested races between crews, on the high seas outside the Heads, many of the boatmen having been recruited from whaling vessels. Another effect of that system was that pilot boats ranged far out to sea to be the first to meet incoming vessels. Some went as far to the southward as Jervis Bay.

In August, 1834, the full-rigged ship *Edward Lombe*, from London, attempting to enter the harbour at night-time without a pilot, ran aground on Middle Head, and was wrecked with a loss of twelve lives. Among those who perished were the Captain, and the Second and Third Mates. As a consequence of this tragedy, the Signal Station was rebuilt, with equipment for night-signalling, and a roster of pilots "round the clock" was inaugurated.

During the Gold Rush of the 1850s, Sydney Harbour became "a forest of masts," as ships converged to the port from all over the world, bringing tens of thousands of adventurous immigrants to seek fortunes on the diggings. The gold boom brought prosperity incidentally to pilots, but the wreck of the full-rigged ship *Dunbar* at The Gap in August 1857, with loss of 121 lives, followed by another wreck, of the Aberdeen clipper *Catherine Adamson* on Middle Head, two months later, with loss of 21 lives, led to a public demand that the Government should take action to improve the pilot service, and to install lighting inside the harbour.

The *Catherine Adamson* (886 tons) had a pilot on board, but was becalmed in the Sound. Her anchors were let go, but did not hold, and she drifted on shore, heeled over, and sank. Among those drowned was the pilot.

In 1858, the Government appointed John Crook as Harbour-master, at a salary of £450 per annum, and decided to pay salaries to the six licensed pilots — £150 a year to the senior pilot and £100 to the others — in addition to which each pilot was allowed to collect tonnage rates for the vessels he handled. The Government also now paid the wages, £72 per annum, of the crews of three pilot boats, each manned by six oarsmen and a coxswain, and erected a building as a Pilot Station at Watson's Bay.

In 1862, a pilot schooner was commissioned to replace the six-oared whaleboats, and in 1863 a second pilot schooner was commissioned. These proved unsatisfactory for their purpose. In that year also Francis Hixson, formerly a sailing master in the Royal Navy, was appointed as Superintendent of the Steam Navigation and Pilot Board and Harbour Department, as the port authority was then cumbrously termed, at a salary of £650 per annum. (He was a predecessor of R.R.P. Hickson, who was Chairman of the Sydney Harbour Trust from 1901 to 1913.)

At the request of the pilots, in July 1864, the use of the schooners as pilot vessels was discontinued, and open boats were again brought into use, but each with a crew of only four oarsmen, in smaller whaleboats than had formerly been used. This change led to a tragedy on 20th July, 1867. Pilot Robinson was attempting to board the full-rigged ship *Strathdon* in a southerly gale when his boat capsized. He was drowned, as also were the four men of his crew, and four men from other boats, two of which capsized when attempting to rescue them.

Progress comes, sometimes slowly, from such mishaps of pioneers. In 1871 the port authority was reconstituted, in the name of the Marine Board, with Francis Hixson as its President. A steam tug, S.S. *Thetis,* 250 tons, was moored at Watson's Bay whenever stormy weather was signalled, and was used as a pilot vessel. In 1875 she was commissioned as a full-time pilot steamer. Then, at last, the system of competition between pilots was abolished. All pilots became employees of the Marine Board at a salary of £350 per annum, and were rostered for duty as required, the Board collecting the pilotage fees.

In 1877, a pilot steamer, *Captain Cook,* was launched from Mort's Dock and stationed at Watson's Bay. She had a wooden hull, 185 tons gross, and was the first steam-driven pilot vessel built specially for that purpose anywhere in the world.

After sixteen years' service, she was taken off station in 1893, and replaced by a second *Captain Cook,* a steel screw steamer, 396 tons gross, which remained in service as the pilot steamer of the Port of Sydney for 45 years, and became world-renowned for her jaunty looks, besides being Sydney's pride for the many rescues she made of small vessels in distress outside the Heads.

Like her predecessor, the second *Captain Cook* had a clipper bow, but this was adorned with a figurehead in bronze, designed and cast by the Sydney sculptor, Nelson Illingworth. It represented Captain Cook, life-size, with his telescope under his left arm, and his right hand shielding his eyes from the glare of the sun as he gazed inquiringly ahead over the seas.

The third pilot steamer to bear the illustrious name of *Captain Cook* came on station in March 1939. She was of 524 tons gross, and also of clipper-bow design, carrying the famous bronze figurehead. She remained in the pilot service for twenty years, being replaced in 1959 by three diesel-powered pilot cutters, of 20 tons displacement and 50 feet overall length, specially built for this service, with radio-telephone equipment and comfortable accommodation for the pilot, coxswain, and crew.

These sturdy cutters, more manoeuvrable than a steamer, and more readily at the disposal of pilots going out separately to meet vessels in the offing, have established the modern pattern, in which on an average the services of sea pilots at Sydney are required annually for 2,100 vessels inward and the same number outward, and for an annual average of 650 piloted removals of vessels from one berth to another within the harbour.

Pilotage remains compulsory for merchant vessels, as it has been at Sydney since 1833, the charges being levied on a tonnage scale, with exemptions granted to masters of vessels engaged in local trading.

Most of the sea pilots of Sydney Harbour live at or near Watson's Bay, and go on duty by roster, or are called as required by telephone. Their rates of pay and conditions of service have been regulated since 1922 by the State Arbitration Court. A new building for the Pilot Station, at Gibson's Beach, Watson's Bay, was opened in May 1959, in conjunction with a wooden-pile jetty at which the diesel cutters are berthed, ready to put to sea at any hour of the day or night.

WRECK OF THE "DUNBAR"

One of the most tragic incidents in the history of Sydney Harbour was the wreck of the *Dunbar*. This full-rigged ship, of 1,321 tons, James Green, Master, with 63 passengers and a crew of 59, left England on 21st May, 1857, and, after a passage of 81 days, was off Botany Bay at nightfall on 20th August.

A strong easterly wind was blowing, and visibility was poor, as Captain Green bore up for the entrance to Port Jackson. The seas were heaped up, and the Captain's intention to run for shelter, instead of "standing on and off" in wind that was rising to gale force, was subsequently considered by other experienced shipmasters to have been a correct decision. Nevertheless, his ship was on a lee shore, at night-time, in stormy weather in which no pilot boat had ventured out to meet him, and in those circumstances his decision had its tragic result.

He could take bearings from the Macquarie Light, but there was no light at that time at Inner South Head. All hands were called on deck, and, with a crew of 59, he had ample manpower for making or shortening sail, but the vessel had more leeway than had been allowed for, and had insufficient room for manoeuvre. Shortly after 11.30 p.m., breakers were sighted at a short distance to leeward, but, with the set of the wind and seas, it was then too late to alter course and haul offshore.

The ship struck the rocks, broadside on, near The Gap, in the cliffs midway between Outer South Head and Inner South Head. The Captain had not mistaken The Gap for the Harbour entrance. Such a mistake would have been impossible for an experienced shipmaster to make, even at night-time, in poor visibility, when he had his bearings from the Lighthouse and from the Signal Station. The only logical explanation of the disaster is that he had miscalculated his leeway. It was a coincidence that the vessel struck the shore near The Gap.

At the first impact she was dismasted, and, lying broadside on to the pounding of the seas, rapidly broke up, with no practical possibility of her boats being launched. The wind increased to gale force, and at dawn the spray from the surf was blowing over the top of the cliffs.

No one on shore had seen the ship strike the rocks. It was not until daylight that wreckage and bodies were sighted in the seething surf at the foot of the cliff. Of the 122 people on board, only one survived — a young Able Seaman named James Johnson, who managed to reach a ledge on the cliff-face and to hold on there. He was rescued with ropes after having been on the ledge for thirty-six hours.

The foreshores to the northward of The Gap were littered for days afterwards with dead bodies and wreckage, some being carried by the wind and the scend of the seas to the beaches of Middle Harbour and North Harbour, and some to North Head and Manly ocean beach. Most of the bodies were mutilated beyond recognition by the pounding of the seas or by sharks. They were buried in a common grave at Camperdown Cemetery.

Much of the flotsam and jetsam was salvaged by various individuals. Some of the timbers were used by James Milson (senior) in building a cattle-slaughtering house at Slaughter House Bay (nowadays known as Careening Cove), Kirribilli.

The sole survivor of the wreck was appointed Lightkeeper at Nobby's Lighthouse, at the entrance to the harbour of Newcastle, New South Wales.

In 1907, the anchor of the *Dunbar* was recovered by local residents of South Head, and was set up as a memorial on the summit of the cliff. In 1958, skin-divers recovered a few other relics of the wreck.

THE SOW AND PIGS

As early as 1836, in consequence of the wreck of the *Edward Lombe* in 1834 on Middle Head, a manned light vessel was anchored off the Sow and Pigs, not only to mark the rocks and shoalwater there, but also as a guide to navigation within the harbour. She was an old schooner named *Rose*. She shone her light there for twenty years.

The fairway leading to the Main Harbour is divided by the Sow and Pigs into two channels. The rocks, and the flat shoal from which they protrude, lie in the centre of the fairway, half a mile from Camp Cove and approximately the same distance from George's Head on the opposite shore. The rocks are covered at half-tide. The clear waters on each side are named the Eastern Channel and the Western Channel. The fairway is similarly divided again by Pinchgut Island (Fort Denison) within a mile from Sydney Cove, but otherwise it is a broad clear channel, navigable from shore to shore.

From the earliest years, the Sow and Pigs Reef — as it was named by the pioneer settlers — has been one of the principal seamarks in the Harbour. It serves also as a rounding-mark in yacht racing. Its first recorded use for that purpose was in April 1827, when the boat-crews of two British warships, H.M.S. *Success* and H.M.S. *Rainbow*, competed in a sailing race, on a course starting from Sydney Cove, round the Sow and Pigs and return, for a purse of Spanish dollars. This naval sporting event inaugurated organized yacht racing and boat racing on the harbour, which developed especially at the annual Anniversary Day Regattas, the first of which was held on 26th January, 1828, the fortieth anniversary of the foundation of settlement.

On many occasions, yachts have grounded on the Sow and Pigs, rounding the reef too fine, and have "disturbed the oysters." The only wreck of a large vessel there occurred on 10th August, 1824, when the sailing ship *Phoenix*, 600 tons, inward from London, struck on the reef, but did not sink. Though badly holed, she was got off on the next tide, and berthed in Sydney Cove, but was afterwards condemned as unseaworthy, and became a hulk in Lavender Bay.

The *Rose* light vessel was replaced in 1856 by the hulk of a former naval surveying vessel, H.M.S. *Bramble*, which, built in England in 1822, had arrived at Sydney in 1842 as tender to

H.M.S. *Fly,* to make a hydrographic survey of the Great Barrier Reef and of the shores of Papua. Commanded by Lieutenant Yule, R.N., the cutter *Bramble* in 1846 had her name placed prominently on the chart, at Bramble Cay, the most northerly point of the Great Barrier Reef, and therefore the rounding mark in the north-eastern channel for shipping on the route through Torres Strait.

When she was put into service as a light vessel at the Sow and Pigs, *Bramble* was thirty-four years of age, and retired from naval service. Her lights shone there for twenty-one years, until she was replaced in 1877 by another light vessel, built for that purpose, which was also given the name of *Bramble.* Attended by a crew of four, the second *Bramble* remained at the Sow and Pigs for thirty-five years, until she was replaced in 1912 by acetylene-gas light buoys.

The modern marking of the Sow and Pigs is by an iron tripod, 27 feet high, surmounted by a ball. The sides of the tripod are covered, and painted with black and white stripes. At the junction of the Eastern and Western Channels, approximately half a mile N.N.E. of the tripod beacon, a conical light-and-bell buoy is moored. The edges of the channels, at the sides of the Sow and Pigs, are marked by buoys and lights: a red conical buoy at the edge of the Eastern Channel, and at the edge of the Western Channel a black conical buoy. The light beacons are connected with the public electricity supply by underwater cables to the shore, as also are the other navigation lights and light buoys within the Harbour, all maintained by the Maritime Services Board.

THE HORNBY LIGHT

The lighthouse at Inner South Head is a tower thirty feet high, painted in red and white vertical stripes. It was originally known as "the Lower Light, South Head," to distinguish it from the Macquarie Light.

This beacon was erected in 1858, as a sequel to the tragic losses of the *Dunbar* and the *Catherine Adamson* in 1857. Its purpose was and remains to light the southern headland of the ocean entrance to the Harbour, and incidentally to mark the South Reef — a ledge of submerged rocks extending approximately a hundred yards from the tip of Inner South Head.

In normal conditions, vessels using the entrance, almost a mile wide, between Inner South Head and Inner North Head, would not be troubled by the South Reef, which is virtually part of the shore, but yachts have been stranded there when tacking out through the Heads and attempting to gybe too close inshore. In a yacht race on 23rd January, 1864, on a course from Farm Cove to Narrabeen and return, the crack Sydney-built yacht *Xarifa,* in the lead beating out through the Heads in light airs, grounded on South Reef, and remained fast until she was assisted off by a Manly ferry steamer. That assistance disqualified her for the race, but she pursued the other yachts, which had all passed her while she was grounded. She overtook them, and sailed home to be first across the finishing line.

The Inner South Head Light was given the name of Hornby Light, in honour of Admiral Sir Phipps Hornby, who in the 1860s was Commander-in-Chief of the British Pacific Fleet. It had originally a kerosene lamp, showing a fixed bright light 90 feet above sea-level. This was changed to incandescent gas-lighting early in the present century, and to electricity in 1933, when it ceased to be a manned light. In 1948 the beacon was given an occulting characteristic and a modern lens.

Its chief purpose being as an entrance guiding light to the harbour and not as a coastal navigation light, the Hornby Light is maintained by the Maritime Services Board of New South Wales, and not by the Federal Government. On the rocky headland, with surf breaking on the reef at its foot, it is a prominent and picturesque landmark. A vessel which has it a beam has entered the port.

MILITARY DEFENCE

The entire peninsular tip of South Head, from The Gap northwards to Inner South Head, is an Australian Commonwealth Government Reserve for naval and military defence purposes, conceived chiefly, in its military aspect, as a garrison artillery and signal post. Its guns are placed to operate in conjunction with other artillery installations on North and Middle Head.

These gun emplacements, on the headlands commanding the entrance to the Harbour, are intended to destroy enemy surface vessels attempting to force the entrance. Their tactical position is so strong that they may be considered a sufficient deterrent to that form of direct attack on the Port of Sydney from seaward. There are anti-submarine defences also. The weapons and tactics of modern warfare, including submarine attack, aerial bombing and the use of guided missiles at long range, may have made the "big guns" of coastal artillery defence to some extent obsolete, but not completely so while prospective enemy powers have in commission surface vessels or submarines capable of bombarding a seaport or of escorting troop-carrying vessels with invading forces.

When Governor Phillip in 1788 selected the site of the original settlement at Sydney Cove, five miles in from the ocean shore, he no doubt took into consideration that this sheltered site would be beyond the range of enemy naval bombardment from seaward with the guns that were used in warships at that time. It would be necessary for an attacking naval force to enter the Harbour and sail up to within a mile or less of Sydney Cove before opening fire effectively with roundshot from muzzle-loading guns.

Ever since Drake had "singed the Spanish King's beard" by bombarding Cadiz from seaward in 1596, it had been considered a wise precaution not only to fortify the entrance to harbours against such raids, but also to place the Seat of Government beyond the reach of naval guns, as far upstream as possible.

On that view of defensive tactics, Phillip intended to make Parramatta the capital of New South Wales, and Government House was built there in 1790. Sydney Cove was then meant to be only a depot for stores, and the outport for the capital; but the difficulty of sailing up to Parramatta in a narrowing channel, in which breezes were obstructed by forests on the riverbanks, caused that idea to be abandoned.

Sydney Cove was fortified by emplacements of naval guns in redoubts on Dawes Point and Bennelong Point. These were manned by marines until the first military garrison troops (a detachment of a specially recruited regiment, the New South Wales Corps) arrived in the Second Fleet in June 1790. Thereafter the garrison artillery defence of the port became a military responsibility.

Because of the difficulties of equipping and maintaining dispersed artillery posts with supplies that would need to be transported across the reaches of the Harbour, the fortifications were restricted in the first few years to the shores of Sydney Cove; but Governor Hunter, who held office from 1795 to 1800, placed a battery on Garden Island, one mile to the eastward of Sydney Cove, thereby flanking a possible approach by enemy naval vessels; and Governor King in 1801 placed a battery on George's Head, commanding the entrance to the Main Harbour at a vital point four miles by water eastward of Sydney Cove.

Those emplacements were temporary — as a precaution against the possibility of a French naval raid on Sydney during Britain's wars against Napoleon — but they were to be renewed in later years, and greatly developed in modern times. Hunter and King, being naval officers, had perceived the tactical value of preventing the enemy from coming within range of the town settlement; but, under Governor Macquarie's administration (1810-21), the military idea of fortifying an inner citadel led to a renewed concentration of the artillery defences at Dawes Point and Bennelong Point (Fort Macquarie), with no outlying defences against approaches from seaward. The question of expense was also relevant in that decision, as Macquarie had limited funds, and many other building works to complete.

In 1819 — four years after the Napoleonic wars had ended — the British Government sent a special commissioner, J. T. Bigge, to report on conditions in New South Wales, and to make suggestions for improvements in the administration of the colony. Among many other suggestions, Bigge recommended that an artillery post should be established on South Head. No immediate action was taken on this recommendation, chiefly because, at that time, Britain was undisputed "Mistress of the Seas," and there was no prospective enemy likely to make a naval attack on a British colony. That lull in Australian defence precautions, under the "sure shield" of the British Navy, lasted for a long time.

Governor Darling (1825-31), who was a military officer with the rank of Lieutenant-General, repeatedly protested to London at the inadequate artillery defences of Sydney — which remained limited to the forts at Dawes Point and Fort Macquarie — but was refused permission to spend money on strengthening, or even on repairing, the forts, or to undertake any new fortifications.

Governor Bourke (1831-37) who was a military officer, with the rank of Major-General, complained to the War Office that the guns at Sydney's only two forts were in need of overhaul. He requested the services of an Engineer Officer; and Captain George Barney was sent to Sydney, arriving in 1835, to establish a branch of the Ordnance Department.

Barney was asked first to undertake some urgent civil engineering work. It was not until 1839, after the arrival of Governor Gipps (1838-46), who was a Lieutenant-Colonel in the Royal Engineers, that Barney put forward his plan for extending the harbour defences by fortifying Pinchgut Island and Bradley's Head, at an estimated cost of £5,000.

While this plan was under consideration by the Legislative Council, before being submitted to London for approval, an incident occurred which caused consternation, but had also its humorous aspects. Two warships of the United States Navy paid a friendly but unannounced visit to Sydney! These warships, part of a squadron of six vessels under command of Captain Charles Wilkes, U.S.N., had been engaged in a United States Exploring Expedition in the Pacific, and had made a thorough cartographic and scientific survey of the Samoan Islands before Captain Wilkes decided to make a courtesy call at Sydney.

Wilkes, in the published narrative of his voyages, stated that his flagship *Vincennes* and her consort *Peacock* sighted the Macquarie Light at sunset on 29th November, 1839. "We had a fair wind for entering the harbour, and, although the night was dark and we had no pilot, it was important to avoid any loss of time, so I determined to run in."

The American officers were unacquainted with the channel, but had been assured that the charts they had on board could be depended upon, so they stood on under press of sail, and at 8 p.m. were at the entrance to the Harbour. "Here, a light erected on a shoal called the Sow and Pigs, since the publication of the charts, caused a momentary hesitation, but it was not long before it was determined where it was placed, and with this new aid I decided to run up and anchor off the Cove. . . . At half past ten p.m. we quietly dropped anchor off the Cove in the midst of the shipping without anyone having the least idea of our arrival."

From that account it appears that the lookout on the Signal Station at South Head was lax, or that the signallers mistook the American warships for British warships familiar with the port and not requiring pilots. Britain was not then at war with any major naval power, but that was no reason for relaxing precautions against naval raids. The news of declarations of war, like all other news, took four months or more to reach Sydney from Britain, and in that time an enemy raiding force could make a strike before the Harbour defences had been alerted.

Captain Wilkes commented: "When the good people of Sydney looked abroad in the morning, they were much astonished to see two men o' war lying among their shipping . . . A few days before 35 our arrival it had been debated in Council whether more effective means of fortification were not necessary for the harbour. The idea of this being wanted was ridiculed by the majority, but the entrance of our ships by night seems to have changed their opinion. Had war existed, we might, after firing the shipping and reducing a great part of the town to ashes, have effected a retreat before daybreak in perfect safety."

The result of the changed opinion was that the plan of harbour defence put forward by Lieutenant-Colonel Barney — he was promoted to that rank in 1840 — was adopted, and work began immediately on fortifications of Pinchgut Island, Kirribilli Point, and Bradley's Head; but those works proceeded slowly and were not completed until 1857, after news of Britain's war against Russia in the Crimea had reached Sydney.

South Head was not fortified until 1859 — nearly forty years after Commissioner Bigge had recommended that precaution. There was some reason to believe that an unofficial "Yankee filibustering expedition" might be organized to make an armed assault on Sydney, in order to rob the banks of literally tons of gold then accumulating in their vaults, the yield of the diggings in that "Golden Decade" of Australian prosperity. This was only a rumour, but it had its effect in the placing of coastal batteries on South Head, and also on Middle Head.

The fortifications were strengthened on the outbreak of the Civil War in America in 1861, when it appeared likely that the Northern States might declare war on Britain for aiding and abetting the Southern States. According to an engraving published in *The Sydney Illustrated News* of 24th July, 1875, the fortifications stood near the Hornby Light on Inner South Head, and consisted of "a battery of three 68-pounders and ten 8-inch guns, mounted one hundred feet above high water mark."

After the withdrawal of British garrison troops from Australia in 1870, and until the federation of the Australian colonies in 1901, military defence was a responsibility of each colony. When the Federal Government took over the defence system in March, 1901, the military establishments of New South Wales had a strength of 669 officers and men of the permanent forces, with 5,549 militia, and 3,493 other volunteer units. The permanent forces were chiefly administrative staff and garrison artillery.

The fortifications at South Head have continued to be manned by garrison artillery forces ever since 1859, and have been strengthened and modernized from time to time, especially during the wars of 1914-18 and of 1939-45. The barracks on Inner South Head are headquarters of an Area Command, which includes a coast battery, a signal troop, and a cadet training centre.

SEE ALSO PART II   H.M.A.S. "WATSON"

At the tip of the Inner South Head Peninsula, on an area of approximately four acres adjoining the military reserve, is a shore establishment of the Royal Australian Navy, which was commissioned in 1945 as H.M.A.S. *Watson*. It is named from its proximity to Watson's Bay; but the name also commemorates the seaman of the Royal Navy, Robert Watson, in whose honour Watson's Bay was named. He was quartermaster of H.M.S. *Sirius* in the First Fleet in 1788, one of the first pilots of Port Jackson, and the first keeper of the Macquarie Light.

H.M.A.S. *Watson* is one of the main operational training centres of the Royal Australian Navy, and one of the principal shore establishments of the R.A.N. at Sydney.

Formed in the early years of the 1939-45 war as a Radar Training School, the establishment was enlarged in 1944 to include a Navigation and Direction Training School. (The word "Direction" here refers to the control and direction of aircraft.) In 1956 the Torpedo and Anti-Submarine Training School — which had formerly been in H.M.A.S. *Rushcutter*, a shore establishment on Rushcutters Bay — was added to H.M.A.S. *Watson*.

Buildings, chiefly of bricks with tiled roofs, were added to serve as accommodation blocks and amenities blocks. On an average, there are 500 naval officers and ratings in residence at H.M.A.S. *Watson*, undergoing training or refresher courses in their special categories in the various schools. In 1960, a naval chapel was added to the establishment.

The site of H.M.A.S. *Watson*, adjacent to the Hornby Light, includes the gun emplacements of the coastal garrison artillery dating from 1859, and other gun emplacements on the clifftop in which guns were mounted during the 1914-18 war. Some of these guns are still in position in the military reserve area with magazines alongside, excavated in the solid sandstone.

On the cliff-edged ridge averaging ninety feet above sea-level, H.M.A.S. *Watson* has extensive views of Sydney Harbour and to seaward. The radio masts and radar masts of the Navigation and Direction Training School are steel structures which stand on the highest point of the ridge. The radar equipment can "see" to a wide horizon.

On the western side of the peninsula, looking across to Middle Head, over the entrance channels to the Port of Sydney, the Torpedo and Anti-Submarine Training School is equipped with the most modern electronic devices for training in anti-submarine warfare and in the handling of torpedoes and anti-submarine weapons. At this School instruction is given also in the operation and laying of explosive sea mines, and in methods of sweeping them. The T.A.S. Training School thus gives training in all forms of undersea warfare.

The accommodation blocks and amenities blocks of H.M.A.S. *Watson* are extensive. They provide living-quarters and recreational facilities for the administrative and instructional staff, and for the trainees. The "galleys" (kitchens) and dining-halls can cater for 400 people to a meal. There is also in H.M.A.S. *Watson* a School of Cookery.

The parade ground is laid out for alternative use as tennis courts and basket-ball courts. The day's work begins at 8 a.m.

in the "Colours" Parade (ceremony of raising the White Ensign and the Australian National flag), with music from the East Australia Area band.

One of the most striking features of H.M.A.S. *Watson* is the Chapel. It is a memorial chapel to all those of the Royal Australian Navy who lost their lives in the 1914-18 and 1939-45 wars, and was built from funds donated by individuals, companies, and institutions throughout Australia, but mainly in the Sydney area. It is dedicated to St George the Martyr and is non-denominational.

The foundation stone of the chapel was laid by a boy whose father, a naval rating, died at sea during the 1939-45 war. The stone is inscribed: "To the Glory of God and in memory of those of the Royal Australian Navy who gave their lives in the service of their country and for freedom, this stone was laid by William, the son of one of that gallant company, on Saturday 30th April 1960."

The site for the chapel evoked an architectural conception that makes this building one of the world's most impressively placed shrines. The building is relatively small, having external dimensions of 88 feet long, 35 feet wide, and 20 feet high; it is beautifully designed and proportioned in a truncated diamond shape. Its walls are of Sydney sandstone, faced with white cement rendering, which, together with its situation, near the cliff's edge and in isolation from other buildings, makes it a conspicuous landmark for the entrance to the Harbour. As such, its position is marked on Admiralty charts.

A cross, thirty feet high, rises in a tapering design from the centre of the roof. The base of the spire is encircled by a Naval Crown. At night the spire is illuminated internally and also by concealed floodlights. Thus it serves as a beacon, visible far out at sea.

The interior of the chapel is of simple but strikingly effective design and construction. It is a nave without transepts, and has a wooden ceiling that is only slightly arched, in modern rather than traditional Gothic conceptions of ecclesiastical design.

In the north and south walls are stained-glass windows, depicting the symbols of the Apostles, but using coloured glass that is "chunky" instead of flat, embedded in veins of concrete instead of the traditional bondings of lead.

The altar is built of stones obtained from many cathedrals and churches throughout the world. The lectern, a gift of the New Zealand Navy, is a wood carving representing the "kea" bird with outspread wings. The organ gallery, which is used also as a musicians' gallery, extends across the nave above the western, or landward-side, entrance.

All these internal features of the chapel are harmonized by the superb conception of the reredos. The entire east wall is formed of glare-resisting plate-glass, which provides not only a clear illumination but also a seascape "picture" of a verisimilitude that no artist could equal, for it is the real thing — the sky, the sea, and the North Head as they are in Nature's ever-changing

38

colours and moods, and a full view of ships entering or leaving the Harbour.

For that reredos alone, the chapel of H.M.A.S. *Watson* deserves to be, and will surely become, far renowned, as a place of pilgrimage for visitors and for Sydney residents who there may see something rare, if not unique, among the world's distinctive small religious shrines.

In its special way, this naval war memorial is a feature of Sydney Harbour that may be compared, in its modern architectural design and boldly imaginative placing, with the much more massive, more costly, and more widely publicized Sydney Opera House on Bennelong Point; but often in small things there is a greatness that comes to be recognized with the effluxion of time. The chapel of H.M.A.S. *Watson* gives every indication of becoming acknowledged in that way as a manifestation of mankind's yearning for the Ideal. It is one of the most perfect examples of the way architects and builders can rise to a scenic opportunity that is to be found anywhere in the world. Sydney Harbour, more than most other large harbours, abounds in sites for striking and unusual architecture.

THE MIDGET SUBMARINES SEE ALSO PART II

In May 1942 Australia had already been at war with Japan for six months. The enemy had made a determined thrust to the southward in the western Pacific, had occupied Hong Kong, the Philippines, Malaya, and Indonesia, and had landed troops in the Australian Mandated Territory of New Guinea. Enemy air-raids had been made on the Australian coast at Darwin and Broome.

On 4th May, a Japanese naval force, escorting troops for an intended assault on Port Moresby and invasion of southern Papua, was encountered by an Australian Naval Squadron and an American Task Force in the Battle of the Coral Sea. Heavy attacks were delivered at long range by the aircraft from the carriers in the opposing surface forces, which were never in sight of one another throughout the battle.

This was the first naval battle in history in which the opposing ships never came within sight of one another. The Japanese ships were compelled to withdraw, and with that result the Battle of the Coral Sea was a strategic victory for the Allies.

Flushed with their early successes in the war, the Japanese had proved to be not only resolute, audacious, and ambitious, but also powerfully equipped for war at sea, on land, and in the air. The mobility of their aircraft carriers enabled them to attack targets thousands of miles beyond the range of aircraft operating from fixed shore bases. Devastating attacks by Japanese aircraft carriers were quickly made upon targets geographically separated as widely as Hawaii and Ceylon.

Sydney was a legitimate target for enemy attack. It was a major terminal of the vital sea communications of the island continent. The Harbour was a fleet base, not only for Australian and British, but also for American and Dutch naval forces. Large merchant vessels, in service as transports of troops and of supplies for the armed services, were continually coming and going to and from Sydney: these included the gigantic transatlantic vessels *Queen Mary* and *Queen Elizabeth* — the biggest ships in the world — besides many other transatlantic liners that had been put into wartime service in the Indian and Pacific Oceans.

The first Japanese attack came on the night of 31st May, 1942. It was made not by enemy surface vessels, but by submarines — and those submarines were of a special kind, constituting a "secret weapon." The Japanese had invented and secretly practised the use of "midget" submarines, only 80 feet long and 35 feet in girth, which could be launched from large long-range submarines acting as their mother ships.

A midget submarine, with a crew of only two men, a short cruising range, and carrying two torpedoes, could sneak into a harbour where surface vessels or large submarines would have had little or no chance of avoiding the shore-based defences.

The anti-submarine defences of Sydney Harbour included a boom-and-net barrage. This was stretched across the entrance channels of the Main Harbour, from Green Point (the headland between Camp Cove and Watson's Bay) to the Sow and Pigs; and from the Sow and Pigs to George's Head.

A "gate" in the barrage had to be opened whenever vessels on legitimate business needed to pass through it. That routine procedure may explain how two Japanese midget submarines passed through the barrage, perhaps in the wake of an incoming vessel — but alternately they may have been very skilfully navigated along the sea-bed at high tide, to pass beneath the net, or may have cut through the net with a saw-tooth net-cutter.

Of four midget submarines, believed to have been launched from Japanese "I" class (long-range) submarines off Sydney Heads, soon after nightfall on 31st May, one was detected and attacked and believed sunk by naval patrol, one was caught in the boom-and-net defence; and two got through into the Harbour.

The crew of the entangled midget, unable to free it from the steel wire mesh of the net, and correctly expecting that depth-charges from naval launches would be dropped on them at any moment, committed *hara-kiri* at 10.30 p.m. by blowing up themselves and their craft.

Of the two that passed through the net-defence, one was detected by naval patrol vessels and destroyed by depth-charges before it could fire its torpedoes.

The other surfaced and was illuminated by searchlights and engaged by gunfire by Australian and U.S. warships. It fired two torpedoes at 400 yards range at the American cruiser U.S.S. *Chicago*, which lay at a buoy off Garden Island.

Both torpedoes narrowly missed the *Chicago*. One ran up on to the shore of Garden Island and did not explode. The other passed under a Dutch submarine lying at Garden Island, hit the sea bottom and exploded, sinking S.S. *Kuttabul*, a former Sydney passenger ferry which had been requisitioned by the Australian Navy for use as a depot ship.

The *Kuttabul* split asunder and sank immediately. Twenty lives were lost and a number of men were wounded. Those men of the Royal Australian Navy were the first casualties from enemy action in Sydney Harbour in 154 years of the Harbour's history.

The Harbour defences had gone immediately into action at the first warning of the enemy attack. Searchlights swept the waters, guns opened fire, and, while the action lasted, for an hour and a half, the normally placid waters of Sydney Harbour had become the scene of violent action.

It is believed that the midget submarine which sank *Kuttabul* — the only one which had been able to fire its torpedoes — was struck by gunfire, but its fate is unknown.

The two which were known to have been destroyed were located by divers and raised from the sea-bed. The bodies of the Japanese crews were cremated with naval honours due to a brave foe, and the ashes were returned to Japan after the war.

The naval defences of the Harbour had frustrated an attack which could have had very serious consequences if all the submarines had been able to make their attack.

A week later, on the night of 7th June, 1942, a Japanese "I" class submarine surfaced offshore, and fired seven shells indiscriminately at Sydney, in an endeavour to shake civilian morale. The effect was the opposite to that intended. The range was too great to reach the centre of the city, or any naval or military targets. The shells fell in the Bondi and Rose Bay suburban residential districts.

Coastal guns opened fire and caused the submarine to break off the action and submerge. Somewhat remarkably, of seven shells fired, five were "duds," and failed to explode. Some dwellings were damaged, but the only casualty was one civilian with a broken leg.

In so far as that bombardment was a continuation of the attack by the midget submarines a week previously, the chief effect of the enemy operation was to demonstrate the importance and value of harbour defences. It drove home the meaning of the old Latin motto: if you want peace, be ready for war.

CLIFF RESCUES

The gold-coloured sandstone cliffs of Sydney have a meaning for Australians similar to that of the white chalk cliffs of Dover for the people of England. They are a landmark and symbol for seafarers homeward or outward bound. Those sandstone cliffs, striated with narrow ledges, rising sheer out of the ocean that breaks in foam at their base, may be the last sight of the beloved land, as it has been for many; or again the first sight of a longed-for destination for homecomers or new arrivals.

The cliffs stretch to the southward from Inner South Head for four miles to Ben Buckler, where their stark line is interrupted by the curve of Bondi Beach. They continue then, for eight miles more to the southward, as a series of bluff headlands flanking in succession Bronte Beach, Coogee Beach, Maroubra Beach, Long Bay, and Little Bay, to Cape Banks and Cape Solander, at the entrance to Botany Bay.

The fine-grained and smooth sands of the ocean beaches, formed from the attrition of the cliffs in milleniums of time, and pounded yet by the breaking seas, provide the people of Sydney with invitations for surf-bathing, within easy access, such as are available so easily to the residents of few, if any, other great cities anywhere in the world.

The alternation of cliffy headlands and curving fine-sand beaches is characteristic also of the ocean shore to the northward of the Harbour, stretching for sixteen miles from North Head to Broken Bay. The large beaches of Manly, Harbord, Curl Curl, Dee Why, Collaroy, Narrabeen, Mona Vale, Newport, Avalon, Whale Beach, and Palm Beach, and several other smaller beaches along that part of the coast, are all flanked by bold headlands, and vie with those to the southward of the Harbour in their invitations for beach picnics and surf-bathing.

With so many and such superb ocean beaches within easy access of the city and suburbs, and in a climate that permits sea-bathing for at least nine months in the year, the people of Sydney have developed recreational habits that are amphibious. Within the Harbour also are many facilities for sea-bathing; and there is large scope for yachting, boating, and fishing inside and outside the Harbour, with picnic grounds in profusion.

Sydney is thus not only a naval and mercantile port and industrial and emporium city, but also a seaside resort with a littoral so extensive and varied that its attractions, so astonishing to visitors who see them for the first time, are taken for granted by the residents, as though such lavish gifts of Nature were a birthright.

"Our Harbour," Sydney people say with pride — but few, even of those who have spent a lifetime on its shores, are closely acquainted with all its components — the ocean cliffs, headlands, and beaches outside; and the many headlands, coves, arms, and occasional islands inside. To visit them all would require more time and more mobility of transport than most residents or visitors have at their disposal. Yet there are watermen — foremost among them the men of the Water Police — to whom all the foreshores and waters are familiar from routine patrols.

Many thousands of people make their living on and by Sydney Harbour, but there have been, in the aggregate of the Harbour's history, large numbers, too, who have met with death in those bright waters and along those picturesque foreshores; and, in the Harbour's history that is now lengthening into vistas of recorded time nearing two centuries, there have been incidents almost innumerable of heroism in the saving of life.

During Captain Cook's short visit in 1770, a seaman of H.M.S. *Endeavour*, named Forby Sutherland, died, and was buried on the shore of Botany Bay. He died on board ship of illness and not of violent mishap; but, in the roll-call of men of the white race who have perished in the vicinity of Sydney Harbour, his name was the first to be called. One of the next was Père le Receveur, chaplain on board the French exploring vessel *Astrolabe,* who died at Botany Bay, on 17th February, 1788, three weeks after the British settlement had been formed at Sydney Cove.

The full toll of fatalities in the history of Sydney Harbour would make a grim chronicle of deaths by drowning, shark attacks, shipwrecks, boat-capsizes, suicides, murders, and other mishaps. The Harbour's story is chiefly of the achievements of the living, and of the security and prosperity that a haven accords, rather than of mishaps and disasters; yet the dead, here as elsewhere, sanctify the living, and especially when stalwart men risk their own lives to rescue the living or to retrieve dead bodies.

The cliffs of the South Head promontory have been the scene of many deaths and also of many rescues from peril. The wreck of the *Dunbar* in 1857, and the difficult and dangerous task of rescuing the sole survivor from a ledge, and of recovering the bodies of 121 dead from the rocks and surf below, haunted the minds of Sydney people for many years, and passed into local lore with a strange after-effect.

It became almost an obsession for people who had decided to resolve in the negative Hamlet's alternative — to be or not to be — to shuffle off this mortal coil by "going over The Gap." Those unfortunates, who, as Thomas Hood had described one in like plight, were "weary of breath," sought a solution to life's intolerable tensions by taking a tram-ride (or in more modern times a bus-ride) from the city to Watson's Bay and alighting at The Gap, not to enjoy the scenery, but to blot it out from their view for ever by plunging to a violent death on the rocks below or in the pounding surf.

The tram-ride (or bus-ride) gave time for further consideration of a drastic impulse; the grand view on alighting may have made some hesitate to quit it; tram-crews and bus-crews, noticing a person alighting in an obvious state of agitation, sometimes stopped their vehicles and remonstrated with or forcibly restrained that person from taking the irrevocable step over the edge.

There is a probably apocryphal story of an inquisitive passer-by, who, seeing a man intending to jump over The Gap, asked him to state his reasons for that dire decision. When those reasons had been carefully explained, they both jumped over!

Whatever the fascination of self-murder — the only felony, which, if successful, is not punishable in the law-courts — it gave The Gap a sinister reputation similar to that with which Shakespeare endowed the cliffs of Dover, where (in *King Lear,* Act IV, Scene 6) the blinded Earl of Gloucester attempted ineffectually to renounce the world and to shake off his great afflliction.

During the Economic Depression of 1929-33, many people spent their last few pence on a one-way tram-ride to The Gap. Others, after the Harbour Bridge was opened in 1932, saved the tram-fare by "jumping over the Bridge," until the bridge-footway was netted to prevent that unlawful use of it. The Gap then came again into favour as a rendezvous of the world-weary. In the early years of the 1939-45 war there were so many suicides there that the task of recovering the bodies — a duty of the police — caused serious concern at a time when many other calls were being made upon the police for war-emergency work.

Until 1942, the bodies of persons who fell, intentionally or accidentally, over the cliffs, were recovered by local police with the help of "rock-fishermen" — intrepid and experienced men who are in the habit of descending the cliffs by tortuous and narrow paths known chiefly to themselves, to fish with lines from the rocks on the ocean foreshore.

Occasionally one of those fishermen was drowned through being swept off the rocks by heavy seas; at other times, fool-hardy persons, attempting to descend the cliffs to fish from the rocks, without knowing the intricacies of the descent, had to be rescued from ledges when their nerves failed them so that they were unable either to proceed or to retire. The recovery of bodies from the surf that seethes among the rocks, or the rescue of people stranded on ledges, is almost impossible from seaward by the use of boats. Dead bodies or persons rescued alive (sometimes injured) have to be hauled to the cliff-top with ropes.

In 1942, the Commissioner of Police (W. J. Mackay) decided to form a Cliff Rescue Unit. This was placed under the instruction of Harry Ware, a civilian who was chief instructor of the rescue and demolition squads of the National Emergency Service that had been formed to protect the population against the effects of possible enemy bombardment of Sydney.

The Cliff Rescue Unit was organized by the Police Department, but it was an emergency service, manned by police who also had other duties. Its equipment included a small swinging derrick with pulley blocks and ropes and a "bosun's chair." The derrick could be mounted only on previously prepared sites at the cliff-top, where holes nine inches in diameter had been excavated at intervals in the rock, and iron-eye bollards had been cemented in position to act as anchorages.

Many bodies were recovered, and living persons rescued, not only at South Head, but at other places along the coast, and on the precipices of the Blue Mountains, fifty miles inland.

So many calls were made for the services of the Cliff Rescue Unit — averaging seventy a year — that in 1945 the Unit was formed into a full-time Police Cliff Rescue Squad. Harry Ware, sworn in as a Special Sergeant, was appointed officer in charge.

The equipment had been improved with a tubular-steel derrick that could be quickly erected at any site of operation. Many police took part in the cliff rescues and recoveries of bodies, but the principal work over the edge, on the cliff-face, was done by Sergeant Ware and Constable Ray Tyson, both of whom were awarded decorations for their courage and endurance.

In course of time, the work of the Cliff Rescue Squad was extended to cope with other emergencies, including the recovery of bodies or the rescue of persons trapped or injured in motor-car accidents, railroad and aircraft disasters, or in other predicaments and dangers.

The Squad was then (in 1954) given the more general name of the "Police Rescue Squad." In 1957 Constable Fahey, and in 1962 Constable Coasby, became permanent members of it. In 1962 Sergeant Ware retired, after twenty years of devoted and heroic service. Sergeant Tyson was then appointed officer in charge.

The work of the Police Rescue Squad, in cliff rescues and the recovery of bodies on South Head, is an outstanding aspect of the policing of Sydney Harbour. Whenever the Squad is in operation on the cliff face, a Water Police launch speeds out through the Heads and stands by, close inshore, to give whatever help may be possible.

These stalwart men of the police force thus risk their own lives in salvage operations of other human beings, alive or dead. The essential duty of the police, at all times, in all departments, is to protect life and property, and not merely to bring law-breakers to justice; but in no other activity is the humanitarian aspect of police work more vividly demonstrated than in the perilous tasks of the Rescue Squad on the cliffs of the headlands of Sydney Harbour.

Those tasks, if not unique, are rare among police activities anywhere in the world: they are a special development of local conditions at Sydney. On the cliffs, especially at South Head, the adventurous, as well as the foolhardy and the desperate, by putting their own lives to the hazard, have called into existence courage of a high order to extricate them from dangers which in some cases could have been avoided, but in many cases are the result of the tragic weakness and cowardice of individuals who refuse to "bear the whips and scorns of time," and so put themselves beyond remedy or rescue, except for the last rites of pious disposal, and the proof of the fact and cause of death that the law requires.

Spectacular though that method of exit from life may seem to persons mentally deranged, it has made no appeal to visitors of normal mentality, who, standing on the cliff-tops of the South Head promontory, have gazed around in delight at the grand panorama of sea, sky, headland, and cove, shipping, and the habitations of men, set in the greenery of the ancient Australian bushland; or (with the Australian poet, William Baylebridge) have, at dawn,

> . . . watched the city, proudly, like a queen,
> Lift from her shoulders fair that marvellous cloak
> Where pearl and opal the pale silvers grain. . . .

or at sunset have watched the golden and crimson glow spreading and fading in the western sky, and reflected in the waters of the Harbour, until

> . . . the swift intercession of high stars
> Makes beautiful the night, with magic dressed.

Then the whirling beams of the Macquarie Light flash far out over the ocean, and wink in their reduced intensity to land- 45 ward over the Harbour and its inhabited shores. The reflections of tens of thousands of house-lights, street-lights, and coloured lights glitter in the ripple of wavelets within the far-spread haven; and, when night has gone, the sunlight sparkles in the waters on a blue-and-gold Sydney day.

In all those lights, Sydney Harbour has an enchantment for those who view it for the first time, and even more so for those who, accustomed to its glittering vistas, are frequently delighted by new facets in its bright scenes. Those onlookers view that grand panorama from South Head, or from any other of the many lookout points around the Harbour's shores, not with the despondent mentality that says "No" to life's challenges and opportunities, but with that which says "Yes." In those bright scenes are no shadowings of the morbid and the sinister, or of failure and defeat: everything spread there speaks of great things accomplished by the human spirit in a comparatively short period of historical time, and of yet brighter promise for the future.

3

WOOLLAHRA

THE MUNICIPALITY OF WOOLLAHRA EXTENDS ALONG THE SOUTHERN shore of Sydney Harbour, westwards from South Head to Rush-cutters Bay. It includes the suburbs of Watson's Bay, Vaucluse, Rose Bay, Bellevue Hill, Point Piper, Double Bay, and Darling Point. These are residential suburbs, with no large factories or commercial wharves. The harbour-front residences include mansions of the "colonial" era, and many dwellings in modern villa styles, surrounded by trees, lawns, and gardens.

There is no "marine drive" or esplanade along the foreshores of Sydney Harbour, except for short distances in a few places. In colonial days the Government granted freehold titles of land with boundaries at high tide mark. Consequently the greater part of the waterfront within the Harbour — with the exception of the naval and military reserves, wharves, and recreation parks — is privately owned. That system of land-tenure precluded the practical possibility of building waterfront roadways or esplanades; but the public has access to the waterfront within the parks, for which some land has been reserved near the heads of most of the bays and coves, and on some of the headlands.

In several of the waterfront parks there are shark-proof enclosures at the beaches for sea-bathing. Many of the private waterfront residences also have sea-bathing pools; but, in the motor-car era since the 1920s, which has provided quick transport by road to the ocean beaches, the sheltered harbour beaches have less popular appeal than they had formerly.

Sydney has more parks and playing-fields, and more spaces of fresh air, than most big cities. The greenery of the parks, alternating with the built-on areas, in which many of the houses have red-tiled roofs, contributes pleasantly to the variety of colour in the harbourside scene.

Most of the bays that are not used for berthing large ships are "boat-harbours," in which moorings are laid for yachts and other small craft, with boatsheds, slipways, and yacht-club build-ings on the shore. These are plentiful in the bays of Woollahra.

Before the development of mechanized road traffic, most of the harbour-front suburbs — including the eastern residential suburbs — had steam-ferry services which ran up and down the Harbour to and from Sydney Cove. There were ferries then to Darling Point, Double Bay, Point Piper, Rose Bay, and Watson's Bay; but the ferry services, unable to compete in speed with modern road traffic, have been reduced to the routes across the harbour between the southern and northern shores, with terminals at Sydney Cove; and even those have been curbed since 1932 by the competition of road traffic across the Sydney Harbour Bridge.   47

The Harbour has thus become less used as a waterway by the residents on its shores than it was in the pre-automobile era; but the reduction in ferry traffic has been accompanied by an increase of yachting and pleasure-cruising, which foster the nautical instincts of a maritime folk, and keep alive the amphibious instincts of a nation of coast-dwellers.

SEE ALSO PART II   ABORIGINAL NAMES

The name "Woollahra" is an Aboriginal word which was spelled in some of the earlier colonial records as "Wilarra." Its meaning, like that of most Aboriginal words used as place-names, has become a matter of conjecture. A place-name, in any language, may have originated in some incident in folk-history that has been forgotten.

Aboriginal names of some of the geographical features of Sydney Harbour have been preserved in use, almost by accident. Among these are "Woollahra," "Woolloomooloo," and "Kirribilli" — euphonious words. Most of the other geographical features of the Harbour have been given names of English meaning, or of association with pioneers of settlement or with British or Colonial officials. The Aboriginal names of some of the capes, bays, and islands have been ascertained by the research of enthusiasts, but are not commonly used.

It is said that the Aboriginal name for Inner South Head was "Burrowaree," of Watson's Bay "Kooti," and of Shark Island "Boambilli"; but no decision has been taken officially to restore the Aboriginal names of those and other places around the Harbour, which seem likely to commemorate in perpetuity the lore of the possessors rather than of the dispossessed.

Very few full-bloods of the Aboriginal tribes of the Sydney district have survived, and those are "detribalized" and assimilated into the modern and civilized way of life. They number not more than one in ten thousand of Sydney's population, which is thus almost completely of white or European racial descent, to an extent which sometimes surprises visitors from other countries, accustomed to multi-racial complexities in big-city life. Sydney is the second largest city of whites in the British Commonwealth.

BAYS AND COVES

Governor Phillip described Port Jackson as "the Bay of a hundred Coves." The distinction between a "bay" and a "cove" has been applied loosely in the naming of the indentations of the shore within the Harbour. A bay in the dictionary definition is "part of the sea filling a wide-mouthed opening of the land"; whereas a cove is defined as "a small bay or creek: a sheltered recess."

On modern maps, fifty-six of the indentations of the shore within the Main Harbour are named as "bays," ten as "coves," and two as "creeks." In Middle Harbour there are nine "bays," two "coves," and one "creek"; in North Harbour one "bay" and three "coves."

48   On that count there is a total of sixty-six "bays" and fifteen

"coves" within the entire Harbour, but they have been named in that way at random. Many of the bays are indentations within larger bays. There are coves within bays, and bays within coves. All are within the large expanse of Port Jackson which Governor Phillip termed a "bay." His count of "a hundred coves" was correct, if "creeks" and "beaches" are added to the "bays" and "coves" of a nomenclature that has developed chiefly in popular usage rather than by official decree.

The names of the inlets, and of the headlands separating them, and of the islands and other features of the Harbour, were in only a few instances officially bestowed in the earlier years of settlement. Names in popular use gradually became officially confirmed — some by Governor Macquarie, and others not until John Crook was appointed as Harbourmaster in 1858. Crook noted some of the popular names in pencil on the original chart which Captain John Hunter, R.N., had made seventy years previously.

As a result of that haphazard procedure, the origin of many of the place-names within the Harbour is nowadays unknown, or is a matter of conjecture. Some of the bays or headlands were named from persons who lived there, or from vessels which lay there, or from incidents which occurred there. Historical research has established the origins of many of the names, but there is scope for much further research in that field. In the present volume, the origins of names are stated only where they are positively known.

We now proceed westwards along the southern shore of the Main Harbour, from Inner South Head, mentioning the principal features of the shoreline in sequence, with as much accuracy as available records and observation permit, but acknowledging that much of the lore of the Harbour is traditional or conjectural, with *lacunae* that remain to be filled.

LADY BAY   SEE ALSO PART II

This slight indentation, with 100 yards of beach, immediately in the lee of Inner South Head, and within the Defence Reserve, adjacent to H.M.A.S. *Watson*, is partly exposed to ocean swell, and fully exposed to northerly winds. The bay faces Middle Head, which is distant three-quarters of a mile from Inner South Head, across the entrances to the two channels leading into the Main Harbour. H.M.A.S *Watson* has anti-submarine defence equipment near the shore of Lady Bay, including mortars for throwing depth-charges. The origin of the name of this bay has not been positively ascertained.

CAMP COVE

Adjoining Lady Bay on the south is the cove in which Governor Phillip's boats were beached on the day when he explored the Harbour, stated in the official narrative of his voyage as 22nd January, 1788.

Camp Cove has a good sandy beach, 200 yards long, and   49 sufficiently in the lee of Inner South Head to be a haven for small craft and boats. A public park adjoins the beach, adjacent to but not within the Defence Reserve. A monument on the shore, erected by the Royal Australian Historical Society, commemorates Phillip's landing, and states that it occurred on 21st January, 1788.

The name of Camp Cove is traditional from the first years of settlement. The earliest pilots, using open boats, were stationed there. The cove is crescent-shaped, and wide-mouthed. The Sow and Pigs Reef lies 800 yards offshore.

Green Point, separating Camp Cove from Watson's Bay, is a distinct promontory, on which an obelisk has been erected as a navigational mark. It is a public recreational reserve, with native trees from which the name of the point was derived in popular usage. It was formerly known also as Laing's Point, from a pioneer settler who lived there. This is one of the clear marks in harbour navigation, especially so for yacht courses on races from up-harbour to Manly Cove and return.

Camp Cove and Green Point reserves are picnic grounds, accessible directly by road, and within a few hundred yards of the bus terminus at Watson's Bay.

SEE ALSO PART II   WATSON'S BAY

Watson's Bay is the main part of a large indentation of the shore between Green Point and Vaucluse Point. The distance between those two points is half a mile. The waters they flank include Watson's Bay and two inlets at its southern side, Parsley Bay and Vaucluse Bay.

The name of Watson's Bay is applied only to the northern part of the larger bay, sheltered between Green Point and Village Point. This is a secure anchorage for seagoing vessels, with soundings of from six to twelve fathoms from close offshore. The distance from Green Point to Village Point is 700 yards. The shoreline between those two points measures three-quarters of a mile, and includes three short sandy beaches, with a shark-proof bathing enclosure, and a public recreational park on the waterfront.

Being the first large bay in secure anchorage for incoming vessels on the southern shore within the Main Harbour, Watson's Bay was used in the days of sail as a clearing-point for inspection of ships' papers, and for Customs and medical inspection, before vessels were allowed to proceed up-harbour. The opening of the Old South Head Road in 1811 gave access to Sydney by land with wheeled vehicles for the small community of pilots, signalmen, port officials, fishermen, and a few landed proprietors, which formed a "village" at Watson's Bay, eight miles by road and five miles by water from Sydney Town.

The name of Watson's Bay came into use officially when Robert Watson was appointed as Harbourmaster in 1811. He had lived there for some years previously as a pilot, and Governor Macquarie adopted the name that had been used unofficially for that anchorage and of the "village" on its shore.

In course of time the name of Village Point was given to the rocky headland on the southern side of the anchorage, separating it from Parsley Bay and Vaucluse Bay.

After the opening of the New South Head Road in 1840, residential settlement extended more rapidly eastwards along the foreshores from Rushcutters Bay to Watson's Bay. All those districts were incorporated into the Municipality of Woollahra in 1860.

Today Watson's Bay is seldom used as an inspection point or for pratique of incoming vessels. Its chief function in the harbour-services is as the site of the Pilot Station. The recreation park and the enclosed swimming-baths at the beach make it a favourite picnic ground. Shops and a modern-style hotel give the one-time "village" the character of a seaside resort, not only for residents but also for visitors and for the personnel of the near-by naval and military establishments. The bay is also a fishing-ground, and a rendezvous for yachtsmen. Two jetties extend from its shore. Memorials on the beach commemorate Robert Watson, and also the building of the Old South Head Road.

Near the beach is the club-house of the Vaucluse Yacht Club. The building is named in memory of Sil Rohu, an ardent yachtsman who made an original and remarkable contribution to the science, art, and sport of yachting.

In 1926 Sil Rohu conceived the idea of an "unsinkable" small sailing yacht, to enable boys and girls to learn and practise sailing in comparative safety. In consultation with a naval architect, Charles Sparrow, he designed, built, and launched the prototype of a sailing boat, eleven feet six inches long, made of plywood, completely decked and with a watertight cockpit and "fin" keel. Even after a capsize, this little yacht could be righted by its crew and got under sail again. It was given the yachting classname of "Vaucluse Junior," soon abbreviated to "V-J."

A large number of these unsinkable yachts were built. In 1931 the Vaucluse Yacht Club was formed, its membership restricted to boys and girls between fourteen and eighteen years; and racing in the one-design "V-J" class was regularly organized, chiefly at and near Watson's Bay. The "V-Js" became internationally known, and their idea was adopted in many other countries. Sil Rohu and Charles Sparrow later designed a larger "unsinkable" yacht, fifteen feet long, for use by adults, and named as the "Vaucluse Senior" ("V-S") class. When Sil Rohu died, his ashes were scattered on the waters of Watson's Bay.

THE "GREYCLIFFE" DISASTER

At St Peter's Anglican Church, Watson's Bay, are the Greycliffe Memorial Gates, erected in memory of those who lost their lives when the ferry-steamer S.S. *Greycliffe*, bound from Sydney Cove to Watson's Bay, was sunk off Bradley's Head on 3rd November, 1927.

This was the worst shipping disaster that has ever occurred inside Sydney Harbour, comparable in its tragic loss of life only with the wreck of the *Dunbar,* outside the Heads, seventy years previously.

The *Greycliffe* had left Sydney Cove at 4.15 p.m., with 125 passengers on board, for Watson's Bay. Many of these were children, returning home from attendance at schools in the city. When the ferry-steamer was off Bradley's Head, and within two miles of her destination, she was overtaken by S.S. *Tahiti,* a mail-and-passenger liner of 7,890 tons, outward-bound from Sydney to San Francisco.

The two vessels were on parallel courses, and the *Tahiti* had a pilot on board. According to her Master's evidence, she was proceeding down harbour at a speed of 7½ knots. For some reason never satisfactorily explained, but believed to have been a failure of the ferry's steering-gear, the courses suddenly converged at the moment when the liner's sharp steel bow was ranging with the ferry's stern.

Within a few seconds there was an appalling collision as the ferry got under the liner's bow, which ploughed right through her, cutting her in halves. The ferry sank almost immediately in fifty feet of water, one part of it to port and the other part to starboard of the liner, which was brought to a stop within a few hundred yards of the collision.

Some of the ferry-passengers had dived overboard on seeing that a collision was imminent. Others freed themselves from the wreckage as it sank, but many, killed outright, injured, or trapped inside the ferry's superstructure and hull, were carried to the bottom with the wreck. Boats were launched from the liner and from the shore, and a Water Police patrol was quickly on the scene. Some swimmers reached the shore at Bradley's Head. Others were picked up in boats.

Eighty-three of the ferry-passengers survived, and of these forty-eight were treated at the Sydney Hospital for injuries. The death-roll as officially stated was forty-two. For some days afterwards, divers were recovering bodies from the wreck on the sea-floor.

The disaster was investigated by a Coroner's Inquest and also by a Special Court of Marine Inquiry. A great deal of conflicting evidence was given, but the Marine Court found that the cause of the collision was "the failure of the *Tahiti* to keep out of the way of the *Greycliffe.*"

Millions of passengers have been, and continue to be, carried safely by the Sydney and the Manly ferry-steamers. The *Greycliffe* disaster was in every way exceptional. All the evidence showed that, a few seconds earlier or later, the ferry would not have been struck abeam by the liner's bow — but that was no consolation to the injured, the shocked, and the bereaved.

PARSLEY BAY

To the southward and westward of Village Point, Parsley Bay and Vaucluse Bay form a double indentation of the shore between Village Point and Vaucluse Point, and are a continuation of Watson's Bay. Though named as "bays," these side-by-side

52

recesses have the character of coves rather than of bays. They are of narrow tapering shape, each with an entrance less than a quarter of a mile wide, facing northwards, the double entrance (as between Village Point and Vaucluse Point) being only 800 yards wide.

The shores of both bays are rocky, except for small beaches at the head of each. They are sheltered from easterly, southerly, and westerly winds — which are the chiefly prevailing breezes at Sydney — but are open to occasional northerly gusts. The bays are used only by small yachts and boats.

The name of Parsley Bay is traditional, and was probably an identification used by the first exploring boat parties in 1788. A rational conjecture is that an edible plant was found growing there, resembling parsley, which would be relished as an anti-scorbutic by the vitamin-starved people of the First Fleet.

Parsley Bay has a netted swimming-enclosure and a municipal park at its head. It is a picnic ground, fishing-ground, and yachting and boating rendezvous, but has no other significant development or special historical associations.

VAUCLUSE BAY

Slightly larger than Parsley Bay, the cove lying adjacent to it on the westward side, Vaucluse Bay, also has a beach and park at its head. It is a boat harbour, and anchorage for small craft, with a jetty at its inner head. A steady red navigational light showing from a white tower on the eastern side of Vaucluse Bay is the front light of two which in transit lead through the Eastern Channel. This cove, and the gully at its head between ridges of sandstone, have romantic associations.

The name "Vaucluse" is a French form of the Latin *vallis clausa,* an enclosed valley. The name has been extended to the residential districts on the crests of the ridges, which are known as Vaucluse Heights, or, literally, "Enclosed Valley Heights."

In April 1801, a prominent and wealthy citizen of Cork in Ireland, Sir Henry Brown Hayes, who had been Sheriff of that city, and Captain of the Militia, was convicted of abducting an heiress. He was condemned to death, but the sentence was commuted to transportation for life. He was put aboard the transport *Atlas,* and arrived at Sydney in July 1802, being then forty years of age. Although some moves were made to humiliate this wealthy and titled convict, Governor King allowed him, in August 1803, to purchase 475 acres of land at South Head, and to attempt to establish a farm there.

In that way the "gentleman-convict" was virtually banished from the precincts of Sydney Town. He named his property "Vaucluse" and built a house in the "closed valley" at the head of the cove which became known as Vaucluse Bay. The sandy soil was not of much use for farming but Hayes could afford to employ some of his fellow-convicts as servants for building the house and clearing and cultivating some of the land.

As snakes were plentiful in the scrubby bush he hit on the

idea of importing from Ireland a shipment of soil, which he sprinkled around the house, in the hope that, as Saint Patrick had banished snakes from the soil of Ireland, this would prove effective in banishing snakes from Vaucluse House. History does not record if the charm worked.

In 1812 Hayes was granted a full pardon. ·He sold his property at Vaucluse to Sir Maurice O'Connell, commandant of the garrison troops of the 73rd Regiment, and then returned to Ireland.

In 1814, O'Connell sold the Vaucluse property to Captain John Piper, a military officer who was in charge of the collection of Customs and Harbour Dues.

In 1827, the house at Vaucluse and a hundred acres of land surrounding it were bought by William Charles Wentworth, the Australian-born explorer, poet, barrister, and fiery advocate of Australian political self-dependence, who within two years built the fine colonial mansion that stands there today, known as Vaucluse House.

Thirty-three years later, in 1862, after a brilliant career in which he had taken a leading part in promoting colonial representative self-government in New South Wales, Wentworth retired to England to live, and died there in 1872, aged eighty-two years. His body was brought home to Australia, and, after a State funeral, was interred on 6th May, 1873 in a vault at Vaucluse House.

In the 1890s, Vaucluse House and part of the landed estate were purchased by the Government; and since then the house has been maintained as an historical museum and a memorial to Wentworth. This is one of the "tourist attractions" of Sydney, visited by large numbers of people annually, the house being a fine example of colonial architecture, in an excellent state of preservation.

SEE ALSO PART II   NIELSEN PARK

The tip of the promontory on the western side of Vaucluse Bay, separating it from Rose Bay, is a public reserve of thirty acres, named Nielsen Park, in honour of N.R.W. Nielsen, who, as Minister for Lands in 1910-11, authorized the purchase of the privately owned land along the foreshores there, for use as a picnic reserve.

The northern foreshore of the Nielsen Park promontory is a rocky headland nearly half a mile long, from Vaucluse Point at its north-eastern end to Shark Point at its south-western end. Within this shore, the rocks are interrupted by a stretch of sandy beach, 300 yards long, in a shallow indentation named Shark Bay. There is a large shark-proof sea-bathing pool at the beach, and also a ferry-wharf, to which excursion steamers run from Sydney Cove in the summer months.

The Aboriginal name of Vaucluse Point was "Morung," and of Shark Point "Burroway." At the tip of Vaucluse Point is a heap of sandstone boulders named the Bottle and Glass. This name,

54

like that of the Sow and Pigs, was bestowed by the pioneer watermen of the Harbour because of its prominence as a navigating-mark. At that time the rock formation had some fanciful resemblance to a bottle and glass, but the rocks have crumbled or collapsed to an irregular heap of boulders.

There is a tradition that, before this part of the shore was inhabited, the Bottle and Glass Rocks were used as a target for gunnery practice with roundshot; but, like many other oral traditions, this is a matter of folklore rather than of documentary proof.

The names of Shark Bay, Shark Point, and Shark Island (in the offing of Shark Point) are traditional, and evidently refer to some incident in early colonial history, in which sharks were sighted or caught, or perhaps attacked a human being.

SHARK ATTACKS   SEE ALSO PART II

Despite the publicity that is invariably given to attacks by sharks on sea-bathers, the fatalities from this cause inside Sydney Harbour and on the adjacent ocean beaches, are rare, in relation to the millions of bathers annually. It is the rarity of the attacks which makes them "newsworthy."

Nevertheless it is true that large sharks of several species, including "man-eaters," cruise in the waters outside the Heads, and occasionally enter the Harbour. According to research by G. P. Whitely, F.R.Z.S., Curator of Fishes at the Australian Museum, Sydney (published in an article in *The Australian Encyclopaedia*, 1956), there are records of only fifteen persons killed by shark attacks inside Sydney Harbour in 165 years (from 1791 to 1956). Of these, eleven were in the Main Harbour, including two in the Parramatta River and one in the Lane Cove River; and four were in Middle Harbour.

There were eight fatal attacks by sharks at the ocean beaches — all since 1922, when surf-bathing was beginning to become popular, and none there since 1935, when mesh-netting for sharks and shark-warning patrols made the ocean beaches almost completely safe from this menace.

There have been no fatal attacks by sharks inside the Main Harbour since 1929. Possibly sharks are scared away by the city lights, noises, and shipping activity. Of the five deaths from shark attacks in the much quieter waters of Middle Harbour, two were in 1942, two in 1955, and another in 1962.

All the sea-bathing facilities inside the Main Harbour are in shark-proof enclosures; the deaths that have occurred in Middle Harbour were all of persons swimming in open waters.

The names of Shark Bay, Shark Point, and Shark Island do not indicate that sharks are more plentiful or dangerous in that vicinity than in other parts of the harbour. In fact, no fatal shark attacks have been recorded there.

ROSE BAY   SEE ALSO PART II

Rose Bay is the largest bay in Sydney Harbour. It is a true bay, with a wide mouth and a curving crescent shore. The   55 distance between its headlands, from Shark Point to Woollahra Point, is one mile. Shark Island lies between these headlands. The shoreline of the bay measures 2¾ miles. The eastern shore, for a mile to the southward of Shark Point, is rocky and elevated, with a small indentation and beach named Hermit Bay.

At the head of Rose Bay is a curved beach stretching for 1½ miles around the foreshores, with an esplanade and a park in flat ground, and the New South Head Road hugging the shore in the nature of a marine drive. The bay has sufficient depth to provide anchorages for ocean-going vessels, but is seldom used for that purpose, and its wide expanse is therefore clear for flying-boats to take off and to alight. A commercial flying-boat base is at the head of the bay. There are no commercial wharves in Rose Bay, but its western side is a boat harbour, with moorings and jetties for small craft.

Rose Bay was named by Governor Phillip in honour of George Rose, Britain's Secretary of the Treasury, who had much to do with financing the First Fleet and the establishing of the colony of New South Wales. (In his honour, also, Phillip named Rose Hill, at Parramatta.) The name is appropriate also, in a poetical sense, when the reflections of dawn or of sunset glow on its broad waters in delicate tints of pink or cerise, evocative of the petal sheen of a rose. That play of light, characteristic of Sydney Harbour in all its reaches, bays, and coves, is seen to perfection on Rose Bay's large expanse, especially when the water is calm, as it is usually at dawn, and often at sunset on a summer's day, before a southerly breeze ripples it at dusk.

Flanked by Vaucluse Heights on its eastern side, and by the promontory of Point Piper (terminating in Woollahra Point) on its western side, and with flat land rising to Bellevue Hill on its southern side, Rose Bay, as a residential district, is considered to be the "dress circle" bay of Sydney Harbour. There are many beautiful dwellings and other buildings on its shores.

On the eastern side, adjacent to Nielsen Park, is the Strickland Hospital. This was a mansion built in 1854 by John Hosking, and named by him "Carrara" because its mantelpieces were of marble imported from Carrara in Italy.

John Hosking was the first Mayor of Sydney when the town was incorporated as a city in 1842. His wealth came chiefly from his marriage to the daughter of Samuel Terry, an ex-convict who became a publican and moneylender. Chiefly through fore-closing on mortgages, Terry became the owner of a large number of landed properties, in town and country. He died in 1838.

"Carrara" was acquired in 1915 by the Government for use as a military hospital, and was renamed in honour of Lord Strickland, who was the Governor of New South Wales at that time. It later became a nursing home for old-age pensioners.

Immediately to the southward of the Strickland Hospital is Hermit Bay, a small indentation of the shore, well sheltered from all breezes except westerlies, used sometimes as a refuge by yachts when strong easterlies or north-easterlies suddenly blow. The bay is presumably named from its southern headland, Hermit

Point, where some individual, whose name is not recorded, made a lonely home in the early colonial years. A house, owned by Alexander Dick, stood on the shore of Hermit Bay in 1840. The property was bought in 1914 by D.H. McCathie, who built a fine home there, that was partly destroyed by fire in 1937, and rebuilt.

Rose Bay is of special interest in the naval history of Sydney, as the naval training ship H.M.A.S. *Tingira* was moored there from 1912 to 1927. She was originally the *Sobraon*, a full-rigged ship of composite iron and teak hull-construction, 2,131 tons, launched at Aberdeen in Scotland in 1866. For twenty-five years she was one of the "crack" flyers among the many large sailing-vessels on the Britain to Australia passenger-and-cargo run.

In 1891, the *Sobraon* was bought by the New South Wales Government for £11,500, and was moored off Balmain, used as a reformatory prison for delinquent boys. In 1911 she was bought by the Australian Commonwealth Government for use as a training ship for boys joining the Royal Australian Navy. Renamed as H.M.A.S. *Tingira*, she was moved to Rose Bay, and began her career as a training-ship in 1912, when the first batch of 37 young trainees began their naval career.

H.M.A.S. *Tingira* was paid off in 1927 and sold to a private buyer. She was anchored in Berry's Bay and then in 1935 was sold to a Sydney company for breaking up. Her figurehead — a lion — was sent to the Flinders Naval Depot, and is preserved there, as a valuable memento of the history of the Australian naval and mercantile marine.

On the eastern shore of Rose Bay, to the southward of Hermit Bay, are two of the best-known boarding-schools for girls in Sydney. "Kambala," a Church of England foundation, was originally a colonial mansion named "Tivoli." It was leased by the church in 1912, and bought in 1927. The school had been conducted since 1884 at "Kambala," a colonial mansion on Bellevue Hill, and that name replaced "Tivoli."

The Sacred Heart Convent was originally a mansion built by a Sydney merchant, George Thorne, in 1851. It was bought by the Catholic Church in 1882, and has since been used as a convent school, with several extensions of the buildings, including a chapel completed in 1900. The convent, which stands in seventeen acres of grounds, is a prominent landmark.

There are also two renowned schools for boys on Rose Bay, on the south-western side, placed on the ridge that runs from Bellevue Hill to Point Piper. Scots College, conducted by the Presbyterian Church, was established on Botany Bay in 1893, and moved to Bellevue Hill in 1898. "Cranbrook," a Church of England boys' school, was originally a mansion built by Robert Towns, merchant and shipowner, who died there in 1873. From 1902 until 1917, "Cranbrook" was the residence of the Governors of New South Wales, under an arrangement by which Government House in the Domain was used as the Sydney residence of the Governors-General of the Australian Commonwealth. The building has been used as a Church of England school since the year 1918.

At the head of Rose Bay are the hangars, slipways, workshops, and landing-pontoon of the Flying-Boat Base, which is controlled by the Department of Civil Aviation. This installation, together with aircraft mooring buoys on the bay, is officially named the Sydney Water Airport. It was opened in July 1938 as terminal of the Qantas Empire Airways mail-and-passenger service with flying-boats on the route between Australia and Britain. This route followed the Australian coast northwards from Sydney to Townsville, thence across Cape York Peninsula and the Gulf of Carpentaria, and along the coast of Arnhem Land to Darwin; thence to Singapore, and, by stages mostly over water, to Poole Harbour, near Bournemouth, in the South of England.

Though slower than land-wheeled aircraft, the flying-boats of that period were considered safer, as they could alight on the water in an emergency, almost anywhere along the route. In April 1940 the flying-boat service was extended from Sydney, across the Tasman Sea, to New Zealand.

The Japanese occupation of Malaya and Indonesia in 1942 cut the Empire flying-boat route. The Qantas flying-boats were then put into service as troop transports. They made a total of 765 flights, carrying 24,000 troops from the Australian mainland to New Guinea. From 1942 to the end of the war in 1945 the Sydney Water Airport saw its maximum activity, in use by American and Australian flying-boats on war service.

In May 1946 the civilian airmail and passenger services were restored, with larger flying-boats that took one week for the journey from Rose Bay to Poole. The services were extended in the following year to Norfolk Island and Lord Howe Island, and subsequently to Fiji, New Caledonia, and the New Hebrides; but gradually, in the 1950s, large land-planes replaced flying-boats on ocean-crossing routes.

In the early 1960s the Sydney Water Airport was used only occasionally, on once-a-week services to Norfolk Island and Lord Howe Island, or on charter-flights; and it appeared that, unless some new technical development occurred, or some new emergency arose, the heyday of flying-boats, in the evolution of air-transport, had passed, and would become only a memory.

To the southward from the shore at the head of Rose Bay, extending for nearly a mile (between the New South Head Road and the Old South Head Road), with a width averaging a quarter of a mile, are the Royal Sydney Golf Club links. The club was founded in 1893. On the western side of its links are the Cranbrook School playing-field and the Woollahra municipal park, in which are the links of the Woollahra Golf Club. These large open spaces of greensward, in a vale flanked by ridges on which the residences are built in substantial styles, add much to the distinctive character of this pleasant suburb.

On the south-western side, at the head of Rose Bay, is the ferry wharf, no longer in use as such, but handy for boatmen using the yacht moorings in that part of the bay. In the three

Southern Bays — Rose Bay, Double Bay, and Rushcutters

Bay — which have no large mercantile wharves, a very large number of small craft — mostly sailing yachts and motor yachts — ride at moorings licensed by the Maritime Services Board, and set out on their courses to take part in racing or cruising, chiefly on Saturdays and Sundays.

The owners and crews of these yachts belong to various clubs, some of which have their club-houses on the shores of the Southern Bays, and some elsewhere around the Harbour. For the building and servicing of the yachts and other small craft there are dozens of boatsheds and slipways on the shores of Sydney Harbour, including several in the Southern Bays. It is not unusual, on Saturday afternoons during the sailing season (from September to March), for a thousand sailing yachts to be out on the Harbour in club and inter-club races. On these occasions the three Southern Bays in particular present a scene of aggregated yachting activity to an extent that is perhaps unequalled anywhere else in the world; yet these three bays provide moorings for only some of Sydney's yachts. There are yacht moorings in many other bays and coves along the Harbour's shores.

The Woollahra Sailing Club has its club-house on the southeastern side of Rose Bay, and the Royal Motor Yacht Club on the western side. One of the oldest and biggest yacht-clubs at Sydney, the Royal Prince Alfred Yacht Club, has its club-house in the city, in Rowe Street, and also a waterfront club-house at Newport (at the mouth of the Hawkesbury River). Many of its members moor their yachts at Rose Bay, Double Bay, and Rushcutters Bay.

The Royal Prince Alfred Yacht Club was formed with twelve members in October 1867, and was named in honour of Prince Alfred, Duke of Edinburgh (the second son of Queen Victoria), who was at that time on a visit to Australia. He consented to become patron of the club, which within two months of its foundation had eighty members, and twenty yachts on its register. By 1965 there were 1,560 members and 230 yachts.

The Club's Admiralty warrant and permission to use the prefix "Royal" were granted in 1911.

The first sailing club formed in Australia was the "Mosquito" Yacht Club, established at Sydney in 1856 for boats limited to thirteen feet on the keel. Its leading members formed the Prince Alfred Yacht Club for larger yachts, with a minimum of 22 ft on the load-waterline.

SHARK ISLAND   SEE ALSO PART II

Lying between the headlands of Rose Bay, a quarter of a mile to the northward of Woollahra Point, Shark Island is 250 yards long and not more than 100 yards wide. It is a prominent seamark in the Lower Harbour, but is not an obstruction to shipping, as it is clear of the channel, and half a mile from the northern shore at Bradley's Head.

The island is a picnic reserve under control of the Maritime Services Board, with a ranger in residence. Its rocky soil sustains some indigenous trees and shrubs, and at various times "hermits" have lived there — among them an author, Con Drew, who in the 1920s made the island his home, describing himself as "a Sydney Harbour beachcomber."

Picturesque, and convenient as a rounding-mark in yacht racing, Shark Island has never been "developed" for any utilitarian purpose. The Aboriginal name, Boambilli, may some day be restored.

POINT PIPER

The promontory on the western side of Rose Bay, separating it from Double Bay, is a ridge with rocky shores, which is exclusively a residential district, and as such has some of the most substantial and elegant private houses on the Harbour shores.

On its northern extremity are two bluff headlands — Woollahra Point and Point Piper — and between them is a small open bay with a short beach, named Lady Martin's Beach, in honour of the wife of Sir James Martin, who was Premier of New South Wales for short periods on three occasions in the 1860s and early 1870s, and Chief Justice from 1873 to 1886. (Martin Place in the city was named as a compliment to him.)

The name of Point Piper is applied not only to the headland but to the entire promontory. It commemorates Captain John Piper, a military officer who was one of the most "spectacular" characters in the early history of Sydney. In 1814, aged forty-one, he was appointed "Naval Officer" of the Port of Sydney. In the terminology of those days, that meant that he was collector of Customs and Harbour Dues, superintendent of the Water Police, and, in general, controller of shipping in the port.

Payment for these services was a commission of five per cent of the dues collected. The "farming" of government revenues in that way was not unusual; it was a spur to zeal in revenue-collecting; but neither Piper nor Governor Macquarie (who appointed him) could have foreseen the rapid increase of shipping and of population and trade at Sydney, which, within a few years, yielded Piper an income of £4,000 a year — equivalent perhaps to £20,000 a year in the currency of the present day.

Piper spent his income lavishly. He built a mansion at Point Piper and entertained there extravagantly, to such an extent that wits referred to him as "the Prince of Australia." He spent money also on breeding horses and on racing them, and was liberal in his gifts to the needy, and to spongers.

He became careless in his duties as "Naval Officer." Governor Darling, who arrived in 1825, investigated Piper's accounts, and found that he had been neglectful in collecting dues. There was no imputation of dishonesty; only of carelessness and neglect. Piper was dismissed from his post, and was soon in such serious financial difficulties that he was compelled to sell his mansion and other properties (including Vaucluse House) to pay his debts.

He attempted to commit suicide by jumping out of his boat, but was rescued by his boatmen. From the wreck of his fortune, he saved enough to buy a pastoral property near Bathurst, but lost this also through extravagant living, and died poor, in 1851, aged 78.

A more distinguished resident at Point Piper was Lawrence Hargrave, a pioneer of aviation, who lived at 58 Wunulla Road from 1902 until his death in 1915.

Born in England in 1850, Hargrave arrived in Australia as a boy of sixteen, and became an engineering draughtsman in Sydney. He accompanied exploring expeditions to Papua, and in 1878 was appointed assistant at Sydney Observatory. In 1884 he began his researches into the problems of aviation, and, after many experiments, invented the box-kite, and built many models of aeroplanes and aeroplane engines. His papers on aerodynamics, published in scientific journals, attracted attention throughout the world. He ranks among the undoubted pioneers of human flight.

Above Lady Martin's Beach is the club-house of the Royal Prince Edward Yacht Club, which was formed in 1920, and named in honour of Edward, Prince of Wales (later King Edward VIII), who visited Australia in that year and consented to become the club's patron. A leading part in the formation of the club was taken by Sir Alexander MacCormick, who became its first Commodore. He was an eminent surgeon who had won distinction especially on military service during the 1914-18 war, and had previously been Commodore of the Royal Sydney Yacht Squadron (which has its club-house at Kirribilli on the northern shore of the Harbour). The Royal Prince Edward Yacht Club was granted an Admiralty Warrant in 1937.

DOUBLE BAY   SEE ALSO PART II

Double Bay is a true bay with a wide mouth and curving shore; although there are two beaches separated by a small headland it cannot be called a "double bay" in any exact topographical sense. A recess on the eastern shore is named Blackburn Cove, evidently after David Blackburn, who was Sailing-Master of H.M.S. *Supply* in 1788.

The mouth of the bay between Point Piper and Darling Point is less than half a mile wide, but the bay has a shoreline of nearly two miles. In its eastern shore is Seven Shillings Beach, whose romantic name is derived from an unrecorded incident. Redleaf Swimming Pool — so named because of a near-by wall covered with a red-leafed creeper — is situated on this beach. It is well appointed for sea-bathing and sun-bathing.

At the head of the bay is another beach, on which the ferry wharf, not now used as such, is handy to a large number of yacht moorings. The bay is generally shallow, its depth of water being for the most part less than three fathoms.

On the flanking promontories of Point Piper and Darling Point, and on the southern shore, which rises to a ridge named Edgecliffe, the mansions of the colonial period have become interspersed with flats in "high-density" population development. Many of the apartment buildings are of striking modern design.

61

This district is three miles by road from the centre of Sydney, and is thus a convenient "dormitory-suburb" for workers in the city.

Near the ferry wharf is the club-house of the New South Wales 18-Ft Sailing League, which was formed in 1934 by an amalgamation of previous existing clubs of yachtsmen devoted to a special kind of yacht racing in "centreboard" yachts of defined dimensions. The "eighteen-footers" are 18 ft long, 6 ft minimum beam, and 20 inches deep, with decking 9 inches wide on each side fore and aft.

They are open boats, with a round bilge construction, and unballasted, except by the weight of the crews. They have a very large sail area, limited in modern times for racing purposes to a mainsail, jib, spinnaker, and ringtail, with a total area of 1,215 square feet.

Racing in the "eighteen-footers" of this class has a special association with Sydney Harbour, and is more keenly developed here than anywhere else in the world. The club at Double Bay conducts a programme of challenge races every Sunday from 1st September to 20th April. The races are followed by spectators in a chartered ferry and in launches, and are watched also by large crowds on the headlands. There is another 18-ft sailing club at Balmain in the Upper Harbour.

The principle of the centreboard, or retractable keel, in yachting was introduced at Sydney in 1854 by S.C. Burt, who imported from America a yacht of this design named *Presto*. Many more centreboard sailing boats were soon built at Sydney. Disputes arose on methods of measuring and handicapping these "skimming-dishes" in races against deep-keel decked yachts. The centreboard boats were suitable for sailing only within the Harbour, and not on ocean courses. Undecked as they were, and of light wooden construction with a shallow depth, and carrying a great press of sail, they were liable to capsize in ocean seas or strong breezes. With their low freeboard they shipped water from overside, to such an extent that a "bailer-boy" was always a busy member of the crew.

Races restricted to centreboard boats became a feature of regatta programmes. In the 1890s the "eighteen-footers" had become well established as a class, with their own clubs, and programmes of racing conducted independently of the deep-keel yacht clubs. One of the clubs, known as the Sydney Flying Squadron, provided spectacular racing that became a notable feature of the life of Sydney Harbour, and world-renowned as a demonstration of the Australian sporting slogan, "give it a go."

These boats, of up to 9 ft beam, carried crews of no more than fifteen men, who acted as "live ballast," leaning far out over the windward side to prevent the craft from capsizing. As many as thirty-two boats started in a race, and there was brisk wagering on the result. On one occasion in 1913, during a sudden squall, twenty of the twenty-one starters capsized, but that holocaust was exceptional.

A "Blue Nose" (i.e., Nova Scotian) yachtsman, Captain Joshua

Slocum, who visited Sydney in 1896 on his round-the-world cruise in his yacht *Spray* — which he sailed single-handed — recorded in his book, *Sailing Alone Round the World,* his impressions of yachting at Sydney: "The harbour was alive with boats and yachts of every class. It was a scene of animation hardly equalled in any other part of the world. The typical Sydney boat is a handy sloop of great beam and enormous sail-carrying power; but a capsize is not uncommon, for they carry sail like Vikings."

The New South Wales 18-Ft Sailing League at Double Bay has continued that tradition. The club operated from a leased boatshed until its club-house was built in 1961. In 1965 it had 600 members and twenty boats on the register.

DARLING POINT

The promontory separating Double Bay from Rushcutters Bay is a ridge terminating in a headland that was named by the Aborigines Yarrandabbi. At some time between 1825 and 1831 Major-General Ralph Darling, who was Governor of New South Wales during that period, conferred on the headland the name, Mrs Darling's Point, in honour of his wife, whose maiden name was Elizabeth Dumaresq.

In course of time that gallant gesture was brushed aside, and Yarrandabbi became known as Darling Point, appearing to perpetuate the name of the Governor, who had already allowed his own name to be put on the map of Sydney at Darlinghurst and Darling Harbour, and on the map of Australia in the naming of the Darling River and the Darling Downs.

Until 1834, the swamp and creek at the head of Rushcutters Bay was uncrossable by wheeled vehicles. A bridge was then built, and thereafter Mrs Darling's Point became an "élite" residential district, in which several fine colonial mansions were built. Among these was "Carthona," on the eastern end of the Point, a splendid two-storey stone building which remains as a prominent landmark. It was the home of Major Thomas Livingstone Mitchell, soldier, explorer, and author (he translated from the Portuguese into English the epic *Lusiad* of Luis de Camoens). Major Mitchell was Surveyor-General of New South Wales from 1828 until his death in 1855. He needed a large house, as his wife bore him twelve children.

Another fine colonial mansion on Darling Point was "Greenoaks," built in 1847 as the home of Thomas Sutcliffe Mort. This Tudor-style manor-house was later bought by the Church of England. Renamed "Bishopscourt," it is the residence of the Archbishop of Sydney.

Among other mansions built at Darling Point was "Retford," the home of Samuel Hordern.

In 1848, the foundation stone was laid of St Mark's Church (Anglican), at the corner of Darling Point Road and Greenoaks Avenue, on one of the highest sites on the ridge of the Darling Point promontory. The church was designed by Edmund Blacket, architect, who, within thirty-five years, from 1845 onwards,

63

designed fifty-eight churches in New South Wales, including St Andrew's Cathedral, Sydney, and St Saviour's Cathedral, Goulburn, besides the main building of the University of Sydney, and is known as "the Christopher Wren of Australia."

Blacket specialized in Gothic-styled church architecture, and St Mark's was one of his best buildings. The church was opened in 1852, and the graceful tower and spire were added in 1875.

The former "exclusive" character of Darling Point — as of the other eastern suburban residential districts along the Harbour shore — has been changed to some extent by the development of mechanized road transport, replacing the horse-drawn carriages and gigs that were not only "fashionable" but almost indispensable for people who could afford to live "out of town," in the heyday of the horse during the second half of the nineteenth century.

With modern road transport has come the "high-density" population of flat-dwellers in multi-storied apartment houses which are becoming more numerous and more prominent each year; they may be seen cheek by jowl with the remaining mansions of the colonial style on those promontories of the Southern Bays, where "a view of the Harbour" was, as it always will be at Sydney, a major aspect in the buying and selling of real-estate properties.

SEE ALSO PART II   CLARK ISLAND

Half an acre in area, Clark Island lies 500 yards offshore, north of Darling Point headland. Like Shark Island, nearly a mile to its eastward, this island is clear of the main navigational channel; it is more than half a mile from Bradley's Head on the northern shore. All the islands in Sydney Harbour were reserved as Crown lands, and in 1901 were placed under the control of the Harbour Trust, passing to its successor, the Maritime Services Board, in 1936.

Like Shark Island, Clark Island is a picnic reserve, with a small jetty by which visitors may go ashore from launches or yachts, and is nicely laid out with rock gardens and native shrubs and trees.

Lieutenant Ralph Clark was an officer in the Marines, who arrived with the First Fleet in 1788. He kept a journal, in which, on 18th February, 1790, he recorded: "After I was relieved from guard, I went down to my island to look at my garden, and found that some boat had landed since I had been there last, and taken away the greatest part of a fine bed of onions. I thought that, having a garden on an island, it would be more secure, but I find that they even get at it there. My corn comes on as well as corn can do, and I hope they will be so good as to let that remain."

Whether the thieves were marines, or convicts, or Aborigines — or seamen of the Navy who had a garden on Garden Island, three-quarters of a mile to the westward — Lieutenant Clark had no means of catching them in the act while he was on guard duty at the settlement at Sydney Cove, two miles away. The Aborigines had canoes of hollowed logs which they used for crossing the harbour and its bays and arms, and they had every right to believe that the island, which they called **Billongoola**, was theirs, including onions for the taking.

Lieutenant Clark had a different view of the rights of property. On 21st March, he noted in his diary: "Soon after breakfast, I went out in my boat, down to my island, and found that some person had been there again, and had taken away all my potatoes. Whoever they are, I wish they were in hell for their kindness."

RUSHCUTTERS BAY   SEE ALSO PART II

In the topographical sense, Rushcutters Bay and Elizabeth Bay constitute a true "double bay" — i.e., two wide-mouthed indentations of the shore side by side — lying between the promontories of Darling Point on their eastern side and Potts Point on the western side. For practical purposes they are considered to be separate identities. This is partly because when Sydney Town was incorporated as a city in 1842 its eastern boundary was fixed at a creek flowing into the western side of the head of Rushcutters Bay. That boundary remained when the municipality of Woollahra was incorporated in 1860.

For municipal purposes, the shores of Elizabeth Bay, and most of the western shore of Rushcutters Bay, are therefore within the City of Sydney, while the southern and eastern shores of Rushcutters Bay are within the municipality of Woollahra. Apart from that aspect, the waters of Elizabeth Bay are geographically separated to a discernible extent from the inner waters of Rushcutters Bay by a small protuberance of the land with two "blunt" points on it, Macleay Point and Elizabeth Point.

In that limited sense, Rushcutters Bay comprises only the waters to the southward of an imaginary line drawn from the western tip of Darling Point promontory to Macleay Point, a distance of approximately a quarter of a mile. The shoreline within that bay measures almost one mile. At its head was originally a swamp and creek, spread inland to the southward for half a mile, and receiving the drainage of the ridges on which the suburbs of Edgecliffe and Paddington have grown.

The swamp has been reclaimed to make parkland and playing-fields, but in its primitive state it was covered in reeds or rushes, and that is how the bay got its name.

From the earliest days of settlement at Sydney Cove, parties of "rushcutters" were sent to that swamp to collect reeds for thatching huts. At first they went there in boats to bring back bundles of rushes, until such time as a foot track may have been cleared over the steep ridge which was designated the Eastern Hill until it was named Darlinghurst.

On 30th May, 1788, two convicts, William Okey and Samuel Davis, who were cutting rushes at Rushcutters Bay, were killed by Aborigines. Their bodies were found and brought by Captain Campbell of the Marines to the hospital at Sydney Cove. Surgeon-General John White, R.N., who examined the bodies,   65 stated in his journal: "From the civility shown on all occasions to the officers by the natives, I am strongly inclined to think that they must have been provoked or injured by the convicts." That opinion was held also by Governor Phillip, who, on making inquiries, found that "The first injury had been offered by the unfortunate men. . . . They had been seen with a 'canoe, which they had taken from one of the fishing-places."

Phillip went in person with an armed party to the place where the bodies were found, not to wreak blind vengeance, but to inquire into the circumstances, in a fair and judicial manner. He gave the natives the benefit of the doubt — one instance among many of his enlightened attitude to those people who had been disturbed in their ancestral hunting-places by invaders who had terrible weapons for dealing out death. The natives' spears were no match for the European guns.

The swamp at the head of Rushcutters Bay was by-passed on its inland side by the builders of the Old South Head Road; but in 1834 a wooden trestle bridge was built, near the foreshore, across the creek. In 1839 this was replaced by a stone arch bridge. From those bridges, the New South Head Road was gradually extended along the shore to the eastward. To maintain the road, a toll-gate was put on the Rushcutters Bay Creek Bridge in 1849, and tolls were collected there until 1894. (The toll-keeper's cottage still stands at 85 New South Head Road.)

The swamp was gradually filled in, and the stone bridge was demolished, but there is still a storm-water drainage channel flowing into the head of Rushcutters Bay from the sportsgrounds, in which are situated the Trumper Park cricket oval, the "White City" tennis courts, the playing-fields of the Sydney Grammar School, and the Rushcutters Bay Stadium.

The Stadium, seating 20,000 spectators, was built in 1907 for the World's Heavyweight Boxing Championship Match between Tommy Burns and Jack Johnson, held on Boxing Day, 26th December, 1908.

Because of silt deposited for æons by the creek which drained the swamp, Rushcutters Bay is shallow inshore. It is — even more so than Double Bay and Rose Bay — a boat haven, with numerous moorings for yachts, and sheds for building and servicing yachts.

On the eastern shore of the bay is a large sea-bathing pool, municipally owned, much used by residents of the densely populated districts near by.

On this shore also is the club-house of the Cruising Yacht Club of Australia, which, since 1945, has organized the annual Sydney-to-Hobart sailing race, on an ocean course of 680 miles. recognized as one of the most strenuous ocean yacht races in the world. The competitors start from Double Bay on Boxing Day in a festive atmosphere, the start attended by a large number of spectator-carrying ferries, launches, and small sailing-yachts.

The Cruising Yacht Club also conducts ocean races to various places on the coast, under strict rules as regards safety at sea, and also under a system of handicapping by time allowances, which gives a chance to yachts designed not only for speed but also for cruising comfort.

In these various ways, Rushcutters Bay, and the parks on its southern shore, provide recreational facilities handy to the city. The head of the bay is two miles by road from the centre of the city, but less than half a mile from the King's Cross district, which is one of the most densely populated districts in Australia.

H.M.A.S. "RUSHCUTTER"

The naval shore establishment, on the eastern side of Rush-cutters Bay, named H.M.A.S. *Rushcutter,* is one of the principal establishments of the Royal Australian Navy at Sydney. It is headquarters for the recruiting and training of the Royal Australian Naval Reserve (chiefly officers of the Merchant Navy who, in wartime, may be called upon to serve in the regular Navy or in auxiliary naval service); it is also the headquarters of the Naval Diving School and of the Naval Divers based on Sydney. Near by is the Naval Experimental Laboratory, concerned chiefly with undersea research.

Before the Australian colonies were federated in 1901 into the Commonwealth of Australia, each of the colonies had some measure of naval defence to support the warships of the British Navy stationed in Australian waters. In 1878, Sir Peter Scratchley, who had been appointed by the British War Office as a commissioner to report on Australian defence, recommended that all offensive action at sea in Australian waters should be left to the Royal Navy, but that the colonies should provide iron-clad gunboats and launches to operate in conjunction with shore batteries in harbour defences; and further that the locally provided vessels should be manned by locally established naval brigades.

A New South Wales Volunteer Naval Brigade had already been formed at Sydney in 1863. The British Admiralty in 1880 gave it a steam screw-driven corvette, H.M.S. *Wolverene,* as a training ship. The headquarters of the Naval Brigade were at Rushcutters Bay. It was a Naval Reserve, to reinforce the British Squadron on the Australian station, if required in any emergency. In 1889 the *Wolverene* was condemned as unseaworthy. She was broken up, and not replaced.

The Naval Brigade struggled on, as best it could, drilling and receiving instruction, to meet contingencies of war that seemed remote.

An opportunity for active service came in June 1900, with the urgent need to send forces to China to cope with the "Boxer Rising," when Europeans were beleagured in the Legation Quarter at Peking. A contingent of 260 of the Naval Brigade from New South Wales, and 200 from Victoria, left Sydney in a troopship, S.S. *Salamis,* on 8th August, 1900, and took part in action against the "Boxers," in what amounted to policing the regions in which troubles had occurred. There were no casualties, and the contingent returned to Sydney in April 1901.

The federation of the Australian colonies had then become an accomplished fact. Naval and military defence was thereafter the responsibility of the Federal Government, which took over control of the former colonial naval and military forces. These included the establishment of the New South Wales Naval Brigade at Rushcutters Bay.

The Naval Brigade continued to function, as an auxiliary and reserve of the Royal Australian Navy. In that sense, the naval shore establishment at Rushcutters Bay is the oldest establishment of the R.A.N. at Sydney. It was commissioned as H.M.A.S. *Rushcutter* in 1920, and continued to serve as a recruiting-and-training depot for the Royal Australian Naval Reserve (which is the successor to the Naval Brigade), and also eventually as the Torpedo and Anti-Submarine Training and Naval Diving Schools.

The Torpedo and Anti-Submarine Training School was transferred to H.M.A.S. *Watson* in 1956. Since then, the principal operational training at H.M.A.S. *Rushcutter* has been that of the Naval Divers, who, under modern conditions of warfare, have an important role to play, not only in salvage operations and mine-clearance, but in underwater combat operations against the enemy.

Ever since the invention in 1886 of the pneumatic diving-suit, made of rubber or "rubberized" fabric, with a copper and glass helmet, supplied with air from a pump, the Navy has had divers, trained to go down to the sea-bed for salvage operations, or to inspect the bottoms of vessels, or for other tasks in the service.

The old-time "suits" are still used on occasions, but the modern-style Naval Diver is equipped with a tight-fitting suit, goggles, flippers, and an air-apparatus which gives great mobility underwater, in the style of the so-called "frogmen," developed during the 1939-45 war.

These Naval Divers are at times asked to assist the Water Police or other Harbour authorities, and their services are made available by the Navy in emergencies calling for the special equipment and training required for underwater work.

Berthed at H.M.A.S. *Rushcutter* are vessels equipped as diving-tenders, used for training and operational service. The equipment on shore includes a pressure chamber for treating divers affected by the "bends" — a result sometimes of rising to the surface too speedily from great depths.

At H.M.A.S. *Rushcutter* also is the depot of the Royal Australian Naval Sailing Club, which trains naval personnel in the handling of naval whaleboats and dinghies under sail.

An interesting historical relic is preserved in H.M.A.S. *Rushcutter*, within an alcove near the gate from the landward side. It is a much larger than lifesize figurehead of Lord Nelson, carved in wood and kept smartly painted in the bright colours proper and necessary on the "wooden angels" that adorned the bows of sailing vessels of yore.

This figurehead was mounted on the bows of H.M.S. *Nelson*, a ship of the line launched in England in 1814. At that time — one year before the final defeat of Napoleon at the Battle of

Waterloo — H.M.S. *Nelson* was the biggest ship that had ever been built in England. She was a three-decker, mounting 120 guns. In 1854 she was cut down to a two-decker, mounting 72 guns, and given an auxiliary screw.

In 1867 she was acquired by the Colony of Victoria as a training-ship for the Naval Brigade, and was stationed at Melbourne, but proved costly to maintain and to work at sea. In 1881 she was cut down to a single-decker, and in 1898 was sold to private owners and used as a storeship.

In 1901, being then eighty-seven years of age, and still carrying the figurehead of the great Admiral, the one-time pride of the Royal Navy was towed to Sydney. Here she was cut down to make a coal-hulk and a lighter. These continued in use for another thirty years.

When the *Nelson* was dismembered at Sydney, the Naval Brigade bought her figurehead, and installed it in the training-depot at Rushcutters Bay. There it remains to this day, in perfect order and condition, without a blemish — a striking reminder of the traditions of the indomitable Admiral who believed that the best kind of defence is to attack.

4

GARDEN ISLAND AND WOOLLOOMOOLOO

THE PROMONTORY THAT HAS ELIZABETH BAY ON ITS EASTERN SIDE, Woolloomooloo Bay on its western side, and the naval establishment of Garden Island at its northern tip, is part of a spur stretching northward from a sandstone ridge that runs from Hyde Park in the city, through Surry Hills, Paddington, Edgecliffe, Bellevue Hill, and Vaucluse Heights, to South Head.

All the promontories of the southern shore of the Lower Harbour are spurs stretching northward from that low range (averaging 200 ft above sea-level), which closes the vistas on the southern ends of the valleys that lie between the spurs. All the bays and coves from Parsley Bay to Sydney Cove are thus the submerged extensions of vales which are enclosed by ridges on their eastern, southern, and western sides, but open at their northern ends, where they sink into the sea.

These vales — or, as they were in their primitive state, gullies — formed separated drainage areas, side by side, through which freshwater streamlets flowed on courses of less than a mile from their headwaters to their debouchures at the tidal marge. The flow of these watercourses was intermittent, depending only on the runoff of rainfall, with very little seepage from the sparse vegetal cover of the sandstone terrain; yet the sandstone, being porous, would keep at least a trickle of water flowing in the gullies, except in times of prolonged drought.

Governor Phillip, on his first inspection, in January 1788, found "the finest spring of water" at Sydney Cove. It was then midsummer, but that "spring" (later to be named the Tank Stream) was — unknown to Phillip on his first view of it at its mouth — a streamlet of less than a mile in length. It was kept filled by seepage from a bowl of marshy ground at its source in the vicinity of present-day Hyde Park, on the southern ridge.

When the Old South Head Road was built, it kept to the crest of that transverse ridge that closes the valleys on the south. The New South Head Road, hugging the foreshores, ran up hill and down dale across the grid of spurs and gullies that constitutes the pattern of the southern shore east of Sydney City.

That pattern was more significant in the days of horse-transport than it is in the era of mechanized vehicles. Its road grades have long ago been reduced by cuttings and by the filling-in of hollows at the crossings of the gullies; yet basically the grid pattern of ridge spurs and intervening valleys remains, and must forever remain, as the chief topographical feature of this part of the shoreline of Sydney Harbour.

With variations of the axial alignment, that pattern extends all around the Harbour. On both the southern and northern shores, each bay or cove is flanked by ridges, with short and closed vales between them at the head of the tidewaters. It is that serration of the terrain that provides so many secluded anchorages in the bays and coves, and building-sites with wide "harbour views" on the promontories.

The alternation of cove and hilly promontory was specially noticeable to the pioneers of settlement at Sydney Cove, who saw the country in its primeval state. To the eastward of the settlement was the vale of Woolloomooloo. They ascertained and adopted the native name, with various attempts at spelling it, ranging from "Woollamulla" to the word with the letter "o" in it eight times, which in that respect is unique among place-names anywhere in the world.

Beyond the Vale of Woolloomooloo, the vista to the eastward was closed by Woolloomooloo Heights, which was known also to the pioneer settlers as the Eastern Hill until Governor Darling named it Darlinghurst. (The word "hurst" in Old English meant "a wooded hill.")

Within the first ten years of settlement, several large wind-mills, for grinding corn, were erected on the Eastern Hill, the better to catch ocean breezes to turn the vanes of the mills; but access to and from the city was not easy. The steep escarpment was one that wheeled vehicles could not ascend or descend. The road from the town to the Eastern Hill therefore kept to the ground with easier gradients southward of the Vale of Woolloomooloo. It followed a track that ran approximately along the line of present-day Oxford Street to Taylor Square, and then turned northward by the track that later became known as Darlinghurst Road.

The crags of Woolloomooloo Heights were more directly approached when a graded carriage road was formed, by cutting and filling, in the 1830s, and named William Street, in honour of King William IV (popularly known as "Sailor Bill"), who reigned from 1830 to 1837. Even then, the steeper parts at the northern end of the spur, looking down to the dockside of Woolloomooloo, had no passage for wheeled vehicles until 1940. The Wharf Roadway was then extended in a hairpin bend to join Wylde Street, and so gave access to Macleay Street and Darlinghurst Road.

Transit for pedestrians was made easier in the 1890s by flights of steps which remain in use today, replacing earlier "goat-tracks." The name of Woolloomooloo Heights remained in general use for that steep declivity at least until the 1880s, when terraces of elegant homes were built along its crest in Victoria Street; but in the 1890s the name of Woolloomooloo became gradually restricted to the dockside district in the vale at the head of the bay.

POTTS POINT

Little is known of J. H. Potts, except that he was a clerk in the Bank of New South Wales, which was founded in 1816. In the 1830s, he bought six acres of land on the tip of the Darlinghurst promontory, which thereafter gradually became known as Potts Point. It appears likely that he subdivided his land after William Street was built, and sold it at a good profit. Several fine residences were erected there, in a salubrious atmosphere, with harbour views, and the district gained a reputation as an "exclusive" neighbourhood.

KING'S CROSS

In 1897, the intersection of William Street and Darlinghurst Road was given the name of Queen's Cross, in honour of Queen Victoria. From this intersection, Victoria Street led northwards to Potts Point, and Bayswater Road eastwards to Rushcutters Bay. The effect was of a "five-ways," which, as the population of Sydney increased, became a busy traffic junction and shopping-centre.

The name of Queen's Cross remained in use after Queen Victoria's death in 1901, until it was changed in 1905 to King's Cross, in honour of her son, King Edward VII. That name became so firmly fixed in long usage during the reigns of Edward VII, George V, Edward VIII, and George VI, that, on the accession of Queen Elizabeth II in 1952, no suggestion was put forward to restore the original name of Queen's Cross.

In the meantime, The Cross — as it is usually termed in speech usage — had become a district of "high-density" population, with flats, apartment houses, hotels, shops, and restaurants in profusion, and a cosmopolitan or "bohemian" character — especially so when large numbers of immigrants from European mainland countries settled there in the 1950s.

The term King's Cross, or The Cross, is now applied to the district with boundaries loosely defined in a radius of a quarter of a mile of the intersection of the five streets on the crest of Darlinghurst; and there is a tendency to apply the name "Darlinghurst" only to the southern end of the ridge.

SEE ALSO PART II   ELIZABETH BAY

On the eastern side of Potts Point the ground slopes, less steeply than on the western side, to the foreshores of Elizabeth Bay. This bay, and the small protuberance of the shore that separates it almost imperceptibly from Rushcutters Bay, were named by Governor Macquarie in honour of his wife, whose maiden name was Elizabeth Henrietta Campbell. In her honour also he named Elizabeth Street, in the city of Sydney, and Mrs Macquarie's Point (the headland between Woolloomooloo Bay and Farm Cove).

The name of Elizabeth Bay is applied not only to the waters and foreshores, but also to the residential district sloping down to those shores. With its easterly aspect and uninterrupted view of the Harbour to the north-eastward, past Bradley's Head, for five miles to the Harbour Entrance and North Head, and northward to the Mosman shore, this is scenically one of the most favoured residential districts within the municipal boundaries of the City of Sydney.

The bay has a shoreline of little more than 300 yards, with a small waterfront park, and also some yacht moorings. The northern end of the shoreline of the bay was altered in 1942-45 by the immense feat of wartime engineering that connected Potts Point with Garden Island, for the construction of the Captain Cook Graving-Dock.

The headquarters establishment of the Royal Australian Navy at Sydney is at Garden Island. Since 1913, the official residence of the Flag Officer in Charge, Royal Australian Navy, Eastern Australia, has been at Elizabeth Bay. (It was previously at Admiralty House, Kirribilli.)

The pioneer land owner and resident at Elizabeth Bay was Alexander Macleay, who in 1826 was granted by Governor Darling, the freehold title of 56 acres of land, comprising virtually the whole of the eastern slope of the spinal ridge of the Darling-hurst promontory, north of Rushcutters Bay, to the water's edge. Macleay built a mansion there, and cultivated a botanic garden that became internationally famous for its rare plants. He named his mansion Elizabeth Bay House, and the garden Elizabeth Bay Garden.

Alexander Macleay was one of the truly great men of early-colonial Australian history. Born in Scotland in 1767, he studied natural history, and in particular plants, insects, and birds. In 1795 he was elected a Fellow of the Linnaean Society, London, and was Secretary of that Society from 1789 until 1825. Then he was appointed Colonial Secretary of New South Wales, at a salary of £2,000 a year. He arrived at Sydney in January 1826.

His wife, whose maiden name was Eliza Barclay, bore him seventeen children. Most of that large brood accompanied the parents to Australia.

Alexander Macleay was Colonial Secretary of New South Wales for eleven years, from 1826 to 1837. In addition to his large salary and his land grant at Elizabeth Bay, he was granted 2,500 acres of land at Ulladulla, and also bought an estate at Camden. He was the first President, and virtual founder, of the Australian Museum at Sydney. He died, aged eighty-one, in 1848.

The subdivision of his estate at Elizabeth Bay brought a fortune to his descendants. Elizabeth Bay House is still standing, with a small walled-in garden. The renowned garden that was there has long ago been replaced by residences and apartment houses, including blocks of flats of modern design.

NAVAL HEADQUARTERS SEE ALSO PART II

The Naval headquarters is housed in two old homes, "Tarana" and "Bomera," which were taken over by the Royal Australian Navy in 1942, situated at the lower end of Wylde Street, Potts Point. The Flag-Officer-in-Charge, East Australia Area, flies his flag from "Tarana."

Within the administration of the Flag-Officer-in-Charge, there are at the various establishments in peacetime, in round figures, a total of 4,300 naval personnel, and a total of 5,400 employed in the civil establishments.

Of these there are normally working, at the Garden Island depot, a total of 500 naval personnel and 2,600 rated in peacetime as civil employees. (These figures do not include the crews of ships of the Fleet.)

Of those rated as "civil employees" at Garden Island, some 2,500 are employed in the dockyard under the General Manager's Branch, in the repair and refit of ships which include alterations and additions.

Most of the naval personnel of the establishment on the active list are rated as crew of H.M.A.S. *Kuttabul*, a name which perpetuates the memory of the men who lost their lives during the attack on Sydney by the Japanese midget submarine on 31st May, 1942.

SEE ALSO
PART II   GARDEN ISLAND NAVAL DEPOT

The part of the Sydney naval base, occupying an area of approximately 50 acres extending from the tip of Potts Point in a causeway to Garden Island, is the most prominent man-made feature of the shoreline of Sydney Harbour eastward of the Harbour Bridge.

The establishment has many components, including Fleet berths and moorings; Naval General Stores; Gunnery, Armament and Machinery Stores; Oil Fuel Installations; Captain Cook Graving-Dock; Accountants; Headquarters; Signal Station; and Headquarters of the Naval Dockyard Police.

As an engineering construction, the causeway and the graving-dock rates with the Sydney Harbour Bridge among the biggest works of man in Australia. The Naval Dockyard, with warships usually alongside the wharves, its engineering workshops, stores, and administrative buildings, its signal-mast and radio-masts, and its gigantic steel crane stretching into the sky above the dock, is in stark contrast with the picturesque residential suburbs along the Harbour shores to its eastward, and with the peaceful green of the Domain to its westward.

The contrast may seem unpleasantly grim to idealists who perhaps believe that the main purpose of a harbour is to delight the eye rather than to serve as a haven for ships. Those idealists would have preferred the naval base and dockyard to have been placed elsewhere than in proximity to the "high-density" residential districts of Potts Point, Elizabeth Bay, and King's Cross; but the answer to such wistful thinking is in the fact that the population and prosperity of Sydney depend on naval protection of the port's seaborne trade.

Naval establishments, and also mercantile wharves and warehouses, must be placed where they can most conveniently serve their purposes. Under modern conditions of naval warfare, in 1940 it became urgently necessary to provide, at Sydney, berthing, docking, and refitting facilities for ships of the largest size. The fact that Garden Island had previously been used as a naval depot and refitting base was not the only factor in the decision that was then put into effect, to enlarge that depot and to make it one of the biggest and best of its kind in the world.

Naval thinking, to be realistic, must consider dire possibilities. If an enemy could succeed in destroying Sydney Harbour Bridge, the ruins, toppled into the water, might obstruct the channel of navigation to and from any naval establishment westward of Dawes Point and Milson's Point. For this reason, and also because ships of the largest size might require to be docked for repairs, needing easy deepwater approaches to the dock, the site at Garden Island was preferred to other sites that were considered.

To a visitor whose first sight of Sydney is from on board ship, there is the strikingly beautiful passage of four miles in from the Heads, between shores of residential suburbs, giving no indication of industrial activity. Then, suddenly, Garden Island is abeam. The incoming passenger sees new vistas, as his ship proceeds through the 600 yard wide channel, between the ultra-modern naval installations of Garden Island and the antiquated martello tower fortress of Pinchgut Island, to berth in Woolloomooloo Bay; or between Pinchgut and Kirribilli to berth at Sydney Cove, or further upstream in Darling Harbour, or elsewhere to the westward of the Bridge.

Wherever his vessel may berth "alongside," within that inner region of the Port of Sydney where the mercantile wharves stretch from Woolloomooloo Bay westwards, the marking-point of that mercantile and industrial region of the port is at Garden Island. There the Navy is on guard, and if that is a stark fact so also is the need for that vigilance.

By Act of Parliament, "Naval Waters" are defined in relation to naval establishments. The regulations under the Act are intended in general to prevent vessels other than naval ships from anchoring, mooring in, or otherwise intruding upon waters reserved for naval use. Under those regulations, the Naval Waters surrounding the Garden Island establishment are marked on Admiralty Charts, and are scheduled in the *Control of Naval Waters Act,* 1918, as also are other Naval Waters within Port Jackson, which are under control of the Senior Naval Officer.

All waters in Sydney Harbour, other than those defined by Australian Commonwealth Government statute as Naval Waters, are under the control of the Maritime Services Board, an instrumentality of the Government of New South Wales.

There is no conflict between these two jurisdictions, since limits are precisely defined; but it happens that, in Woolloomooloo Bay, the Naval and M.S.B. waters are contiguous. This bay has the naval oil wharf, cruiser wharf, fitting-out wharf, and Captain Cook Graving-Dock on the eastern side of its approaches, and some of the most important mercantile wharves and sheds of the Port of Sydney—including a large passenger-liner terminal—at its head.

The concentration of naval and also mercantile shipping activity within the relatively narrow, but deep, waters of Woolloomooloo Bay, in proximity to the densely peopled district of King's Cross, has created an enclave of busy movement, isolated by the expanse of the Domain from the centre of the city at Sydney Cove, a mile to the westward. That green Domain intervening between the waterfronts of Woolloomooloo Bay and Sydney Cove, with an open promenade on its own waterfront of Farm Cove, is typical of the lavish layout of Sydney and its Harbour. What other great seaport city could afford to have a recreation park of 177 acres on the waterfront next to the centres of commercial lading, and to disregard commercially a spacious and deep bay such as Farm Cove, reserving it for naval occasions?

Sydney can afford to make gestures of that kind. There are sixteen miles of deepwater wharves in Sydney Harbour, and most of them are westward of the Bridge—out of sight of visitors who disembark at Woolloomooloo or at Sydney Cove.

So lavish is Sydney Harbour's natural endowment of bays and coves that, eastward of the Bridge, only those two are used, for berthing large vessels "alongside." The other twenty-three bays and coves of the Lower Main Harbour are, in a sense, more ornamental than useful. Commercial wharves could be constructed, if required, in most of those bays fronting the waterfront residential suburbs—but there has been no need to do that with so much good wharf frontage available further upstream, more convenient to railroad transport.

It was Governor Phillip's choice of Sydney Cove—five miles in from the Heads—as the site of settlement, that determined the pattern of the Harbour's mercantile development. The sheltered anchorage and deep water close inshore in Woolloomooloo Bay soon brought that bay also into use commercially; but any further expansion of commerce to the eastward was blocked by the precipice of Woolloomooloo Heights (Darlinghurst), impossible for drays and carts to surmount. Wharfage was therefore sought to the westward of Sydney Cove, in Cockle Bay (later named Darling Harbour) — "around the corner" of Dawes Point — and that trend set the pattern for all subsequent commercial development of the Harbour.

The wharves of Woolloomooloo Bay, and more especially the naval base obtruding at the entrance to that bay, constitute an outpost of the immense berthing installations of the Port of Sydney, most of which are not in sight on the "showy" and picturesque reaches of the Lower Harbour. It is that contrast with its surroundings that makes the naval base at Garden Island so impressive. Like the Harbour Bridge, it is a reminder that Australia has moved strongly and boldly beyond the pastoral and agricultural pioneering phases into the Age of Steel. That gigantic crane—its girders etched against a background of new ferro-concrete apartment buildings reaching in cubes for the sky at Potts Point—is a symbol of modernity, ugly to the eye of a nature lover, beautiful to the eye of an engineer.

THE ORIGINAL GARDEN ISLAND

In its original state, and until 1940, Garden Island was approximately 600 yards long, and 200 yards wide at its widest point. It lay in a south-to-north alignment, as though it were a continuation of the promontory of Potts Point, but it was separated from the extremity of Potts Point by a channel 330 yards wide.

The island consisted of two rocky hummocks, each approximately 60 feet above sea-level, with a "saddle" of lower ground between them. On 11th February, 1788, sixteen days after the settlement was established at Sydney Cove, an entry was made in the log-book of H.M.S. *Sirius*: "Sent an officer and party of men to the Garden Island to clear it for a garden for the ship's company."

The garden was cultivated and maintained by parties from other naval vessels in port from time to time. The crew of H.M. Brig *Lady Nelson* "obtained supplies" from Garden Island, after her arrival at Sydney in December 1800.

In 1801 Governor King had a battery of garrison artillery posted on the island, presumably with hutments for the gunners. The unofficial naval garden had by then sufficiently served its purpose as an emergency source of supply of fresh vegetables. The soil was poor, the level ground (between the hummocks) was of limited extent, and naval vessels at that time could obtain fresh vegetables in the market at Sydney Town.

In September 1811, Governor Macquarie issued a proclamation, appropriating Garden Island to the civil establishment. He intended it to be a quarantine station, and possibly also a military garrison outpost, and in any case to prevent the island from being sold to any private buyer. That proclamation had the effect of interrupting the Navy's slight association with the island.

Naval vessels that visited Sydney Harbour, or were on the Australian station from time to time, usually anchored in Farm Cove. Naval stores were usually maintained in storeships or hulks, but there was also a naval depot in part of Fort Macquarie, to which there was access by Man-of-War Steps—a landing-stage in Farm Cove.

In 1818, the Burial Ground of Sydney—in the vicinity of the present-day Town Hall—was overcrowded, and a new burial ground was opened on the site later to be occupied by the Central Railway Station. At a date not ascertained, the body of Ellis Bent was removed from a vault in the old Burial Ground and placed in a vault on Garden Island. He had arrived with Governor Macquarie in 1810 as Judge-Advocate of New South Wales, and practised also as a barrister. He died at Sydney in 1815.

In 1825, another body was placed in that vault, when Brigade-Major John Ovens, military engineer and explorer, died. He too had arrived with Governor Macquarie in 1810. In 1821 he had become aide-de-camp to Governor Brisbane. It seems likely that Ovens had been responsible for moving the body of his friend Bent from the Old Burial Ground to Garden Island, and that, on his own deathbed, Ovens had asked to be buried there.

Until the 1850s, the naval defence of the Australian colonies was a responsibility solely of the Imperial Government. A squadron of the Royal Navy was based on Sydney, under command of the Flag Officer on the Indian station. The large increase of wealth and population, following the Gold Rushes of the 1850s, and the development of colonial representative self-government, gave rise to a public demand for some measure of Australian self-defence. From small beginnings then, Australian defence forces on sea and on land gradually developed their individuality, but within the imperial pattern.

In 1856 the Government of New South Wales offered, and the Admiralty accepted, the use of Garden Island as a depot for H.M. ships in Australian waters. Much delay occurred in completing the formalities of the transfer, which was not gazetted until 1866. A start was then made with the building of a rigging-shed and a sail loft, but difficulties of determining responsibility for expenditure continued until 1887, when the *Australian Naval Defence Act* of the British Parliament gave effect to an agreement between the Australian colonies and Britain for maintaining Australian naval defence in part at Australian expense.

Some fine buildings were then erected on Garden Island. In addition to the rigging-shed and sail loft, there were added barracks, administrative offices, stores, boatsheds, spar shed, blacksmith shop, and other installations, including a hospital— the "sick-bay." There was some reclamation also of the foreshore. As part of the planning for naval space, the bodies of Ellis Bent and John Ovens were removed to St Thomas's Churchyard, North Sydney.

When the six Australian colonies were federated in 1901, defence powers were among those relinquished by the colonies ("States") and vested in the federal ("Commonwealth") government.

During a transition period, Australian naval defence continued to be a responsibility of the British Admiralty until, in 1909, it was agreed at an imperial conference in London that an Australian fleet unit should be paid for, maintained, and controlled by Australia, and should eventually be manned entirely by Australians.

On 10th July, 1911 the title "Royal Australian Navy" was granted by King George V to the naval forces of the Commonwealth of Australia. On 4th October, 1913 the Australian Fleet — consisting of a battle cruiser, two light cruisers, and three destroyers—entered Sydney Harbour for the first time. All naval establishments on the Australian station were then handed over by the Admiralty to the Royal Australian Navy.

These included Garden Island and the buildings there that had been erected by the Government of New South Wales in the years before federation. Litigation followed when in 1923 the Government of New South Wales claimed the island as its property! After seven years, the High Court and the Privy Council both held that the claim of New South Wales was valid.

In the meantime the naval installations on the island had been largely extended. Soon after the outbreak of war in 1939, the Australian Commonwealth Government resumed the island under wartime powers, and in 1945 purchased it for £638,000.

EXTENDING THE PENINSULA

In its early years, from 1911 onwards, the Royal Australian

Navy relied largely on the British Navy for ships, equipment, training, and even to some extent for personnel, especially for senior officers. It was understood that in the event of war the R.A.N. would automatically come under control of the British Admiralty. That situation gradually changed in the 1930s. On the outbreak of war in September 1939 the Royal Australian Navy was officered and manned chiefly by Australians, and was under the sole control of the Australian Government.

At that time, British naval policy in the Pacific relied on a main fleet based on Singapore, intended to protect sea-communications in southern and eastern Asia, and in the south-western Pacific, including Australia. The growing naval strength and expansionist policy of Japan led to a request by the British Admiralty, in 1938, that a graving-dock be built at Sydney, capable of accommodating the largest capital ships of the British Navy, for repairs or refit. (A "graving-dock" is defined as a dry dock in which vessels can be careened by being "laid on shore" for bottom-cleaning and painting; but that meaning has been extended to include any repairs to the hull requiring dry-docking.)

The Australian Government agreed to pay the expenses of constructing the dock to British Admiralty specifications and plans. This work was, therefore, in its conception and planning, an example of Australia's dependence on Britain, at that time, in some technical aspects of naval engineering.

The site at Garden Island was recommended in January 1940, and construction of the dock began in July 1940, as a matter of wartime emergency. The work proceeded in shifts "round the clock," employing on an average between 2,500 and 4,000 workers.

The principal feature of the plan was the reclamation of 33 acres of the sea-bed between Potts Point and the southern shore of Garden Island, to include the basin in which the graving-dock would be constructed. With this also went the levelling of the southern hummock of the island, and excavations of the cliff at Potts Point to allow the building of an access-road, past the Woolloomooloo wharves.

After the coffer-dam of rock filling was built, the basin was pumped dry, and the immense task of lining the walls and bed of the dock with concrete, and of installing caissons and machinery, was begun. In all, 330,000 cubic yards of concrete were placed.

The dock was ready for use in March 1945, and from then until the end of the war was used for docking and servicing units of the British Pacific Fleet, including battleships and aircraft-carriers, and also for refitting ships of the Royal Australian Navy. The Captain Cook Graving-Dock, as it is named, is one of the biggest dry docks in the world.

With an overall length of 1,139 ft, and breadth of 147 ft, this dock could accommodate the Cunard liner *Queen Elizabeth* (1,031 ft long and 118 ft beam). As the *Queen Mary* and *Queen Elizabeth* were both calling at Sydney, in service as troop transports, while the dock was being built, it must be considered likely that the dimensions of the dock were intended to accommodate either of these mammoth vessels if required; but fortunately the need did not arise.

The gigantic "hammer-head" crane, capable of lifting 250 tons, was installed in 1951. It is one of the biggest cranes in the world, and certainly by far the biggest in Australia.

NAVAL WHARVES AND WORKSHOPS

The Garden Island establishment, in its industrial aspect, is not a shipbuilding yard, but a repairing and refitting dockyard. In times of peace, the need for repairs and refitting of naval vessels is much less apparent than in times of war; but such a dockyard must be maintained for any emergency.

On the outbreak of war in 1939, the Royal Australian Navy had a total of sixteen ships in commission, and a manning strength of 5,440. At the end of the war, the R.A.N. had 317 ships in commission, and a manning strength of 40,000.

Most of the additional naval vessels were built in Australian shipyards during the war. They included three destroyers, sixty corvettes, and twelve frigates, besides a large number of motor-launches.

After the war ended in 1945, there was a reduction in naval strength, as is usual in the immediate aftermath of wars; but, in the 1960s, the Royal Australian Navy was again building up its strength to the requirements of our national defence and of our commitments to Allies.

Anti-submarine and anti-aircraft defences are paramount in modern naval strategy and tactics. The re-equipment of Australian naval units with guided missiles, modern minesweeping apparatus, and anti-submarine weapons, to keep the Navy up-to-date, provides steady employment at shipbuilding yards and refitting depots, such as Garden Island, even in peacetime. These workshops, and the skills of the workers employed there, provide the basis for whatever expansion may be required in the event of war.

The 2,500 employees in the Dockyard at Garden Island, in the General Manager's Branch, are civilian workers, not under naval discipline. Their conditions of employment are regulated by Arbitration Court awards and by trade union organization. To the Australian way of thinking there is nothing unusual in this. The Government is an employer like any other, even when the Government represents the people, including the employees.

Berthing facilities "alongside" at Garden Island include the Cruiser Wharf, the Oil Wharf, the Fitting-Out Wharf, and the West Dock Wall. All these are in Woolloomooloo Bay, on the western side of the "Island" that has become a peninsula. There are small wharves and jetties on the eastern side also. These will eventually be enlarged.

There are fleet berths at moorings and "dolphins" in several other places in the Harbour, including Farm Cove, Athol Bay, Shell Cove (Kirribilli), and Pyrmont.

Among the older buildings remaining on what was the northern hummock of Garden Island are the signal station, the administrative buildings, the sail loft and rigging-shed, and the "sick-bay." These are well-designed, well-built, and well-preserved examples of colonial architecture, all completed in 1887. The sick-bay (not now used as a hospital) is a three-storied building, with verandas supported by iron pillars on each storey. It is the best-preserved building in its distinctive style to be seen anywhere in Sydney.

The old sail loft is now used as a Dockyard Church. In a stone-paved courtyard near the administrative buildings is a "wooden angel" — the figurehead of the clipper-ship *Windsor Castle*, which was built in 1869 and sailed for twenty years in the Australian trade. She was sold in 1889 at Sydney and converted into a coal-hulk. Presumably the naval authorities acquired her figurehead, and installed it at Garden Island.

The figurehead is an effigy of none other than Queen Victoria in her regal robes. It is kept brightly painted, as a figurehead should be. The great Queen could still look young and beautiful at the age of fifty, when this figurehead was carved, idealizing her, as was only right and proper. She was the Queen of the Australian Colonies for sixty-four years, and of the Commonwealth of Australia for twenty-one days (she died on 22nd January, 1901); and, throughout her long reign, all the ships of the Royal Navy were the Queen's ships.

It was a good idea to preserve that figurehead at Garden Island, as a reminder of the imperishable traditions of the great days of sail. Even there, among all the paraphernalia of modern mechanized seafaring, the figurehead of Victoria smiles benignly and encouragingly as she looks out of the past into the present and the future.

WOOLLOOMOOLOO BAY SEE ALSO PART II

During the first five years of settlement at Sydney, the deep, narrow, and landlocked recess that is nowadays known as Woolloomooloo Bay was known to the pioneer colonists as the Garden Cove.

That name came from the naval garden on the island at the mouth of the cove. Of all the recesses within Sydney Harbour, this one most deserves to be described as a "cove" and not as a "bay." It has a breadth at its entrance of only a quarter of a mile (between Mrs Macquarie's Point and Garden Island), narrowing to 250 yards as the inlet stretches for three-quarters of a mile to the southward. It is thus almost completely landlocked.

Sydney Cove, Farm Cove, and the Garden Cove were the first three anchorages of ships in Port Jackson. On their shores the first permanent settlement of white men in Australia took shape, with dwelling-houses and cultivation of the soil.

The land on which that settlement and cultivation were made is a peninsula, of a little more than one square mile in area, bounded on the east by Woolloomooloo Bay and on the west by Darling Harbour (which the pioneers called Cockle Bay). That peninsula, on which is situated the inner city of Sydney and the Domain, is a grid of ridges terminating in Miller's Point, Dawes Point, Bennelong Point, Mrs Macquarie's Point, and

Potts Point, with valleys between them which, in their primitive state, held watercourses flowing into the coves.

The foreshores have long ago been fixed by dredgings and fillings, and by the building of retaining walls and wharves; the streamlets have been channelled underground; the slopes of the ridges have been gentled by cuttings and gradings; millions of tons of concrete have been poured to pave streets and to erect the pinnacled office blocks, hotels, flats, department stores, and warehouses, which make the city's skyline craggy in the Manhattan manner: yet all that ant-heap architecture stops, as it must, at the water's edge. Beyond the shoreline, the waters of the Harbour come and go with the tides, and fish swim, and gulls swoop and scream, and the sunlight plays on the wavelets, and the Harbour is as it was before any human beings, white or black, settled and hunted for a living on its shores.

Sydney is not a river port; it is a seaport. There is that distinction to be made, among the world's great ports, between those that have muddy water and those that have clean, oceanic water, such as Sydney has, renewed by every tide. Despite everything that man has built on the shore, altering the levels of the land, there has been nothing done here to alter the level of the water, which varies only with that of the great ocean outside, not far away; and into the Harbour from that ocean fish swim exploring, as they have done from time immemorial: not only fish, but even whales are sometimes sighted in Sydney Harbour. If that is not unique to Sydney, it is something that rarely happens elsewhere in the world's great havens of ships.

The Sydney City Peninsula—as the square mile of ridge and vale between Woolloomooloo Bay and Darling Harbour may be called for purposes of description—was intended by Governor Phillip to be reserved entirely as Crown Land, and never to be sold.

A map drawn in 1807 by James Meehan, assistant to the Surveyor-General, shows the landward boundary-line of the Town of Sydney. This line is drawn from the head of Woolloomooloo Bay, south-westward to the head of Cockle Bay (i.e., at the western end of present-day Bathurst Street). It is marked:

> Boundary-line within which all the ground is reserved for the Crown and for the use of the Town of Sydney. N.B. It is the orders of Government that no ground within the boundary is ever granted or let on lease, and all houses built within the boundary-line are, and are to remain, the property of the Crown.
>
> (Signed) A. PHILLIP, December 2nd, 1792. Sydney

That description of Meehan's map of 1807 was evidently copied from an earlier map, drawn from a survey made by the first Surveyor-General, Baron Alt, in 1792, and signed by Governor Phillip.

The date of Phillip's signature, 2nd December, is noteworthy. He left Sydney nine days later, on 11th December, 1792, to return to England. The marking of that boundary-line of the

Town of Sydney was one of the final administrative acts of the Town's founder.

His edict that no land was ever to be alienated to private ownership within that boundary-line was disregarded by later Governors; but only gradually, and in small blocks. It was from Governor Phillip's decision of 2nd December, 1792 that the Domain and Botanic Gardens were reserved in perpetuity for public ownership, and also the sites of most of the present-day public and municipal buildings and wharf frontages of Sydney.

Governor Phillip's reason for marking that boundary-line was not only to reserve land for the Crown, but also to make land available, outside the boundary, for free grants to officers of the garrison, officials of the administration, well-behaved convicts, and free immigrants.

After Phillip's departure, the acting-administrator, Major Francis Grose, in February 1793, made a grant of 100 acres of land in the Vale of Woolloomooloo to John Palmer, who was Commissary-General of the colony. The grant, outside the town boundary, was at the head of the Garden Cove.

Palmer adopted the native name of Woolloomooloo—and its spelling with the letter "o" eight times—as the name of his estate. He was a "First-Fleeter," having arrived in 1788 as purser of H.M.S. *Sirius,* and had been appointed Commissary-General (keeper of the Government stores) in 1790.

In 1796, Palmer went to England, but he returned to Sydney in 1800, bringing with him his wife (an American) and children. He then in 1801 built a house on his Woolloomooloo estate—one of the best homes in Sydney—and lived there for twenty years. Apart from his duties as Commissary-General, he became a flour miller, and also a ship owner and a rural land owner.

In 1804, Palmer owned three schooners—two of them hunting seals in Bass Strait and the third trading up the Hawkesbury River. These schooners were the first, or among the first, commercial vessels to anchor in Woolloomooloo Bay, which became known by that name, instead of Garden Cove, when Palmer built his home there.

In 1822, Edward Riley, a merchant, who was a director of the Bank of New South Wales, bought Palmer's Woolloomooloo estate for £2,290. Palmer then went to live at Parramatta, and Riley lived in Woolloomooloo House until 1825, when he committed suicide by shooting himself.

Riley left a widow and seven children, who inherited the Woolloomooloo estate. It was subdivided in 1842 and sold for £100,000. Two of the main streets in the subdivided district were named Palmer Street and Riley Street.

THE MERCANTILE WHARVES

Woolloomooloo Bay has depth of water for vessels of the largest size, with soundings of 40 feet close inshore. Being exceptionally well sheltered, it was a favourite anchorage for sailing vessels awaiting cargoes or charters, but had no good facilities for wharfage until the 1860s.

As early as February 1804, an official list of "schooners and sloops belonging to individuals" showed that one of these vessels had been built at Woolloomooloo.

In the 1850s a boat-builder named Dan Sheehy had a shed on the shore of Woolloomooloo Bay. In 1858 he built there a 30-ft yacht, *Australian,* to the design of R. H. Harnett: This design was decidedly unorthodox. Harnett stated:

> I caught a mackerel in Woolloomooloo Bay for the purpose of obtaining correct lines. Opening its mouth, I cut the fish into two parts. Leaving the back, and laying the incised portion on a sheet of paper, I took for my load-waterline the horizontal lines of the fish, which were segments of a circle, the garboard strake corresponding with the water-lines and the mid-section of a right-angled floor.

That discovery of streamlining in the hull design of yachts eventually influenced yacht design throughout the world, and remains the basic principle in the design of racing-yachts today. *Australian* sailed on Sydney Harbour for thirty-five years. Despite difficulties of agreeing on her unorthodox measurements for handicapping purposes, she was unbeatable in open racing, and remained a champion to the end of her days.

Until the 1860s, there was a mudbank at the head of Woolloomooloo Bay, caused by silt brought down from Surry Hills and Darlinghurst. This was dredged, and a semi-circular wooden wharf was constructed at the head of the bay, in 1861-63, when Charles Cowper was Premier. He was Member of Parliament for East Sydney, which included Woolloomooloo.

That wharf, known as Cowper Wharf, was later extended along the eastern side of Woolloomooloo Bay. In the 1890s, the "Coal Baron," John Brown, mine owner, built Brown's Wharf on the western side at the head of the bay. Because of Governor Phillip's reservation of the Domain, there has been no further building of wharves along the western side of the bay.

When Cowper Wharf was built, the Municipal Fish Markets were opened in a brick building at the head of Woolloomooloo Bay. For various reasons, the fishing industry in New South Wales, and especially at Sydney, has never been organized in the large way it is conducted in the North Atlantic Ocean.

The fish that swim in the waters of Australia are different from those in the North Atlantic, and methods of catching them are different; there are no "banks" in the Tasman Sea like those of Newfoundland, or of the North Sea.

The fish market at Woolloomooloo was supplied in the 1880s and 1890s chiefly by fishermen who used small sailing boats. It was eventually found to be more convenient to send fish to Sydney by rail from fishing-ports along the coast than to bring them in boats to Woolloomooloo. For this reason, the fish market was moved to the Municipal Markets near the railway goods-yard at Darling Harbour. The old fish-market building at Woolloomooloo is now used as a factory.

Although the wharves at Woolloomooloo have no railroad connection, motor transport enables cargoes of general merchandise to be handled there; and passenger-liners regularly use the large and modern berthing facilities.

There are eleven berths at the Woolloomooloo Wharves, with a total length of nearly a mile. Four of these, on two sides of a jetty structure, include a passenger terminal, built in 1956, designed for liners of up to 20,000 tons.

This is one of three similar passenger terminals for large liners at Sydney, the others being at Sydney Cove and at Pyrmont. The principle is of a two-storey structure, the cargo being handled at wharf-deck level, and the passengers and their baggage passing to and from the upper floor by means of gantries or gangways.

Elevators and luggage conveyors enable passengers and their visitors to be moved smartly on board or off ship, and cleared through Customs. On an average, 150,000 passengers arrive at or depart from the Port of Sydney each year—and about one-third of them pass through the Woolloomooloo terminal.

THE DOCKSIDE DISTRICT

After the subdivision of Riley's Woolloomooloo estate in the 1840s, the district was for twenty years an "exclusive" residential suburb, especially on the Woolloomooloo Heights in Victoria Street.

The great increase of shipping that followed the Gold Rush of the 1850s, and the building of Cowper Wharf in the early 1860s, made Woolloomooloo Bay a busy resort of sailing-vessels, especially for the unloading of general merchandise and the loading of wool.

In the 1880s, rack-renters introduced the worst type of Victorian English slum tenement buildings to provide accommodation for dockside workers and sailors; and in the 1890s Woolloomooloo—known, in the Australian way, for short, as "the 'Loo"—was already becoming famous, or notorious, for its gangs of "larrikins."

These young hoodlums were no worse in their anti-social activities than their counterparts in large seaport cities such as San Francisco, New York, Boston, and Glasgow at that time, but they were given a special reputation in Australia by journalistic and literary descriptions that exaggerated their importance.

The members of the larrikin "pushes" ("mobs") were usually youths who roamed the streets and "got into mischief"—which frequently involved vandalism and offensive behaviour, including street fights with other "pushes," and assaults on police.

The "uniform" of the larrikins was a black suit with bell-bottom trousers, short coat, flat-crown hat, and high-heeled fancy boots. Possibly the chief causes of larrikinism were lack of recreational and educational facilities, and the pleasant climate of Sydney which encouraged "larking" out of doors among bands of city-bred youths.

The larrikins were also known as "leers" or as "leery coves"— pronounced in the German way, from *leer*, meaning "empty," "empty-headed," or "good-for-nothing." Referring to this, and to the steep ascent of Woolloomooloo Heights, the poet Montague

85

Grover wrote of

> . . . *the fairy, leery 'Loo,*
> *Where the streets stand up on end,*
> *And the sky is always blue.*

There are some, but only a few, cases of vicious crimes committed by larrikins. Most of the members of the "pushes" married their "donahs" and settled down to a respectable and hardworking life.

The reputation of "the 'Loo" as a "tough" quarter of Sydney continued to some extent until the 1930s; but in modern times the slum tenement type of housing has gradually been abolished. Better education and recreational facilities and better conditions for wage earners in general have made Sydney a city that has no "slums" in the European or American sense of that word.

In 1937, the first Police Boys' Club in Australia was opened at Woolloomooloo, to counteract juvenile delinquency by providing healthy recreational activities. The idea quickly spread to other suburbs of Sydney, and to other cities in Australia.

SEE ALSO PART II   FISH OF SYDNEY

Present-day Australians sometimes feel surprised when they read that the pioneer settlers at Sydney Cove suffered from starvation, while waiting for supplies of food to arrive from South Africa or from England. Evidently those pioneers did not know how to add fresh fish and game to their rations of salt pork and ships' biscuits. They did not know how to "live off the country" as the Aborigines had lived for thousands of years, finding plenty to eat.

The shores of all the bays and coves of Sydney Harbour were thick with oysters, cockles, mussels, and pipis. The waters teemed with crayfish and prawns, and with fish of many kinds. These marine fauna being different from those of the North Atlantic, the "newchum" colonists either did not recognize that a large supply of seafood was readily available to them; or they did not have the equipment—boats, nets, hooks, lines—to gather the harvest of the sea, or the knowledge of the methods of gathering that harvest, which required local experience.

The failure to increase the rations amply with fish was all the more remarkable after early experiments with seine nets had yielded good hauls. Surgeon-General White recorded that fish were caught in that way at Botany Bay on 20th and 23rd January, 1788, including "bream, mullet, large rays, besides many smaller species." On 27th January, the day after the fleet had moved to Sydney Cove, White mentioned that "the boats sent this day to fish were successful."

In the meantime, two French ships, commanded by La Pérouse, at anchor in Botany Bay, used a seine net, and caught "nearly 2,000 light horsemen in one day." (The name "light horsemen" was later replaced by "snapper"—one of the tastiest fish of Eastern Australian waters.)

A Cornish convict, William Bryant, was appointed official fisherman to the settlement. On 28th March, 1791 he sailed away in the fishing boat, accompanied by his wife, their two small children, and seven male convicts. They achieved the remarkable feat of sailing 2,500 miles to Koepang in Timor, in sixty-eight days.

Before he left without notice, Bryant had served for three years as fisherman at Sydney. It is apparent therefore that some regular supply of fish was obtained to supplement the rations of the starving pioneer colonists, but not enough boats and fishermen were available to provide fully for the needs of a community of a thousand souls. It is likely also that the pioneer colonists were unaware that Sydney Rock Oysters are edible, or did not have knowledge of the way to gather or "open" them. These bivalves became recognized, in course of time, as the world's most palatable oysters. The Aborigines had feasted on them for milleniums, as is proved by the deposits of shells in millions, in the heaps which anthropologists call "middens."

The name "Sydney Rock Oysters" is to some extent inaccurate, as the habitat of these oysters extends along the entire coast of New South Wales and of southern and central Queensland. Nowadays they are cultivated on "oyster farms"—leases of estuarine waters along the coast, away from Sydney Harbour. The average harvest from the oyster farms of New South Wales is 50 million oysters a year. On the rocks around the shores of Sydney Harbour, the oysters grow in profusion, but seldom to maturity, as beachcombers—especially boys—open them *in situ*.

Prawns are abundant in Sydney Harbour, as in other estuaries of New South Wales and Queensland and in the waters offshore. These are the most prolific prawning-grounds in the world. Up to 10 million pounds of prawns are caught and sold annually in Australia—chiefly in New South Wales, to such an extent that, in Sydney, prawns are an important item in the diet of the people, comparable with herrings in Europe.

The immense proliferation of prawns is indicated from the fact that one female lays as many as half a million eggs. The young prawns swim in schools of millions, practically invisible to the human eye, as for the first three months of their existence they are of glassy appearance and less than a quarter of an inch in length. They grow to four inches long at seven months, and migrate into estuaries, especially on dark nights. It is then that they are easily caught by fishermen with scoop nets. "King prawns," up to nine inches long, are netted from trawlers offshore.

Marine crayfish are crustaceans which, along the shores of New South Wales and Queensland, often attain a length of twenty-four inches and weigh eight or ten pounds—sometimes more. Though crayfish, like prawns, are hatched in tremendous numbers, they are preyed upon by pelagic fish until they grow their spiny shell and settle on the sea-bed, where they search for food. They are caught in bamboo or wire "pots" baited with flesh. Many crayfish—sometimes termed "local lobsters"—are caught in Sydney Harbour, especially in Middle Harbour.

Apart from molluscs and crustaceans, Sydney Harbour is visited by several kinds of estuarine fish. These are caught by amateur sea-anglers, who are to be seen fishing with lines from the shores and jetties, or sometimes from boats, in all the reaches of the Harbour, at all hours of the day or night, in every season of the year, and in all weathers.

Net fishing is prohibited within Sydney Harbour. The professional fishermen who supply the Sydney markets operate from trawlers outside the Heads, or in estuarine waters along the coast. The most commonly marketed kinds of fish are sea-mullet, mackerel, snapper, "John Dory," blackfish (luderick), bream, garfish, flathead, and leather-jackets.

All these may be caught with hand lines also inside the Harbour, but bream, blackfish, and leather-jackets are the most usual hauls of the rock-fishermen.

Deep-sea or pelagic fishing is of recent origin in Australia, and not yet fully developed. It is known that immense shoals of pilchards (sardines), anchovies, sprats, mackerel, and tuna swarm in the Tasman Sea, but their migratory habits are not yet known sufficiently to provide a basis for big canning factories or preserving industries which would require a large fleet of trawlers and steady supply for efficient working.

There are more fish in the sea than ever came out of it. Sydney cannot fairly be described as a fishing-port. Its catch of fish is for local consumption, and not sufficient for that: its most typical, and most distinctive, seafoods are prawns and oysters. The abundance of the sea harvest has never yet been fully reaped anywhere in Australia. It is there, waiting, whenever the need for it may arise.

5

FARM COVE

THE PROMONTORY ON THE WESTERN SIDE OF WOOLLOOMOOLOO BAY, separating it from Farm Cove, is a ridge 200 yards wide, terminating in the headland named Mrs Macquarie's Point. Along that ridge, in June 1816, Governor Macquarie had a carriage road built, so that his wife could better enjoy the harbour view. Near the headland lookout, a seat was carved from a sandstone outcrop, and named Mrs Macquarie's Chair.

The driveway and the seat remain today, within the Public Domain, a park of 177 acres, of which 66 acres are enclosed and reserved as the Botanic Gardens. That large space of greensward has a water frontage on its eastern side on Woolloomooloo Bay, with a men's bathing enclosure, the Fig Tree Baths, named from the Moreton Bay fig trees near by.

The Domain and Botanic Gardens occupy two undulating ridges and the shallow vale that stretches between them. One of the ridges is that which terminates in Mrs Macquarie's Point; the other terminates in Bennelong Point. The vale between them is a basin that forms a watercourse flowing through the Botanic Gardens into Farm Cove. This creek is dammed to form a series of pools in which aquatic plants from many countries flourish. It is almost the only creek on the south side of the Harbour which has not been channelled underground.

The distance between the headlands of Farm Cove is 750 yards. The shoreline sweeps in a symmetrical curve that has been artificially formed with a stone retaining wall. Having no buildings, but only parkland, on its foreshore, this Cove is, in that special aspect, the most beautiful within Sydney Harbour. Its beauty is man-made, and not untamed like that of some of the other headlands and bays, or scarred with wharves and buildings.

The anchorage at Farm Cove is occupied by mooring buoys which are reserved for naval use. On the western side of the Cove is Man-of-War Steps—a jetty under naval control, originally giving access to Fort Macquarie, and also to Government House.

On the eastern side of Farm Cove also is a landing-stage, known as Fleet Steps. Adjacent to it is a plinth, indicating that Queen Elizabeth, as Queen of Australia, stepped ashore there on 3rd February, 1954 — the first time in 166 years of British settlement in Australia that a reigning sovereign had set foot on Australian soil.

THE BOTANIC GARDENS   SEE ALSO PART II

In more ways than one the shores of Farm Cove have historical distinction. The first cattle, horses, and sheep in Australia grazed there. They were landed at Bennelong Point — which was at first

89

named Cattle Point—on the western side of Farm Cove, the present-day site of the Sydney Opera House—and from there were depastured on the site of the Domain and Botanic Gardens. There too the first farm in Australia was established and the first crops grown.

Governor Phillip reported, in July 1788, "a farm, nine acres in corn." The site of that first cultivation of the soil in Australia is marked by a small obelisk and plaque (erected in 1952) in the "Middle Garden" of the Botanic Gardens.

Some of the plants and seeds brought in the First Fleet from Rio de Janeiro and Capetown were established in the garden of the first Government House, on a site that later became the intersection of Phillip Street and Bridge Street. That garden extended westward to the vicinity of Macquarie Place, northward to the shore of Sydney Cove, and eastward to the Domain.

In 1810 Governor Macquarie laid out Macquarie Street, describing it as "the easternmost street in the town." It has been the boundary of the Domain ever since. Macquarie in 1816 appointed Charles Fraser as "Colonial Botanist," and set aside part of the Domain as the Botanic Garden.

Fraser held that position for fifteen years, until his death in 1831. He, and those who followed him, extended the gardens. The greatest changes were made by Charles Moore, who was Director for forty-eight years, from 1848 to 1896, and was chiefly responsible for filling in the foreshore of Farm Cove and the building of the semi-circular sea-wall—a work which was begun in 1848 and completed in 1878.

Though the wildflowers of Sydney are of surpassing beauty, variety, and botanical interest, the Sydney Botanic Gardens are renowned for their preservation not of Australian flora, but of plants from almost every other country in the world. On this "farm" at Farm Cove, a clean sweep was made of native plants, and one of the biggest collections of non-Australian plants in the world was steadily built up. Remarkably, too, the soil of the Sydney Botanic Gardens was originally poor and sandy. It has been enriched by topsoil, compost, and humus.

The outstanding feature of the Botanic Gardens is the "Spring Walk," established in 1856 with a large display of azaleas and other non-Australian spring-flowering plants. It is only in recent years that Australians have begun to take an interest in Australia's own floral wonders and beauties.

THE GARDEN PALACE

On the western side, within the Botanic Gardens, is the site of the Garden Palace—a huge building which had a central dome and four towers, and was chiefly of wooden construction.

This "Palace" was built to house Australia's first International Exhibition, opened in September 1879. After the exhibition ended in April 1880, the Garden Palace was used for concerts and also to house some government departments and records. On 22nd September, 1882 the building was completely destroyed by fire, in the biggest blaze ever seen at Sydney. Among the records destroyed in the conflagration were government papers of the convict system. Arson was suspected, but never proved.

On the site of the Garden Palace stands a bronze statue of Governor Phillip, larger than life-size, the work of the Italian sculptor Simonetti, who lived in Sydney in the 1870s. There stands the founder of civilization in Australia, high on his pedestal, looking out across the land where he began the cultivation of the soil, to the Harbour beyond, into which he was the first sea-captain to sail.

PINCHGUT ISLAND

A quarter of a mile to the northward of Mrs Macquarie's Point is Pinchgut Island, a bare rock crowned by the masonry of a martello tower, known officially as Fort Denison.

This is one of the most prominent seamarks of Sydney Harbour, standing as it does in the stream at the approach to Sydney Cove and also in the offing of Woolloomooloo Bay. The island was probably given its unofficial identifying name of Pinchgut by Captain Hunter on his first survey in 1788. The name "Pinchgut" was a common nautical term for a point at which a channel narrows.

For the first fifty-three years of settlement, Pinchgut Island remained as a rocky peak, rising to a sharp pinnacle. Another unofficial name for it was Rock Island.

At the first criminal court held in Australia, at Sydney on 8th February, 1788, Thomas Hill, a convict found guilty of stealing biscuits from another convict, was—as Surgeon White noted—"ordered to a barren rock, or little island, in the middle of the harbour, there to remain on bread and water for a stated time."

In nautical parlance, "bread" meant ships' biscuits. Hill was released after one week, but subsequently other convicts were sent there—usually as punishment for stealing food—and the nautical name of "Pinchgut" became appropriate in another way.

In 1797, Governor Hunter decided to make an example of a murderer named Morgan by ordering him to be hanged in chains on a gibbet erected on the pinnacle of Pinchgut Island. The skeleton was allowed to remain there for three years. It was said that this horrible sight scared the Aborigines, who avoided going to the island, which had previously been a favourite fishing-ground for them.

In 1841, on the orders of Governor Gipps, in accordance with a recommendation from Colonel Barney, the pinnacle was cut away, and the island levelled to make a fort. That act of vandalism infuriated Dr John Dunmore Lang, Minister of the Scots Kirk at Sydney, who declared:

> This natural ornament of the harbour, which no art could have equalled, this remarkable work of God, which has stood like a sentinel keeping watch for thousands of years, has been destroyed by the folly of man.

Governor Gipps did not complete the fort, but in 1856, during the Crimea War, when it was thought that a Russian fleet might attack Sydney, the thick stone masonry of a martello tower was built as a gun-mounting, and stands there today. It was named Fort Denison, in honour of Sir William Denison, who was Governor of New South Wales, 1855 to 1861.

The guns of the fort have never been fired in anger. The island is maintained by the Maritime Services Board as a picturesque tourist attraction, visited by many thousands of people each year.

GOVERNMENT HOUSE

The residence of the Governor of New South Wales stands prominently on the ridge at the western side of Farm Cove. It is of stone, in Tudor Gothic style, with turrets, and was built between 1840 and 1845, when its first occupant was Governor Gipps.

Governor Phillip's residence in 1788 was a hut of laths and canvas erected within a palisade on the eastern side of the Tank Stream, at the head of Sydney Cove. In July 1788 he reported that a cottage of three rooms was being built for him. That dwelling, enlarged from time to time, served as Government House until 1845. Its site is marked by a stone and plaque at the intersection of Bridge Street and Phillip Street.

In 1832 Governor Bourke complained that "a new House must be built, as this which I now inhabit is extremely inconvenient, subject to bad smells, and irrepairable." He suggested selling for £15,000 the land on which the old House stood, to finance the building of a new House.

This was done, and plans were prepared in 1836 by a London architect. The building was completed in 1843, and Governor Gipps moved in, with a house-warming party, on 26th June, 1845. Because of its castellated structure and prominent situation— standing in the Domain, apart from other buildings—Government House is a landmark at the approach to Sydney Cove.

In the first half-century of settlement at Sydney, New South Wales was a Crown Colony of an extreme type, and the Governors had almost dictatorial powers; but from the 1840s onwards those powers were curbed by the Constitution. The Governor, as representative of the Crown, is the formal and visible Head of the State. He has extremely limited powers, and he is "neutral" in party-political conflicts.

THE CONSERVATORIUM OF MUSIC

On the western side of the Botanic Gardens also, and within the Domain, is the New South Wales State Conservatorium of Music. It is housed in a fine Gothic building that was erected in 1821, to the order of Governor Macquarie and the design of Francis Greenway—intended to be used as stables!

Though Macquarie caused many fine buildings to be erected, including this magnificent edifice as stables for his own carriage horses and riding horses, and for the horses of the trooper police, he was too modest to build a new residence for himself, his family, and his entourage.

The stables continued to house horses until 1914, when the

building was handed over to the then newly established State Conservatorium of Music. This is the only Conservatorium of Music anywhere in the world installed in a stable; and, at that, it is a better building for a Conservatorium of Music than most cities can show.

THE DOMAIN SEE ALSO PART II

All that part of the Domain (111 acres) which is not enclosed for the Botanic Gardens is a park, chiefly of greensward with some avenues of trees, preserved by the pressure of public opinion against the encroachments that threaten parklands in cities.

Considered as an open space between Macquarie Street and Woolloomooloo, the Domain since 1810 has been encroached upon by the Botanic Gardens, the Government stables (Conservatorium of Music), Parliament House, the Sydney Hospital, Government House, the Garden Palace, the National Art Gallery, and the Public Library.

The National Art Gallery, erected between 1885 and 1906, and the Public and Mitchell Libraries, erected 1939-1943, are the most modern of these "stealings of the common from the goose." They would be considered justifiable land grabs by all except zealots of civic pride who maintain that green spaces within a city should be forever inviolate.

Apart from those encroachments, the Domain retains its character as a common. Although sheep and geese do not graze there, the broad open spaces of turf give scope for playing-fields, for ceremonials, and for holding large and small public meetings in the open air. The "Domain orators," especially on Sunday afternoons, let off steam in the traditional outlet of the socio-political and religious "safety valve" of Free Speech; and at any season of the year "Domain dossers"—homeless through misfortune or perhaps through folly or laziness—sleep out beneath the trees.

The people of Sydney feel keenly that this large open space, within such easy reach of crowded commercial and residential districts, should not be further encroached upon—on the surface. That has not prevented the burrowing of tunnels underneath the Domain for the Underground Railway, and the Cahill Expressway, and the excavation of a large underground automobile parking-station.

Those subterranean borings and rumblings have not disturbed the rural look of Australia's oldest farm, set in the midst of Australia's oldest city: the farm with a "harbour view."

That is the Sydney Domain. It has statues of Governor Phillip, of Shakespeare, and of Henry Lawson, and a memorial to the beloved actress, Nellie Stewart (who was born in Woolloomooloo). It has also a memorial to the 20,000 Australian horses that were sent overseas in the 1914-18 war for the Australian Light Horse regiments of the Desert Mounted Corps.

To understand what the Domain means to Sydney, try to imagine what Sydney would be if the Domain had all been densely built on, with wharves and sheds around the shores of Farm Cove. Sydney without its Domain would not be the city that it is—the city that can afford the space and the time to bask in the sunshine.

BENNELONG POINT

The promontory between Farm Cove and Sydney Cove is an extension of the ridge along which Macquarie Street stretches. In its original state the headland was rocky, with a small island at its tip separated from the headland by a shallow and narrow tidal channel. H.M.S. *Supply,* the first vessel to arrive (with Commodore Phillip on board) at Sydney Cove, anchored at the mouth of the Cove, near that point, at nightfall on Friday, 25th January, 1788, and so was in a position next day to signal the other vessels to their anchorages.

On Monday, 28th January, the cattle and the horses were landed on that headland, which was thereupon unofficially named Cattle Point. There were one bull, four cows, one bull-calf, one stallion, three mares, and three colts, brought from South Africa. It may be assumed that the vessel, or each of the vessels, from which these animals were landed was laid along-side the shore so that the animals could be conveniently disembarked from the 'tween-decks where their stalls had been fitted up.

Historians have supposed that Governor Phillip's first landing and raising of the King's Colours was on the western side of Sydney Cove; but, as the cattle and horses were landed on the eastern side, it is probable and even likely that Phillip himself went ashore there, to erect a signal to the other vessels approaching the anchorage. Perhaps it was on that promontory that he raised the Colours.

The name of Cattle Point continued in use for two years. In November 1789, an Aborigine, Bennelong, was persuaded to join Governor Phillip's household retinue. He was kindly treated, but was closely guarded until he learnt enough English to act as an interpreter.

Bennelong was the first Australian Aborigine to become "civilized." Phillip had a hut built for him on Cattle Point, which thereafter gradually became known as Bennelong Point. In 1792, Bennelong accompanied Governor Phillip to England. He returned to Sydney three years later, and for eighteen years afterwards was a "character" in the town. He died at Kissing Point, on the Parramatta River, in 1813. He is one of the few Aborigines whose names have lived on.

FORT MACQUARIE

An outcrop of sandstone on Bennelong Point was humorously given the name of the Tarpeian Rock—an allusion to that rock on the Capitoline Hill in ancient Rome from which traitors were hurled to death.

In 1817 the Tarpeian Rock of Sydney was quarried, to level the site for a strong fortification, which was given the name of

94

Fort Macquarie. Those earthworks consolidated the peninsula by joining the small island at the tip of the headland to the mainland.

Fort Macquarie was a square building, 130 feet on each face, on a solid base of masonry. At high tide, its walls were washed by the sea. It mounted fifteen guns, and remained manned as a regular garrison artillery post and ordnance store until 1902.

The fort had then become obsolete. It was demolished, and a red brick turreted edifice was built on its site, for peaceful use as a tramway depot. That turreted structure—which continued to bear the name of Fort Macquarie—remained for fifty-seven years as an adornment of the entrance to Sydney Cove, a bogus fort, intriguing in its bizarre pseudo-feudal design.

In 1959 it was demolished to make way for a building that would be recognized as one of the most remarkable in the world.

THE SYDNEY OPERA HOUSE SEE ALSO PART II

It has often been suggested that Sydney Harbour's splendours should be enhanced by some colossal work of art—erected on Pinchgut Island or on the Sow and Pigs, in the manner of the Statue of Liberty in New York Harbour—to symbolize Australia, and perhaps to demonstrate that natural beauties are not as significant as contrived beauty.

The building of the Sydney Harbour Bridge (opened in 1932) may have satisfied some of the yearnings of those who could feel that at last a work of man had been completed on these shores to assert the superiority of human effort; but though that gigantic construction in steel had spanned the Harbour with an arch in the sky that seemed to dwarf the distances, it was not enough yet to prove that man can embellish nature's best works.

Another vision took shape—of an Opera House on Bennelong Point—a building which, in the setting of Sydney Harbour, would be one of the wonders of the modern world. As Venice was "the Bride of the Sea," so too is Sydney: and whatever has been done well anywhere else may be surpassed here.

The concept of the Sydney Opera House is of a building which will take rank among the world's greatest architectural constructions. The plan is not simply of an Opera House—but rather of an aggregate of auditoriums in which opera, ballet, music, and drama may be performed, but also where public meetings, conferences, exhibitions, and lectures may be held. In that modern acropolis the life of Sydney may be compared to that of ancient Athens in dedication to ideals more permanent than those of the market place.

Being committed to such an immense enterprise, Sydney will have to live up to it. It will not be enough to build the Opera House. The test will be in the use that is made of it.

The site is unique among the world's opera houses. It was an inspiration to Joern Utzon, the Danish architect whose design won the prize in a competition in which 223 designs were offered by architects from thirty countries. The principal feature is in the discarding of conventional walls and roof. The auditoriums 95 are protected by gigantic vaulted "shells" of elliptical parabolic shape, which, in silhouette, suggest the sails of yachts. It is that conception chiefly which makes the Sydney Opera House, in its harbourside setting, not only distinctive, but startlingly unique.

Within those shells are the four auditoriums—a main hall to seat 2,000 persons; a smaller hall, 1,000 persons; a "little theatre," 430 persons; a recital hall, 300 persons.

Each auditorium is acoustically insulated, so that four different performances may be going on, side by side, at the same time. This is not "a building," but a group of buildings spread over a site of six acres, within a comprehensive design.

In addition to the auditoriums, there are canteens, a restaurant (seating 250 persons), bars, cloak-rooms, offices, machinery-rooms, store-rooms, dressing-rooms, library, terraces, foyers, concourses—and parking-spaces for a large number of cars.

The Opera House is approached not only from the landward side, but also from wharves for ferries and launches. The immense cost of construction has been met chiefly from "mammoth" lotteries. The immediate and long-term effect can only be to give a great impetus to the arts—not only of drama and music, but of all the allied arts—in Sydney, and so throughout Australia.

There, where the first cattle were landed in 1788, on the point between Farm Cove and Sydney Cove, and where Bennelong's hut was built, one of the world's greatest Temples of the Arts will have become well established before the 200th anniversary of civilized settlement in our continent is celebrated in 1988.

6

SYDNEY COVE   SEE ALSO PART II

WHEN GOVERNOR PHILLIP DISCOVERED AND NAMED SYDNEY COVE, on 23rd January, 1788, and decided to establish his settlement on its shores, he was influenced in that decision by the fact that it provided a perfectly sheltered anchorage, with deep water (five and six fathoms) close inshore, and that it had a freshwater stream flowing into it, through a forest of large trees, indicating fertile soil and a handy supply of building timber and fuel.

With a naval tactician's eye, Phillip would not have failed to consider that this Cove, being five miles inland from the ocean entrance to Port Jackson, was beyond the reach of enemy bombardment from the open sea. An enemy raider, to come within range, would need to sail up, in narrow waters, and so become vulnerable to shore batteries, where there would be no wide sea-room for manoeuvre to make his escape.

Important though considerations of defence were, the facilities for wooding and watering, and for anchoring close inshore, to provide for the ultimate development of a commercial port, were more immediate.

Phillip had left the nine transports of the First Fleet, under guard of H.M.S. *Sirius* and H.M.S. *Supply*, at anchor in Botany Bay while he made his exploration of Port Jackson in two open boats. Having decided to make the settlement at Sydney Cove, he acted promptly on that decision. He returned on 24th January in the boats to Botany Bay. On 25th January he sailed around from Botany Bay to Sydney Cove in H.M.S. *Supply*, with an advance party of trusty convicts and a guard of marines, to prepare for the arrival of the rest of the fleet.

The anchor of the *Supply* was let go at 7 p.m. on 25th January, in the entrance to Sydney Cove, a cable's length from the rocky promontory later to be named Bennelong Point. Next day all the nine merchant vessels of the fleet, chartered as transports, lay securely within the Cove, each with two anchors out, or mooring lines made fast to trees on shore, to prevent them from swinging with the tide, while *Sirius* and *Supply* rode at the entrance to the Cove, their guns commanding the approaches, while two French warships—of a scientific expedition—lay at Botany Bay.

The English colours—the naval ensign with the red cross of St George on a white field—were displayed on either a tree or a flagstaff. The exact site is a matter of dispute among historians, argued sometimes dogmatically from the insufficient data. It is assumed that the first landing was made on the western side of the Cove, and that subsequently the Governor decided to establish his camp at the head of the Cove, on the eastern side of the stream which flowed into the Cove in the south-western corner.

The official narrative of Phillip's *Voyage* stated:

> In the evening of the 26th, the colours were displayed on shore, and the Governor, with several of his principal officers and others, assembled round the flagstaff, drank the King's health, and success to the settlement, with all that display of form which on such occasions is esteemed propitious, because it enlivens the spirits, and fills the imagination with pleasing presages.

Although some eminent artists have depicted this scene with a modern Union Flag (popularly termed the Union Jack) as the "colours" that were "displayed," a sketch drawn by Captain Hunter in August 1788 shows only the cross of St George displayed at the Government Camp on the eastern side of the stream. It is possible that a composite flag, including the crosses of St George and St Andrew, symbolizing the union of England and Scotland in 1707, was used by Governor Phillip at Sydney Cove, but the red saltire of St Patrick was not officially included until Ireland joined the United Kingdom in November 1800, and the flag of the triple cross was not raised at Sydney until the King's birthday celebration on 4th June, 1801.

The "pleasing presages" of the original flag-raising ceremony on 26th January, 1788, established the shores of Sydney Cove as the birthplace of civilization in Australia. There and then the task began of subduing and occupying a continent. The date gradually came to be remembered and celebrated as Anniversary Day, and in recent years has become more suitably known as Australia Day.

The immensity of the task was quickly realized as the pioneers, with inadequate tools, tried to fell or grub out the tough Sydney Red Gum and Banksia trees to make clearings for tents and huts.

As Governor Phillip remarked:

> Though in this spot the trees stood more apart, and were less incumbered with underwood than in many other places, yet their magnitude was such as to render not only the felling, but the removal of them afterwards, a task of no small difficulty.

Captain David Collins of the marines wrote lyrically of the scene:

> . . . the run of fresh water stole silently along through a very thick wood, the stillness of which had then, for the first time since the creation, been interrupted by the rude sound of the labourer's axe, and the downfall of its ancient inhabitants— a stillness and tranquility which from that day were to give place to the voice of labour, the confusion of camps and towns, and the busy hum of its new possessors.

The male convicts and guards of marines were landed on 27th January and were put to work clearing the ground, pitching tents, and building huts. In ten days the settlement had taken shape. The women and children were then brought ashore.

98   Collins recorded:

The women did not disembark until the 6th of February, when, every person belonging to the settlement being landed, the numbers amounted to 1,030 persons.

The 210 naval and 233 mercantile seamen, in the eleven vessels of the fleet, continued to live on board, but their shore parties, unloading the cargoes and fetching wood and water for the ships, added to the activities described by Collins:

> Parties of people were everywhere heard and seen, variously employed—some in clearing ground for the encampments, others in pitching tents or bringing up such stores as were wanted; and the spot which had so lately been the abode of silence and tranquility was now changed to that of noise, clamour, and confusion.

It had been intended to give the name of Albion to the settlement, but that name was never proclaimed or adopted. Instead, the name Sydney Cove was used unofficially, and also in official correspondence. From that usage the settlement became known as Sydney Town, and eventually as the City of Sydney (incorporated in 1842).

Sydney Cove, as the pioneers saw it, was an indentation, roughly U-shaped, approximately a quarter of a mile wide and a half a mile long, facing due north. It was perfectly sheltered by rocky ridges on its western and eastern sides, and by the timbered valley of the freshwater rivulet (later to be named the Tank Stream), and sloped gently from the head of the Cove to a ridge half a mile inland on the southern side. No ocean swell or running seas could ever disturb the calm waters of the anchorage; the land mass on the northern side of Port Jackson would break the force of any northerly gale. In this most secure, most perfect of all havens, vessels could lie at anchor or at moorings, in waters rippled only by wavelets, and, as Governor Phillip had noted, "so close to the shore that at a very small expense quays may be constructed at which the largest vessels may unload."

On 7th February—eleven days after the arrival of the fleet at Sydney Cove—all the settlers were mustered, presumably on the parade ground of the marines on the western side of the Stream at the head of the Cove, and the King's Commission was read by Captain Collins, as judicial officer, constituting the Colony of New South Wales and appointing Captain Arthur Phillip as Governor.

The Territory of New South Wales was originally defined as comprising the whole area of the present-day States of Queensland, New South Wales, Victoria, and Tasmania, and most of South Australia and the Northern Territory, and "all the islands adjacent in the Pacific Ocean."

This was approximately the eastern half of the continent that had been vaguely delineated by map-makers, such as Mercator and Ortelius, in the sixteenth century, and named *Terra Australis Incognita* (the Unknown South Land). The entire continent had been renamed New Holland by the Dutch sea explorers of its northern and western coasts, and part of its southern coasts, 99 early in the seventeenth century, 150 years and more before Captain Cook visited its eastern coast.

After Captain Cook's discovery, the eastern coast of New Holland was renamed New South Wales, as a prelude to its annexation by Britain. The continent continued to be known as New Holland until 1826, when Major Lockyer ·annexed the western part also for Britain. Thereafter the name of Australia for the whole continent came into general use.

That euphonious and suitable name was adopted enthusiastically in the 1820s by colonial-born men of merit, such as Phillip Parker King and William Charles Wentworth—both born in Sydney's first sub-colony, at Norfolk Island—who objected to being called New Hollanders, or New South Welshmen. They proclaimed themselves Australians, and used the name of Australia—which had been suggested by various writers in earlier times—as much more appropriate than the Dutch Imperial and British Imperial designations.

The modern meaning of the name of Australia took shape in that pioneering settlement on the shores of Sydney Cove—not in the cruelties of the British Imperial Convict System, or in the arrogance of a minority of the pioneers there who attempted to inaugurate a new feudalism based on the virtual enslavement of their fellow Britons; but rather in the development of an Australian way of life in which those cruelties were eliminated and that arrogance was curbed.

The wider vision of Australia as a new homeland for immigrants from the white or European nations and their descendants began at Sydney in 1788, and has been extended and intensified to the present day. The task of those pioneers who could fairly have called themselves "New Australians" was to establish civilization in a continent that had remained latent and intact for æons in the "Dreamtime" of the Aborigines, the only people who could truly be called "Old Australians."

The extent to which that task has been accomplished in seventeen decades may be seen more vividly at Sydney Cove than anywhere else in Australia; for here History speaks from the contours of the shores and the silhouetted skyline of the city, with a dramatic impact that belongs only to the oldest city, the first city, in any national or geographical region.

As the Ancient Romans based their history on the foundation of the City of Rome, so modern Australians must begin their annals of the occupation of the Great South Land with the pioneering settlement at Sydney Cove. That history, which soon will have two centuries of achievement to record, was expanded within seventeen decades from the one small nucleus settlement of 1,030 persons, to eleven and a half million people occupying the continent's area of three million square miles. Always Sydney was the Mother City—at first a camp, then a township, then a town, then a city—from which most of the other settlements in Australia were initially explored, then guided, supplied with livestock and stores, protected, and nursed in their infancy.

Here then is the city which can never be superseded in its

renown as the oldest civilized settlement in Australia. It is the Mother City not only of a State but of a Continent. With a population of two and a third million, Sydney ranks as one of the great cities of the world. That status has been accomplished within the span of three human lifetimes, and of six generations of the Australian-born, yet this city is already old; for it did not spring from nothing, but from the knowledge, experience, and accumulated ability of the two thousand years of European civilization that had preceded its foundation.

The pioneers of Sydney Cove have left on record a full description of the foundation of the settlement. We know from the large number of documents, journals, maps, and pictures that were written, or drawn as "eye-sketches," at that time, exactly how Port Jackson and Sydney Cove looked to the first and subsequent early settlers there.

To compare those old "views" with the Sydney scene today is a thought-stimulating exercise. The headlands and vales of the Harbour's shores that were covered densely with trees, shrubs, ferns, and flowering plants of rare and delicate beauty have been replaced today—especially on the shores of Sydney Cove and in the Vale of Sydney—by the "concrete jungle" of monster-city architecture, in which towers of glass, steel, and concrete have been erected in the 1950s and 1960s, on sites where solid sandstone buildings of "the Golden Age" of a century previous have been demolished.

"I destroy and I build"—that motto of the anarchist, Bakunin, could well be the motto of the City of Sydney, as perhaps of many other cities of the modern era. It is a process deemed deplorable by conservatives, admirable by "progressives," but in either case it is fascinating to the historian, or to any other disinterested onlooker who can see in his mind's eye the contrast of past and present, but can scarcely dare to envisage the future.

To enter Sydney Cove today from seaward—whether in a passenger-liner from overseas or in a ferry-steamer from the northern side of the Harbour—is an experience that could not fail to stimulate the imagination. Flanked by the Opera House on Bennelong Point and the Harbour Bridge abutments on Dawes Point, Sydney Cove is a city's sea-portal as strikingly adorned with the wonders of modern engineering as any berthing place of ships in the world. The scurrying ferry-steamers, customs launches, and police launches; the Overseas Terminal for liners of up to forty thousand tons; the Cahill Expressway and City Overhead Railway transforming Circular Quay to Rectangular Quay, the tall new oblong buildings of glass, steel, and concrete; the glimpses of older classical stone buildings such as Government House and the Customs House; and the crowded vistas of Manhattan-like architectural complexity of the city beyond the Quay: all this is the modern setting of the scene where, as Collins remarked in 1788, "the spot which had so lately been the abode of silence and tranquility was now changed to that of noise, clamour, and confusion."

If change always means progress, then there has been very

101

great progress here; but to those who realize that there can be changes for the worse as well as changes for the better, the altering appearance of Sydney Cove may bring the sombre reflection that progress is not only inevitable but also sometimes deplorable.

Falling back then on the consolations of philosophy, the somewhat dazed beholder of Sydney's Front Door in this second half of the twentieth century may well consider that what he sees there demonstrates that life never has been, and never can be, static. A community of human beings can be expanding or declining, but can never be at a standstill. While Sydney is being destroyed and rebuilt by its own inhabitants so that its face is changed in each generation, there is at least a restless striving for adaptation to new ideas, and that spirit is not a symptom of the inertia of decay, but of national growth and expansion.

At Sydney Cove we have arrived at the heart of the Mother City of Australia. Here the primitive bushland has been utterly destroyed and replaced by an agglomeration of architectural constructions symbolizing and embodying the aspirations of commercial greed and of the nobler yearnings that have moved men in successive generations to build and rebuild a city.

In the vista of history we see that everything passes, everything changes—but no!—skimming over the roof of the Opera House or under the deck of the Bridge to alight on the wavelets of the Cove, screaming in excitement to feast on a school of prawns visible only to their keen eyes, a flock of seagulls swoops just as the ancestors of the bird swooped there in Governor Phillip's day and for millenniums before.

Everything changes, but not the sea and its creatures, which existed before Man evolved or was created, and will probably continue to exist long after the last man has perished from the earth. Men can move mountains, or erect mountainous buildings on land, but they cannot stop the movements of the winds and tides, or pump the oceans dry, or basically alter the habits of sea creatures. So the permanent, unchanging aspect of life at Sydney is in the Harbour; and Sydney is basically a seaport and a seaside resort.

On the shores everything changes, everything passes and is replaced; but the Harbour remains. As it was in the beginning, so it is now. It has been dredged a little, embanked a little, pushed back a little here and there, and churned by innumerable hulls, great and small; yet the tides ebb and flow as they have done since before human time was reckoned, and will continue to do so until time ends: and with the tides the fish and sea birds come and go, in and out of the Harbour, indifferent to the millions of dollars that are made, spent, and wasted, by the ephemeral people on the shore.

THE TANK STREAM

The "spring" of fresh water, which had been one of the principal reasons for Governor Phillip's decision to form the settlement at Sydney Cove, was a ferny creek, only half a mile long, draining a small, closed valley that was typical of the corrugation of ridge and vale surrounding the "Harbour of a Hundred Bays." Into each of those bays a streamlet poured the runoff from a catchment seldom more than a quarter of a square mile in area; but even in time of drought there was a run of clear fresh water in each streamlet, fed and filtered from the seepages of the humus, mosses, and ferns that provided a spongy cover to the porous sandstone subsoil.

The Vale of Sydney, like all the other vales that drained into the bays and coves on the Harbour shore, was covered in a forest of wide-branching myrtles (*Angophora lanceolata*, the Sydney Red Gum), with Banksias, Acacias (wattles), some Eucalypts, and Bangalow and Cabbage Tree Palms shading an undergrowth of flowering shrubs and smaller plants, including grasses, orchids, ferns, and mosses. It was remarkable that such a profusion and variety of plants could have evolved in that sandstone terrain; but in aeons the sandstone had become covered with a topsoil of the decayed vegetation that a forest builds up from shed leaves and bark and the rotted boles and boughs of fallen trees.

In that spongy topsoil and in the porous sandstone subsoil were natural storages of fresh water that the removal of the trees and shrubs and smaller plants would quickly deplete. Soil erosion was not understood by the pioneers, who, bred in the lore of damp islands, believed that "springs" of fresh water were perennial.

Nor could they understand that the clearing of the trees and the "underbrush," and the cultivation with spades and hoes of the shallow topsoil, would cause that loosened topsoil to be washed away by heavy showers of rain, leaving the sandstone subsoil exposed. So British settlement in the Vale of Sydney quickly destroyed the "spring" of fresh water and the fertility of the soil —two of the principal features that had caused Governor Phillip to decide to form the settlement there.

That first settlement was a base camp from which explorations were made in quest of "better country farther out." Governor Phillip himself, in an exploration of the Upper Harbour by boat, in April 1788, discovered good farming country at Rose Hill (Parramatta). He decided to establish his capital there, intending that Sydney Cove should be only a depot for what he expected to be the principal city, fourteen miles farther upstream. That idea proved impractical, through the difficulty of sailing in the narrow forest-enclosed upper reaches of the Parramatta River; and so it was Sydney, not Parramatta, that became the seat of the colonial government.

The permanent reason for the development of Sydney as the administrative and commercial centre of the Colony was not in the facilities for "wooding and watering," or in the suitability of the soil for the garden cultivation of food crops, but chiefly in the excellent scope for anchoring and berthing ships in Sydney Cove. For that reason Sydney Cove remains today, as it was in Governor Phillip's day, the focal point of the settlement: it is the nucleus that has expanded to the monster emporium-city and industrial city of today, with its many suburbs spread over an area of 640 square miles around the Harbour's shores.

The Vale of Sydney, drained by the "spring" that flowed into Sydney Cove, was a catchment basin almost exactly a quarter of a square mile in area. It was enclosed on the western side by a ridge extending from The Rocks (Dawes Point) along the sites of present-day York Street and Clarence Street, to the vicinity of the Town Hall. There the ridge curved to form the southern wall of the vale, extended in the vicinity of present-day Park Street and Bathurst Street to a small plateau that Governor Macquarie in 1815 humorously named Hyde Park.

The eastern wall of the vale was a ridge extended from Hyde Park along the present-day sites of Phillip Street and Macquarie Street to the eastern side of Sydney Cove (Bennelong Point).

The "spring of water" rose in a spongy swamp on the Hyde Park plateau, and flowed down in a northerly direction, between the sites of Pitt Street and George Street, to enter the Cove in a tidal estuary that had its head in the site of present-day Bridge Street.

The watercourse determined the alignment of the principal streets of Sydney. The track along the western bank of the stream, first known as Spring Row, was later officially named George Street. The track along the eastern bank became known as Pitt Row—in honour of Britain's Prime Minister, William Pitt—and later was officially designated Pitt Street.

A log bridge across the stream at the head of the tidewater explained the naming of Bridge Street.

The "longitudinal" streets of Sydney were surveyed parallel to George Street and Pitt Street, and the "latitudinal" streets parallel to Bridge Street.

The log bridge gave access by land from one side of Sydney Cove to the other. With that as the connecting link, Governor Phillip laid out the first settlement of Sydney in two parts. His residence and official headquarters were on the eastern side of the estuary at the head of the Cove, in the vicinity of present-day Macquarie Place. The main camp of the convicts and their guards was on the western side of the estuary, in the vicinity of present-day Grosvenor Street and Essex Street, with a track to a hospital on the western side of the deepwater part of the Cove, in the vicinity of the present-day Maritime Services Board building.

During the first few weeks of settlement, all the eleven vessels of the fleet sent boat parties daily to the head of boat navigation at Bridge Street, to fill casks with fresh water as soon as the ebb-tide had swirled the salt water away.

Parties of convicts hauled casks for the shore establishments on sledges along Spring Row or Pitt Row to watering-places higher up the stream, in the vicinity of the present-day General Post Office.

Within twelve months, the clearing of the timber and underbrush from the Vale of Sydney had dried the Spring to a trickle. In the summer of 1789-90, convicts were put to work excavating three storage tanks in the sandstone, near the intersection of present-day Bond Street and Pitt Street. Thereafter, the Spring became known as The Tank Stream.

The shortage of water, and also of food, became so acute at Sydney that Governor Phillip shipped almost half the population to Norfolk Island, and many also to Parramatta. The population at Sydney was reduced to between two hundred and three hundred, but then the arrival of a Second Fleet from England in 1790 brought approximately a thousand new settlers, many of whom were elderly or ill. Those "new chums" were quartered in the hospital and the convict baracks at Sydney, and thereafter the population of the settlement on the shores of Sydney Cove steadily increased.

To improve the water supply, wells were sunk, and water was carted from the Blackwattle Swamp (on the Parramatta Road, south of the town, at present-day Broadway), and from swamps to the eastward, at present-day Moore Park. In the meantime, the increase of population caused the polluting of the water in the Tank Stream, which gradually took on the appearance and quality of an open drain, rather than of a water supply.

In 1827, work began on Sydney's first big engineering project, the excavation of a tunnel to bring water from the swamps to the eastward (in present-day Centennial Park), a distance of two and a half miles, to a standpipe in Hyde Park. This work, effected in stages, was completed in 1837. Thereafter, until the 1860s, the Tank Stream was a smelly and ugly open drain. It was gradually enclosed in stone-walled channels, then arched over, and finally built over, so that it disappeared from sight.

Today the Tank Stream is a stormwater drain, entirely covered and hidden below street level, with its debouchure into Sydney Cove at the western end of the ferry jetties at "the Quay." The ferny gully where once lyrebirds sang and danced has vanished forever.

SEMI-CIRCULAR QUAY   SEE ALSO PART II

The tidal estuary of the Tank Stream had its western shoreline between present-day George Street and Pitt Street, as far as Bridge Street. Its eastern shoreline stretched alongside present-day Macquarie Place and across the site of the Customs House to join the eastern side of the deepwater Cove. The estuary was thus triangular in shape, covering approximately ten acres of shallow water at the head of the Cove. It was navigable for boats, and in parts for vessels of up to two hundred tons. A landing-stage, named the Government Wharf, was built out from the shore near the present-day Customs House.

Sydney's first shipbuilding dock was on the western side of the Tank Stream estuary, where present-day Underwood Street joins Pitt Street. From that dock a convict shipwright, James Underwood, launched, in 1789, the first vessel built in Australia, the *Rose Hill Packet*, a sailing craft of ten tons, which was put into service to convey passengers, mails, and some cargo between Sydney and Parramatta. Of the several other vessels built there, the largest was the *King George*, 185 tons, launched in   105

1805 for seal hunting in Bass Strait and New Zealand waters.

As Sydney Town grew, and its seaborne trade increased, the Tank Stream estuary, with its mudflats partially exposed at low tide, was an obstacle to the convenient handling of passengers and cargoes. In 1838 Sir George Gipps took office as Governor of New South Wales. A military engineer (with the rank of Lieutenant-Colonel), he had the assistance of another military officer of the Royal Engineers, Captain George Barney, to supervise several important works, including the remodelling of the Harbour fortifications.

Barney had been appointed by Governor Bourke as Colonial Engineer in 1835. His greatest work was the building of a seawall along the shores of Sydney Cove, with a horseshoe-shaped semi-circular quay approximately in the position of the present-day ferry jetties, and the filling-in of all the estuary of the Tank Stream except its deepwater channel on the western side.

The formation of the Semi-Circular Quay and the reclamation of ten acres of mudflats behind the sea-wall was one of the biggest enterprises of foreshore reclamation in the world at that time. It employed the labour of many thousands of convicts for seven years, from 1837 to 1844.

The mudflats were filled in with sandstone rubble brought in lighters from Cockatoo Island and Pinchgut Island, and also from the Argyle Cut quarries in "The Rocks" (on the western side of Sydney Cove) and the Tarpeian Rock (on the eastern side of Sydney Cove).

The monumental task, which in the perspectives of Australian history may be compared with the building of the pyramids of Ancient Egypt or the Great Wall of China, was possible only because convict labour was virtually slave labour.

During the progress of the work, in 1841, the system of Imperial Convict Transportation to New South Wales ended. At that time there were 26,977 convicts (of whom 23,844 were males) in the Colony, comprising one-fifth of the total population. The building of the Semi-Circular Quay, and the reclamation of the foreshore at the head of Sydney Cove, was the last and greatest work of construction done by convicts in New South Wales, and could well be viewed today as the most enduring memorial to those men, who so often have no other memorial than stigmas of infamy unjustly applied to them by sensation-mongers and prigs.

There, at Sydney's Front Door, is the biggest and most enduring engineering construction among the several great engineering and architectural constructions adorning that portal; but because that work was done without fuss or publicity, and without great public expense, the building of "the Quay," and those who built it, are seldom mentioned by historians, and therefore remain generally unacclaimed.

The horseshoe-shaped sea-wall at the head of the Cove was correctly described as "the Semi-Circular Quay." In the heyday of sailing-vessels, from the 1850s to the 1890s, dozens of windjammers were to be seen at all times berthed alongside the sea-wall, which served as a quay of almost perfect U-shape along the entire waterfront of Sydney Cove.

Gradually the name of Semi-Circular Quay was altered in lazy speech to Circular Quay—an absurdity, for a circular quay would have no landward access. Visiting sailors carried the fame of Sydney's Circular Quay throughout the world, and it remains world-renowned to this day.

Early in the twentieth century, the quay space converted to wharfage at the head of Sydney Cove was reserved for ferry-steamers, and the arc of the sea-wall was gradually straightened to provide docks. In the 1950s another great reconstruction was completed at the head of the Cove, with the building of the City Loop overhead railway and the Cahill Expressway (overhead road) above the ferry terminals.

In this work the Semi-Circular Quay was completely straightened, and became a Rectangular Quay, but the old name of Circular Quay remains in use, a romantic misnomer.

ALFRED STREET

The large and wide open space in front of the Quay is officially named Alfred Street, in honour of Prince Alfred, a son of Queen Victoria, who visited Australia in 1867. Wider than Martin Place, but also, like Martin Place, connecting George Street and Macquarie Street, the broad thoroughfare in front of the Quay is increasingly becoming the facade of the City of Sydney, and could better be designated a "Place" than a "Street."

It gives access not only directly to the ferry wharves and the Quay railway station, but beyond them, on the eastern side, to the Sydney Opera House, and on the western side to the Overseas Passenger Terminal.

On the southern side of Alfred Street is the Customs House, a fine sandstone building erected in 1885 on the site of a smaller Customs House that was built in 1844 when the foreshore was reclaimed. The classical architecture of the Customs House, with its stone-masonry construction, makes a strong contrast with the A.M.P. Building—head office of the Australian Mutual Provident Society, a life assurance company—which stands near by, an edifice of steel, concrete, and glass, twenty-nine stories (380 ft) high, which, when completed in 1961, was the tallest building in Australia.

Other large "egg-box" buildings of this style have been built, and more are planned, around the foreshores of Sydney Cove and in the vicinity of "the Quay." These blocks of modern offices have revived commercial activity at "the Quay end" of the City of Sydney. That district had become somewhat decrepit at the end of the 1940s—a century after Barney's foreshore reclamation—yet in that now almost vanished decrepitude was a certain charm of Old Sydney that is remembered with the sentimental affection of times past and beyond recall.

MACQUARIE PLACE

Set back from the waterfront by the construction of the Semi-Circular Quay in the 1840s, Macquarie Place and its surroundings were the original hub of Sydney. Near by, at the intersection of present-day Phillip Street and Bridge Street, the Governors had their residence for the first fifty-seven years of the Colony's existence, from 1788 to 1845.

All the ground between the Governor's residence and the waterfront was occupied by government gardens and residences of senior officials. Official buildings were erected along Bridge Street, and elsewhere in the vicinity, and this district continues today to be the site of some of the finest sandstone buildings in Sydney, including the admirable buildings of New South Wales Government Departments: Education, Agriculture, the Treasury, and the Lands Office. The former Royal Exchange Building was demolished in 1964 to make way for a modern-style office block.

So much of Sydney has been demolished and rebuilt in the 1950s and 1960s that those who respect antiquity can only hope that the remaining beautiful sandstone buildings in the vicinity of Macquarie Place will be preserved for posterity.

Macquarie Place, originally an enclosure for the vegetable garden of Government House, was thrown open as a public park by Governor Macquarie in October 1810, and named by him in honour of himself—an honour that was well deserved, for he was the first great townplanner of Sydney. He viewed Macquarie Place as the hub not only of the administration but also of commerce. Adjacent as it was to the Government Wharf at the head of Sydney Cove and to the navigable reaches of the Tank Stream, this open space also fronted the residences and warehouses of prominent pioneer merchants, including Simeon Lord and Thomas Reiby.

In 1817 the first bank in Australia, the Bank of New South Wales, was opened for business in a cottage at Macquarie Place. Since then, and to the present day, the vicinity has had many banks, shipping offices, insurance offices, and wool-broking firms.

In Macquarie Place, in 1818, Governor Macquarie erected an obelisk from which "all the public roads leading to the interior of the colony are measured." This obelisk has become one of the most venerable historical relics in Sydney.

Another relic of Australian antiquity, dating from the First Fleet of 1788, is the anchor of H.M.S. *Sirius*, mounted on a pediment in Macquarie Place. The anchor was salvaged in 1890 from the wreck of the *Sirius*, which had run aground and broken up on a reef at Norfolk Island a century before. The anchor was brought to Sydney, and was mounted in Macquarie Place in 1907.

That large and rusted bower—now well preserved by anti-corrosive paint—is the oldest relic of British settlement at Sydney. To the eye of the historian, or of any person endowed with historical imagination, it is an object to be regarded with awe. The men who hove up or let go that anchor, in Rio de Janeiro, in Table Bay, in Botany Bay, in Sydney Cove, and in the offing of Norfolk Island, were seamen of the greatest tradition of seamanship that the world has known. When H.M.S. *Sirius*, in October 1788, sailed from Sydney, bound for Capetown, rounding Cape Horn, and returned to Sydney by "running the easting down" to round the South Cape of Van Diemen's Land, she became the first vessel in history to circumnavigate the globe in the high southern latitudes of the Roaring Forties and Howling Fifties by taking advantage of the prevailing westerlies on the entire route.

That large hand-forged anchor was lashed on her bows on that passage, and, beyond that, it is the only anchor now remaining of all those that were let go at Sydney Cove on 26th January, 1788. Its sentimental value for Australians is great, and will become greater with the passing of time.

THE FERRIES   SEE ALSO PART II

If a "public opinion poll" were taken to ascertain the most distinctive feature of the Sydney scene, many would vote for the ferries. That would certainly have been true before the opening of the Sydney Harbour Bridge in 1932, when seventy ferry-steamers operated on routes from Circular Quay across the Harbour to the north shore, and also along the southern shore to Watson's Bay, in addition to the Manly ferries; and other ferries operated from Erskine Street (Darling Harbour) to Balmain and the Parramatta River.

The opening of the Bridge drastically reduced the ferry traffic for passengers, and eliminated the punt ferries for vehicles; yet in the 1960s there remained fifteen ferry-steamers operating from the Quay to the north-side suburbs—chiefly to Neutral Bay, Cremorne, Mosman, and Taronga Park—and seven larger steamers were on the run from the Quay to Manly.

The picturesque design of the ferry-steamers, their bright colours, and their bright lights at night, caused at least one awe-struck child to call them "fairy boats," but even the most blasé adult could clearly remember, in places far from Sydney, those gay steamers converging on Sydney Cove, or emerging from it, on a blue-and-gold Sydney sunlit day, or with their lights reflected in the waters at night beneath a starlit cloudless sky.

As gondolas are to Venice, so are the ferries to Sydney. A time must come when the fleet of coal-burning or oil-burning double-ended steamers will become obsolete, to be replaced perhaps by hydrofoil craft or hovercraft, or by motor-driven speeders, or by helicopters, or by more bridges across the Harbour or tunnels beneath it—yet while the old-style Sydney Harbour ferries maintain their traditional services they will remain a delight to residents and visitors.

Five two-sided piers at the head of Sydney Cove comprise the Circular Quay Ferry Terminal to which all the Harbour ferry services now converge.

The first Sydney ferry was the *Rose Hill Packet*, built and launched from Underwood's yards in 1789. A clumsy "hoy," propelled by oars and sails, she took a whole day to make the passage of fourteen miles to Parramatta. She carried chiefly government passengers and cargoes, and did not run to a schedule.

Other sailing craft and rowing boats were soon brought into service as ferries across the Harbour, or up and down the Harbour. These were operated by "watermen" whose boats, which could be hired for special occasions, were not scheduled ferry services. In 1830 an eighty-two-year-old Negro ex-convict, Billy Blue, established a regular row boat ferry service between his home at Blue's Point on the north side and Dawes Point. His sons maintained the service for twelve years until a steam ferry (a paddle-wheel vehicular punt) began operating there in 1842.

The first Australian-built steamer, the S.S. *Surprise*, a paddle wheeler, began a ferry service from Sydney to Parramatta in 1831. Thereafter more and more ferry-steamers were gradually brought into commission. In the 1860s the North Shore Steam Ferry Company began cross-harbour services from Circular Quay to Milson's Point, a service that was steadily expanded as residential suburbs developed at Kirribilli, Neutral Bay, Cremorne, and Mosman.

In the 1880s a regular steam ferry service was inaugurated from Sydney Cove eastwards along the southern shore of the Harbour, to Darling Point, Double Bay, Rose Bay, and Watson's Bay. This service was discontinued in 1938, when the development of motorized road traffic had made the waterway unprofitable.

In 1889 the North Shore Ferry Company was reorganized financially in the name of Sydney Ferries Limited. It ran most of the ferry services on the Harbour except for the Manly ferries and the Balmain ferries. The opening of the Sydney Harbour Bridge in 1932 affected the cross-harbour ferry services so adversely that in 1951 the business of Sydney Ferries Limited was taken over by the Government of New South Wales, to be conducted under subsidy as a public utility.

The opening of the Harbour Bridge did not adversely affect the Manly ferries. Manly, with an expanding population, is served by a fleet of seven large steamers, providing one of the best passenger ferry services in the world. The Port Jackson and Manly Steamship Company Limited was incorporated in the 1890s to take over previously existing ferry services to Manly, which had been inaugurated in 1847 with a wooden-hulled paddle-steamer, S.S. *Brothers*.

In the 1960s the Manly ferries were making on an average eighty trips a day, carrying seven million passengers a year. The steamers make the six-mile passage between Sydney Cove and Manly Cove in half an hour.

At any hour of the day, and most hours of the night, there is at least one Manly ferry, and two or three of the smaller Sydney ferries, to be seen proceeding on their courses, adding distinctively to the animation of the general Harbour view. They converge on Sydney Cove, and emerge from their berths there, so frequently that the waters of the Cove are almost perpetually churned by their screws and cut by their bows.

Sydney without its ferry-steamers would not seem to be Sydney. The ferries, the Customs launches, and the Water Police launches, all add to the movement at the Cove, from which pleasure yachts and other small craft are excluded. Usually a large passenger liner occupies the berth at the Overseas Terminal on the western side of the Cove, and one or two cargo vessels may be berthed at the few other commercial wharves which are nowadays used at Sydney Cove; but most of the sea-borne trade of the Port of Sydney is handled at Woolloomooloo and on the many miles of wharves at Darling Harbour, Balmain, Pyrmont, and at other places upstream from the Bridge, out of sight of the citizens who live along the shores in the lower reaches of the Harbour; while Sydney Cove and the now archaically named Circular Quay are being perennially embellished as the Front Door of a city and of a nation.

The installations on the western side of the Cove, including the Harbour Bridge, are of such historic and present-day importance that they merit a separate description.

7

SEE ALSO PART II   THE ROCKS

THE PROMONTORY ON THE WESTERN SIDE OF SYDNEY COVE, SEPARATING
the Cove from Darling Harbour, and terminating in Dawes Point,
is a ridge which was known to the pioneer settlers as The Rocks.
It continues to be known affectionately to the public by that
name, which flatters no bygone panjandrum, but is aptly descriptive in more senses than one: for, in the waterfront pubs and
harpies' dens that formerly flourished on that ridge, many a
stranded sailor has found himself financially as well as physically
"on the rocks" until he could sign articles with a shipmaster to
go to sea again in a teetotal forecastle.

The carousals of sailors in port were typical of the era of
ocean-crossing sailing-vessels, in the days when Sydney Town
was founded, prevailed in the world's seaborne trade and commerce, and continued to prevail, even against the competition of
steamers, until the 1890s. A goodly number of sailing-vessels
continued to call at Sydney until the European War of 1914-18
put them into the discard.

It was never understood by landlubbers that "the drunken
sailor" in port had not tasted grog for months while at sea.
Perfect sobriety was required in men who risked their lives daily
in all weathers, working aloft on swaying yards at dizzying
heights, frequently in gales of wind, rain, sleet, or hail, when one
slip of foot or hand could mean death.

For the first half-century of the history of Sydney Town, the
wharves at Sydney Cove were the only berths in the Harbour
where large vessels could lie alongside to load or unload
merchandise. It was in this period that The Rocks district
became a notorious resort of "drunken sailors"; and it continued
in that reputation, but with diminishing intensity in the "steam
boat" era, almost to the present day.

That rocky western shore of Sydney Cove is famous for much
more than sailors' carousals in the numerous taverns that thrived
there in those olden days. Here stood the first hospital, the first
fort, the first observatory, the first cemetery, the first mercantile
wharf, the first warehouses, the first flourmill, the first bakery,
and the first military camp in Australia; and along this shore the
first whitemen's footpath, which became the first city street in
Australia, had its starting point at a rough landing-stage for the
boats of the First Fleet.

Above all, since the 1930s The Rocks Peninsula has borne the
weight of the southern abutments and approaches of the Sydney
Harbour Bridge; and it is proposed that in the late 1960s whatever then remains of old-style buildings in that vicinity, will be
demolished, and replaced by a gigantic "planned development"

of Tower-of-Babel architecture, in which tiers of apartments, serried in glass, steel, and concrete honeycombs, will once again make The Rocks a high density residential district, as it was in those earlier years when it was a crowded dockside slum.

That "development," the developers say, will balance the modernity of the Opera House on the opposite shore, to make the foreshores of Sydney Cove architecturally so startling that the general scenic effect will be acknowledged as a worldwide wonder. If that is accomplished, it will revive in the modern age the fame that formerly belonged to the Semi-Circular Quay as an engineering achievement of large scope and striking originality of design; but, even without a dense development of skyscraper apartments on The Rocks, the Cove that is flanked by the Sydney Opera House on one side and the Sydney Harbour Bridge on the other is so startlingly different in its surroundings from any other berthing place of ships, or bay of the same size, elsewhere in the world, that it may be fairly claimed as a sight unique, wonderful, and unforgettable. The world's three thousand million inhabitants may then be divided into two classes—those who have seen Sydney Cove and those who have not.

So Sydney people believe in their hearts; but they may be too modest to make such a bold claim, which is nevertheless occasionally voiced by world tourists and seafarers of wide experience, qualified to make comparisons.

CIRCULAR QUAY WEST   SEE ALSO PART II

The western side of Sydney Cove, though perfectly rectilinear, continues to be officially designated, by force of habit, as Circular Quay West. As the pioneers viewed it, on that side of their anchorage was a rocky ridge rising steeply to 150 feet above sea-level, forming the spine of a peninsula half a mile wide that separated Sydney Cove from the much larger bay to the westward that, forty-five years later, was to be named Darling Harbour.

That rocky ridge, with large red-boled trees and smaller grey-green shrubs growing on it with surprising tenacity, their roots embedded in stone, sloped down to a northern point (later named Dawes Point) opposite a promontory on the other side of the Harbour (Milson's Point), reducing the width of the Harbour there to a gut only 500 yards wide.

At the base of the rocky ridge, along the western foreshore of Sydney Cove, was a ledge of sandstone, fifty feet wide, a few feet above high tide mark. This formed a natural landing place for anyone coming ashore by boat. The waterfront was not a beach sloping to shallows; it dipped steeply to five or six fathoms close inshore, so that, as Phillip had noted, "at very small expense quays can be constructed at which the largest vessels may unload."

That remark applied to both sides of the Cove; but the western side, with its level ledge, was a natural quay. It was there that the first settlers were landed, the first patches of ground cleared, and the first tents and huts erected.

Rocky protuberances on the shore were gradually cleared away, and the waterfront became more sharply defined by a sea-wall and by wharves and docks. That work was consolidated when the Semi-Circular Quay was formed to Barney's grand design in the 1840s.

In the 1950s and 1960s, most of the older buildings, wharves, sea-wall, and other constructions were replaced by modern works of waterfront engineering and architecture. The waterfront at the base of The Rocks ridge is occupied nowadays by the Maritime Services Board Building and its esplanade; the Sydney Cove Passenger Terminal; two docks for smaller commercial vessels; the Water Police dock; and a park on Dawes Point in which stands the South Pylon of the Harbour Bridge.

Most of those modern installations are on ground that has been reclaimed by the filling-in of the original shoreline. They stand between the present waterfront and George Street North, which follows the original shoreline. It was the pioneers' track along the ledge between the shore and the base of The Rocks ridge, and today it follows the same line of country that it did then.

THE HOSPITAL

The First Fleet had been eight months on the passage from England. Most of the convicts had been on board the transports for at least ten months from the time of their embarkation in England to their disembarkation at Sydney Cove. They had not been allowed ashore at Rio de Janeiro or Capetown. It was a long time to be confined on shipboard, with salt rations and restricted use of fresh water.

Remarkably, only forty-eight persons died on the passage; and some of those may have been incurably ill when they were embarked. The good health of the people was due to care by the eight "surgeons"—naval term for all medical officers, including physicians and surgeons—in the fleet, and to the plentiful supplies of fresh meat, vegetables, and fruit taken on board at the ports of call.

But when the fleet arrived at Sydney Cove, seventy-three days out from Capetown, many of the people were ill, with scurvy or dysentery. Others became ill soon after landing, perhaps from unaccustomed hard labour in the heat of midsummer; or from eating berries or the leaves of plants; or from the after-effects of a long diet of weevily biscuits and "high" salt pork; or from sheer excitement at stretching their legs on shore again, with unlimited quantities of fresh spring water to drink.

Of the eight surgeons in the fleet, four were appointed to remain in the Colony on the government payroll. They were John White, Surgeon-General, and his assistants, Dennis Considen, Thomas Arndell, and William Balmain. Under their supervision, the first hospital in Australia was established on the western side of Sydney Cove, on the level ground at the foot of The Rocks ridge. Its site was at or near the intersection of present-day Argyle Street and North George Street.

Surgeon-General White, in his journal on 29th January, 1788, stated:

> The laboratory and sick tents were erected, and, I am sorry to say, were soon filled with patients afflicted with the true camp dysentery and the scurvy. More pitiable objects were perhaps never seen. Not a comfort or convenience could be got for them, besides the very few we had with us.
>
> His Excellency, seeing the state those poor objects were in, ordered a piece of land to be enclosed, for the purpose of raising vegetables for them. . . .
>
> The sick have increased since our landing to such a degree, that a spot for a general hospital has been marked out, and artificers already employed on it.
>
> A proper spot, contiguous to the hospital, has already been chosen, to raise such vegetables as can be produced at this season of the year, and where a permanent garden for the use of the hospital is to be established.

As that entry was dated only three days after the arrival of the fleet at Sydney Cove, it indicates that the hospital was one of the first buildings erected in Australia, and that its garden was the first, or certainly one of the first, gardens cultivated in Australia.

A plan of Sydney Cove drawn by an officer of H.M.S. *Sirius*, Lieutenant William Bradley, R.N., and dated 1st March, 1788, shows the Hospital and Garden, with two wells sunk, and a bakehouse and oven and a guardhouse near by.

That plan indicated that the lines of "Convicts' Tents" were on the western side at the head of the Cove, near the intersection of present-day George Street and Essex Street; and the Marine Encampment was near the intersection of present-day George Street and Grosvenor Street.

George Street thus began as a track connecting the Hospital with the Convicts' Tents and the Marine Encampment. It was used also by water carriers bringing fresh water in pails, or in casks dragged on sledges, from the "Spring" above the tidal range, in the vicinity of present-day Martin Place, to the tents and huts along the shore.

Its original name of Spring Row was humorously altered unofficially to Sergeant-Majors' Row, and then officially to High Street by Governor King, and to George Street by Governor Macquarie.

THE FIRST CEMETERY

An official report, dated 27th September, 1788, shows that, in the first eight months after the landing, fifty-two people had died. These comprised three marines, twenty-six male convicts, twelve female convicts, and eleven children. They were buried in a small unconsecrated cemetery on The Rocks ridge, probably near the site of the present-day St Philip's Church (which was built in the 1850s).

The original cemetery became lost to memory in course of time. Another cemetery was opened—on the site of the present-day Sydney Town Hall—early in the year 1789, and continued in

115

use for thirty years. It was then that the first cemetery on The Rocks was neglected, and eventually streets or buildings obliterated all trace of it.

Somewhere in The Rocks ridge are the skeletons of the pioneers who died at Sydney in the first year of British settlement. Exact records were not kept, or are no longer extant, but in all probability the total number of skeletons in that "lost" cemetery would be between sixty and seventy.

SEE ALSO PART II   DAWES POINT

William Dawes, a Lieutenant in the Marines serving in H.M.S. *Sirius*, was thirty years of age when the First Fleet arrived at Sydney Cove. He had been trained as an astronomer, and was recommended for service in the *Sirius* by the Astronomer Royal (Doctor Maskelyne) and equipped with a small telescope and other instruments, to observe that part of the heavens visible from New South Wales, and in particular to keep watch for a comet expected to be visible in the Southern Hemisphere in 1788.

Dawes accompanied Governor Phillip's advance party in the *Supply*, the first vessel to anchor in Sydney Cove. Within a few days after the arrival of the *Sirius* and the other vessels of the fleet, he had erected a temporary shed for his observatory on the point of The Rocks Peninsula, which he named Point Maskelyne, in honour of the Astronomer Royal; but the settlers renamed it Dawes Point, and that name passed into general use and became officially recognized.

Alongside the observatory, eight naval carriage-guns were mounted in a redoubt—a square earthwork, breast-high. This gun emplacement, manned by marines and gunners of H.M.S. *Sirius*, was under command of Lieutenant Dawes, and became known as "Dawes Battery." It was Australia's first fortification.

On 23rd May, 1788, Dawes was discharged from the *Sirius* and transferred to the shore establishment of the marines. On 9th July, Governor Phillip wrote in a report, "On the point of land which forms the west side of the cove an Observatory is building, under the direction of Lieutenant Dawes." This presumably referred to a stone building with a more substantial house for Dawes and his detachment than the tents or rough shelters in which they had camped for five months.

Dawes' Battery, 500 yards beyond the hospital and 1000 yards from the main camp of the marines, was an outpost of the settlement. It was near the site of the South Pylon of the present-day Harbour Bridge. A path led to it from the hospital along the foreshore—the present-day northern end of George Street North.

Soon after July 1788, a flagstaff was erected on the highest point of The Rocks ridge, on the site of the present-day Sydney Observatory. The flagstaff was manned as a signal station and lookout point for the expected arrival of the Second Fleet. The lookout men were marines from Dawes Battery. The path between Dawes Point and the Flagstaff later became known as Fort Street, and continues to be so named today.

After the signal station had been established and manned, The

Rocks ridge became officially known as Flagstaff Hill, but the older name of The Rocks persisted, and ultimately prevailed.

SHIPBUILDING

In addition to Underwood's shipbuilding yard established in 1789 on the western side of the Tank Stream estuary, a government shipbuilding yard was established in 1796 by Governor Hunter. It was on the western side of Sydney Cove, with its slipways at the site of the present-day Water Police dock, near Dawes Point.

From that shipyard were launched several ocean-going sailing-vessels, including the schooner *Cumberland*, 28 tons, in 1801, the schooner *Integrity*, 59 tons, in 1804, and the brig *Elizabeth Henrietta*, 150 tons, in 1816.

These vessels, and others which were built at Underwood's yards, and at Woolloomooloo, and on the Hawkesbury River, were used in government passenger and cargo services to the settlements on the Hawkesbury, and for longer voyages to Norfolk Island, Van Diemen's Land (Tasmania), and the Hunter River. Some were sold to private individuals engaged in seal hunting in Bass Strait and in New Zealand waters. There was also a schooner trade between Sydney and Botany Bay, and up the George's River to Bankstown and Liverpool; and a regular and busy waterborne trade between Sydney and Parramatta.

An official return in 1804 showed a total of "twenty-one schooners and sloops belonging to individuals in his Majesty's territory of New South Wales." Of these, fifteen had been built at Sydney Cove, one at Woolloomooloo, and five on the Hawkesbury.

The Government shipyard continued in operation for thirty-seven years, until it closed down in 1833. It had always one or more vessels under construction on its slipways. These were shown prominently in sketches, paintings, and lithographs of "Sydney Views" from 1796 onwards.

The timber from trees growing at Sydney was not suitable for shipbuilding, but logs and pit-sawn planks of various kinds of eucalypts were rafted, towed, or brought as deck cargo to Sydney from the Hawkesbury, Parramatta, Lane Cove, and George's rivers, and from Botany Bay, Brisbane Water, and the Hunter River.

In the 1820s and 1830s, shipyards were established at Brisbane Water and on the Hunter River and the Northern Rivers, near the forests from which the timber was obtained; and larger vessels, including steamers, were built there; but in the perspective of history it was at Sydney Cove that the Australian shipbuilding industry began. The shipwrights of the government yard were among the first residents on The Rocks ridge.

CAMPBELL'S WHARF

The first wharf in Australia was a landing-stage named the King's Wharf, on the western side of Sydney Cove, built in 1788 near the site of the present-day Maritime Services Board building. Soon afterwards a jetty, which became known as the Government Wharf, was built at the head of the Cove, on the eastern side of the Tank Stream, near the site of the present-day Customs House. These two wharves were used chiefly for landing passengers and government stores.

In 1798 Robert Campbell, a Scot aged twenty-nine, arrived in Sydney from Calcutta with a cargo of general merchandise. He saw opportunities for developing an export and import trade, and so became Australia's first fully established merchant.

Military officers, government officials, shipmasters, and emancipated convicts had engaged occasionally in trade, as opportunities offered; but Robert Campbell was the first merchant at Sydney to build his own warehouses, and to engage in the export and import trade as a regular occupation.

Obtaining a lease of land on the waterfront on the western side of Sydney Cove—near the site occupied by the present-day Overseas Passenger Terminal—he built Campbell's Wharf and a warehouse there in 1800, and maintained an increasing trade for more than forty years. His warehouses—extended to a series of gabled buildings, some of which were extant in the 1960s— were stocked not only with general merchandise, including grog, imported chiefly from India, but also with whale oil, sealskins, and cedar, which he bought from local shipmasters, and eventually with wool, bought from graziers, enabling him to develop an export trade as well as an import trade.

In 1801 Robert Campbell had married Sophia Palmer, daughter of the Commissary-General, John Palmer, who had charge of all government stores. This was an advantageous alliance; Campbell received many government contracts from his father-in-law. By these and other fair means he prospered greatly.

In 1834 he was granted 5000 acres of land on the Molonglo Plains, including much of the site of the present-day city of Canberra. The homestead of his property, which he named Duntroon, was acquired from his descendants in 1910 for the Australian Military College.

In 1846, Robert Campbell died at Duntroon, and was buried in the churchyard of St John's, Canberra.

SEE ALSO PART II   FORT PHILLIP

In 1804, apprehensive of the possibility of an insurrection by Irish political prisoners who had been sent to the Colony, Governor King had a strong citadel built on Flagstaff Hill. A hexagonal fort of stone, it was named Fort Phillip. It continued to be manned by artillerymen for forty years. Its guns, commanding the seaward approaches to Sydney Cove, were never fired in anger.

When, in 1818, Governor Macquarie established military barracks at what is now Wynyard Square—a walled area of ten acres, including the parade ground—a road named York Street led from the barracks to Fort Phillip, and thence by way of Fort Street to Dawes Point.

Fort Phillip was demolished in the 1840s, and the Fort Street School, serving The Rocks district, was established near by. In the 1950s it became a Girls' High School.

SYDNEY OBSERVATORY   SEE ALSO PART II

After Lieutenant Dawes returned to England at the end of 1791, after nearly four years' service at Sydney, there were no trained astronomers in New South Wales until Sir Thomas Brisbane arrived as Governor in December 1821.

Governor Brisbane, who was an astronomer himself, equipped an observatory at Government House, Parramatta, and engaged two skilled astronomers, Carl Rumker and James Dunlop, to assist him in compiling "The Parramatta Catalogue" of 7,385 stars.

After Sir Thomas Brisbane returned to Britain in 1825, Rumker and then Dunlop served as government astronomers of New South Wales until Dunlop retired in 1847. The Parramatta Observatory was then closed, and a new observatory was opened eleven years later (in 1858) on the site of Fort Phillip, on Flagstaff Hill.

This building, extended, and with new equipment added from time to time, is still the Sydney Observatory. It stands in a park, on the western side of the approaches to Sydney Harbour Bridge. For many decades a feature of the Observatory was the "time-ball" signal, which gave exact local time daily at noon. This signal was visible to shipmasters in all parts of the Harbour, who could set their chronometers to it, but radio broadcasting of time signals has made the time-ball service unnecessary.

Since 1892 the astronomers at Sydney Observatory have been compiling an "astrographic catalogue" of stars in accordance with an international plan.

MILLER'S POINT

The Rocks Peninsula has its northern termination in Walsh Bay, a crescent-shaped indentation between Dawes Point and Miller's Point.

Miller's Point is 800 yards to the westward of Dawes Point. In all probability it was so named by Governor Phillip in honour of Andrew Miller, the Governor's Secretary, who was also the first Government Commissary of New South Wales.

During Governor Hunter's term of office (1795 to 1800), a flourmiller named John Leighton—known as "Jack the Miller"—had three windmills on that point, to catch the westerly breezes, for grinding corn. According to some historians, Miller's Point did not take its name from Andrew Miller, but was originally named Jack the Miller's Point, in honour of Leighton. It is an open question.

A track across the head of the peninsula, from Sydney Cove and Dawes Battery to Miller's Point, became Windmill Street, and bears that name today.

WALSH BAY   SEE ALSO PART II

The crescent-shaped bay between Dawes Point and Miller's

Point had no distinguishing name until the 1920s, when it was given the name of Walsh Bay, in honour of Henry Deane Walsh, who was Chief Engineer at the Sydney Harbour Trust from 1901 to 1919.

Nowadays there are five docks in Walsh Bay, separated by piers, with berths for ten large vessels, in depths· of from five to seven fathoms alongside the wharves.

SEE ALSO PART II   SAILORS' TAVERNS

In the heyday of the whaling industry, from the 1790s to the 1870s, it was usual for whaling-vessels when they visited Sydney to sell oil, to refit, to obtain provisions, and to anchor in the bay between Dawes Point and Miller's Point.

The whaling crews gave The Rocks district its reputation for drunken carousals, but sailors from merchant vessels at Campbell's Wharf, and after 1840 from the various berths at the Semi-Circular Quay, also went on wild sprees in the taverns there.

Among the most renowned or notorious of the sailors' taverns on The Rocks were the Black Dog, the Brown Bear, the Whaler's Arms, the Hit or Miss, the Lord Nelson, the Mermaid, the Erin go Bragh, the Cat and Fiddle, the Jolly Sailor, the Rose of Australia, the World Turned Upside Down, the Hero of Waterloo, the Sheer Hulk, the Labour in Vain, and the Sailor's Return.

Most of those "pubs" have disappeared, but a few remain, patronized by waterside workers and seamen, who drink less uproariously than did their forbears of bygone days.

LARRIKINS AND CHINESE

In 1838, James Maclehose, in his descriptive book, *Picture of Sydney,* stated:

> Although The Rocks were among the first parts of the township of Sydney to be built on, this quarter has been but little improved. Many wooden skillings and mean huts are still standing, inhabited by the poorer parts of the community. The roads and footpaths are in such bad repair, and so filthy, that no respectable person will pass through them if avoidable.

The hygiene of The Rocks was not improved in the 1850s and 1860s, when large numbers of Chinese settled there, in transit to and from the goldfields. An outbreak of smallpox, which created a panic in Sydney, began in the "Chinatown" at The Rocks. This plague scare contributed to the public opinion that gave rise to the White Australia Policy.

Larrikin "pushes" at The Rocks were notorious in the 1880s and 1890s for their raids and street fights against the "pushes" of Woolloomooloo, Surry Hills, the Glebe, and Balmain.

FAMOUS RESIDENTS

Despite the sailors' taverns, the harpies, the Chinese, and the larrikins, some streets on The Rocks ridge, in remarkable contrast with the adjacent slums, were lined with residences of wealthy merchants and professional people.

Maclehose noted this as early as 1838, when he remarked:

> In Windmill Street a number of respectable dwelling houses have lately been erected, and are mostly occupied by opulent persons. As a whole, it is probably one of the best neighbourhoods in Sydney.

Some good terrace houses were built in the 1850s, along Argyle Street and in Argyle Place. An Anglican Church, Holy Trinity, was built in Argyle Place in 1843 and enlarged in 1855. It served as the Garrison Church of British regiments stationed at Sydney.

Among famous residents of the upper-class part of The Rocks were Edmund Barton, who became Australia's first Prime Minister, and David Scott Mitchell, founder of the Mitchell Library. The artist, Conrad Martens, lived there for two years (1835-37) when he first arrived in Sydney. Joseph Conrad, in the 1890s, and Jack London, in 1908, stayed at the Mermaid Inn.

Those were famous men, but none surpassed in renown "Young Griffo," who, according to his own statements, was born at Miller's Point on 31st March, 1871. According to other accounts, he was born at Bendigo in Victoria, brought as a baby to Sydney, and was reared by foster parents in the slums on The Rocks. His name was Albert Griffiths, but he became known as "Young Griffo," and later simply as "Griffo."

Perhaps through undernourishment due to poverty, Griffo was only five feet four inches tall, and eight stone in weight at fifteen years of age, when he became a professional bare-knuckle pugilist, and soon afterwards learned to be a glove-fighter under the tuition of Larry Foley at Sydney.

In six years, from 1886 to 1892, Griffo had forty-six fights—mostly at Sydney, but some also at Melbourne and at Adelaide—and was never beaten. His successes were all against opponents older and heavier than himself.

In 1892, he was persuaded to leave for America. He embarked in a sailing ship at Sydney Cove, but when she was passing Pinchgut Island, he became homesick, dived overboard, and swam ashore.

In the following year (1893), he went to the U.S.A. In the next ten years he had more than sixty fights, most of which he won, in many different American cities, and was considered to be the World's Featherweight Champion. He was so quick on his feet, and in "bobbing and weaving" to evade his opponent's blows, that he came through even the most arduous fights unscathed; but, small though he was, the power of his punches was such that on one occasion—at Sacramento, California, 27th April, 1896 —his opponent, Bill McCarthy, after being knocked out in the twentieth round, died next day from injuries received during the fight.

Griffo retired from prizefighting in 1904, and lived in New York, a drunkard, until his death in 1937. The names of only two

121

Australians are inscribed in the "Boxing Hall of Fame" (greatest pugilists of all time) at the Ring Museum, in New York City— Griffo and Les Darcy.

SEE ALSO PART II   THE ARGYLE CUT

Argyle Street, so named by Governor Macquarie in 1810 in honour of his own birthplace (the Isle of Mull, in the County of Argyle, Western Scotland), was at that time a foot track, too steep for wheeled vehicles. It led over the crags of The Rocks ridge, from the waterfront at Sydney Cove to Fort Phillip on the crest of the hill, and beyond to Miller's Point.

During Governor Macquarie's term of office (1810-21), The Rocks ridge, though officially known as Flagstaff Hill, was unofficially renamed Bunker's Hill. This was a humorous reference to the Battle of Bunker's Hill, near Boston, Massachusetts, where, in April 1775, the American War of Independence began, with a victory of the colonists against British troops. The name was presumably approved by Governor Macquarie, as it appeared on an official map of Sydney drawn on his instructions, though dated August 1822; but it was discarded, perhaps on the instructions of Governor Darling (1825-1831), who may have thought that the "revolting colonists" of Sydney might have been inspired to emulate the Americans.

In 1838 Maclehose stated that Argyle Street was "in two divisions, separated from each other by a precipice of considerable height." Steps were hewn in the stone to make the ascent or descent of the "precipice" easier. These were "the Argyle Steps," which remain today.

In 1843, under Barney's grand plan of reclaiming the foreshores to form the Semi-Circular Quay, a deep cutting was made through The Rocks ridge to form a road for handcarts and horse-drawn wheeled vehicles between the waterfronts of Sydney Cove and Darling Harbour. The stone from this cutting—hewn with handtools by the labour of hundreds of convicts—was used to form the sea-wall and foreshore reclamation of the western side of Semi-Circular Quay.

Known as The Argyle Cut, this large excavation is not only one of the most impressive achievements of convict slave labour at Sydney, but is also an instructive exhibit of the solid rock foundation on which the City of Sydney is built.

The Argyle Cut remains in use today as the main east-west thoroughfare through The Rocks. It is spanned high overhead by an arch supporting the approaches to the Harbour Bridge on the north-south axis of traffic.

SEE ALSO
PART II   THE MARITIME SERVICES BOARD

On the waterfront, at the south-western corner of Sydney Cove, stands the Maritime Services Building, a five-storey sandstone edifice in classic architectural style, completed in 1949. It is in the spacious surroundings of an esplanade with lawns and gardens, between the Sydney Cove Passenger Liner Terminal

and the Harbour Ferry Terminals. It may fairly be considered as the handsomest public building erected in Sydney in a classical style in the modern era.

The Maritime Services Building stands on the site of a Government Commissariat Store building that was erected by order of Governor Macquarie in 1812. The old building, designed to be useful rather than ornamental, but nevertheless gracefully proportioned and of solid stone construction, was a landmark at Sydney Cove for 128 years until it was demolished in 1940 to provide a site for the larger, more handsome, and much more useful and necessary building which is the headquarters of one of the most important functional authorities of the State Government of New South Wales—the Maritime Services Board.

Under the federal constitution of the Commonwealth of Australia, promulgated on 1st January, 1901, the Federal Government was granted power to control "trade and commerce with other countries, and between the States," and also some fields of maritime or partly maritime activity, including Immigration, Defence, Customs, Lighthouses, and Quarantine; but those powers, while applying to ocean navigation and to coastal shipping between the States, did not apply to the control of trade and commerce, or of shipping *within a State.*

Consequently, the State Governments have retained control of commercial navigation, and of the waters and foreshores *inside* ports and harbours, and within navigable rivers and lakes of the inland, and along the coast between ports within each State. The maritime jurisdiction of a State thus covers all aspects of shipping and boating and longshore handling that have not been expressly delegated to the Federal Government.

The State Government controls pilotage, wharfage, dredging, moorings, harbourside installations, and other services to shipping of many kinds. The responsibility to incur expenditure implies also the right to collect port dues as revenues to cover such expenditure, some of which is financed from loan funds as capital works, repaid from revenues over extended periods.

Control of the waters and foreshores of Sydney Harbour, and of the shipping and shore installations, is therefore divided between the Federal and State Governments in defined fields of activity. The Federal Government controls all naval and military or other defence installations; the South Head Lighthouse (which is for "oceanic" not "harbour" navigation); the Quarantine Station and other health services related to passengers in overseas ships; and the collection of Customs dues. As usual in federal constitutions, all rights and powers not expressly conveyed by the States to the Federal authority remain with the States.

This means that the Maritime Services Board and the Water Police, as instrumentalities of the State Government of New South Wales, work in conjunction with instrumentalities of the Federal Government, including the Defence forces and the Federal Departments of Health, of Customs and Excise, and of Immigration, in practical ways that have been arrived at by experience, and depend on co-operation.

For example, though the Maritime Services Board of New

South Wales controls all commercial wharfage and facilities for handling passengers and cargo inwards and outwards in the ports of New South Wales, no cargo may be discharged from an overseas vessel or removed from a wharf until Customs requirements have been met, and an overseas vessel may not leave port without a Customs clearance. Likewise, movements of passengers are subject to the over-riding control of the Federal Departments of Health and of Immigration.

Yet the residual powers vested in the Maritime Services Board are very wide. The Board is, for practical purposes, the paramount authority in the control of the Port of Sydney as a mercantile seaport, and incidentally of Sydney Harbour as one of the greatest pleasure yachting-grounds in the world. As an example of the Maritime Services Board's powers, though all bridges across the Harbour, or any of its saltwater arms, are under control of the Main Roads Board (a State Government instrumentality), no such bridge may be built across navigable waters, including inland rivers and lakes, unless the plans are approved by the Maritime Services Board (i.e., to ensure that the bridge is not an obstruction to navigation).

As custodian of the State Government's residual rights, the Maritime Services Board was constituted under that name in 1936 to take over and co-ordinate the work of the previously existing authorities in the control of navigable waters, ports, and harbours in the State of New South Wales. The Board's jurisdiction includes the inland navigable waters of rivers and lakes, including the Murray and Darling Rivers, on which there is now very little traffic.

Governmental control of ports and shipping began in the earliest years of settlement at Sydney. During Governor Phillip's term of office, the Colonial Government provided a signal station and beacon at South Head, made some provision for pilotage, and built two wharves or landing stages in Sydney Cove. No port dues were charged until October 1800, when Governor King, to raise funds for an orphanage, levied a charge on all vessels entering the Harbour.

In 1811 Governor Macquarie appointed a Harbourmaster to supervise pilotage, and in 1813 he fixed the pilotage fees. In 1814 he appointed Captain John Piper (a military officer) to be "Naval Officer" of Port Jackson, with authority to collect Customs duties and also harbour dues, and to supervise pilotage, anchorage, berths, and the Water Police; but this "Naval Officer" had no authority over vessels of the Royal Navy or over Naval shore establishments: he had control only of the mercantile marine and of civilian activities on the Harbour. The name "Naval Officer" was an anomaly.

Throughout the nineteenth century, as the trade and commerce of the Port of Sydney increased, most of the commercial wharves were owned by or leased to private individuals or companies. In 1852 a "Steam Navigation Board" was constituted, as a government authority, to regulate steam ferry services, but its functions were soon extended to the control of all shipping movements within the Harbour, and eventually to other ports and harbours along the coast of New South Wales, and in general to coastwide navigation.

In 1858 the pilotage service was reorganized under full government ownership and control, with a salaried Harbourmaster and salaried pilots and boat crews. The revenues and expenditures of this service were controlled by a Pilot Board.

In 1871, a Marine Board was constituted to supervise and control the handling of seaborne trade and commerce in all the ports of New South Wales; but a different authority, the Navigation Board, controlled the movements of vessels, including the pilotage services at all ports.

When the Federal Government took over its delegated fields of control in 1901, the Government of New South Wales drastically reorganized its large residual powers in control of the ports and harbours. It constituted the Sydney Harbour Trust, with special powers to control and develop the Port of Sydney—in particular by taking over and enlarging the privately owned wharves. The supervision of all other ports in the State, and of seaborne trade between ports within the State, and of the pilotage services at all ports, including the Port of Sydney, was entrusted to a different authority, the Department of Navigation, successor of the old colonial Navigation Board.

That arrangement continued until 1st February, 1936, when the Maritime Services Board of New South Wales was constituted to co-ordinate in one authority the port and navigation services which had previously been administered by the Sydney Harbour Trust and the New South Wales State Department of Navigation.

In its thirty-five years of control from 1901 to 1936, the Sydney Harbour Trust had reshaped the commercial wharves and docks of the Port of Sydney, with large new installations to keep pace with the ever-increasing seaborne trade of the port. That work has been continued since 1936 by the Maritime Services Board with many modern waterfront engineering and architectural constructions, including its own headquarters, and the Overseas Passenger Terminal, on the western shore of Sydney Cove.

The Maritime Services Board is responsible for the administration and control of all the ports, harbours, etc., in New South Wales of which the major ports are Sydney, Newcastle, Port Kembla, and Botany Bay. In addition to being the Port Authority and the Navigation and Conservancy Authority, the Board is also the Pilotage Authority at the various ports where pilotage facilities have been established. The Board is the construction and maintenance authority for wharfage, port facilities, etc., at the Ports of Sydney, Newcastle, and Botany Bay, but in the other ports of the State this task is the responsibility of the Department of Public Works. In addition to the major ports mentioned, there are 29 other proclaimed ports in the State administered by the Board, but of these only the ports of Richmond River, Clarence River, Coff's Harbour, Trial Bay, and Eden are still regularly visited by trading vessels. Of these ports, Trial Bay is the only one where a pilotage establishment is not maintained.

The Board is a corporate body of seven commissioners, of whom three are full-time members and four are part-time members representing various special interests. All are nominated by the Government of New South Wales. The extent of the enterprise that they control may be understood from the statistical fact that the Board's net income from shipping dues and other services in a typical year (1964-65) was £8,508,408, and in that year the capitalized value of its assets was £32,168,545.

Although these figures cover the Board's control of all the ports in New South Wales, the largest revenues are earned at Sydney.

Vessels Entered, and their Description, 1964-65

	Overseas	Interstate	Intrastate	Gross Tonnage
Sydney	2,489	494	1,041	24,810,768
Newcastle	702	588	609	9,960,998
Port Kembla	466	687	—	8,013,687
Botany Bay	333	—	—	4,907,984

Much of the trade of Newcastle and of Port Kembla is interstate—exports of coal and imports of iron ore—and there is a large trade in coal from Newcastle within the State, viz., to Sydney. The Port of Botany Bay, neglected for 150 years after Commodore Phillip rejected it in 1788, has been developed in the modern era, but almost exclusively as an oil port, to which tankers bring crude petroleum for treatment at the large refineries on the shores of the bay.

Sydney handles almost two-thirds of the overseas trade.

These totals are of the vessels calling at the ports and subsequently clearing out. Each vessel on short runs within the State or in the interstate trade would usually be entered and cleared out several times in a year. Vessels plying between Newcastle and Sydney are entered statistically at both ports.

Cargo handled at the Port of Sydney in that specimen year amounted to a total trade of 13,046,456 tons, made up of exports and imports in the three main categories as follows:

Tonnage of Cargo Handled at Sydney, 1964-65

	Overseas	Interstate	Intrastate
Imports	4,440,742	1,372,953	2,046,115
Exports	4,809,710	332,183	44,753

The comparatively large quantity of imports to Sydney from within the State included 1,432,847 tons of coal, almost entirely from Newcastle.

The principal items of export from Sydney to overseas destinations during 1964-65 were coal (1,558,862 tons), wheat (1,475,004 tons), and wool (1,211,387 bales). The largest items of imports from overseas and interstate ports, in terms of tonnages, were bulk oils, paper, and timber.

The revenue of the Maritime Services Board from cargoes is based on tonnage, not on values as merchandise. For this purpose a "ton" may be calculated, at the discretion of the Board, either as 40 cubic feet or as 2,240 lbs. The charge is known as "Wharf-age and Harbour Rates," but there are many other charges and fees collected by the Board, including pilotage, "tonnage rates," berthing charges, storage, and various certificates and licences, including registration of many kinds of small craft, mooring fees, and rents of wharves, jetties, sheds, warehouses, and other buildings.

Tonnage rates are charged on the gross registered tonnage of all vessels entering the port and berthing at a wharf vested in or controlled by the Board, while berthing charges are applicable to vessels of under 240 tons.

The number of sea-passengers in a typical year was as follows.

Passenger Traffic, Port of Sydney, 1964-65

	Arrivals	Departures
Overseas	74,830	62,295
Interstate	14,676	15,702
Totals ...	89,506	77,997

The Maritime Services Board has found it necessary, in order to handle the administration and physical work at the ports under its control, to employ a staff of more than 2,500, including an average of 1,300 men on "outside" works of maintenance, construction or reconstruction at the ports of Sydney and Newcastle.

The ever-increasing trade at Sydney has been acompanied by extensive port improvements since the Maritime Services Board was constituted in 1936, and when the present wharf reconstruction programme is completed the facilities available to shipping will be among the best in the world.

For that achievement, the Maritime Services Board, as a public authority that has efficiently and enthusiastically accepted its responsibilities and risen to its opportunities, deserves a full meed of praise.

On the façade of the Maritime Services Building are carved three symbols—a steering-wheel, a propeller, and an anchor. Below them on the lawn is a bust of Governor Phillip, not of special artistic merit, too small for its impressive surroundings. Yet that is the ideal place for a commemoration of the founder of civilization in Australia. The larger than life bronze statue of Phillip, by the Italian sculptor Simonetti, which stands in the Botanic Gardens, could appropriately be moved to a more suitable position on the Maritime Services Concourse at Sydney Cove, to replace the small and nondescript bust standing there now.

THE PASSENGER TERMINAL

Adjoining the Maritime Services Building, on the western side of Sydney Cove, is the Passenger Terminal, opened in January 1961.

Built at a cost of two million pounds, it has a "wharf apron" 720 feet long and 40 feet wide, with a depth of water alongside of 42 feet at low tide. The Terminal, which provides a berth for vessels of up to 45,000 tons, is regularly used by the largest liners to visit Sydney. Similar terminals had previously been constructed for liners of up to 30,000 tons at Pyrmont, and of up to 20,000 tons at Woolloomooloo; but the Sydney Cove Terminal is not only the biggest at Sydney, but one of the best designed in the world.

Being a two-storeyed structure, it handles passengers on the upper deck, and cargo at wharf-level. It has facilities for embarking or disembarking 2,000 passengers and their luggage within a very short time, and also for accommodating the crowds of friends and relatives of passengers who congregate to welcome a large overseas liner or give it a send-off.

The site of this terminal, at Sydney's front door, has many advantages not usually to be found in the passenger-liner terminals of large seaports. It is adjacent to public transport by train, bus, and ferry to all parts of Sydney and the suburbs, and within easy walking distance of the city's commercial centre. Its surroundings are picturesque, with no suggestion of the dockside squalor that mars the approach from seaward to most of the world's big seaport cities.

Though the site of the Sydney Cove Passenger Terminal is rich in historical associations for those who can envisage them in imagination, the immense modern reconstructions of the foreshores of the Cove present to the mind's eye the image of a modern and progressive nation, here at its portico lavish in its display of confidence in its future.

SEE ALSO PART II   GEORGE STREET NORTH

Passengers who disembark at the Sydney Cove Terminal enter the City of Sydney by the oldest street in Australia, George Street North, which curves like a dog's hind leg to connect Dawes Point with what was originally the head of the Tank Stream estuary at Bridge Street, a distance of nearly three-quarters of a mile.

There, George Street North becomes simply George Street, and continues southward, as one of the main arteries of the City, to Railway Square, at Central Station, the terminus of the country and interstate trains. Beyond Railway Square, the thoroughfare continues southward to the Prince's Highway, forking south-westward to the Hume Highway, westward to the Great Western Highway. So George Street is the main exit from and entrance to Sydney on the landward or southern side, while at its northern end it is, as it was originally, the main City corridor from seaward.

Considered as an incorporated municipality, the City of Sydney has an area of only 7,161 acres, approximately one-sixtieth of the far-spread metropolitan area. That inner City is entirely on the south side of the Harbour. Its boundary is the shoreline, extending westwards from Rushcutters Bay to Rozelle Bay (an arm of Darling Harbour). Viewed broadly, most of the City is on a composite peninsula spread between Rushcutters Bay and Darling Harbour, with a serrated northern shoreline, in which Woolloomooloo Bay, Farm Cove, Sydney Cove, and Walsh Bay are indentations.

George Street, including its beginning in George Street North,

The *Dunbar*, which was wrecked in 1857 with the loss of 121 lives, now has its anchor as a memorial at South Head.

Traditionally a favourite spot for suicides — the Gap at North Head.

One of the pleasant experiences of Sydney is eating at a harbourside fish restaurant like this one at Watsons Bay.

Greycliffe House, in Nielsen Park, now the headquarters of the Sydney Harbour National Park, was built in 1850 for a daughter of the explorer and politician, William Charles Wentworth.

Fort Denison, popularly known as Pinchgut, was built on Rock Island between 1841 and 1857 from sandstone quarried at Neutral Bay.

One of the world's great architectural constructions, the Sydney Opera House. Designed by the Danish Architect, Joern Utzon, in 1957, it was opened in 1973, and cost $102 million.

Sydney Cove as Captain John Hunter drew it on 20 August 1788 *(from a photograph of the original, Public Library of Victoria).*

Circular Quay, 1874.

Sydney Cove in 1980

Circular Quay from Fort Macquarie in the 1880s.

Circular Quay, 1890 *(Photo: National Library, Canberra).*

Circular Quay, 1940 *(Photo: National Library, Canberra).*

Circular Quay, 1956 *(Photo: National Library, Canberra).*

When the *South Steyne* was launched in Scotland in 1938 it was the largest and fastest ferry in the world. Fire damaged it in 1974, but a group of enthusiasts later took over its restoration.

Built in stages between 1838 and 1895, Campbell's storehouse now contains a tavern and restaurant complex. The restoration of the area cost over $1 million.

Right

The Maritime Services Board tower rises 87 m above sea level at Millers Point.

Cadman's Cottage was the home of John Cadman, a convict who later became superintendent of Government boats. It was built in 1816 on the water's edge, but it is now some distance from the shore.

A highly spectacular and apparently dangerous stage of the construction of the Sydney Harbour Bridge — in fact, unobtrusive cables supported the two halves of the arch.

Right

Number 1 Walsh Bay, the first wharf west of Sydney Harbour Bridge, was scheduled for conversion in 1980 into a restaurant and shopping complex.

Placing the centre road panels during the construction of the Sydney Harbour Bridge, 1930.

The Thames Street ferry wharf and shelter at Balmain, in an area where huge container vessels are usually moored, is classified as part of the National Estate.

The Dawn Fraser Swimming Pool, the oldest pool in the harbour, dating back to 1881, was originally called Elkington Park Baths, after a former Mayor of Balmain.

Birkenhead Point, an old rubber factory, has been redesigned as a shopping complex, marina, and maritime museum.

Gladesville Bridge was the longest concrete arch bridge in the world until 1979, when it was outstripped by one built in Yugoslavia.

Chalwin Castle, in Middle Harbour, built in 1951, has been designed in the eighteenth-century style with Georgian neo-classical interiors. It has a picturesque theatre used for chamber music, opera and plays.

Blues Point Towers, designed by Harry Seidler. The name commemorates Billy Blue, a part-Jamaican Negro convict who became Sydney's first ferryman.

is an axis that probes from the City's most northerly point (Dawes Point) to the southward. The distance from Dawes Point to the Town Hall is a mile and a half, and to the Central Railway Station two miles. Parallel to that corridor is the grid of the other longitudinal streets, with names commemorating English dukes and political celebrities of a bygone era—Sussex, Kent, Clarence, York, Pitt, and Castlereagh. All those streets, for topographical reasons, are shorter than the original High Street that Governor Macquarie renamed in honour of "the Mad Monarch," George the Third.

In George Street North, behind the resplendent new waterfront buildings, the atmosphere of the nineteenth century lingers in the Victorian Baroque architecture of the Coroner's Court (the Morgue) and of a police station where many a sailor and many a larrikin spent "a night in the cooler" in the rip-roaring days of the full-rigged sailing vessels. There remains a flavour of those days, too, in the emblazoned names of the "Fortune of War" hotel and of the "Flying Angel"—the church Mission to Seamen, next to the Sailors' Home.

Near the northern end of George Street North are rows of gabled red-brick bond stores, some of which were built in the 1820s and 1830s by Campbell of Campbell's Wharf. Others in the same architectural style were built in the 1840s along the opposite (eastern) side of Sydney Cove, but most of the warehouses on that side were demolished in the 1950s to make space for blocks of office buildings in the modern glasshouse Tower-of-Babel oblong box style, fronting the landward approach to the Opera House.

While the gabled bond stores and other specimens of archaic architecture remain standing in George Street North, in contrast to the large designs of modern waterfront engineering and of the soaring shapes of the Harbour Bridge and its abutments, that medley of building styles symbolizes the lengthening scroll of Australian history. On that track along the shore that grew to a street, throngs of ocean-crossing adventurers for seventeen decades have set foot in the Great South Land, hopeful of finding a better life than was possible in their ancestral homelands. George Street North was, for many, the Gate of Opportunity; for others, the Gate of Disappointment; but for sailors, usually, one of the best places in the world for a wild spree.

There, where the Aborigines for millenniums had speared fish and roasted oysters, successive cohorts of invading Europeans— sailors, marines, soldiers, officials, prisoners of the Crown, free settlers, gold-seekers, and their Australian-born descendants— have, according to their duties or inclinations, marched or strolled, or rambled with the rolling gait of the sailor, along that ledge between the sandstone ramparts of The Rocks ridge and the wharves where the masts, yards, and rigging of berthed windjammers made intricate patterns against the sky. There, where merchants "undid their corded bales," and old chums, new chums, and native sons worked as shipwrights, stevedores, shipchandlers, carters, and wood and water joeys; where the diggers of The Argyle Cut trundled sandstone blocks in barrows and hand-carts to build the sea-wall, and the larrikins roamed and fought and the harpies preyed; surely *there* the Spirit of the Place will remind the percipient observer of the rich pageant of Australian history. If those stones could speak, they would tell the epic of the civilizing of a continent, and of the acclimatization of millions of "New Australians" within two centuries in a new Homeland — the longest sustained mass migration across such great ocean distances in all the history of the world.

SEE ALSO PART II CADMAN'S COTTAGE

The oldest building extant in The Rocks district, and also one of the oldest buildings remaining anywhere in Sydney, is a two-storeyed four-roomed stone cottage with its entrance in George Street North, near The Argyle Cut. By the mercy of the men of sentiment on the Maritime Services Board, that relic of Old Sydney was preserved for posterity when the Passenger Terminal was built adjacent to it in 1960.

The cottage was erected in 1813 as living quarters for the coxswain and crew of the Governor's gig, who manned other government boats also. The back door of the cottage was then only eight feet from the water's edge, but today, by the reclamations of the foreshore, it is 300 feet from the wharfside.

In 1817, Governor Macquarie officially appointed as his coxswain John Cadman, an ex-convict, aged 41, who had been sentenced in England, in 1798, to transportation beyond the seas for life. Being well-behaved, as most of the convicts were, Cadman had been granted, like most of the convicts, a pardon. Being free then to return to England if he wished to do so, he had preferred to remain in Australia. He was appointed by Macquarie at a salary of £30 a year and living quarters in the coxswain's cottage.

He lived there for twenty-nine years, as Superintendent of Government Boats, during the terms of office of Governors Macquarie, Brisbane, Darling, Bourke, and Gipps. The cottage, which was government property, became known as Cadman's Cottage, and retains that name today.

When Cadman retired in 1846, aged 70, he went to live in the Hunter River district, and died there in 1848. From 1847 until 1865, Cadman's Cottage served as headquarters of the Water Police. It was then made available on loan to the Sailors' Home, and was used as quarters for officers of merchant vessels who for any reason required quarters on shore—and it is still occasionally put to that use.

The Maritime Services Board, recognizing the historic value of Cadman's Cottage, preserved it as an enclave in the reconstruction of the waterfront for the Passenger Terminal.

The original cottage had a roof of thatch, or of tiles, or of shingles, but a galvanized-iron roof was put on it in the 1890s or later, and was therefore not historically congruous. The cottage may eventually be transformed into a small historical museum and so opened to public inspection inside as well as outside.

THE WATER POLICE

Near the tip of the Dawes Point peninsula, where George Street North takes a dog-leg turn to avoid what was from 1796 to 1833 the Government Shipyard, are two docks which were formerly the slipways of the Shipyard. In the 1860s those docks were dredged and formed into wharves for berthing steamers of small size, with depths of 24 feet of water alongside. They are still so used, especially for small passenger and cargo vessels trading to the Pacific Islands. The berths there are numbered as Sydney Cove 6, 7A, and 7B.

The more northerly of those two docks, almost at Dawes Point, and therefore directly opposite the Opera House on Bennelong Point, commanding the entrance to Sydney Cove, has accommodation for the launches of the Water Police and for the Customs Patrol launches, with jetties, slipways, and workshops. Here are the headquarters of the New South Wales Water Police, one of the oldest, biggest, and best Water Police organizations in the world.

From the earliest days of settlement at Sydney, especially between April and November 1788, when the transports of the First Fleet were putting to sea at intervals to return to England, boats manned by marines patrolled the shores to prevent convicts from stowing away on board the returning transports.

On 7th August, 1789, Governor Phillip established a civilian police force of twelve "watchmen," recruited from well-behaved convicts, to patrol on shore at night-time, in order to prevent stealing from gardens, thefts from huts, assaults, or other offences. This force of watchmen was enlarged, and eventually took over the patrols in the government boats, not only to prevent the escape of prisoners, but also, when merchant vessels began calling at the port, to prevent smuggling, especially of grog.

After the appointment in 1817 of John Cadman as Superintendent of Government Boats, the Harbour Patrol became known as the Rowboat Guard.

Governor Macquarie extended the land patrols by building watch-houses. The watchmen were then called "constables," and placed under the control of the magistrates. In 1833 a regular police force was organized, and the Rowboat Guard was described officially for the first time as "the Water Police."

The boat patrols remained under the general supervision of John Cadman until he retired in 1846 and vacated his cottage. That little building remained as a Water Police station until 1865, when a move was made to the larger premises at Dawes Point, in the old shipyard dock.

Additional Water Police stations had been established in 1852 at Watson's Bay and at Goat Island. At each of those stations, as also at Sydney Cove, there was a four-oared skiff, manned by four constables and a coxswain. The principal task of the Water Police was to prevent smuggling; they also arrested offenders of any kind in boats, on board ships, or on the wharves.

When the Gold Rush was in full swing in the 1850s, hundreds of large sailing-vessels lay unmanned at anchorages in the

Harbour, the crews having deserted to go to the diggings. The prevention of theft from vessels which were guarded by only one watchman, or sometimes left unguarded, put a heavy strain on the Water Police.

The Water Police office was in the same building as the Police Court in Phillip Street, which was known as "the Water Police Court," even though the magistrates there dealt with all kinds of lawbreakers. In 1852, the Water Police were merged temporarily with the Land Police, but the Police Regulation Act of 1862 established the Water Police as a separate division of the police force, as it still is.

Two steam launches, the *Biloela* and the *Argus*, were put into service by the Water Police in 1865, from the new headquarters at Dawes Point. From that time to the present day the powerful and speedy police launches, on their regular or special patrols, have been an added spectacular feature in the always lively Sydney Harbour scene.

With a fleet of five high-powered motor launches, painted blue and white and always spick and span, equipped with two-way radio-telephones and all other equipment necessary for the work, the Water Police maintain a continuous patrol of the Harbour. At least one launch is always out on patrol, by day and by night, and on occasions more than one launch—even the entire fleet—is called out for special tasks.

The best-known police vessel, the *Nemesis,* was one of the prettiest sights on Sydney Harbour as she cruised, or sped with a foaming bow-wave, not only to apprehend lawbreakers, but to rescue victims of mishaps and to save lives and property on or in the water.

The biggest vessel of the police fleet, the *Colin J. Delaney*—so named in honour of a retired Commissioner of Police—was launched in 1962. This vessel, 45 feet long, and capable of a speed of 20 knots, puts to sea outside the Heads when cliff rescue operations are in progress, or otherwise when called to the rescue of vessels in distress or to save lives or recover bodies of persons drowned in the ocean.

One of the principal activities of the Water Police is to rescue the crews of yachts or rowing boats that capsize in the Harbour, and to salvage capsized craft. Such accidents usually happen when gales blow suddenly during yacht races on a Saturday afternoon. On one afternoon in the 1920s, the Water Police rescued 110 people from capsized yachts. In an average year, 400 people are rescued from drowning in Sydney Harbour. On the water, as on land, the police are required to save people from the dangers of their own folly as well as from crime.

Water Police patrols, called by radio-telephone or acting on their own initiative, salvage many yachts and dinghies that break loose from their moorings, especially during gales. There are more than 3,000 licensed yacht moorings in Sydney Harbour. It is therefore not surprising that yachts or small boats occasionally go adrift, often becoming a danger to shipping.

The recovery of dead bodies, and of objects from the bed of

the Harbour that may provide evidence of murder, robbery, or other crimes, is a special task for the Police Diving Squad, acting in conjunction with the Water Police. There are twelve divers, who use modern techniques and apparatus for underwater work.

The Flood Rescue Squad, like the Cliff Rescue Squad, is a special branch of the Police Force, which works in conjunction with the Water Police.

The Diving Squad and the Flood Rescue Squad are mobile by land, with a motor vehicle that can convey the trained men and their equipment to any part of New South Wales, including the rivers of the far inland, 600 miles from Sydney, where the special abilities of Water Police may be required.

There are Water Police Stations at Newcastle, at Botany Bay, and on the Hawkesbury River, each with patrol launches. The Water Police from those stations act, as in Sydney, in conjunction with Customs officials—who also have speedy launches—in detecting smugglers and in confiscating contraband goods.

Very large hauls of contraband are frequently made on board vessels in Sydney Harbour—not so much of alcoholic spirits as of drugs, cigarettes, transistor radios, watches, and other manufactured articles on which the smugglers seek to evade payment of tariff dues.

As with the work of the land police in Cliff Rescues, so with the Water Police at Sydney, the special circumstances have brought into existence a skilled body of men, dedicated to their tasks. The Sydney Water Police are equal in efficiency, discipline, seamanship, and smartness to the world's best. These are men to be regarded with pride. The Rowboat Guard of the past established a tradition that has developed to a maturity of knowledge and courage in our time. The full history of the Water Police of Sydney will never be told, for those men, who frequently risk their own lives to make the Harbour safe, do not seek acclaim. The satisfaction for them is in knowing that their work is necessary and that they do it effectively.

THE SYDNEY HARBOUR BRIDGE

SEE ALSO
PART II

The first poem of Australia, *Visit of Hope to Sydney Cove*, by Erasmus Darwin, published in London in 1789 as an epigraph to the official volume, *The Voyage of Governor Phillip to Botany Bay*, contained a remarkable prediction:

There the proud arch, Colossus-like, bestride
Yon glittering streams, and bound the chafing tide. . . .

Erasmus Darwin (born 1731, died 1802) was a medical practitioner, botanist, and poet, who lived at Lichfield, in Staffordshire, England. He was the grandfather of Charles Darwin (born 1809, died 1882), who became renowned as formulator of the doctrine of biological evolution.

It is evident that Erasmus Darwin was given an opportunity to read Governor Phillip's manuscript journal and dispatches. These had been sent to England in the *Alexander*, which left Sydney on 13th July, 1788 in company with three other returning transports of the First Fleet. The journal was edited in London, perhaps by Erasmus Darwin at the suggestion of Sir Joseph Banks, to transform the first person narrative to third person.

The reading of Phillip's narrative inspired Doctor Darwin to write his poem of twenty-six lines in the highfalutin style of the period, with rhymed couplets in which the poet envisaged the allegorical figure of Hope standing "high on a rock" at Sydney Cove and declaiming her belief in the great future of the Colony then and there established:

Visit of Hope to Sydney Cove

Where Sydney Cove her lucid bosom swells,
Courts her young navies, and the storm repels;
High on a rock amid the troubled air
Hope stood sublime, and waved her golden hair;
Calmed with her rosy smile the tossing deep,
And with sweet accents charmed the winds to sleep;
To each wild plain she stretched her snowy hand,
High-waving wood, and sea-encircled strand.
"Hear me," she cried, "ye rising realms; record
Time's opening scenes, and Truth's unerring word!
There shall broad streets their stately walls extend,
The circus widen, and the crescent bend;
There, rayed from cities o'er the cultured land,
Shall bright canals and solid roads expand.
*There the proud arch, Colossus-like, bestride
Yon glittering streams, and bound the chafing tide;**
Embellished villas crown the landscape scene,
Farms wave with gold, and orchards blush between.
There shall tall spires and dome-capped towers ascend,
And piers and quays their massy structures blend;
While with each breeze approaching vessels glide,
And northern treasures dance on every tide!"
Thus ceased the nymph. Tumultous echoes roar,
And Joy's loud voice was heard from shore to shore;
Her graceful steps descending pressed the plain,
And Peace, and Art, and Labour joined her train.

* My italics—P.R.S.

This first poem of Australia, though written in England by an Englishman who had never seen Australia, was far superior in its poetical expression and feeling to the first poems that were written in Australia by resident Englishmen—the *Odes* of Massey Robinson (published at Sydney in 1810), and the so-called *First Fruits of Australian Poetry,* by Barron Field (published at Sydney in 1819). Erasmus Darwin's *Visit of Hope to Sydney Cove* was published thirty years before Barron Field made his false claim of priority for his dreary doggerel that rhymed "Australia" with "failure"—not a true rhyme. . . .

The prediction by Erasmus Darwin of "the proud arch, Colossus-like" became a reality in 1932, when the Sydney

Harbour Bridge was opened for traffic, 143 years after he had predicted it. Few poets, other than Nostradamus, have such a good claim as Erasmus Darwin to be considered a long-range seer. The poet's comparison of the prophesied bridge with the Colossus of Rhodes is apt; for if the enormous bronze statue of Apollo at Rhodes was one of the wonders of the ancient world, who could deny that the enormous steel arch bridge across Sydney Harbour is one of the wonders of the modern world?

Familiarity breeds respect: the more the Sydney Harbour Bridge is examined, the more it must be admired. It was, when it was built, and it remains, the biggest single-span arch bridge in the world; and even though there are chronic decriers of everything in Australia, who quibble that there are arch bridges in the U.S.A. with slightly longer spans, those other bridges could not carry the load that the Sydney Harbour Bridge is designed to carry—43,000 tons deckload within its span of 1,650 feet. Only a colossal arch could carry such a colossal weight.

The perfect proportioning of the Sydney Harbour Bridge has the effect, by optical illusion, in some perspectives, of making it appear smaller than it is, and likewise of making the Harbour, thus spanned, seem narrower than it is. Anything colossal—such as Ayers Rock in Central Australia—dwarfs the middle distances of the human eye's perspectives: it is only when the observer is either very close to it, or at a long distance from it, that a colossal object is seen to be colossal. There are several places, on hills on the northern side of the Harbour, a few miles from the Bridge, where its immense size suddenly looms at a street corner; or, on a large view of the Harbour from the Heads, or from an aeroplane, it is realized that the Bridge, by far the most prominent object in the scene, is, as a work of human hands, tremendous.

From the earliest years of British settlement at Sydney, and for the Aborigines from time immemorial, the Harbour stretched like a chasm between the southern and northern shores. For nineteen miles in from the Heads, it could be crossed only by boats, or by canoes, or by swimming in waters where sharks lurked. There were no fording places shallow enough to wade across, and, except where the stream narrowed in the upper reaches of the Parramatta River, near the head of the tidewater, there was no easy place to build a bridge.

Not only the main Harbour, but its many tidal arms, were unfordable and not easily bridgeable. A transit by land on foot, or on horseback, or in a wheeled vehicle, from Sydney Town to the North Shore—only 500 yards distant across the water from Dawes Point, would have required, in pioneering days, a trip of thirty or more miles to "head" the Parramatta and Lane Cove rivers. That fact was discovered by Captain Hunter's boat explorations within a few weeks of the arrival of the First Fleet, when he completed a working chart of the entire Harbour and its arms.

Governor Phillip himself led a party in April 1788 which made explorations on the northern side of the Harbour, but found the country there "high and rocky, the soil arid, parched, and inhospitable."

135

In February 1794, after Phillip's departure, the Lieutenant-Governor, Major Grose, decided to establish a farm settlement for old soldiers on the northern side of the Harbour, at a place which was jocularly named "the Field of Mars," in the vicinity nowadays known as St Leonards and Artarmon. Eighteen old soldiers were given grants of land there. The settlement did not prosper, for the soil was unsuitable for farming, but it was from that experiment that boat transits across the Harbour began.

The country on the northern side, between the Harbour and the Hawkesbury River, was—as it remains today—unsuitable for farming, except in a few places. It was "Blackfellows' Country" —rough ridges of sandstone with scrubby vegetation and very little topsoil, except in the gullies; yet gradually settlements were formed there, in occasional patches of fertile soil, at Kissing Point and Lane Cove, and elsewhere.

The promontory on the northern shore, opposite Dawes Point, acquired its name of Milson's Point in 1806, when a free immigrant from Lincolnshire, James Milson, aged twenty-three years, was given a grant of 50 acres of land there, and built a cottage. He attempted farming, but with little success. Then he took to selling sandstone ballast to the masters of sailing-vessels. He quarried the sandstone from the hillside, and lightered it in a punt to vessels at anchor or at berths in Sydney Cove. He also sold the shipmasters fresh water that he collected after rain in the sandstone quarries on his "estate." Very likely he also sold firewood, fruit, vegetables, eggs, and poultry. His ship-chandling punt service across the Harbour was the forerunner of ferry services, and eventually of the Sydney Harbour Bridge.

In 1817 Billy Blue, a Negro boatman, was granted eighty acres of land on the northern shore, at Blue's Point. He grew produce for sale in Sydney, and took it across the Harbour in his boat to Miller's Point. A cart-road was cleared to Blue's Point from the few farms in the hinterland; and Billy Blue then made a charge for ferrying passengers and goods in his boat to and from Miller's Point.

In 1827 a vehicular punt service, known as Wiseman's Ferry, was established by Solomon Wiseman at a crossing-place on the Hawkesbury River, 25 miles northward of Parramatta and thirty miles northward of Blue's Point.

Wiseman's Ferry was a link in the Great North Road from Sydney to the Hunter River Valley. It enabled cattle to be droved from the Hunter River to Sydney, and wool and station stores to be transported by road. Most of the traffic by that route was through Parramatta, but some cattle were droved to Milson's Point to be slaughtered there for the market across the water, and for providoring ships.

In 1842 a large paddle-wheel steamer punt began operating a vehicular ferry service between Dawes Point and Blue's Point. That route from Sydney to Wiseman's Ferry was twelve miles shorter than the old road that headed the Harbour at Parramatta.

With the increase of population and prosperity that followed the ending of the Imperial Convict System in 1841, settlements began to spread along the North Shore of Sydney Harbour, and ever since then have developed their present-day character chiefly as residential or "dormitory" suburbs, housing people whose breadwinners cross the Harbour to earn their living in the City.

As population grew, a second steam-ferry service for vehicles was established in 1860, crossing the Harbour from Bennelong Point to Milson's Point. This ferry contributed to the development of North Sydney, Kirribilli, Neutral Bay, Cremorne, and Mosman, as residential suburbs, while the Blue's Point ferry likewise served the suburbs of Crow's Nest, St Leonards, Artarmon, Chatswood, and other districts to the northward and westward.

The two punt-ferry services from Sydney Cove to the North Shore, each with two large punts in operation, together with an ever-increasing number of steam passenger ferries shuttling in and out of Sydney Cove like bees at the door of a hive, caused so much congestion at the "Quay" that in 1890 a Royal Commission was appointed to report on the alternatives of a bridge or a tunnel to connect the North Shore directly with Sydney by road, rail, and tramway.

There were already road and rail connections between the City and the North Shore, but by roundabout routes, "heading" the Harbour.

The railway from Sydney to Newcastle, and beyond to the Great North, branched from the Western line at Strathfield, to cross the Parramatta River at Ryde, where the stream was only 700 feet wide. That bridge, eight miles up-harbour from Dawes Point, carried the rail traffic northwards through Epping and Hornsby, and so to the Hawkesbury River Bridge, which was built in 1889 as a vital link connecting the southern and northern railway systems, previously operating independently.

The Hawkesbury River Bridge, constructed by an American company, was one of the world's biggest bridges. It crossed the river at low level with seven spans, each of 416 feet at a place where the river was 2,910 feet wide. Five of the piers were sunk in water 150 feet deep, a world's record at that time. That style of construction could have been applied also to a bridge across Sydney Harbour from Dawes Point to Milson's Point, but the Royal Commission of 1890 recommended that "the connection shall be by a high-level bridge not obstructing the navigation of the Harbour."

The railway bridge at Ryde gave access via Strathfield to the western suburbs on the northern side of the Harbour, but it was useless to the residents of North Sydney, Mosman, and the adjacent suburbs in the hinterland of Milson's Point.

Road-connection between the City of Sydney and the northside suburbs had been made possible, but only with a long detour, when a road bridge was built in 1881 across the Parramatta River at Gladesville, four miles up-harbour from Sydney Cove. By that route it was twelve miles from Sydney to North Sydney, crossing the Harbour and its arms by bridges at Pyrmont, Glebe Island, Iron Cove, Gladesville, and Fig Tree—a detour known as "the Five Bridges Road," which was completed by the building of the Fig Tree Bridge across the Lane Cove River in 1885.

The report of the Royal Commission of 1890 stated that five million crossings of the Harbour were made annually by persons, 378,500 by vehicles, and 43,800 by horsemen. These figures referred to crossings by ferry services, and not to users of the "Five Bridges" route.

The need of a bridge or a tunnel directly connecting Sydney with North Sydney had become obvious. The Commissioners rejected the proposal for a tunnel "in face of the fact that so little is known as to what the waters of the Harbour hide from view."

The proposal for a bridge that would carry road traffic, railways, and trams, besides pedestrians, at a sufficient height above water-level to enable sailing-vessels (some with masts 180 feet tall) to pass beneath it, seemed to present insuperable financial and engineering problems.

The width from shore to shore, Dawes Point to Milson's Point, 1,650 feet, would require a colossal arch, cantilever, or suspension bridge of one span. It was assumed that the depth of water, averaging between 50 and 60 feet, would make the building of piers in the stream, for shorter spans with a central swing-span, too costly, or perhaps impossible, since at that time there was no data on the geological structure of the harbour-bed. Delays to navigation and to bridge traffic by the use of a swing-span would be intolerable.

A further problem was that a railway line across the proposed bridge could be connected with the general railway system, on the southern side of the Harbour, only by extending the line for two miles to the bridge from the terminal at Central Station. That extension would have to pass through the most densely built-on part of the inner city of Sydney, either by a subway or as an "elevated" railway, in either case requiring a great expense.

Despite all those problems, the Government of New South Wales in 1900 called for competitive designs and tenders for building a bridge connecting Dawes Point and Milson's Point. In all, thirty-six designs were submitted, but all were rejected for various reasons. In 1908 a committee of inquiry recommended that two tunnels—one for railway traffic and one for road traffic —should be excavated beneath the Harbour, with a subway for the railway through the City.

The sceptics considered that tunnels under the Harbour would flood or cave in. In 1911, the Government announced a further proposal for a bridge. This was referred to a Parliamentary Works Committee, which sought advice from an Engineer on the staff of the Public Works Department, Dr J. J. C. Bradfield.

John Job Crew Bradfield, born in Queensland in 1867, and trained in Engineering at Sydney University, was appointed in July 1912 as Chief Engineer in charge of the design of an electric railway system for Sydney and its suburbs, including a design for a bridge to connect the City with the North Shore.

For twenty years thereafter J. J. C. Bradfield was the person most directly concerned with details of the design and erection of the Sydney Harbour Bridge. He visited Europe and America in 1914 to study the design of underground railways and long-span bridges. His proposal for a Harbour Bridge was completed in 1916, but as the 1914-18 War in Europe was then raging, the proposal was shelved.

In 1922, an enabling bill for the construction of the Bridge was enacted by the Parliament of New South Wales. Tenders were called in accordance with the general plans and specifications prepared by Bradfield. Twenty tenders were received from six countries, and the contract was awarded to a British firm, Dorman Long & Co. Ltd, of Middlesbrough, England.

Bradfield's design for a single-arch steel bridge, with a span of 1,650 feet, was modified in some respects by Dorman Long's consulting engineer, Sir Ralph Freeman; but, despite attempts by decriers of Australian efforts to minimize Bradfield's work, the basic design of the Sydney Harbour Bridge was Bradfield's, and all details of the contractors' work were subject to Bradfield's inspection and approval.

The work of construction began in April 1923, and proceeded for nearly nine years, employing an average of 1,400 men on the site, apart from the many thousands employed in supplying materials, which included 52,000 tons of steel, and an immense quantity of stone and concrete.

The specifications included, in addition to the main arch span of 1,650 feet, five steel approach spans averaging 212 feet long, leading to the main arch on each side. The overall length of the actual bridgework would then be 3,770 feet (nearly three-quarters of a mile). Most of the steel used in the main arch (37,000 tons) was imported from Britain, and all the other steel, including principally that used in the approach spans (15,000 tons), was made in Australia.

While the work of building the bridge was in progress, the government Department of Public Works was constructing the underground City Railway, burrowing below George Street and York Street, to connect with the bridge, and beyond it with the North Shore Line that had been opened some years previously. The North Shore Line ran from the ferry wharf at Lavender Bay, on the western side of Milson's Point, through the suburbs of Waverton, Wollstonecraft, Crow's Nest, St Leonards, Artarmon, Chatswood, Roseville, Lindfield, Killara, Gordon, Pymble, Turramurra, Warrawee, Wahroonga, and Waitara, to join the Northern Trunk Line at Hornsby. Residents of those suburbs would greatly benefit, in speed of railway transit to and from the City, by the opening of the Harbour Bridge.

The approaches to the bridge on both sides were principally of reinforced concrete work including arches—one of which spanned The Argyle Cut—and tunnels and cuttings lined with concrete. Those approaches were designed to carry railway and tramway tracks, and road traffic. The railway and tramway tracks built from Wynyard station towards the bridge ran for half a mile through concrete-lined subways before ascending through open air to the deck-level of the bridge, 192 feet above sea-level. The length of the bridge-crossing by railway, measured from Wynyard station, on the southern shore, to Waverton station on the northern shore, is 2½ miles.

The roadway for vehicular traffic is likewise necessarily elevated on a gradual slope on both sides to reach bridge deck-level. On the City side, the special road construction begins at the intersection of York Street and Grosvenor Street, on what used to be called Church Hill (the approximate site of the original "lost" Sydney Cemetery), and extends to the bridge, passing alongside Observatory Park. The entire length of roadway, crossing the bridge, measured from Grosvenor Street on the City side to the Pacific Highway on the northern side, is officially, and aptly, named Bradfield Highway. It is 8,040 feet (approximately 1½ miles) in length. This is the shortest and most-used highway in Australia.

Construction of the approaches to the bridge transformed the appearance of The Rocks Peninsula. For ninety years there had been vehicular traffic, mostly horse-drawn, through The Rocks district to the Miller's Point ferry terminal; but the Motor Age, beginning to "boom" in the 1920s, was imperative in its demands for better roads and bridges everywhere. The passengers on the vehicular ferries "wasted" much time which the Harbour Bridge would "save"; but what would be done with the time thus saved needed no consideration in a civilization based on a belief that "time is money." If time were equated with thought instead of with money, it would not be so necessary to "save time"; but, whatever the implications, it was obvious that the Sydney Harbour Bridge would save millions of man-hours of time per annum: time that had been "spent," if not "wasted," on ferry crossings or on heading the Harbour by the "Five Bridges" route.

As the enormous structure of the Bridge arose, The Rocks Peninsula was not only transformed; it was dominated by the roadway and by the arches of concrete and steel erected along its spine, and by the tunnels and cuttings that chewed its innards. Then at last the songs and brawls of the sailors and of the larrikins became only a memory. The skyline of prehistoric turrets and ramparts of sandstone rock had at last been smoothed to the balustrades of an elevated road on an arched viaduct more impressive than any that the Ancient Romans could have built; and the entire peninsula seemed now to be taking the weight of its end of the colossal arch that reached for the sky.

That main arch of the bridge thrusts its weight on two gigantic steel bearings, on each side of the water, set in foundations of concrete, forty feet deep, embedded in solid sandstone. After the bearings had been set, abutment towers of Moruya granite were built to bridge deck-level, as bases for a ramp from which creeper cranes could operate to enable the steelwork of the arch to be built out over the water, from each side, at increasing heights.

Until those two halves of the arch met in the centre and supported one another, the steelwork reaching out from each side was supported by steel cables passed through a horseshoe-shaped tunnel excavated in the solid rock, sloping at an angle of 45 degrees from the horizontal to a depth of 132 feet. In each tunnel there were 128 cables. Each cable, 2¾ inches in diameter and 1,200 feet long, weighed 8½ tons, and had a breaking strain of 350 tons. Beginning with a few cables, more were attached as the two halves of the arch lengthened and reached far out over the water. To laymen, this aspect of the construction seemed highly spectacular and dangerous, even inexplicable, since the cables were not obtrusive.

The gigantic arch was closed on 30th August, 1930, seven years after work had begun on the approach spans. The worldwide Economic Depression had begun in 1928, and continued until 1933. That Depression—also known as "the Slump"—was spreading misery and despondency far and wide in Australia, and throughout the world, while at Sydney one of the greatest, and financially most costly, engineering feats of the modern world was carried through to completion, as though in defiance of the worldwide despair, and as a gesture of faith in Australia—a new "Visit of Hope to Sydney Cove," confirming Erasmus Darwin's prediction. In that sense, the Sydney Harbour Bridge, coterminous with the Economic Depression of 1928-33, stands as a monumental reminder of that grim period.

The crown of the arch is 440 feet above sea-level. The trusses of the arch, 98 feet apart, are braced together vertically and laterally with an intricate, but symmetrical, web of steel girders. The bridge decking is suspended by steel hangers from the lower chord of the arch. The clearance for ships underneath the bridge-decking is 172 feet 6 inches. Very few power-driven vessels have a top hamper reaching to that height above the waterline. The great height of the bridge decking has therefore allowed the commercial development of wharfage on the Upper Harbour to continue.

The Bridge was officially opened for traffic on 19th March, 1932, by the Premier of New South Wales, the Hon. J. T. Lang, who was the centre of much controversy and political tension caused by "the Depression." Wits promptly named the Bridge "Jack Lang's Coat Hanger"—a contribution to Australian folklore which endowed the polemical Premier with a stature of brobdingnagian proportions: not so incongruously, since Swift's *Gulliver's Travels* had identified Australia as the land of the gigantic Brobdingnags.

Others, more poetically, think of the Bridge as "the Harp in the Sky." In daytime it is impressive rather by its gigantic size than by its beauty; but at night-time—especially since the whole structure was delicately floodlit in 1961—it has become, in the words of the International Society of Illuminating Engineers, "a joy for many . . . a filigree of light, a most delicate tracery spanning the blackness of the Harbour."

The pylons erected on the abutments at each end of the bridge reach to 290 feet above ground-level, and are solidly built of Moruya granite. They measure 225 feet by 162 feet at the base; but, though the abutment towers were temporarily useful as a base for the creeper cranes during the construction of the arch, the pylons that were afterwards added to them have no structural value in the bridgework. They were built in the belief that they would enhance the bridge's appearance. That point is debatable; for, as Keats has stated, "Beauty is truth, and truth beauty." As the pylons only *pretend* to give the Bridge stability, but do not serve that purpose in the slightest, they lack the sincerity of truth, and therefore lack beauty. Only at night-time, when it is not easy to see that the arch does not rest on the pylons but on hinges set into the solid rock, the floodlighting gives an illusion that the pylons are an integral part of the Bridge. Then the whole effect of the illuminated bridge, in conjunction with the multi-coloured advertising sky-signs on the shores, and with all the glittering lights of the "twin cities" of Sydney and North Sydney, makes a night scene with a quality of magic in it.

The capital cost of the Bridge and its approaches was, in round figures, £7 million. With other expenses, including the acquisition of land, and interest on loans during the construction, the cost mounted to £10 million in pre-inflation currency values, equivalent perhaps to £50 million in the inflated currency of thirty years later, before the change-over to decimal coinage in Australia made all historical currency comparisons difficult or impossible; yet ten million pounds in 1932 was a large sum of money to be raised during a Depression, from loan funds.

The amortization of the capital debt, and the costs of mainten-ance and of improvements, are met by road tolls on vehicles, and by passenger tolls which are included in the price of rail and omnibus tickets. In its first thirty years, to 30th June, 1962, the accounts of the Bridge showed a total income of £20 million, and total loan charges of £12 million. Of the capital debt, some £3½ million had been paid off. It was hoped that the Bridge would be free of debt by the year 1985; but it was considered that in all probability passenger tolls and vehicle tolls would then be continued in perpetuity to cover the costs of maintenance and repairs, though at a rate not as high as that required for service of the loan funds.

During the year 1961-62, thirty million crossings of the bridge were made by vehicles, not including omnibuses. The toll on vehicles, since April 1960, had been at a flat rate for each class of vehicle, irrespective of the number of passengers; but an average of two persons per vehicle would be a minimum, making 60 million crossings by road-users, to which are to be added 25 million crossings by railway passengers and 14 million by omnibus passengers. Increases of traffic subsequently raised the number of crossings of the bridge by persons in each year to more than a hundred million.

In the maintenance of the Bridge one of the most important items of expense is the repainting, which proceeds almost con-tinuously. The surface to be painted is 580,000 square yards (approximately 120 acres), requiring 7,000 gallons of paint for one coat. Most of the steelwork to be painted is at great heights and in awkward situations. The painters use travelling cranes and gantries to reach all parts of the bridge. These are used also by expert riggers and ironworkers who systematically inspect all riveted connections and bearings. Six million rivets were used in the building of the bridge. There are more than one hundred sliding bearings in the structure, to allow for expansion or contraction of the steel in changes of temperature, and according to the load carried by weight of traffic at different times of the day. Maintenance of the bearings by greasing and in other ways is essential to the life of the bridge.

Constant vigilance in upkeep is essential. Steel is subject to corrosion, and possibly to fatigue. Even with the most careful maintenance, a steel bridge has not a fraction of the life of a stone bridge, or of a concrete bridge; but no one knows how long, with proper care, the Sydney Harbour Bridge may stand. It may live for a very long time; and, if its parts are replaced seriatim, it may last for ever, or for as long as those replacements are periodically made; yet it is more likely that new techniques of concrete-arch construction, and of underground tunnelling, may make the Sydney Harbour Bridge obsolete before the year 2000. If it lives to its centenary in A.D. 2032, it will continue until then to be one of the world's wonders of the Age of Steel, which may be also a passing historical phase in the long and varied history of mankind.

With the ever-increasing pressure of road traffic under the increased motorization of Australia, the Bridge and its approaches became so crowded in "peak" hours that two extra lanes of road track were provided in 1959, by removing the tramway tracks. This was also in conformity with a general policy of replacing trams by motor-buses throughout the Sydney metropolitan area. The Bridge then, in its overall width of 160 feet, carried two pedestrian footpaths, two lines of railway, and eight lanes of road traffic.

To enable a freer movement of traffic at the southern approaches, an overhead roadway, named the Cahill Expressway in honour of the Hon. J. J. Cahill, Premier of New South Wales, was built in 1958-62, as a branch from the Bradfield Highway. This work was done in conjunction with the completion of the City Loop railway and the remodelling of the Circular Quay ferry terminal. The cost of the Cahill Expressway, which distributes traffic from the northern suburbs to the eastern part of the city, was £8½ million. It passes under the Botanic Gardens in a four-lane vehicular tunnel 1,300 feet long, and then on the surface through the Domain, to Woolloomooloo.

On the northern side of the Harbour, also, the approaches to the Bridge have required large plans of street reconstruction. It is the Bridge which has been mainly responsible for the commercial development of North Sydney as a "twin city" of Sydney, and has intensified the density of population in all the northern suburbs.

In 1932, when the Bridge was opened, J. J. C. Bradfield uttered a prediction:

The Bridge will make it possible for upwards of a million people to reside in the Northern Suburbs, and will provide adequate facilities by rail and road for the transit of this population to and from the City.

The City proper will become a New York in miniature, with skyscrapers exceeding 150 feet, whilst North Sydney and Mosman will merge into a second Brooklyn with property-values in places equalling those of the City.

Within the next twenty years the population of Metropolitan Sydney should increase by over 1¼ million, of whom about half will find homes on the northern side of the Harbour.

That prediction was almost exactly fulfilled, not in twenty years but in thirty years, which was near enough to be a very good prophesy. Bradfield could then take rank with Erasmus Darwin as a major prophet of Australian expansion, or more precisely as the man of action who put into effect one of the earlier prophet's visions of hope.

8

COCKLE BAY

THE LARGE, DEEP, AND EMBAYED SHEET OF WATER THAT STRETCHES along the western side of the Sydney City Peninsula was known for the first forty years of British settlement as Cockle Bay. The name was then changed to Darling Harbour, in honour or in flattery of Lieutenant-General Sir Ralph Darling, who was Governor of New South Wales from 1825 to 1831. He was perhaps already sufficiently honoured, or flattered, by having his name commemorated in the Darling River, the Darling Downs, the Darling Ranges, and Darlinghurst. To confer his name on Cockle Bay was an excessive compliment. No individual, other than a national emancipator of the first magnitude such as George Washington, could be so important in a nation's history as to have so many great natural features named for him. Governor Darling was not an emancipator of Australians. In a thousand years, or less, the name of Cockle Bay may be restored.

During the first two years of British settlement at Sydney Cove, the pioneers suffered from shortages of food, and many of them died of starvation, in a place where the Aborigines for milleniums had found food plentiful. With primitive but effective weapons, those old Australians had lived chiefly on game and fish, including the "shellfish"—oysters, mussels, and cockles—that proliferated along the shores of Sydney Harbour.

The "new chum" immigrants—who were later described as "Jimmygrants" and then as "Pomegranates" or "Pommies"—starved on their daily issues of putrid pickled pork and weevily meal that they had brought with them from Britain. Perhaps they were prevented by their taskmasters from roaming the harbour-shores to knock oysters and mussels off the rocks, or to dig for cockles in the mudflats between the tides.

Some who were sent in boats, from Sydney Cove round Dawes Point to that large bay on the western side of The Rocks ridge, to gather wattles for the walls of adobe huts or reeds for thatching roofs, found an opportunity there to lift cockles from the mudflats; and some boats' crews were sent there specially to gather them. That stretch of water became known as Cockle Bay.

Those small but tasty bivalves were a basic food for the Aborigines, known to them as *pipis*, a name that has been adopted widely, except in South Australia, where they are known as "Goolwa Cockles." To detach oysters or mussels from the rocks would have required special implements or skill; but the cockles could be dug from the mud with bare hands or feet. They saved some of the First-Fleeters and Second-Fleeters from dying of starvation; and the name of Cockle Bay had that good memory until Governor Darling, or his advisers, decided that the popular name was not good enough.

That stretch of water, an inland sea rather than a bay, is the biggest and most landlocked indentation of deep water within Sydney Harbour. It is "a Harbour within the Harbour." Although its entrance channel—between Miller's Point and the peninsula of Balmain—is only a quarter of a mile wide, its enclosed waters extend to the southward for a mile and a quarter along the western shore of Sydney City, and also it has arms stretching further to the westward and south-westward for a mile and a quarter in Johnston's Bay and White Bay, and then another mile and a quarter to the southward in Rozelle Bay and Blackwattle Bay.

The shoreline of that interconnected series of basins measures ten miles. Considered as an inland sea, the whole basin is enclosed between the peninsulas of Sydney City on its eastern side and Balmain on its western side; but on its southern side its waters are partitioned by the peninsulas of Pyrmont and the Glebe, which are the shores of the innermost wharfages.

The five contiguous and interconnected basins are all navigable, with no reefs or shoals, and there is deep water—18 feet or more—close to the shores, extending to the head of each of the basins. Along those shores, by the construction of wharves and jetties, are berths for a total of not less than a hundred ocean-going vessels, ranging in size from small coasters to passenger liners of 20,000 tons, and some special cargo vessels of up to 40,000 tons register.

The name Darling Harbour is applied nowadays only to the waterfront along the western shore of the Sydney City Peninsula, where there are berths for approximately fifty ocean-going vessels. The berths along other parts of the shores of the large composite basin are locally identified as the wharves and jetties of Pyrmont; of Blackwattle Bay; of Rozelle Bay; of Glebe Island (which is not an island but a peninsula); and of White Bay—but all share one entrance, in the channel between Miller's Point and Balmain, on the course passing under Sydney Harbour Bridge from or to the main Harbour, and the ocean six miles distant.

In the placid waters of those five spacious deepwater basins conjoined, with the adjacent Walsh Bay added, the wharves and waterfront districts of West Sydney, Pyrmont, the Glebe, and Balmain provide two-thirds of the mercantile wharfage of the Port of Sydney, as calculated in total tonnages of cargoes handled annually.

When Governor Phillip selected Sydney Cove as the site for his settlement, remarking on its facilities for berthing ships, he was not aware that, only half a mile away, on the other side of the rocky ridge crowning the western shore of that Cove, were anchorages and deepwater berthing spaces ten times greater in extent and even more landlocked and sheltered than those of Sydney Cove.

Soon after the pioneers had landed, the ridge of The Rocks was climbed, and the vast extent of the Inner Harbour beyond was discerned. The emotions of those who from that lookout were the first Europeans to sight that inland sea stretching away to the westward and southward must have been like those of Balboa, "silent upon a peak in Darien." Within a few days, Captain Hunter of H.M.S. *Sirius* and his crew had begun their chartmaking, and had taken soundings of those bays beyond The Rocks.

By good chance, Governor Phillip had chosen for the settlement a site with far greater port facilities than he had been aware of when he made that choice. Beyond that ridge to the westward was scope, a century and more later, for miles of wharves, and for the loading and unloading of cargoes in vessels which to Phillip would have seemed preposterously gigantic, and their cargoes—of coal, timber, wheat, wool, sugar, and general merchandise—of grotesquely immense tonnages.

The scope for expansion was latent there; and without that large extra range of wharfage the Port of Sydney could never have become one of the world's greatest seaports; yet, strange but true, many residents of Sydney, and visitors to Sydney, are scarcely aware of the immensity of the Upper Harbour, westward of the Bridge, where most of the mercantile shipping activity of the port, is, in a sense, concealed from view.

There is a reason why—whereas the Lower Harbour, eastward of the Bridge, has residential suburbs along its shores—the Upper Harbour, westward of the Bridge, is chiefly "industrial," especially along its southern shore. The cause of that specialization is railway access, an imperative advantage in the bulk handling of export cargoes such as wheat and wool, which come from the inland, and of coal, sugar, and timber, whether imported to the wharves in Sydney or exported from them.

As the City of Sydney, in the limited municipal definition, is on the southern side of the Harbour, all the railroads from the west and south—and even from the north, via the Ryde Bridge— were built to converge to the first rail terminus, at Redfern. From there, and from other points on the trunk line, branch lines for goods traffic were built to the wharves at the head of the Darling Harbour, and later to Pyrmont, Rozelle, Glebe Island, and White Bay, with marshalling yards and facilities for delivering trains of goods-wagons alongside vessels berthed at wharves.

The southern shore of the Harbour, westward of Redfern, is fairly level—not corrugated in sandstone ridges—and therefore that region has been convenient for railroad construction and for commercial wharfage. That was the basic factor affecting the commercial development of the Port of Sydney, for the ridgy terrain on the shores of the Lower Harbour made railroad construction difficult there.

Eastward of the Bridge, there are no large commercial wharves, except those at Sydney Cove and Woolloomooloo; but neither of those havens has railroad connections for handling cargo alongside vessels at berths. The steep terrain on the western side of The Rocks ridge also has prevented railroad connection with the wharves at Walsh Bay and along the Sydney City shore of Darling Harbour.

Those older wharfages, established before railroad transport was introduced, were originally served by horse-drawn lorries, drays, wagons, and carts, and are now served by motor-lorries and trucks. They load and unload chiefly general merchandise, which may be placed in the many bond and "free" stores adjacent to the waterfront, or taken direct from wharf-sheds to factories, or from factories to wharves or to or from the nearest railway goods yards; but for bulk handling of wheat, coal, sugar, timber, and some other cargoes more conveniently handled by rail-transportation, vessels berth at the wharves with railway lines alongside—at Pyrmont, Glebe Island, and Balmain.

Today, from any high lookout point, such as the deck of the Harbour Bridge or its pylons, or the roof of any of the new tall buildings in the City, the panorama of the Inner Harbour to the westward can be seen more synoptically than was possible before the 1930s; yet even though the general view of the expanse of water and of the shore installations is large, it is not until the details are seen in a near view that the great extent of human achievement along that waterfront can be appreciated.

So Sydney Harbour does not put all her goods on show in the front window. The reaches between the Heads and the Bridge are much more picturesque than the commercial reaches of the Upper Harbour westward of the Bridge; but there, in the grime and clang of trade and industry, the main wealth of the Port of Sydney is accumulated, and there the heaviest work of handling ships and their cargoes is done.

A wharf, at the edge of the land and of the sea, is the starting or finishing point of almost all seaborne venturing. As Australia is an island continent, wharves are our chief points of contact with the outside world. To seamen, port workers, and shipping people generally, wharves are the focus points of all significant movements of ships, cargoes, and passengers, clearing outward or inward. A great part of the life of a seaport city converges on the wharves and radiates from them. That teeming and specialized life of the waterfront is to be seen in all its variety at Sydney, chiefly along the shores of Walsh Bay, Darling Harbour, Pyrmont, Blackwattle Bay, the Glebe, Rozelle, Glebe Island, White Bay, and Balmain. In that large harbour-within-a-harbour, *pipis* continue to thrive in mud marges underneath wharves, despite the immense intrusions of international, interstate, and intrastate seaborne trade, which churns the originally placid and secluded waters with the throb of propellers and the bow-waves of tugs, police and customs launches, ferries, and the large displacements of water by weighty hulls as the leviathans of modern seaborne trade make fast "alongside," or cast off moorings to put to sea with their Plimsoll marks awash. Around the shores—where for æons kookaburras cacchinated, currawongs carolled, and vivid parrots flashed and screeched in the interlaced boughs of gnarled red-gum trees, while wallabies hopped and goannas basked in the ferny gullies where cascades of limpid water splashed—there, today, the silhouette is of silos, smokestacks, gantry-cranes, conveyor-belts, and ships' derricks in the industrial forest of clanging, puffing and panting, mechanical installations dedicated to commercial get-and-grab and Quick Turn Around.

Within 150 years from the first settlement at Sydney Cove, all traces of primitive Australia had been eliminated from the shores of West Sydney, the Glebe, Pyrmont, and Balmain. A waterfront district of cosmopolitan quality had come into existence there; for ships in their nature are international, and ships of every seafaring nation visit the Port of Sydney.

There they lie at their allotted berths, loading or unloading. At almost any hour of the day, the "stranger vessels" are to be seen passing, with tugs in attendance, under the Harbour Bridge, making for their berths or putting to sea. That is the unceasing pageant of any large mercantile seaport, but nowhere else in the world is that pageant so well displayed as in the Port of Sydney. Here every vessel that approaches a berth or leaves one must show herself, as a beauty or as a drab, for five miles along the scenic reaches of the Lower Harbour, observed—some carefully and some only with a glance—by a million pairs of eyes. She may lie unobtrusively at her berth in the Inner Harbour, but when she is under way she has her hour of pride or of shame as she shows her paces, her lines, her garb, and her paintwork, as publicly as in a fashion parade.

WHARVES PUBLIC AND PRIVATE SEE ALSO PART II

In the first years of settlement, there were only the Government Wharves in Sydney Cove; but when, in 1803, Robert Campbell was granted a freehold title to land on the waterfront for building a wharf and storehouses for his own commercial enterprises, a system of private ownership of wharves and wharf-sheds and stores was inaugurated which, within a hundred years, had allotted many miles of the foreshores of Sydney Harbour, either for residences or for mercantile wharves.

Until the 1880s, only a few of the wharves of the Port of Sydney were owned by the Government, and all others had been built by shipping or trading companies or individuals.

Wharfage fees were collected by the Government at the government-owned wharves only. At the privately owned wharves there were reduced charges, or no charges when a vessel was owned by the owners of the wharf at which she berthed. This was considered unfair competition. In 1880 an Act of Parliament (the Wharfage and Tonnage Rates Act) imposed uniform rates of tax on all cargoes, wherever landed. The collection of these revenues and the control of wharves was then vested in the Public Wharves Department.

Many of the government-owned wharves, and some of the privately owned wharves, were leased to shipping companies, and so were used as berths exclusively for vessels of the lease-holding companies. Some of the best berths in the port were vacant for weeks on end. Some of the leased wharves, allowed to fall into disrepair, became dirty and dangerous.

In 1901, when the Sydney Harbour Trust was constituted as a successor to the various port authorities of the nineteenth century, the Government of New South Wales took the strong action that was necessary to develop the wharfage facilities of the port on a systematic plan, under a unified administration. All privately owned wharves in the port were resumed, and were vested in the Sydney Harbour Trust.

The wharves thus acquired were a miscellaneous collection of rickety wooden structures, poorly equipped with gear and sheds for handling cargo and for embarking or disembarking passengers. For thirty-five years thereafter the Harbour Trust energetically rebuilt wharves and developed the waterfront facilities of the port under a long-term plan. The Trust's work has been continued and expanded since 1936 by its successor, the Maritime Services Board, so that today the wharfage of the Port of Sydney compares favorably with that of any other seaport in the world; especially in mechanization and "automation" in the handling of a variety of cargoes in bulk, but also in facilities for disembarking and embarking overseas passengers, at an average yearly rate of 77,000 arrivals and 69,000 departures.

On an average, seventy ocean-going mercantile vessels enter Sydney Harbour each week, and a corresponding number clear out each week. That is thus the average number of large vessels lying at berths alongside the wharves of Sydney Harbour at any time; but on occasions there are as many as 120 large vessels in the port, some at moorings awaiting berths.

The cargo-carrying sailing-vessels of the nineteenth century usually remained in their destination ports for many weeks, unloading and loading cargoes and taking in water, provisions, and ship's stores; but in the modern age of mechanical propulsion, when time is considered to be the equivalent of money, a Quick Turn Around of a vessel in port is required. Few vessels remain in port longer than a week. Some are entered and cleared out in as little as two or three days.

The planning of the Quick Turn Around is the responsibility of the port authority, which co-ordinates the activities and interests of all the parties concerned in each vessel's arrival, berthing, unloading, loading, and departure. Those parties include shipowners, shipping agents, wharf managers, stevedores, waterside workers, carriers, consignees, shippers, warehousemen, ship chandlers, tugmasters, pilots, and the Government Departments of Railways, Customs, Health, Immigration, and the Water Police.

All those varied parties are notified of the expected time of arrival and departure of each vessel, and of the berth and of the nature and extent of her cargo to be unloaded or loaded.

Radio communication from and to vessels approaching the port enables details of their berthing and other handling to be prearranged, and all parties concerned may then be warned to stand by at the prearranged times and places for handling each vessel without any waste of that most valuable factor, time. A failure, neglect, or delay by any of the parties concerned to do its part at the required time may throw out of gear the entire operation of the Quick Turn Around, with the further consequence that when a vessel is delayed in leaving her berth another vessel is delayed in occupying it.

In the planning of the large "combined operations" of berthing and clearing an average of seventy large vessels a week, the work of the Maritime Services Board may fairly be compared to that of a Naval or Military Headquarters Staff. Few members of the general public realize how extensive those operations are. The old-time haphazard methods of berthing overseas and coastal vessels and of handling their cargoes has been replaced by a modern system of co-ordinating all waterfront activities, not the less remarkable because it is taken for granted.

Since 1901 there has been a complete reconstruction of the commercial wharfage at Woolloomooloo, Sydney Cove, Walsh Bay, Darling Harbour, Pyrmont, Blackwattle Bay, Rozelle, Glebe Island, and Balmain. That work was actively continuing in the 1960s with further constructions and reconstructions of wharves, wharf-sheds, access roads, and the installation of modern cargo-handling machinery and gear. The annual revenue of the Maritime Services Board, from wharfage rates, berthing charges, and other port charges, amounting to between £6 million and £7 million a year, enables the Board to spend an average of £1½ million a year on capital works.

Shipowners, and those who use the services of ships—including passengers, and shippers, and consignees of cargo—pay for the longshore facilities that the port authorities provide. When those facilities are continuously being improved, enlarged and modernized, as is the rule at Sydney, no complaints are heard that the port charges are excessive. The whole community benefits when time saved means costs reduced.

EPIDEMICS AND RATS

In April 1789—fourteen months after the arrival of the First Fleet—an epidemic of smallpox killed large numbers of the Aborigines near Sydney. On 8th May, Lieutenant Bradley, R.N., of H.M.S. *Sirius*, reported:

> From the great number of dead natives found in every part of the Harbour, it appears that the small pox had made dreadful havoc among them. We did not see a canoe or a native the whole way coming up the Harbour, and were told that scarce any had been seen lately, except laying dead in and about their miserable habitations.

As there had been no case of smallpox in the First Fleet, or among the British settlers at Sydney Cove, Governor Phillip surmised that the disease had been brought to Botany Bay in the French ships of Admiral La Pérouse, which lay at anchor there for six weeks from 26th January to 10th March, 1788. This was possible, since the French ships had visited Macao in China and had called also at the Philippines, Formosa, and Samoa; but there was no mention in the French Admiral's journals of any case of smallpox on board either of his two vessels during twelve months since he had left Macao. The actual cause of the epidemic among the Aborigines at Sydney in April 1789 is therefore a mystery. It is possible that the disease which killed them so tragically, in such large numbers, was not smallpox, but measles

151

—a disease to which Europeans had developed a resistance which the Aborigines had not developed.

As most of the serious infectious diseases, such as smallpox, plague, cholera, leprosy, and typhoid fever, are of Asian origin, or endemic in Asian countries, it is usually considered that any outbreak of these diseases in Australia has been caused by infection on the waterfront from ships which have come from Asian ports. In conformity with international procedures of quarantine, if a vessel has been at sea for fourteen days from its last port of call, and no case of infectious disease has occurred on board, then pratique is granted, and the passengers and crew are allowed to go ashore.

That procedure is adequate in all except the rare cases in which a "carrier" of the disease may spread it without being himself or herself a sufferer. Whether from that cause, or through laxity in a quarantine inspection, there was in May 1881 an epidemic of smallpox at Sydney, chiefly among Chinese living at The Rocks, but the disease spread also to white people.

As an emergency measure, the Government hastily built an isolated hospital for the sufferers, on the clifftop overlooking the Pacific Ocean, near Little Bay, a mile to the northward of the north head of Botany Bay, and nine miles by road from Sydney. That was the origin of the Coast Hospital, which from that time onwards specialized in the treatment of infectious diseases. In the smallpox epidemic of 1881, 154 cases were notified, and of those 38 died. The spread of the disease was checked by the strict isolation of sufferers and their "contacts."

In 1886 there was an outbreak of typhoid fever, originating in the waterfront districts of West Sydney. This was checked also by isolating the sufferers at the Coast Hospital.

A panic was caused in 1900 by an outbreak of Bubonic Plague at Sydney. The epidemic was spread by rats that infested the waterfront, brought to Sydney in ships trading with China. The sufferers were removed to the Quarantine Station at North Head, where ninety persons (of 303 cases) died. In 1902 there was a further outbreak of Bubonic Plague. On this occasion the sufferers were sent to the Coast Hospital, where twenty-six (of 128 cases) died.

Compared with the dreadful mortality during epidemics in Asian countries, the prompt preventive measures that have been taken in Australia have curbed and quelled the outbreaks. The panic caused by the outbreak of Bubonic Plague in 1900 was one of the factors that induced the Government to establish the Sydney Harbour Trust in 1901 and to resume all wharf properties. The immediate first task of the Harbour Trust was to wage war on rats, which infested the decrepit wharves and wharf-sheds, and were presumably descended from rodents that had swarmed ashore from ships which did not have rat shields on their mooring lines.

Gangs of rat-catchers were employed, using every device of art and science—including traps, poison baits, cats, terriers, carpet-snakes, pea-rifles, and air-guns—to exterminate the rats, not only as carriers of plague-germs, but also as destroyers of cargo, especially of flour, wheat, and other foodstuffs. Ships and wharf-sheds were fumigated with sulphur dioxide and sometimes with cyanogen or other poisonous gases. The regulations for fitting rat shields to berthing hawsers were strictly enforced, with heavy fines for neglect.

In consequence of a long-sustained and vigorous offensive, the rat population of the waterfront was greatly reduced, though never completely exterminated. In the 1960s the Maritime Services Board was spending £4,000 a year on rat extermination.

In that Sixty Years War of men versus rats, it seemed that men were winning, and that rats were becoming rare; yet the price of liberty from rat infestation is eternal vigilance. A few survivors could breed up to hundreds of thousands if they were left to multiply uncurbed. The rats that infest wharves are of two kinds —the black or ship rat, and the brown or sewer rat. Both are imported pests, not indigenous to Australia, brought here as "stowaways" in ships.

From evil sometimes good may come. The Plague Scares of 1900 and 1902 led to a clean-up, and eventually to the complete rebuilding of Sydney's wharves—a consequence, direct or indirect, of the wide powers urgently given to the Harbour Trust to exterminate rats.

WHARF TIMBERS AND BORERS

Until the 1950s, all commercial wharves in the Port of Sydney were built of timber. Some wharves had concrete-slab decking, but the basic structure—of piles, headstocks, and girders—was of timber. Not until the late 1950s were some large new wharves built entirely of concrete, and these were exceptional.

Repairs and renovations of existing wharves usually conform with the basic timber structures, of the traditional design that had been used, as in many other ports of the world, throughout the nineteenth century and previously.

In no other port in the world was timber used more extensively for wharf-building than at Sydney. This was partly because long and straight-stemmed hardwood logs were obtainable at no great expense in the primeval Australian forests within easy distances from Sydney. That source of supply dwindled as the forests were thinned. Wharf-building was not as rapacious in its demands for hardwood as some other kinds of construction—such as the use of hardwood timbers for telephone poles, railway sleepers, bridge girders, fence posts, scantlings and weatherboards for house-building, wood-block street pavings, and (in more recent years) paper-making—which led, cumulatively, to the denudation of Australia's natural forests; yet the use of timber in the wharves of Sydney Harbour has been extensive, and will continue to be so, in renovations of existing structures, until perhaps eventually all the wharfage of the port shall have been replaced by concrete constructions.

In the 1960s there were not less than forty thousand timber piles standing in salt water, supporting the wharves of the Port   153 of Sydney. As each pile was the bole of a felled turpentine tree, ranging in lengths from 40 feet to 115 feet, driven into the sea-bed in rows, the piles spaced ten feet apart, the visual effect beneath each wharf was of a drowned grove; yet it could be seen also that wharf-carpentry is a skill of a special kind, in which the carpenters work from punts, and expertly handle heavy logs and beams in and out of the water.

The Australian "turpentine" tree, so-called, is an indigenous myrtle (*Syncarpia laurifolia*) which grows only in New South Wales and Queensland, and has no resemblance to the conifers of the Northern Hemisphere, from which the oleo-resin, Venetian turpentine (used in paints), is obtained. The name "turpentine," as applied to the Australian tree, is a misnomer. Its resin is a sweet-smelling gum, not inflammable. The remarkable feature of *Syncarpia laurifolia* is that its timber resists attacks by the marine worms or borers known as "Teredo," which are plentiful in the waters of Sydney Harbour. With the bark left on, this timber, though not completely impervious to attacks by Teredo and other wood-eating marine organisms, resists those attacks for much longer periods than any other timber. The trees grow tall and straight; this is the world's best timber for wharf piles.

A wharf extending 120 feet out from the sea-wall and 200 feet wide requires 240 turpentine piles—a large grove of full-grown trees. The sea-bed usually slopes from ten or twenty feet deep at the sea-wall to forty feet on the outside, or may be dredged to that depth. The piles are lowered one at a time from a pile-driving punt, and are "driven" by the traditional process of a weight dropped on the pile-head within a frame or tower, operated by a winch.

The piles are forced through the silt on the sea-bed, to rest on bedrock or in firm material such as clay or compacted sand. They are then "capped" with beams of ironbark timber, 14 inches square, known as headstocks, tied together longitudinally with heavy ironbark girders. These support a decking of hardwood planks, nine inches by four inches, or (more usually nowadays) of pre-cast concrete deck-slabs each 10 feet square and weighing three tons.

To prevent the whole structure of the wharf from moving, it is "tied" to the foreshore with steel rods anchored in concrete blocks, and also buttressed with "raker piles" which are set on a slant to act as struts supporting one in three of the vertical piles on each face of the wharf. Fenders and kerbs of heavy timber are fitted around the edges of the deck.

Everything in the wharf structure is above water except the turpentine piles, which are submerged at high tide for as much as seven-eighths of their length. The marine borers attack the piles chiefly between high-water and low-water levels in the "tidal zone," which at Sydney has an extreme range of seven feet. Despite the resistance of *Syncarpia laurifolia* to Teredo infestation, there are other organisms also which attack the piles, so that the piles have an average "life" of only fifteen years under water.

Treatment of the tidal zone on the piles with creosote, in a "floating collar," discourages the borers, but it is necessary to replace at least 1,000 wharf piles each year. The expense of that replacement is high; so, as suitable hardwood timber is becoming scarcer and more expensive, the Maritime Services Board has developed techniques for building all-concrete wharves, including the use of reinforced concrete piles of up to 100 feet in length.

These have proved satisfactory since they were first used in 1957, but only time will tell whether the eroding forces of the ocean will allow reinforced concrete piles to stand upright, submerged to their necks, and bearing a heavy burden, for as many years as did the Australian turpentine myrtle boles.

WALSH BAY

The small open bay between Dawes Point and Miller's Point— one of the few wide-mouthed crescent bays in Sydney Harbour —is occupied by twelve berths in docks between piers. The piers extend 800 feet from the shore, so that the whole of the bay is partitioned into docks. The berths have depths of water from 30 to 48 feet alongside, and can thus accommodate large ocean-going vessels. The Walsh Bay wharves, which have no railway connections, are used chiefly for unloading general merchandise, and for loading baled wool. With the Harbour Bridge and its approaches soaring in silhouette high overhead, the eight lines of motor traffic on the Bridge seeming to crawl like orderly beetles on that skyline, and the electric trains at intervals emitting a steely roar in the air that begins and ends like a growl of thunder, the ships berthed in those usually fully occupied docks, loading or unloading with the rattle of winches and the rumble of gantry-cranes, present a scene of concentrated longshore activity that comes as a surprise when it is first sighted from a vessel proceeding upstream under the Bridge, immediately after passing Dawes Point.

That revelation of the beginnings of Sydney's hidden Inner Harbour may be sighted from the Lane Cove ferry-steamer that plies upriver from Sydney Cove, or from the "Harbour Cruise" ferries. To the crews and passengers of overseas vessels proceeding to berths at Walsh Bay or in Cockle Bay beyond, the wished-for destination has abruptly come into sight, and very soon a gangplank will stretch to the shore.

The waterfront at Miller's Point, in its natural state, was steep-to, and inaccessible to wheeled vehicles. When John Leighton ("Jack the Miller") erected his three windmills there between 1795 and 1800, to grind wheat to flour, or maize to hominy, his mills were on the clifftops, to catch breezes from any point of the compass. The grain was landed from boats on a narrow ledge at the foot of the cliff, and hauled up with block and tackle gear.

The whaling vessels that lay at anchor in that bay in the lee of The Rocks ridge obtained their wood, water, provisions, and stores by boats. Their crews used footpaths up the cliffs and over the ridge to the taverns of Sydney Town.

Gradually a cart-road was formed by a roundabout route from   155

Sydney Cove through George Street North to Fort Street and then to Windmill Street. In the 1840s, wharves for ocean-going vessels were built in the bay at Miller's Point, which had no other name than that. Access roads had then to be improved.

In 1845, Captain Robert Towns, one of the most enterprising South Seas traders—who later became the founder of Townsville in North Queensland—established his own wharf and warehouse on the site now known as Central Wharf (Berths 8 and 9), Walsh Bay. There was then some excavating of the cliff to form a level space—now called Towns Place—at the foot of steps, and of a cart-ramp that gave access to and from Windmill Street, and from there to the city via Kent Street.

During the next fifty years, other privately owned wharves were built in that vicinity—among them Dalgety's, Moore's, and Dalton's. These provided berths chiefly for sailing-vessels unloading general merchandise and loading wool. The road access to the wharves was gradually improved, but extra horses were kept handy to help haul vehicles up the ramps. There was also a hydraulic lift which could raise or lower a dray and its load of wool or merchandise, and the draught-horses were unyoked and led up or down the cliffs by a narrow path. Adjacent to the wharves were several large bond-stores — the Argyle Bond, Dalgety's, and Parbury's—which continue in existence, in enlarged premises, today.

Road access to Walsh Bay today is by a wide and level marine driveway skirting the foreshores from Sydney Cove to Dawes Point, and then passing under the Harbour Bridge deck, between the pylons and the sea-wall, to connect with all the Walsh Bay wharves, and beyond to the wharves of Darling Harbour. This road was one of the first major engineering feats of the Sydney Harbour Trust from 1901 onwards. It was formed by a wide cutting at the base of the cliff on the western side of The Rocks ridge. The excavated stone was used for reclamation of the foreshore and building of sea-walls as bases for reconstructing the wharves at Walsh Bay and Darling Harbours.

That part of the Port Roadway is well named Hickson Road, in honour of P. R. P. Hickson, who was Chairman of the Sydney Harbour Trust from 1901 to 1913. He had much of the responsibility for rebuilding the wharves and for building the access roads to them, and it is fitting that his name should be remembered.

DARLING HARBOUR

From Miller's Point southwards to Bathurst Street, the waterfront of Darling Harbour stretches for a mile and a quarter along the western shore of Sydney City. With fifty berths for ships, it has its head 400 yards west of the Town Hall. It is crossed, at the foot of Market Street, by the Pyrmont Bridge, one of the "Five Bridges" of the old roundabout route across the Harbour and its arms.

At the southern end of that long row of wharves and jetties is the Darling Harbour Railway Goods Yard, occupying an area of

56 acres, with a total of 30 miles of tracks, and handling four million tons of goods a year.

The Railway Goods Yard was increased to its present area in the 1920s by reclamation of the tidal mudflats at the head of Darling Harbour, where the pioneer settlers of 1788 had found cockles, and had cut rushes (reeds) for thatching their huts. The filling material was the sandstone excavated from the tunnels of the City Railway.

Along the crest of the western ridge of Sydney, York Street and Clarence Street, giving access from and to the Harbour Bridge, are "longitudinal" streets, parallel with George Street. Below Clarence Street, the ridge slopes steeply to the waterfront of Darling Harbour, with two additional longitudinal north-south streets, Kent Street and Sussex Street, built as terraces parallel to the waterfront.

The principal cross-streets, leading down from the crest of the ridge towards the wharves, are Margaret Street, Erskine Street, King Street, Market Street, Druitt Street, and Bathurst Street.

All the streets on that western slope of the western ridge of the City of Sydney are dominated by the busy life of the wharves. In that zone are most of the warehouses of the importers of merchandise, the bond and free stores, the wool stores, the offices of stevedores and of shipping and customs agents, the depots of carriers and of ship providores, the engineering workshops connected with wharves and shipping, and the pubs where seamen and waterside workers quench their thirsts; but there are in this district very few dwellings, or retail shops, or large blocks of offices tenanted by members of the learned professions. At the dockside most of the work of moving cargoes inwards or outwards is done by men of brawn; the traffic in the streets is chiefly of motor trucks laden with merchant-goods and driven by burly, muscular men; the object of life here is to "deliver the goods" without delay or fuss. The buildings are drab and lack architectural graces or distinctions—they are for use, not for show, as also is the working garb of the people who earn a living in this part of the city. But even though there is little that is spectacular in the drab façades of the dockside streets, it is there that the wealth of a seaport emporium-city accumulates and the profits of trade originate, to be spent more showily elsewhere.

The streets and wharves on the Darling Harbour side might be likened to the back door or tradesmen's entrance of that city which makes such a glittering show eastwards of the Harbour Bridge and of York Street; but all is not gold that glitters: there is more real wealth along Darling Harbour than in Darlinghurst.

For the first twenty-two years of settlement at Sydney, the hillslope frontage of Cockle Bay, being too steep for cart traffic, remained uninhabited, uncleared of its trees, shrubs, ferns, and wildflowers, and unsurveyed; but when Governor Macquarie took office he energetically planned an expansion of Sydney Town.

One of his first reforms was to move the town market-place from the western side of Sydney Cove (where the present-day Cahill Expressway crosses George Street) to a new site at the corner of George Street and Market Street. There a row of market sheds was erected. Country people could bring their produce to market in carts from the farming districts of Petersham, Canterbury, and Bankstown, or in boats from up-harbour or across the harbour to a landing-stage at "Wharf Street" (near present-day Pyrmont Bridge), and so, in market-baskets or in hired carts, up Market Street, 400 yards, to the market sheds.

During his term of nearly twelve years in office, Macquarie supervised the laying-out of Kent Street and Sussex Street (both named by him in honour of Royal Dukes), on the hillslope on the western side of the military reserve in which he ordered "the biggest barracks in the British Empire" to be built, near the site of present-day Wynyard Square. The barracks remained there, as headquarters of the British Garrison troops in Australia, for forty years, until the 1850s. A track led down the hill from the barracks, in the vicinity of present-day Erskine Street, to Soldiers' Point, where the troops enjoyed sea-bathing in the Military Bath House—the first bathing enclosure erected on the foreshores of Sydney Harbour.

In 1813 an engineer named John Dickson arrived at Sydney in the sailing ship *Earl Spencer*, bringing with him the components of a steam engine, the first in Australia. At that time there were dozens of windmills on the ridge-tops of Sydney, to provide power for grinding grain. Dickson proposed to set up a flour mill driven by his steam engine; Governor Macquarie allotted him a site at the head of Cockle Bay, and granted him sixteen acres of land there, between Bathurst Street and Liverpool Street.

There, on 29th May, 1815, in the presence of Governor Macquarie, the steam mill was officially opened, and began crushing grain at the rate of 260 bushels a day, in comparison with the average output of a windmill, twelve bushels a day.

The site of Dickson's mill is indicated in the name of Steam Mill Street, at the edge of the Darling Harbour Goods Yard. It deserves a monument, for it introduced the Industrial Revolution to Australia. Within ten years most of the windmills had disappeared from Sydney's skyline, and several more steam mills were erected in Sussex Street, handy to jetties on the shore of Cockle Bay, where shipments of grain from Parramatta, and from the Hawkesbury River and George's River settlements, could be landed from sloops and schooners; and from Van Diemen's Land (Tasmania) in brigs and other larger vessels.

The Market Wharf, and the various small jetties serving the steam flourmills, inaugurated the waterfront activities along Sussex Street. In 1830, when Governor Darling conferred his own name on Cockle Bay, the shipping activity there was already fairly well developed, with importations not only of grain for the flourmills, and of every sort of farm-produce for the markets, but of coal (from the Hunter River) for the steam engines of the flourmills and for supplying to masters of sailing-vessels as galley-coals, and for domestic heating.

Other industries were established along that shore, including a brewery owned by John Dickson adjacent to his flourmill.

This was given the name of the Darling Brewery. It was bought in the 1860s by John and James Toohey, and removed to another site.

In 1838 James Maclehose, in *Pictures of Sydney*, stated:

> Sussex Street, throughout its whole length, is but slightly elevated above the level of Darling Harbour. It forms the main thoroughfare between the wharves, warehouses, flour-mills, shipbuilding yards, and manufactories, which are posited between it and Darling Harbour.

He added that there were eight flourmills, several shipbuilding yards, and "upwards of a dozen large wharves" in that vicinity, and expressed the opinion—which may be true also today—that "more valuable merchandise and other property is conveyed through Sussex Street than through any other street in Sydney."

The "several shipbuilding yards" were slipways where small vessels were built for the coastal and upharbour and cross-harbour trades. The site of one yard is shown in the name of Slip Street, on the waterfront near the foot of King Street.

In Governor Darling's day, when the town gaol at the corner of Essex Street and George Street was overcrowded, some of the men who were "reconvicted" (i.e., convicted of crimes committed in the Colony) were confined on board a prison hulk, *Phoenix*, which for a time was moored in Darling Harbour, near the foot of Erskine Street. The name is retained in Phoenix Wharf (Berths 14a and 14b, Darling Harbour). Convicts quartered in the hulk worked on shore in chains, mostly at road building, under military guard.

In 1836 the first Gaslight Company was formed in Sydney. The gasworks were built on a freehold property on the water-front, between Kent Street and the shore, below the northern end of Clarence Street, where the name of Gas Lane now indicates the site. Sydney was first lit by gas in 1841. The Darling Harbour Gasworks were the first in Australia. Coal was brought from the Hunter River, in sailing-vessels and later in steamers, and un-loaded at the Gas Wharf on the site of the present-day berths 6a and 6b, Darling Harbour. Two large gas-holders were built on the shore adjacent, and remained there, with the gas-making retorts and huge dumps of coal, until the works were removed in 1922 to Mortlake on the Parramatta River.

From the 1850s to the 1890s, many privately owned wharves were built along the foreshore of Darling Harbour, chiefly by shipping companies engaged in the Australian coastal trade, in which steamers ran on regular schedules, with passengers, cargo and mails, between Sydney and ports in the other colonies, but also between Sydney and the outports of New South Wales, including the steamer services to and from Newcastle, Grafton, and other North Coast ports, and to and from the Illawarra and South Coast ports. On these routes also many sailing-vessels were in service, carrying coal and timber.

It was the coastal trade that chiefly developed the waterfront of Darling Harbour, with farm produce for the markets, timber for the shipyards, wheat and coal for the flourmills, and coal for the gasworks and for bunkering. Not until the Hawkesbury River railway bridge was opened in 1880, providing a direct rail link between Sydney and the North, did the coastal sea-trade gradually fall into decline.

In the 1890s, some of the wharves were enlarged for overseas vessels, especially for the loading of wool, and larger wharves were built also at Pyrmont, Glebe Island, and Balmain, in conjunction with the extension of railroad sidings.

The energetic reconstruction, by the Sydney Harbour Trust, of the entire wharfage and road access, from 1901 to 1936, and since then by the Maritime Services Board, has provided the Darling Harbour waterfront with berthing accommodation and cargo-handling facilities of the highest standards, chiefly for loading and unloading overseas cargo vessels. In the latest rebuilt wharves and sheds, these facilities are acknowledged to be equal to the world's best.

PYRMONT

In December 1806 the *Sydney Gazette* reported that "a select party of ladies and gentlemen, twenty-one in all, made an aquatic excursion from Parramatta to Captain Macarthur's estate at Cockle Bay." There they examined "the picturesque beaches" of the "romantic scene" and enjoyed a picnic "beneath the shelter of a spreading fig tree."

The *Gazette* report continued:

> To this enviable retirement one of the young ladies was pleased to give the name of Pyrmont, from the pure and uncontaminated spring, joined to the native beauties of the place. . . . Pyrmont, near Hanover, in Germany, has medicinal springs.

Drastic has been the transformation of that rustic and idyllic scene, to one of the most intensely industrialized districts of Sydney. There is apparently no record of the right or title that Captain Macarthur had to that "estate," or of when it lapsed or was sold; but the romantic name of Pyrmont remained.

In 1840 a shipbuilder named Russell had a large shipyard at Pyrmont, from which was launched a steam dredge, *Hercules*, used in 1842 to dredge the mud at the head of Sydney Cove, to enable the sea-wall of the Semi-Circular Quay to be built.

Other industries developed at Pyrmont, requiring water transport, or accessible by road from George Street West and Harris Street, Ultimo. In 1804 Governor King had made a grant of land to Surgeon John Harris, comprising most of the district which is now the suburb of Ultimo, so named from the mansion Harris built there. He died in 1838, aged eighty-four years. His estate adjoined the peninsula of Pyrmont, through which Harris Street is extended.

In 1855 an incorporated company, with a capital of £50,000, was granted the right by Act of Parliament to build a bridge

160

across Darling Harbour from Market Street to Pyrmont, and to charge tolls for using it. The Act of Parliament stipulated that the bridge should have a moveable panel "capable of admitting vessels of all classes to pass and repass through it."

The bridge, a wooden structure with a "swing panel" operated by hand-gears, was opened for traffic on 17th March, 1858. It was operated profitably by the Company for twenty-six years, until 1884, when it was bought by the Government, and the toll system abolished. A new bridge, of steel, was built in 1902, and continued in service in the mid-1960s, but plans were then in hand to abolish it, and to send traffic to and from Pyrmont by the Port Roadway around the foreshore at the head of Darling Harbour —no great extra distance.

The complex of wharves and piers at Pyrmont, with twenty-one berths for large vessels, many of the wharves with railroad sidings, makes this the most densely concentrated industrial and mercantile shipping zone along all the foreshores.

The modern development at Pyrmont began in 1891, with the building of coaling-jetties along the shore of the peninsula on the seaward side of the Pyrmont Bridge. These were connected by railroad with the Darling Harbour Goods Yard. There were six berths, with narrow jetties, permitting the unloading of colliers or bunkering of steamers directly from or into rail wagons. These berths remained in use for coaling until the 1950s, when two large coal wharves with modern "automation" were completed at White Bay, Balmain.

The reconstruction of the Pyrmont wharfage for large vessels, including "rail berths" and cargo-sheds, proceeded steadily from 1901 to 1919. Berths 7 to 10, constructed in 1906, were used extensively for the shipment of bagged wheat direct from railroad wagons. In 1928 the wheat export trade was specialized at Glebe Island; but the wheat silos and flour mills at Pyrmont continued to be operated for the export trade in conjunction with the shipping of wool and the importation of general merchandise.

During the 1939-45 war, the cargo wharves at Berths 12, 13, and 14, Pyrmont, were used largely for the embarkation of troops going overseas on active service, and also for the shipment of large quantities of war material. A Memorial Plaque commemorates that special war service.

After the war had ended, those three adjacent berths were equipped as the first modern passenger terminal in Australia. This was done by building an upper deck on the cargo-sheds, so that passengers and their luggage could be handled at that upper level, while cargo and ship's stores were simultaneously handled at the lower level. An overhead road bridge across the railway-tracks enabled motor-cars, taxis, and buses to drive to and from the upper-deck level. The length of berths and depth of water alongside enable passenger-liners of up to 30,000 tons to use the Pyrmont Terminal.

By a misnomer, a promontory of the Pyrmont Peninsula is named "Darling Island." If it ever was an island, the channel dividing it from the main shore has long ago been filled in. The 161 promontory has the Passenger Terminal (Berths 12, 13, and 14, Pyrmont) on its eastern side, and the Naval Stores and Royal Edward Naval Victualling Yard on its western side, with berths for naval storeships, and others also for wool-loading, with a large number of rail-sidings and shunting lines handy.

On the western side of the Pyrmont Peninsula ·is Johnston's Bay, where the principal water frontage is occupied by the large buildings of the sugar refinery, established there in 1878. This group of buildings, with its own wharves and coal storages, and prominent transporter-cranes for handling raw sugar in bulk (not bagged), includes, in addition to the sugar refinery, a distillery, a factory for making wall-boards from pressed sugar-cane, and a large engineering workshop.

The bulk sugar is brought to Pyrmont by sea, chiefly from Queensland and from the northern ports of New South Wales. Intense automation, with grabs lifting four tons of raw sugar from the hold of a steamer at each "bite," and transferring it to hoppers, from which it is carried by conveyor-belts to the storage-sheds in the refinery, has practically eliminated the manual handling of heavy bags of sugar, and is eliminating also the use of jute bags for shipping sugar.

SEE ALSO PART II   GLEBE ISLAND

In August 1789, Governor Phillip made a grant of 400 acres of land to the Reverend Richard Johnson, Chaplain of the First Fleet, not for the clergyman himself, but as "church land or glebe." The land was, as the Chaplain remarked, "covered with large green trees." It was at the head of the inner recesses of Cockle Bay, where hunting parties, landed from boats, had shot kangaroos and emus for food for the starving settlers. For this reason it was known as "the Kangaroo Ground."

In December 1792, the Chaplain agreed to accept a smaller grant, of only 100 acres, but in more open country, at a place a few miles away, which later became known as Canterbury. The Kangaroo Ground was then granted in small allotments to various military officers, but in 1825 it was vested again, as "glebe," in the trustees of the Church Lands Corporation, which eventually sold parts of it, and leased other parts, as building sites. In the 1870s an industrial suburb, retaining the old name of The Glebe, began to be densely populated there.

The Glebe, adjacent to Pyrmont and to Ultimo, extends along the southern shores of the two most southerly and most land-locked arms of Sydney Harbour used for navigation, Blackwattle Bay and Rozelle Bay.

Glebe Island, so-called, is not an island, and is not part of The Glebe, geographically, municipally, or historically: it is a peninsula on the opposite side of Rozelle Bay from The Glebe. The western boundary of the City of Sydney is at the head of Rozelle Bay. Glebe Island is within Leichhardt municipality, and thus "belongs" to Balmain, rather than to The Glebe. It is separated by a passage or strait (800 ft wide) from the western side of Pyrmont.

That strait is part of an arm of the Inner Harbour named Johnston's Bay, not in honour of the Reverend Richard Johnson, but of Lieutenant-Colonel George Johnston, who was a captain in the Marines with the First Fleet in 1788, and, after lengthy and varied service in the Colony, retired in 1813 to his estate, which he named Annandale, where he died ten years later. The present-day suburb of Annandale is on the western side of The Glebe, separated from The Glebe by Johnston's Creek, which flows into Rozelle Bay.

On the western side of Glebe Island is White Bay, so named in honour of the Surgeon-General of the First Fleet and of the pioneer settlement at Sydney Cove, John White, who retired and returned to England in 1794, being then succeeded by Doctor William Balmain. In the year 1800, Doctor Balmain was granted 500 acres of wild bushland on that large peninsula to the westward of Cockle Bay that now bears his name. It seems likely that it was Surgeon Balmain who conferred the names of his friends, Johnston and White, on the bays that were on the eastern shore of his property. He sold his estate cheaply in 1801, and died in 1803.

In 1857 a wooden bridge was built from Glebe Island to Pyrmont, to shorten road communications between the city and Balmain, which were further shortened in the following year when the Pyrmont Bridge was opened. The Glebe Island Bridge, which had a swing span to permit vessels to enter or leave the two backwaters to its southward, Blackwattle Bay and Rozelle Bay, was replaced in 1901 by a steel bridge.

The wharves at Glebe Island, having deep water close inshore, and being connected by railroads to the main western line and to the Darling Harbour Goods Yard, have become specialized, since the 1920s, in the handling of wheat and flour for export. Huge storage silos have been built, visible from afar, like a modern Parthenon or a Temple of Ceres. The storage capacity of the silos is 7½ million bushels (a bushel weighs 60 pounds). Exports of wheat from the Glebe Island Terminal average 30 million bushels a year, valued at £23 million.

Elaborate mechanization enables wheat to be loaded, either "in bulk" (i.e., loose) or in bags, almost "untouched by human hands." The bulk wheat is loaded into a vessel alongside at the rate of 1,800 tons an hour. In 1963 one vessel loaded 22,000 tons of wheat (for China) in twelve hours.

A monument at the wharves, in the form of a plain block of granite with a cast bronze plaque, commemorates the arrival of armed forces of the U.S.A. in the Port of Sydney on 28th March, 1942. They came in the *Queen Mary* from Boston. She anchored in Athol Bight, and the 8,398 troops on board were taken in Sydney Harbour ferries to Glebe Island, where troop trains waited to take them to camps outside the city. That was the first large contingent of U.S. troops to arrive in Australia, in transit to the war zones in the north-west Pacific. Subsequently Glebe Island became the principal U.S. Army depot at Sydney for disembarking and re-embarking troops, and for unloading, storing, and reloading immense quantities of war material. All except the "mammoth" troop transports could berth at Glebe Island, which was chosen for its military value as a transit depot because of its combination of wharfage and railroad communications. Those considerations had led also to the use by the Australian armed forces of the berthing facilities at Pyrmont for the transports.

WHITE BAY

In conformity with the modern trend to mechanical loading of specialized cargoes, most of the seaborne coal trade of the Port of Sydney has been concentrated at White Bay, Balmain. This trade depends, like the wheat trade, on the combination of transport by rail and by sea.

On an average, one and a half million tons of coal are brought to Sydney annually, by sea, chiefly from Newcastle-upon-Hunter, in a fleet of colliers known as "the Sixty Milers"—sixty miles being the distance along the coast from Sydney to the Hunter River port. A large quantity of coal is brought to Sydney also by rail, from mines in the Burragorang Valley and the Illawarra. The distribution of coal for industrial uses, gas-making, electric-power generation, ship-bunkering, rail-locomotive use, and for export, requires a large organization of transport and handling, by sea and by rail, or by sea and rail in combination.

There are coal wharves at various places in Sydney Harbour, but by far the higgest concentration of coal-handling, both for local distribution and for export, is at White Bay, which in that respect could more appropriately be called *Black* Bay, for there, inevitably, the grime inseparable from the handling of "black diamonds" is the obtrusive feature of the scenery.

Coal-mining was conducted at Balmain for sixty years (until the 1940s), and it was this fact that brought the coal wharves into special functioning there; but in modern times the export of coal from Balmain is a re-export. The huge black stacks at the wharves have been built from consignments by sea and rail. From that depot-source, nearly one million tons of coal are exported annually, chiefly to Japan and other Asian countries. The coal is loaded from the stacks into the holds of the foreign going colliers by mechanical equipment, consisting of cranes, grabs, hoppers, bins, conveyors, and chutes. Big Japanese colliers are loaded with 22,000 tons of coal within thirty-two hours—at the rate of nearly 700 tons an hour.

Apart from that export trade, there is a large re-handling of coal from White Bay for railway and industrial purposes, and especially for the generation of electricity at Sydney in the power-houses of White Bay, Balmain, Pyrmont, Ultimo, and Bunnerong —all connected by rail with the White Bay wharves.

SEE ALSO PART II   BLACKWATTLE BAY

Originally there was a swamp at the head of Blackwattle Bay, filled partly by the tides and partly by a freshwater creek that drained into it from Surry Hills. The name of the bay was evidently conferred on it by boat parties sent there from Sydney Cove in 1788 to gather wattles and reeds for hut-building. When a road was built towards Parramatta in 1789, a log bridge crossed the Blackwattle Creek.

The creek was not fully channelled underground until the 1890s. The swamp, filled in, forms Wentworth Park, a fine open space for the recreation of the residents of Ultimo, the Glebe, and Pyrmont.

Wharves were built in Blackwattle Bay in 1890, replacing earlier ramshackle jetties. The wharves, which were later extended, are used by small coastal vessels for loading and unloading coal, timber, potatoes, and other farm produce, and by fishing trawlers. All vessels have to pass through the swing-panel of Glebe Island Bridge to enter or leave this secluded bay.

ROZELLE BAY

Adjacent to Blackwattle Bay is the backwater haven of Rozelle Bay, which has greater depth (24 ft) in its channel and alongside its wharves than its neighbouring innermost recess of Sydney Harbour. The origin of the name of Rozelle Bay is not positively known, but is believed to have been associated with a schooner, the *Rozelle*, which may have been built or berthed there. She was wrecked in 1914 at Narrabeen.

On the western side of Rozelle Bay are the biggest timber-handling wharves of Sydney, and also the concrete construction plant and depot of the Maritime Services Board. There, with ample space available, and railroad communication alongside, the concrete is mixed and pre-cast for slabs, piles, ferry pontoons, and other material for wharf-building. The mixing, curing, and handling of this heavy material is done by large mechanical equipment, including travelling cranes, and the finished products are moved in lighters to the required places along the Harbour shores.

The timber wharves (i.e., wharves for handling freighted timber in logs or sawn) at Rozelle Bay are the largest in Sydney Harbour, but there are others elsewhere. Sawmills operate alongside the wharves. The accumulation of huge stacks of logs—brought from Australian ports and from New Zealand, New Guinea, Canada, the U.S.A., Sweden, and Finland—makes a distinctive sight, yet another reminder of the complexity of a seaport's life, and of the denudation of forests by civilization's demands. Whereas in bygone years timber was one of the principal exports from New South Wales—cedar, hardwood for railway sleepers, and turpentine piles—no timber is exported nowadays from Sydney. On the contrary, an average of 360,000 tons is imported annually from overseas countries, and 15,000 tons from Australian ports, chiefly from North Queensland and Tasmania. (The tonnage of timber is calculated by cubic measurement, not by weight.)

PEACOCK'S POINT   SEE ALSO PART II

Along the eastern, or Inner Harbour, shore of Balmain, approximately a mile from the head of White Bay to Peacock's Point, with frontages on Johnston's Bay, are the depots of oil companies, and some large factories, including soap-making and pharmaceutical works, some of which have wharves or jetties for their own use. The Balmain Ferry runs across Johnston's Bay and Darling Harbour to the City at Erskine Street Wharf, as it has done since that service was inaugurated by three of the first Australian-built steamers (paddlewheelers), the *Experiment*, the *Emu*, and the *Australian*, in succession from 1840 to 1843.

The inner harbour of Cockle Bay, with its complex of intercommunicating bays, and of bays within bays, ends at Peacock's Point, where the shore trends away to the northward and westward. The channel between Peacock's Point and Miller's Point provides the only sea-ingress to, and exit from, that large, sheltered, and secluded series of havens in which most of the sea-trade of the Port of Sydney is concentrated.

Peacock's Point was named after John Thomas Peacock, who in 1846 was authorized to collect wharfage and tonnage dues at the then newly built Semi-Circular Quay in Sydney Cove. He presumably had his residence at Peacock's Point, Balmain; but, like much else of the lore of Australia, the naming of some of the features of Sydney Harbour in popular usage—later officially adopted—leaves scope for conjecture when pioneers are forgotten, or remembered only in names that have almost lost their meanings.

9

BALMAIN

THE UPPER HARBOUR IS NAVIGABLE BY OCEAN-GOING STEAMERS FOR
seven miles upstream from the Sydney Harbour Bridge. There,
twelve miles from the ocean, the Ryde Bridges (a road bridge
and a railway bridge) mark the head of navigation for vessels
with high top-hamper; but the clearance under the bridges is
enough to allow barges, lighters, launches, small yachts, and
boats to proceed farther upstream, in a narrowing river channel,
to the head of tidal waters, within Parramatta City, eighteen
miles from the ocean.

The main channel of the Upper Harbour is conjoined, on its
northern side, two miles upstream from the Harbour Bridge,
with the Lane Cove River, a creek that is tidally flooded in its
lower reaches. It forms an arm of the Harbour, navigable (though
seldom used for commercial navigation) by vessels of medium
size for two miles to the Fig Tree Bridge, and beyond that point
for five miles by small craft (chiefly pleasure-launches and boats),
in a narrow channel.

The Upper Harbour, above its junction with the Lane Cove
River, is named the Parramatta River, but this is a matter of
tradition rather than of apt description. The waterway has the
appearance of an arm of the Harbour, rather than of a "river,"
at least until it narrows to 200 yards from bank to bank, a mile
and a half above the Ryde Railway Bridge.

In the general geographical sense, the entire expanse of Sydney
Harbour is a sunken estuary at the confluence of three small
freshwater streams—the Parramatta River, the Lane Cove River,
and Middle Harbour Creek—and of the many smaller creeks and
gullies that drain into the coves and bays of the serrated shore-
lines of those three arms in their estuarine reaches. It was not
strictly logical to refer to two of those tidally flooded arms as
"rivers" and to the third as (Middle) "Harbour"; but those loose
designations, conferred in the earliest pioneering days, became
conventionally accepted.

The low-lying nature of the country along the southern shore
of the Upper Harbour, which caused the tidal flooding of Cockle
Bay, has likewise caused the flooding of several other large inlets
along that shore, including Iron Cove, Hen and Chicken Bay,
and Homebush Bay; but, along the northern side, the ridgy
corrugations have formed coves of the characteristic Sydney
Harbour configuration—the sunken effluents of short gullies, in
addition to the large flooded valley of the Lane Cove River.

The southern shore, with easy access by rail and road to
Sydney City, has developed chiefly as industrial suburbs, whereas
the northern side has chiefly residential suburbs. The distinction 167

is not absolute: there are some pleasant residential districts along the southern shore, and some few industrial enclaves along the northern shore.

The municipalities to the westward of the City of Sydney, on the southern shore, are: Leichhardt (including Balmain); Drummoyne (including Five Dock and Abbotsford); Concord (including Cabarita, Mortlake, Yaralla, and Rhodes); and Auburn (including Homebush, Newington, and Silverwater).

Westward of Auburn is the City of Parramatta, extended on both sides of the upper narrow reaches of the Parramatta River, at the head of the tidal water, the head of boat navigation, and therefore, in the strict geographical sense, the head of Sydney Harbour, approximately sixteen miles inland by rhumb-line, or eighteen miles by mid-channel course.

East of Parramatta, along the northern shores, are the municipalities of Ryde, Hunter's Hill, Lane Cove, and North Sydney.

There are thus eight municipalities and a city on the shores of the Upper Harbour, to the westward of Sydney Harbour Bridge. Half a million people live there, and cherish the local lore, which is different from that of the Lower Harbour. In those more sheltered inland waters, less ruffled by oceanic zephyrs, rowing, rather than sailing, is the traditional aquatic sport; there, some of the most important industries of the metropolis employ large numbers of workers in making goods for the Australian market, rather than in handling exports and imports; there too are some of the biggest hospitals and boarding-schools of the Greater Sydney region; there the Harbour was crossed by two road bridges and a rail bridge long before the Sydney Harbour Bridge was built; and there the place-names are rich in historical associations, evoking incidents and men of renown in the pioneering era. But, perhaps because the whole extent of Sydney Harbour, in all its arms and reaches, is much greater than is generally realized, the scenic and other pleasing and interesting aspects of the Upper Harbour have never been given as much publicity as those of the Lower Harbour, and consequently—especially since the ferry service to Parramatta was discontinued in 1928—remain partially or almost completely unknown to many visitors to Sydney, and even to many residents of the City and of its suburbs that stretch from the City eastwards towards the ocean.

SEE ALSO PART II   GOAT ISLAND

Three-quarters of a mile upstream from the Harbour Bridge, and 200 yards offshore from Balmain Peninsula, is the island which the Aborigines called Mel Mel; but the pioneer British settlers, not knowing or caring about that, for reasons of their own, not difficult to surmise, called it Goat Island. There, it seems likely, the three goats which were brought with other livestock from Capetown in the First Fleet in 1788 were put ashore, to forage for themselves in a place from which they could not stray.

There is no documentary proof of that surmise. The name Goat Island was not used in official reports until 1826, when the island was mentioned by that name in a despatch from Governor Darling, in relation to a project for building a dock there; but, as with many other place-names of Sydney Harbour, a popular usage had, in course of time, become officially adopted. That usage was evidently based on a tradition that, during the early years of British settlement at Sydney, the island had been used as a goat pasture. A rocky knoll, thirteen acres in area, covered with trees and shrubs, less than one mile from Sydney Cove by boat, it certainly had, in its primeval state, some rockpools of rainwater where goats could drink until they had nibbled or trampled the shrubs and other herbage that shaded the pools from quick evaporation. Exactly when and by whom a goat was, or some goats were, placed on that island, and for how long it or they remained in occupation, are facts that have not been recorded precisely in historical documents. After those who knew the facts at first hand had died, there remained only the tradition preserved in a place-name, with the quality of lore, to arouse conjecture perhaps for centuries yet to come.

Towards the end of Governor Darling's term of office (1825-31), the prison hulk *Phoenix* was moved from her berth at a wharf near Sussex Street, and was laid alongside Goat Island's western shore. The prisoners, colonially reconvicted men who were awaiting transportation to the "ultra"-penitentiary of Norfolk Island, worked on shore in fetters at Goat Island, quarrying building-stone and rubble that was lightered to Sydney City, and other places along the Harbour shores, for government and private contractors.

The Surveyor-General, Major Mitchell, complained in 1831 that Goat Island—a most valuable site, in his opinion, for a fort to defend Sydney and the Parramatta River—was "likely to be quarried away." That statement was exaggerated. The quarries had made a comparatively small scar in the cliffs on the western side of the dome-like structure of the island, which rose to a crown 120 feet above sea-level, with cliffs 80 feet sheer on the eastern side; but Mitchell's warning brought the quarrying to a stop. The *Phoenix* was towed to Lavender Bay (so named from her bosun, George Lavender), on the north side of the Harbour. For two years, the white cockatoos that had nested from time immemorial on Mel Mel could screech in the trees there, free of fear, and undisturbed by the lugubrious sights and sounds of Britons in chains and slavery: but the island's days as a sanctuary for cockatoos were numbered with the onset of civilization.

In 1833, Governor Bourke, a humane and enlightened administrator, decided to move the prisoners from their unhealthy quarters on board the *Phoenix* hulk to huts on shore at Goat Island. There they would be put to work building a naval and military ordnance store, guardhouses, and other defence works, and a wharf, all of solid stone construction from materials quarried on the island. For five years (1833-38), while that work was in progress, Goat Island was a penitentiary and transit depot for the "hard cases" (colonially reconvicted Imperial convicts), and also for offenders born in the colony, or free immigrants colonially convicted. Bourke relaxed the regulations to allow well-behaved convicts to work without leg-irons. He also appointed a resident schoolmaster on the island to improve the education of the convicts: a reform in accordance with the humanitarian ideas that were being applied at that time, when the Imperial Convict System was nearing its end in New South Wales.

Most of the stone buildings erected on Goat Island by convict labour in that period (1833-38) remain in use today, in a perfect state of preservation. The biggest building, the arsenal (gunpowder magazine), has walls of hewn sandstone six feet thick, and is 100 feet long and 35 feet wide. It has a vaulted ceiling of stone, roofed with tiles. This and the other buildings near by, including homes for the officers and a guardhouse, all of stone, with cedar doors and mahogany floors, are rated among the best remaining buildings of the convict era in Sydney.

In 1838, the convict establishment was removed from Goat Island to Cockatoo Island, a mile and a quarter up-harbour. The buildings at Goat Island were then occupied by troops of the British garrison, guarding the ammunition and ordnance stores, for thirty-two years, until British troops were withdrawn from Australia in 1870. Thereafter, the island was manned by Australian colonial troops until 1893. Commercial, as well as naval and military, explosives were stored in the magazine. The naval stores were removed in 1884 to Spectacle Island, and the military explosives in 1893 to Newington.

After 1893, the powder magazine on Goat Island was used chiefly for storage of bulk supplies of blasting powder, dynamite, and small-arms ammunition owned by merchants or mining and quarrying companies. The island had thus reverted to civilian use, but remained a Crown Reserve, closed to unauthorized persons. In 1852 a Water Police station had been established on the eastern side of the island, with a skiff manned by four oarsmen constables. The station received and sent messages from and to Dawes Point by semaphore.

During the outbreak of bubonic plague at Sydney in 1900, the explosives were hastily removed from Goat Island to hulks at Bantry Bay, in Middle Harbour. All the buildings were vacated, including the Water Police station, and the island was put into emergency use as a bacteriological station, under control of the New South Wales Government Department of Health. The arsenal was equipped as a laboratory for the preparation of serums and for the testing and diagnosis of plague infection. The residential quarters were occupied by the laboratory superintendents and staff. As the island was exclusively in use for that purpose on 1st January, 1901, when the Colonies of Australia became federated as States, the Government of New South Wales refused to hand it over to the Federal Government, which claimed that it was a military post.

The Federal Government's claim was not pressed. When the outbreak of plague ended, the bacteriological station was closed, and Goat Island was handed over in 1901 to the newly constituted Sydney Harbour Trust, which used its buildings immediately as the headquarters of the Port Fire Brigade.

Additional premises were built on the island to house officials and staff members of various other port services established there, with large installations, by the Harbour Trust and its successor, the Maritime Services Board. In the 1960s, there were 120 employees of the Maritime Services Board resident on Goat Island, and many more were conveyed to and from work there daily in ferries and launches. The island had become the principal depot for the Board's fleet of 170 harbour-services craft, including pilot vessels, dredges, tugs, lighters, barges, launches, and work-boats of many special purposes. Large workshops, slipways, wharves, and docks had been installed for the building and maintenance of harbour craft. The old-time powder-magazine had become a modern shipyard store and chandlery.

The Port Fire Brigade's headquarters and residences remain at Goat Island, where four vessels equipped as fire-fighting units are berthed in readiness to be called out instantly to fires in ships or longshore buildings. These vessels, able to pump water at the rate of 8,000 gallons a minute, are equipped with chemicals for quelling oil fires.

Tugs owned by the Maritime Services Board, built and stationed at Goat Island, are not normally used for commercial towage, but only for moving the Board's lighters, barges, dredges, and other floating plant. Several commercial tug-owning companies operate towage services on Sydney Harbour with powerful modern tugs, most of which are stationed and serviced at Balmain.

The shipyard at Goat Island, established in 1919, has been expanded to a large establishment, with several slipways (for vessels of up to 500 tons), a fitting-out wharf, large workshops, a sawmill, cranes, winches, coal-bunkers, and a modern "amenities block" with a dining-room for 150 men. In addition to building its own vessels of many kinds, the M.S.B., at its Goat Island shipyard, has built the fast and powerful patrol launches of the Water Police.

The pride of Goat Island is the Commissioners' launch, *Captain Phillip*, built there and completed in 1965, to replace the venerable steam yacht *Lady Hopetoun*, which, built in 1902 for use by the Commissioners of the Harbour Trust as an inspection vessel, and taken over and maintained in operation by the Maritime Services Board in 1936, had become in 1965 the oldest steamer remaining in active service anywhere in the world. Stylish and graceful, the *Lady Hopetoun* was one of the most interesting and most pleasing features of the Sydney Harbour scene. She was used not only by the Port Officials on tours of inspection, but to carry visiting dignitaries from many countries on harbour trips as guests of the Government of New South Wales.

The *Captain Phillip*, 76 feet long overall and with a 20-foot beam, powered with twin diesel motors, though not as pretty to look at as the *Lady Hopetoun*, is well designed as a large modern passenger launch, and has luxurious accommodation for entertaining distinguished visitors to Sydney on harbour tours. It is appropriate that, 177 years after Captain Phillip discovered Sydney Harbour, his name should have been commemorated in this way. In the 1830s and 1840s there was a colonial government brig, the *Captain Phillip*, sailing from Sydney to Norfolk Island and to Van Diemen's Land. She was wrecked in Bass Strait in 1848, and since then there had been no vessel in·service with that name.

Strangely, too, there is not one headland, cove, bay, or island in Sydney Harbour named in honour of Governor Phillip. No honour conferred posthumously upon that upright man who was the founding father of Sydney, and of European settlement in Australia, could adequately commemorate the strength of his character, his common sense in judgments of the practical, and the magnitude of his achievement. An island was named for his goat, but he was too modest to allow his own name to be used there, or anywhere else in the Harbour he had discovered.

SEE ALSO PART II   BALMAIN PENINSULA

The metropolitan agglomeration of the City of Sydney and its 480 suburbs (i.e., postal districts), spread over an area of 670 square miles, is divided, for purposes of local self-government, into forty-five municipalities. Each municipality thus consists of several suburbs, which are distinct vicinities for postal or other identifications. One such suburb is Balmain, which, being a peninsula, has a strong local identity; but it is merged administratively with the suburbs of Rozelle, Lilyfield, Annandale, and Leichhardt, on its southward side, to form the municipality of Leichhardt, one of the most densely peopled industrial districts of the entire metropolitan region. Including, as it does, the wharves and dockside vicinities of Rozelle Bay, Glebe Island, White Bay, and all the foreshores of Balmain, the municipality of Leichhardt is one of the commercially busiest of the fifteen municipalities which have frontages on Sydney Harbour and its arms. (As the metropolitan region extends from Broken Bay to Port Hacking, there are municipalities with ocean frontages, and on the shores of Botany Bay, not described in the present volume.)

The people of Balmain have a strong feeling of local pride, with traditions of toughness, cheerfulness, sportsmanship, and self-dependence, due to their peninsularity, which sets them a little apart from Sydney City; but their feeling of local pride is enhanced by the fact that Balmain has among its residents a larger proportion of workmen skilled in shipbuilding, engineering, stevedoring, and waterfront trades generally, than could be found in any other suburb of the Harbour frontages.

Balmain has, or has had, everything, even a coal mine, which is more than any other suburb of Greater Sydney can boast; it has various light industries, too, including flourmilling and soapmaking; but shipbuilding and the engineering trades are, and have been for more than a hundred years, the mainstay and mainspring of Balmain's industrial life. In the 1830s, and earlier, there were shipyards and boatsheds on the shores of Balmain; but when iron and steel replaced timber in the hulls, and when steam engines replaced sails, in ocean-going vessels and in harbour ferries, then the skills of the engineer became allied with those of the shipwright, and the biggest shipyards in Australia (Mort's Dock and Cockatoo Island) were developed at Balmain and in its vicinity.

The men who were employed in those shipyards, and in railway locomotive building, and in the coal mine, and in the huge electric power-house, and on the wharves, or in manning tugs, barges, lighters, and other harbour vessels, all helped to create the tradition of Balmain's self-respect and craftsman pride. The man who has the skill to make something that is useful or necessary need never apologize for his existence or his way of life. He gives more than he gets, and can look anyone in the eye: that's how it is at Balmain. . . .

DOCTOR BALMAIN'S LAND GRANT

Of the eight naval surgeons (medical officers) who served in the First Fleet, only one, William Balmain, achieved the distinction of having his name perpetuated in a suburb. The Surgeon-General, John White, is commemorated at White Bay, within the suburb of Balmain; but the other six pioneer doctors of Australia—Worgan, Callam, Arndell, Considen, Altree, and Bowes—are commemorated not at all in place-names, unless perchance Arundel Street, Glebe, was named for Surgeon Thomas Arndell. The commemoration of Surgeon Balmain's name and fame was not intentional, but, rather, the result of a land deal that was somewhat irregular, and, at best, decidedly unusual.

Born in Perthshire, Scotland, in 1762, William Balmain was twenty-six years of age when he arrived in New South Wales in 1788 as Surgeon in the ship *Alexander*, the largest of the convict transports in the First Fleet. After serving as a medical officer of the civil establishment at Sydney for three years, he was appointed in 1791 as medical superintendent at Norfolk Island, and remained there for four years. He returned to Sydney in 1795, and served there for six years as Principal Surgeon (chief medical officer) of New South Wales, acting also as a magistrate.

Like other officers and officials of the military garrison and civil establishment, William Balmain was given large free grants of land, and also engaged in trade, especially in the sale of imported alcoholic spirits. These practices had developed to a scandalous extent only after Governor Phillip's departure in 1792.

Doctor Balmain was awarded free grants of 270 acres of farmland at Windsor (on the Hawkesbury River), and 425 acres at the Field of Mars (on the north side of Sydney Harbour, in what is now Ryde municipality). After his return to Sydney from Norfolk Island he engaged extensively in trading, especially in imports of rum and tea from India. This was during the term of office as Governor of Captain John Hunter, R.N., who was so friendly with Doctor Balmain, or so highly appreciative of his services, that on 26th April, 1800 he made an additional grant to him of 550 acres of land, comprising practically the whole of the peninsula on the western side of Cockle Bay.

173

That stretch of country, a low ridge of sandstone bushland, unsuitable for farm cultivation, had been by-passed by applicants for land grants during the first twelve years of settlement at Sydney. A rough foot-track led to it, branching to the northwards for two miles from the Parramatta Road at Petersham. The distance from Sydney to Balmain's land by that route was six miles; but by boat it was only a mile from Sydney Cove, or 500 yards from Miller's Point. The waterway would always be the best way there.

In the sequel it soon appeared that Surgeon Balmain had applied for and obtained that land grant, not in order to develop it as a farm, or as an out-of-town residence for himself, but to transfer its ownership to a merchant at Calcutta, John Gilchrist, in payment for a cargo of trade goods. In September 1800 Governor Hunter was succeeded in office by Governor King, who immediately issued an order prohibiting officials of the civil establishment from engaging in trade. It appears likely that Balmain had already arranged to pay Gilchrist for a cargo of trade goods by transferring to him, for a nominal sum, the title-deeds of the 550 acres of freehold land that he had been granted by Governor Hunter at Cockle Bay. After Governor King's decree against trading by officials, Gilchrist may have agreed to deliver the goods to Balmain's order in Britain.

It was, however, managed; the official records indicate that in July 1801 John Gilchrist bought 550 acres of land from William Balmain for five shillings. In the following month (August 1801), the doctor left Sydney and returned to Britain, where presumably the cargo from India awaited him. By a private agreement between himself and Gilchrist, this would be considered as payment in full for the land sale.

William Balmain died in London, aged only 41, in 1803. He was unmarried, but had two illegitimate children at Sydney—a son and a daughter—to whom he bequeathed his estates. They had no financial interest in the ultimate resale by Gilchrist of the land that continued to be known as "Balmain's Grant"—eventually to become the suburb of Balmain.

John Gilchrist settled in New South Wales as a merchant and shipowner. He decided, during the term of office of Governor Darling (1825-31), to develop his Balmain property for sub-division and resale. His first move in that direction was to improve the "Balmain Road," which branched from the Parramatta Road at Petersham. He extended that road through the middle of his property for the entire length of the peninsula to a boat-jetty across the water from Miller's Point, and named it—the intended main street of the suburb-to-be—"Darling Street," as could have been expected, and as it remains to this day.

That done, some residential blocks and cross-streets were surveyed, and the blocks were gradually sold off at prices that steadily increased. The first blocks were sold in 1836 at £56 an acre—that being the usual size of a suburban building block in those days when each householder had at least one cow and one horse. Eventually Gilchrist took a profit of more than £50,000 from developing the suburb; but, subdivided further into cheek-by-jowl residential and industrial lots, that same land is worth millions today. It is not unusual that the "unearned increment" of increasing land-values yields large profits to investors and speculators in land; but there could be no more striking example on the record than Surgeon Balmain's sale of 550 acres of land for five shillings, on a site that in the fullness of time would increase in money-value to incalculable millions of dollars in elastic currencies that would become useless for measuring comparisons. Yet there is a saying at Sydney that a man who is lucky or clever in business "has bought all Balmain for five bob and sold it for a quid." So lore lingers sometimes when its origins are forgotten.

THE SHIPBUILDERS OF BALMAIN

During the first thirty years of British settlement in New South Wales, many small ocean-going sailing-vessels were built at the shipyards in Sydney Cove; but from 1818 onwards it was realized that wooden vessels could more conveniently be built handy to the forests from which suitable timber for their hulls, decks, and spars could be cut and hauled out as required. Shipbuilding then declined at Sydney, but was developed extensively in "country shipyards" on the Hawkesbury River, the Hunter River and its tributaries, the "Northern Rivers" (to the northward of Newcastle-upon-Hunter), and on the South Coast (or Illawarra, southward of Sydney). There was also considerable shipbuilding in Van Diemen's Land (Tasmania), for the whaling and sealing industries.

The introduction of steam-engine paddlewheel propulsion, as auxiliary to the use of sails, in the 1830s, caused a revival of the industry at Sydney. The old shipyards at Sydney Cove were closed. New shipyards came into existence, at Balmain, and elsewhere in that vicinity, where the artisan skills of engineers and other metalworkers became allied with the skills of timberworkers in that new development of the shipwrights' craft.

The first steamer in Australian waters, the S.S. *Surprise*, was built at Sydney and launched in March 1831. After a few successful trips on the Parramatta River, she sailed and steamed to Hobart, and went into service there as a ferry on the Derwent River. Two months later, on May 1831, an auxiliary paddlewheel steamer, S.S. *Sophia Jane* (250 tons), built in England, arrived in Sydney under sail, and was put into service with sail and steam propulsion on the sixty-mile coastal run between Sydney and Newcastle. In October 1831 a "colonial steam packet," S.S. *William the Fourth,* was launched on the Williams River (a tributary of the Hunter) and entered the coastal trade between Sydney and Newcastle early in 1832. She was a handsome vessel of 300 tons, with a wooden hull, clipper bow, schooner-rigged on two masts, the twin paddlewheels and steam engine amidships—the typical design of steamers until screw propulsion was introduced in the 1850s, and sails were gradually discarded.

The early steamers used their engines and paddles only as

auxiliary to their sails, for making headway in calms or against adverse winds, or for steering courses without tacks in narrow waters, especially on entering or leaving harbours, and when proceeding to and from berths inside harbours. It was that manoeuvrability of steamers which made them specially suitable for use as ferries: a fact that was quickly appreciated at Sydney. Within twenty years, before the first steam-engined mail and passenger liner, S.S. *Chusan*, arrived in Sydney from England in 1852, there were already a dozen or more steamers operating to and from Sydney on coastal and "inter-colonial" services, and a rapidly increasing number of steam-ferries in operation on Sydney Harbour. Some of these steamers had been imported from Britain; others had engines, or engine components, that had been imported; a few, especially the ferries, were entirely Australian-made.

From the 1830s to the 1850s, shipyards established at Balmain, at Pyrmont, at Miller's Point, and at Cockatoo Island (off the western shore of Balmain) were concerned chiefly with building steamers, including ferries and coastal vessels, at first with wooden hulls, and later with iron, and then with steel hulls. Most of the workers in these shipyards lived in the then newly developed suburb of Balmain. The growth of population in all the suburbs along the shores of the Upper Harbour was stimulated by that development of Balmain, and even more so by the steam-ferry services which came increasingly into operation after the mid-1830s. For a hundred years thereafter, until electrified and motorized road and rail transport, and the Sydney Harbour Bridge, provided speedier transits between the Harbourside suburbs and the City, the steam-ferries on the grand waterway of the Harbour were essential to the life and growth of those suburbs, and so of the City and of the metropolis as a whole.

Historically, the introduction of steam propulsion in sea-going vessels marked the change of an era, at Sydney as elsewhere throughout the civilized world. That change was focused in Sydney Harbour at Balmain, where, in Thomas Chowne's shipyard on Johnston's Bay, many vessels, including steam-ferries, were built in the 1840s and 1850s. Corcoran's yard at Miller's Point, established in 1844, was taken over by John Cuthbert in the early 1850s, and some large vessels were built there until the yard closed in the 1870s.

Steamers with iron and steel hulls, with screw propulsion, of large size, and with the engines to drive them, were built for many years at the Pyrmont Shipyards (established in 1853), at Mort's Dock at Balmain (1854), and at Cockatoo Island (1857). It was this industrial activity, combined with flourmilling and other light industries, and the general development of mercantile wharfage for overseas and coastal shipping at Darling Harbour, Pyrmont, Glebe Island, and elsewhere in Cockle Bay, that was mainly responsible for the high population-density and "working-class" composition of those Western Suburbs; but a Sydney dockside district—such as Balmain, the Glebe, The Rocks, or Woolloomooloo—was never grim and dreary, like dockside districts in other countries. There were no "slums" in Sydney to be compared with those of London, Glasgow, Liverpool, or New York, as districts of despair.

The industrial wage-workers, living on the shores of Sydney Harbour, have always had access to the recreations of the "Aquatic Sports"—as they used to be called—of rowing, sailing, fishing, and sea-bathing, within walking distance of their homes; and facilities for other outdoor sports in parks and playing-fields amply provided. Those recreations, with the mild climate, bright sunshine, clean air, and plentiful food, have built the character of Australian wage-workers within a framework of cheerfulness and friendliness that left little scope for social and political resentments imported from Europe. The Australian wage worker is not a cringer. Anyone who doubts that statement should take a trip to Balmain.

No detailed study of the history of shipbuilding, or of the ferry services on Sydney Harbour, is available in print. Much that passes for historical study in Australia is based on the official *Historical Records* of the Convict Era, which ended in New South Wales in 1841. Those *Records* are chiefly Governors' despatches to the British Government in London, and other official papers, in which the problems of the administration, rather than the real life and work of the people, are chronicled. The history based on those *Records* is of the Governors and not of the governed; of tax-collectors rather than of taxpayers; of bureaucrats rather than of wealth-producers, of an attempt that failed to make a continent into a penitentiary, and freeborn people into slaves. It is a British-Imperial and not an Australian-national view of Australian history; but unfortunately that view has prevailed at Australian universities, where studies of Australian activities of basic importance, such as the history of shipbuilding, have been neglected. If ever that history is written, it will be found that the shipyards of Balmain, and the men who worked there, will be accorded a large meed of recognition.

BALMAIN AQUATIC SPORTS SEE ALSO PART II

The history of Aquatic Sports, especially of rowing and sailing, at Balmain, "would fill a book," but can be mentioned here only briefly, as a reminder that each part of Sydney Harbour has its wealth of local lore; but Balmain is second to none in its traditions of water sports, including professional boat racing and sculling, and centreboard sailing. The Balmain Regattas were in their heyday in the nineteenth century, but some of their aura remains today, in legends that do not die.

For forty years before steam-ferries were introduced, the passenger services on Sydney Harbour were provided chiefly by "watermen," who plied for hire in skiffs and small sailing boats; but, even after the steam-ferry routes had become well established, the watermen continued to carry paying passengers up and down the Harbour, across the Harbour and its arms, and to and from vessels at anchor, until the turn of the century, and some continued in operation until the 1920s. The service they provided was, in effect, a water-taxi service, though not so-called. (Their successors, in the modern era, are the numerous hirers of motor-launches, for pleasure-trips, fishing expeditions, or for following yacht races.)

The original Sydney watermen plied for hire in skiffs manned by one or two oarsmen, each using a pair of sculls. The skiffs were built of light timbers, and were long and narrow, the passengers being seated in the sternsheets and bows, the oarsmen amidships. Skiffs were frequently hired for long pulls, from Sydney Cove, to meet vessels anchored at Watson's Bay, a distance of five miles each way, or on various trips up the Harbour. There were also watermen with sailing dinghies of up to sixteen feet in length, plying for hire on the longer routes within the Harbour, and sometimes bringing farmers and farm produce to market from Parramatta and other places on the Harbour's upper reaches.

The Sydney watermen were highly skilled as boat-handlers. Many of them had served in whaling-vessels and on bay-whaling stations, and were experienced in handling whaleboats on the high seas; some had served, from time to time, as crewmen of the pilot boats at Sydney Heads. All by long practice had developed not only skill but also stamina as oarsmen. There was keen competition and rivalry among them, especially when several boats were rowing or sailing on the same course, to meet a newly arrived vessel from overseas, anchored at Watson's Bay, or in the stream, awaiting a berth.

From 1805 onwards, challenge races were held, for stakes and side wagers, not only among the Sydney watermen themselves, but between watermen and crews of ships in port. In 1818, Captain John Piper, collector of Customs, who had a smart crew of four watermen in his gig (each man pulling one oar) won a challenge match against the Captains' gigs of three merchant vessels then in port, for a stake of 200 guineas. The course of 3½ miles was from Bradley's Head to Sydney Cove. The time was fifteen minutes, with the tide.

In April 1827, a regatta was held at Sydney Cove, with rowing-races and sailing races for the crews of two visiting British warships, H.M.S. *Success* and H.M.S. *Rainbow*. Though this was a naval occasion, it attracted such a large crowd of spectators that, in the following year, on 26th January, 1828—the fortieth anniversary of the foundation of the settlement—a regatta was organized by a citizens' committee, with rowing and sailing races in several classes, on Harbour courses, from Farm Cove. Thereafter, regattas were held on Anniversary Day in 1830, 1831, 1832, 1834, 1835, 1837, and in every year since then, to the present time. The "Anniversary Day" Regatta—in recent years renamed the Australia Day Regatta—is the oldest regularly organized regatta in the world.

Aquatic sports boomed to such an extent that a newspaper report of the 1841 Regatta stated:

The Harbour presented a splendid spectacle. The steamers *Maitland, Kangaroo, Rapid,* and *Sophia Jane* plied about the Harbour crowded with passengers. Sailing vessels were present of all sizes, from 70 tons down to half a hundred-weight, whilst 10,000 persons viewed the spectacle from the Government Domain and Dawes Point. The flagship, [a steamer] *Australian*, was handsomely decked with flags.

That was the year when the British Imperial Convict System ended in New South Wales. So keen was the interest in aquatic sport that citizens' committees and clubs were formed to organize additional regattas annually at Double Bay, at Woolloomooloo, at Balmain, and at Lane Cove.

The first Balmain Regatta was held on 30th November, 1849, and continued to be held annually until 1914. It was chiefly at the Balmain Regattas, from the 1850s to the 1870s, that professional rowing races and sailing races were encouraged with such large cash prizes that eventually the world's professional sculling championship was won many times by Sydney Harbour watermen who had begun their racing careers at Balmain, or had gained their earliest big successes there.

Professional boat racing in Australia was developed chiefly in Sydney, where, for many years, especially during the Gold Rush decades, it was the principal "spectator sport" (and opportunity for betting). Before the many other forms of outdoor sport and recreation, so familiar a century later, had become established in popular favour, the challenge-matches, frequently rowed on Sydney Harbour by the professional watermen, attracted big crowds on the headlands overlooking the courses, and following the races in chartered steamers. Championship titles—of Sydney, of New South Wales, of Australia—with large stakes and side-bets, were challenged and lost or won amid tremendous public excitement, the competitors having the status of heroes, if only temporarily during their reigns of excellence, that would in later times be accorded to the paragons in other sports; but it would remain forever on record that the first Australian to be recognized as a World Champion in any kind of sport was the Sydney waterman, Ted Trickett, who, on 27th June, 1876, beat the English Champion, J. H. Sadler, in a sculling match on the Thames, London, over the traditional course, Putney to Mortlake, 4¼ miles, in 23 minutes 24 seconds.

Ted Trickett, who was born on the shores of the Parramatta River in 1850, was a "native son" who deserved the fame that came to him. He stood 6 ft 3½ ins tall and weighed 13 stone. When he returned to Sydney, on 9th November, 1876, after winning the World Championship, it was said that the entire population of the city lined the streets to give him a hero's welcome. The enthusiasm, a symbol of Australian national sentiment, was later to be similarly expressed in Test cricket matches.

Professional scullers who were popular heroes at Sydney from the 1850s to the 1870s included George Mulhall, Dick Green, John McGrath, William Hickey, Jim Punch, Mick Rush, and Elias Laycock. Most of the early championship races were organ- 179 ized by the Balmain Regatta Committee, on courses from Balmain round Pinchgut or Clark Island and return. Later, a course in smoother water on the Parramatta River was preferred. Between 1876 and 1914 there were forty-five contests for the World Professional Sculling Championship, of which Australians won thirty-two, either in challenges or in defence of their titles. The Australian winners of the title after Trickett were: Bill Beach, 1884; Peter Kemp, 1887; Harry Searle, 1887; John McLean, 1890; Jim Stanbury, 1891; George Towns, 1901.

Professional sculling matches were at their zenith of popularity in the 1880s. Thereafter, other sports gained public patronage; and amateur scullers and rowers, not competing for money prizes, gradually caused public interest in the professional sport to wane. Sailing races, in which large numbers of crewmen could participate, replaced rowing matches, especially on the lower reaches of the Harbour, where choppy water was unsuitable for the very light racing skiffs that were used after the 1860s.

At Balmain, the sport of sailing developed its special quality with the "eighteen footers." These were flat-bottom dinghies of "skimming dish" design, 18 feet long by nine foot beam, with retractible centreboards, and crews of up to fifteen men and boys serving as "live ballast." These boats were not eligible for registration with the Deep Keel yacht clubs, and consequently were barred from the yacht-club races. The owners of the "eighteen-footers" then formed their own club, the Sydney Flying Squadron, and held races on Saturdays and public holidays on a course from Long Nose Point, Balmain, round Clark Island or Shark Island and return. They carried an immense spread of sail, and there were frequent capsizes in gusty weather. As many as forty boats would start in a race, for cash prizemoney and wagers, the race being followed from Balmain by chartered ferry-steamers, crowded with spectators and bookmakers briskly betting on the results. These races were regarded as the most "spectacular" sailing races in the world; but in 1913, when twenty of twenty-one starters in a race capsized during a squall, regulations were made limiting the sail area. There are still many "eighteen-footers" sailing on Sydney Harbour, including some at Balmain, for the sheer joy of it.

Balmainers are renowned also for non-aquatic sports, such as Rugby League football, and cricket. The Balmain footballers wear jerseys of black-and-gold stripes, whence they are known as "the Tigers." A Sydney Harbour fish, the Banded Sea Perch, which has black and gold stripes, is known as "the Balmainer"; and the Sydney mud crawfish or flapjack, which has black and gold markings when cooked, is popularly and humorously called "the Balmain lobster."

MORT'S DOCK

One of the most enterprising and public-spirited capitalists in the history of Sydney was Thomas Sutcliffe Mort. He was born in Lancashire in 1816, and immigrated to Sydney, aged 22, in 1838, as a woolbuyer. In 1841 he became a foundation shareholder in the Hunter River Steam Navigation Company. In 1843 he became a woolbroker, and established the first regular wool-auctions held in Australia. That business prospered greatly, and in the 1850s he made extensive investments in mining, in railways, and in dairy farming.

When mail-steamers (with auxiliary sail) began arriving from Britain in Australia in 1852, there was no dry dock at Sydney large enough to accommodate them for the overhaul and bottom-painting that was considered advisable before they set out on the long return passage. T. S. Mort saw the opportunity and seized it. He bought ten acres of land on the foreshore of Waterview Bay, Balmain (at the north-western end of the Balmain Peninsula), and there, in 1854, employed a large gang of men in excavating, with pick and shovel, a dock 400 feet long and 50 feet wide, in the solid sandstone. Most of the men employed on this work were immigrants who had returned to Sydney after unsuccessfully "trying their luck" on the gold diggings beyond the Blue Mountains.

The first vessel to enter Mort's Dock for overhaul was S.S. *Hunter*, a coastal steamer, in 1855. Engineering workshops, and also shipbuilding slipways, were erected alongside the dock, and within a few years 700 men were regularly employed there, not only in shipbuilding but in general engineering, including the building of railway locomotives. Many coastal steamers were built there, and in 1872 the enterprise was formed into a public company, Mort's Dock and Engineering Co. Ltd, at that time the biggest industrial establishment in Australia.

T. S. Mort retained his interest in that company, but was also a shareholder in many other companies, notable among those being one which experimented in refrigeration of meat for export and pioneered that innovation, which developed a large export trade from Australia in frozen beef and mutton. He also owned an estate of 38,000 acres at Bodalla, near Moruya, on the South Coast, where he made large-scale experiments in dairying, especially cheesemaking. He died at Bodalla in 1878, aged 62.

Mort's Dock and Engineering Co. Ltd greatly expanded its activities. The original graving-dock was enlarged and in 1898 a floating dock was taken over from another company at Woolwich (Lane Cove River). Additional docks and slipways were built at Waterview Bay and at Johnston's Bay, Balmain. Many ships were built and repaired there; for a hundred years Mort's Dock was the pride of Balmain, and the principal source of local employment; but, during the 1939-45 war, the development of shipbuilding elsewhere, at government-owned shipyards, pushed the company into financial difficulties. When it went into liquidation in 1959, the large plants at Balmain and Woolwich were closed, and the fixed assets and waterfront properties were sold.

The skilled shipwrights and other artisans of Balmain had no difficulty in obtaining employment at other shipyards and engineering workshops in Sydney or elsewhere in Australia during the industrial boom in Australia in the 1960s; but the one-time far-famed Mort's Dock of Balmain quietly ceased to be, and passed into historical memory with scarcely more than the sighs of regret of men of the older generation who had known it in its heyday.

COAL UNDER THE HARBOUR

According to geologists, one of the biggest deposits of black (bituminous) coal in the world is in a saucer-shaped basin which has its rims near the surface of the ground on the north in the Hunter River valley, on the west at Lithgow in the Blue Mountains, on the south near Wollongong in the Illawarra; and its centre nearly 3,000 feet below Sydney. (Its eastern edge, beneath the Tasman Sea, is not known.) Though immense quantities of coal have been, and are still being, mined in the northern, western, and southern coalfields, those are only the easily accessible outcrops of the vast, continuous, seams of coal in that geologic basin, which has an area of perhaps 15,000 square miles, and its centre below Sydney.

This geological structure was announced as early as the year 1847 by the Reverend W. B. Clarke, one of the best of the pioneer geologists of Australia: it was confirmed subsequently by others, including Edgeworth David in the 1880s. The theory was tested in a practical way in 1893, when a diamond-drill bore at Cremorne, on the northern side of the Harbour, discovered a ten foot seam of coal at a depth of 2,917 feet.

Further test bores indicated that the coal-beds lay everywhere beneath Sydney and its suburbs and the Harbour. In 1903 the Sydney Harbour Collieries Co. Ltd was formed to work the seam. Balmain was chosen as the best site for a shaft, which was sunk to a depth of 2,784 feet. Coal was found plentifully, of good quality. The mine was worked for fourteen years, with drives far out beneath the bed of the Harbour; but operations ceased in 1917, because of technical problems caused by seepages of water, or financial problems caused by the competition of the bigger mining companies which were shipping coal to Sydney from the Hunter River fields.

At various times since 1917, there have been temporary mining operations in the workings at Balmain. It appears likely that, with mechanized methods of mining, the immense coal deposits that lie half a mile below the surface of Sydney may some day again be commercially exploited: in the meantime there are many people who do not realize that Sydney has a coal-mine, and that the "Sydney Basin" is one of the biggest and richest coalfields in the world, mined only on its outer edges. Nature has been so prodigal in endowing Australia with the riches of the soil that some large reserves can be left for the enrichment or sustenance of future generations and centuries.

SEE ALSO PART II LONG NOSE POINT

At the extreme north-western end of Balmain Peninsula is Snails Bay, so named for a reason that may be surmised, but is apparently not known, for it is lost in the mists of Australian antiquity. If molluscs of the genus *Aplysia*, known as "sea-snails," were found there in large numbers by early exploring parties—

as would be quite likely—the name, unofficially conferred, would have been intended for provisional identification; later it became traditional, and finally official.

The water in the centre of Snails Bay is from four to five fathoms deep, sufficient to float cargo vessels of medium size in which log timber is brought to Sydney from New Zealand, New Guinea, North Queensland, America, and Baltic countries. The Maritime Services Board has provided five "Dolphin berths" (mooring structures of buttressed piles) in Snails Bay, where logs are unloaded from freighters, either into lighters or directly into the water, to be towed to the various sawmills and timber-depots on the shores of the Upper Harbour.

Along the western side of Snail's Bay is a spit of land named Long Nose Point, 500 yards long and averaging 100 yards wide. It is traditionally so named, and well named, for it is one of the most important geographical features of the Upper Harbour. Between the tip of Long Nose Point and Mann's Point on the opposite shore, the main channel of the Harbour narrows to 300 yards, the smallest gut encountered from the Heads to that point, but beyond it the channel opens again to a broad sound, at the confluence of the two arms of the Upper Harbour named the Parramatta River and the Lane Cove River.

Long Nose Point was presumably formed originally as a spit or bar at the junction of the Parramatta River and the Lane Cove River, by the sand, silt, or other detritus brought down in floodwaters. In that sense it is a landmark in the Harbour, as by convention the two arms of the Harbour to the westward of it are named traditionally, and also on the charts of the Australian Navy Hydrographic Branch, as "rivers." From this it would appear that Long Nose Point is regarded as the western limit of the estuarine part of Sydney Harbour; but for purposes of navigation it is only another headland, though a prominent one: large vessels can and do proceed far beyond it.

Nevertheless, for all purposes of description and reference, the Main Harbour to the westward of Long Nose Point is tradition-ally called the Parramatta River, and that usage is therefore followed here. In the overall view of the topography of Sydney Harbour, Bradley's Head and Long Nose Point are the most significant headlands within the Harbour, in the sense that they are turning-points and therefore "breakwinds" and perfect barriers to oceanic seas and swell. There are sometimes slight seas whipped up within the Harbour by winds of gale force eastwards of Long Nose Point; but to the westward of that Point the waters are so fully landlocked that their smoothness could never be disturbed by more than local ripples. That fact was appreciated by the pioneer chartmakers, who considered that, on rounding Long Nose Point, they had left the Harbour and had entered the River.

COCKATOO ISLAND   SEE ALSO PART II

Beyond Long Nose Point, the western shore of Balmain Penin-sula trends to the south-westward for three miles to the head of

Iron Cove, a large indentation of the southern shore of the Parramatta River, separating Balmain from Drummoyne. In the offing, 400 yards from the shore of Balmain, and almost in the centre of the river which is here a deepwater sound a mile wide, is Cockatoo Island, with two graving-docks, a floating dock, and extensive shipyards and workshops. Owned by the Australian Federal Government, this is the biggest shipyard in Sydney Harbour. It is also the biggest island in Sydney Harbour.

In its natural state, Cockatoo Island—known to the Aborigines as "Biloela"—was a knoll of sandstone, forty acres in area, with a crown approximately thirty feet above sea-level, covered in shrubs and large red-gum trees, in which white cockatoos congregated, festooning the boughs of the trees like living blooms, or large burst pods of cotton. There they nested, and were safe to some extent from snakes, goannas, marsupial cats, and other tree-climbing enemies. The island, somewhat circular, had a ledge around its shore, like the brim of a hat. Two islets, which became known as Spectacle Island and Snapper Island, lie in the passage between Cockatoo Island and the mainland shore of Drummoyne Peninsula. All three islands are within the Parramatta River, off the entrance to Iron Cove.

Cockatoo Island remained uninhabited until the prison establishment on Goat Island was closed, and the prisoners removed, at the end of 1838 and early in 1839, to new quarters on the larger island up-river. At that time the only jail in Sydney for colonially convicted offenders was at the corner of George Street and Essex Street. A large new gaol was being built at Darlinghurst: it was completed in 1841.

Prisoners sent to Cockatoo Island were the "hard cases" awaiting transportation to Van Diemen's Land or to Norfolk Island. Governor Gipps (1838-46) had decided to use the labour of those convicts for building large grain stores on Cockatoo Island. These were to be pits, excavated "in the shape of bottles," twenty feet deep, in the solid sandstone on the crown of the island. Twenty of the "bottles" were excavated, and were in use as government grain stores for many years. The rubble was used as filling of a stone quay, where bagged wheat was unloaded from sailing-vessels bringing it from the Hawkesbury River, the Hunter River, and Van Diemen's Land.

In 1841, when the British Imperial Convict System ended in New South Wales, arrangements were made to transfer the penitentiary at Norfolk Island to the control of the Government of Van Diemen's Land. (This was done in 1844.) Governor Gipps then decided to constitute Cockatoo Island formally as a penal establishment of New South Wales. It was proclaimed as such in June 1841. The prisoners there were put to work building a strong stone-walled gaol for themselves on the island, and also in quarrying stone, which was lightered to Sydney Cove as filling for the reclamation of the Semi-Circular Quay.

The island remained in use as a prison for convicts sentenced to hard labour, who could not be employed (after the mid-1840s) on the roads or other publicly frequented places. In 1842,

William Westwood, known as Jackey-Jackey, an Imperial Convict who had turned bushranger, attempted to escape from the island by swimming, but was captured by the Water Police. In 1851, the prisoners were put to work excavating a large graving-dock on the eastern side of the island, to be used by naval vessels. Named the Fitzroy Dock, in honour of Sir Charles Fitzroy (Governor of New South Wales, 1846-55), it was first used as a naval dock in 1857, but it continued to be used also as a prison.

On 11th September, 1863, an Australian-born bushranger, Frederick Ward, known as Thunderbolt, who had been sentenced to life imprisonment for cattle stealing, swam to freedom from Cockatoo Island. Taking to the bush in north-western New South Wales, he lived there by robbery under arms for six years until he was shot dead by a police constable in May 1870.

In 1871, the prisoners were removed from Cockatoo Island, and the former prison buildings, surrounded by a high stone wall, on the crown of the island, were put to a new use as a "reformatory" for women prisoners and female juvenile delinquents.

In 1884, work began on the excavation (but not with convict labour) of a second and larger dry dock at Cockatoo Island, on the western side. Completed in 1890, it was named the Sutherland Dock, in honour of the Minister for Public Works in New South Wales at that time. Both docks at Cockatoo Island were used by British warships on the Australian station, but it was not until 1908 that a shipbuilding yard and workshops were installed, and the female reformatory closed. The island, which had then become solely a defence establishment, was handed over to the Australian Federal Government in 1913, and was used as a naval dockyard and shipyard throughout the 1914-18 war, when four destroyers and two light cruisers were built there. That achievement, in conjunction with the establishing of steelworks at Newcastle-upon-Hunter in 1915, was an indication of Australian industrial maturity. In 1923 and 1924, two cargo vessels of 12,500 tons, the *Ferndale* and the *Fordsdale*, owned by the Australian Commonwealth Government, were completed and launched there.

In 1933, following the Economic Depression when work had been brought almost to a standstill in the shipyard, Cockatoo Island and its installations were leased to a company which became a subsidiary of the English shipbuilding firm, Vickers Limited. The Australian Federal Government pays the leasing company a "management fee," based on turnover. General shipbuilding and engineering work is done, with naval priority.

In the 1930s, four sloops, eight corvettes, two frigates, and four destroyers were built at Cockatoo Island for the Australian Navy. During the 1939-45 war there were 3,600 men engaged on naval shipbuilding and repair work at the Cockatoo Island docks and workshops, where also merchant vessels were converted to use as auxiliary cruisers, troop transports, and hospital ships. A floating dock was added to the facilities for ship-handling.

Since 1945, much of the naval work at Sydney has been transferred to the large new graving-dock and workshops at Garden Island; but the facilities at Cockatoo Island have been kept in working order. In 1965, the motor vessel *Empress of Australia*, 9,850 tons, entirely built at Cockatoo Island, was completed and placed in service as a passenger and vehicular "ferry" on the Sydney-Hobart route. She is designed to carry passengers and their motor-cars, principally for the Tasmanian "tourist" trade. Owned by the Australian National Line, she operates from a terminal in Waterview Bay, Balmain (also known as Mort's Bay), near the disused Mort's Dock.

Spectacle Island, which is approximately 300 yards to the westward of Cockatoo Island, is a Naval Armament Supply Depot, which has been used for that purpose since 1884.

Snapper Island, which lies at the mouth of Iron Cove, southward of Cockatoo Island and of Spectacle Island, is an islet used as a training depot for Sea Cadets. There are some relics of Australian naval historical interest in its drill hall, which serves to that extent partly as a naval museum.

The names of Spectacle Island and Snapper Island are traditional: anyone is entitled to guess who named them, when, and why.

SEE ALSO PART II   IRON COVE

The inlet or gulf, a mile and a half long and 400 yards wide, separating Balmain from Drummoyne, was evidently given its name after 1839, when convicts from Cockatoo Island were at times sent to work in irons (fetters) on its shores; but that is a surmise. Who knows?

The inlet is spanned near its entrance by the Iron Cove Bridge, originally erected in 1884 to connect the suburbs of Balmain and Drummoyne, and also to provide a route across the main Harbour via the Gladesville Bridge from Drummoyne (on the "Five Bridges" route). The old Iron Cove Bridge, of wrought-iron lattice girders, was replaced by a steel and concrete construction in the 1950s.

Near the head of Iron Cove, on the Balmain Shore, are the large grounds and group of buildings of the Callan Park and Broughton Hall Mental Hospitals. The Callan Park Hospital, formerly a mansion named Garryowen, was acquired by the Government of New South Wales in 1878, for use as "An Asylum for the Insane," and as such is the biggest institution of its kind at Sydney, having accommodation for nearly 2,000 patients. The neighbouring Broughton Hall, opened in 1921, is for voluntary patients suffering from nervous or mental breakdown. There are three other large Mental Hospitals on the upper reaches of Sydney Harbour (at Gladesville, Rydalmere, and Parramatta), besides the huge "Repatriation" Hospital at Concord, and several large boarding-schools.

The hospitals, schools, and other institutions on the shores of the Upper Harbour were placed conveniently "out of town" for large ground space, yet originally were within easy access of the city by ferry-steamers. Industry has encroached on those placid reaches of the Upper Harbour in the Western Suburbs, where now factories, oil-depots, gasworks, and other industrial installations range along the Harbour front, in alternation with the beautiful, park-like grounds of the large public institutions and the streets of suburban residences, many of fine architecture, classical or modern, and nearly all with gardens.

Beyond Balmain, the Upper Harbour stretches to Parramatta with a life of its own. The tempo of living is calmer, it seems, in the smoother waters there, so completely landlocked that breezes can scarcely ripple its surface; yet there, too, much has happened, and is still happening; and the place-names speak of men and events that have passed into history, or sometimes faded into oblivion.

IO

ASHFIELD

AT THE HEAD OF IRON COVE, THE MUNICIPALITY OF ASHFIELD HAS A harbour frontage of only a quarter of a mile, in the suburb of Haberfield. With that narrow corridor of access (squeezed between the boundaries of the municipalities of Leichhardt and Drummoyne), Ashfield has a limited, but undeniable, claim to be rated as a waterfront municipality. Its councillors have taken that responsibility seriously. They have channelled two creeks, drained and filled a swamp, built a sea-wall, an esplanade, a marine drive, and a picnic park in their short stretch of the Harbour frontage, and so they have co-operated with the neighbouring municipalities in beautifying the shores of Iron Cove (southward of the Iron Cove Bridge), to provide the residents of the industrial and densely populated surrounding and adjacent suburbs with a due share in Sydney Harbour's lavish gifts to all who dwell within cooee of its shores: its sea-side air and the recreations of swimming, boating, fishing, lazing in the sun, and picnic-making "to see the sea," beloved of the amphibious folk Australian shore-dwellers have become.

Although Sydney is a world-city and a "megalopolis," it has also the permanent qualities of a sea-side resort or fishing village. Even here, seven miles in from the ocean entrance to the Harbour, and a good two miles westward of the Harbour Bridge, the waters of Iron Cove sparkle and ripple, clear and clean, translucently blue or green in a basin of golden sandstone, a mile and a half long and 500 yards wide, with soundings of from eight to eighteen feet. Those waters, replenished by ample tides, are protected by laws and regulations and civic pride from pollution by industrial effluents and sewerage and from the discharge of oil, dirty water, and garbage from ships. There are parks with trees, grass-swards, and flower beds, reserved for public recreation along the shores, enclosures for sea-bathing (Iron Cove has an Olympic Pool), boat-sheds and boat-moorings, sailing clubs and rowing clubs, and every other indication, here as elsewhere in many places around the shores of the Harbour and its arms, that the Harbour and the people of Sydney belong to each other.

What other great seaport city in the world has its harbourwater so clean, and kept so clean, and foreshore parks, freely accessible to everybody, within easy walking distance of its most densely inhabited industrial suburbs, and facilities for aquatic sports at every season of the year? The cleanliness and beauty of the strangely named Iron Cove are worthy of remark, not because that Cove is exceptional in those qualities in Sydney Harbour, but because it is typical. There are sixty foreshore public parks, some at the heads of coves, some on headlands, all around the Harbour. Iron Cove is one of the biggest coves in Sydney Harbour: it is used, not for trade and commerce, but for pleasure.

Being almost completely landlocked, it makes a stretch of sheltered and usually smooth water, perfect for boat racing practice. At its head is the boat-shed of the Haberfield Rowing Club; on the Balmain shore is the boat-shed of the Leichhardt Rowing Club; and on the Drummoyne shore the boat-shed of the Drummoyne Rowing Club. These are three of the seven clubs of the New South Wales Rowing Association that have boat-sheds on the shores of Sydney Harbour. In addition, nine boys' schools maintain boat-sheds on the Harbour shores. Practically all the boat-sheds of the rowing clubs, senior and junior, are on the Upper Harbour, where, in narrower and more sheltered waters, the courses are smoother, and the commercial traffic much less, than in the wider reaches of the Lower Harbour.

On the Parramatta River and Lane Cove River, and in their bays, almost any afternoon, especially in the summer months, eights, fours, pairs, and single scullers are to be seen practising for regattas, interstate matches, Olympic Games or other international contests, or for the schools' Head-of-the-River races. The rhythmical flashing of oars in the westering sun—a sight familiar in all the river-side State capital cities of Australia—evokes special historical memories at Sydney, where the oarsmen of the amateur rowing clubs are the heirs of the great traditions of Sydney's watermen of bygone years, who were the champions of the world. And now the amateurs of this clean-limbed sport are building their own traditions, and training like galley-slaves, not for the prizes, not for renown, but for the zest of the sport itself.

Rowing and yachting on Sydney Harbour, engaging thousands of ardent and healthy recreation-seekers with their expertly built craft and gear ranging over the many courses that the Harbour's twenty-two square miles of water offers, make a composite scope of aquatic sport, sustained throughout the year, unequalled in extent on any other waterway in the world—sport for sport's sake.

Rowing in racing boats requires such a perfect co-ordination of crew effort, such rhythmical harmony of mind and body, and such discipline for a purpose, that of all sports it is the one most entitled to be considered, when it is practised for its own sake, an art, and not for its usefulness or for any other motive. In every reach of Sydney's Upper Harbour, then, that art is to be seen demonstrated, daily, by crews of strong young Australians, driving their racing shells or skiffs skimming over the water, by muscle-power and will-power, with the zeal that only art-for-art's-sake, or rowing-for-rowing's-sake, can attain.

This is part of the lore of Sydney Harbour that cannot be known to anyone who thinks of the Harbour only in its broader and more breeze-ruffled lower reaches where the big ships come and go; but, in these narrower and quieter waters of the Upper Harbour, and along their shores, the art of rowing is followed keenly by the many who know that in a well-trained racing eight the poetry of motion has rhythm.

DRUMMOYNE

As the Drummoyne Peninsula has a shoreline of eight miles, with harbour frontages on its eastern, northern, and western sides, its suburbs are caressed by salubrious sea-side airs, and blessed by harbour vistas at the end of almost every street. The municipality of Drummoyne includes the suburbs of Drummoyne, Chiswick, Abbotsford, and Five Dock. Incorporated in 1890, it then had a total population of 1,000, but today has more than 30,000. There are pleasant residential vicinities along the waterfront, interspersed with industrial enclaves including timber-mills, a box-factory, a wire-works, a chocolate-factory, and a very large rubber-factory that employs 1600 workers. Most of the residents are thus locally employed, but some travel by road daily to and from the City, a distance of four miles by the short-cut that crosses Iron Cove Bridge, Glebe Island Bridge, and Pyrmont Bridge. As motorized congestion on the roads became more baffling to traffic in the mid-1960s, these travellers waited hopefully for the restoration of ferry services that would take them by the waterway to the Quay, as their fathers and grand-fathers travelled, in peace and ease.

It is a privilege of pioneers to bestow place-names. In the year 1806, Governor King made a free grant of 750 acres of land to Surgeon John Harris, an Irishman who had arrived in Sydney in 1790 as medical officer to the troops of the British garrison, and had acted also as a police magistrate and collector of shipping-dues. Harris, who had been granted land also at Parramatta (Harris Park) and at Sydney (Ultimo), named his new property "Five Dock Farm." It was the site of the present-day suburbs of Five Dock, Abbotsford, and Drummoyne.

Nobody now knows what was Harris's reason for choosing the apparently ungrammatical name of Five Dock, which has remained in use, a solecism in nomenclature, ever since. There were no docks for shipping in Sydney Harbour at that time: only open anchorages and wharf berths. Doctor Harris had a strong sense of humour, as he had shown in naming his Sydney town estate "Ultimo." Probably he had some private joke in naming his farm "Five Dock," perhaps referring to the *dock* in which prisoners stood in the court to be tried before him as a magistrate; or to the weed well known in Ireland and Britain as *dock*, which has some medicinal uses; or to the stump of a horse's tail; but none of these surmises explains how a noun in the singular came to be used with a plural numeral. As good a guess as any is that "Five Dock" was an Aborigine's way of saying "Five Dogs."

Surgeon Harris did little to develop Five Dock Farm as a farm, for the soil was not suitable for farming, but he did something to develop his property as real estate, by opening communications to it. We may surmise that it was by his influence that a cart-track was cleared through the bush, branching from the Parramatta Road six miles west of Sydney, leading through Five Dock Farm to a punt-ferry with a landing stage at the north-western promontory of the Five Dock Peninsula.

That branch road, two miles long, became known as the Great

North Road, and continues to be so named today, long after its original meaning has become obsolete. In the 1820s, it was a significant link in the development of communications between Sydney Town and the hinterland. The punt-ferry, operated by winch and cable, crossed the Parramatta River where the stream narrowed to a gut 250 yards wide, between what is now known as Abbotsford Point on the southern side and Bedlam Point on the northern side.

Bedlam Point was so named when a "lunatic asylum" was established there in the 1820s, on the site of the present-day Gladesville Mental Hospital. The punt-ferry gave access not only to the lunatic asylum, but also to the farm settlement beyond, known as the Field of Mars (Australia's first experiment in "soldier-settlement" on the land), later to be named Ryde. This was the first crossing of Sydney Harbour by a ferry that could transport a cart or a riding-horse. The distance from Sydney to Bedlam Point, by way of the Parramatta Road, the Great North Road, and the ferry, was eight miles, as compared with five miles by the waterway from Sydney Cove. Though farm produce was taken to market in schooners and boats and barges, and in watermen's skiffs, from the Field of Mars, and even from as far upstream as Parramatta, there were occasions on which settlers on the northern side of the Harbour wished to drive carts to Sydney or to ride there, or to the outlying settlements on the southern side of the Harbour. It was for them that the Bedlam Point ferry and the Great North Road provided the first answer to the problem of cross-Harbour transport for road traffic; and though that route was roundabout, as compared with the direct route of the Sydney Harbour Bridge in modern times, it opened the way between Sydney and the Great North for wheeled transport, at a time when the Great South Road to Goulburn and beyond, and the Great West Road across the Blue Mountains, were also being extended, like tentacles of the Octopus of Sydney, to embrace, maybe, or to crush in a too-loving grip, the vast regions of the Inland.

Surgeon Harris sold his Five Dock Farm in 1836, after he had held it as a speculation for thirty years. He was then eighty-two years of age. He died two years later, in 1838, childless, and one of the wealthiest men in the Colony. Part of Harris's land was bought by William Wright, a shipowner who had made a fortune from sealing and whaling. He was presumably connected with the engineering firm of Wright & Co., of Birmingham, England, who in 1852 obtained a large contract for supplying rolling stock to the Sydney Railway Company, which was then building the railroad from Sydney to Parramatta—opened to traffic in 1855.

In 1854, William Wright built a mansion on a headland which became known as Wright's Point, a mile and a half to the eastward of the Bedlam Point ferry crossing. He named his estate Drummoyne, a Gaelic word meaning a flat-topped ridge. In that same year he had obtained the contract for building the railroad in the Hunter Valley, from Newcastle to East Maitland, and had begun construction there.

On Wright's Point, in front of his Drummoyne mansion, William Wright built a private landing stage of stone, with carved stone balustrades and stone steps. It remains today, in a good state of preservation, as one of the most striking and pleasing ornamental landmarks along the Parramatta River shore.

When Wright's estate was subdivided in the 1880s, the name of Drummoyne was applied to the whole vicinity; and it was adopted as the name of the municipality in 1890; but the old name of Five Dock was retained for the suburb that developed on the western side of Wright's estate, and, like other names of legendary origin, is accepted in official and general use.

The Drummoyne Sailing Club, near Wright's Point, marks almost the western limit of organized yachting on Sydney Harbour. On days when fresh breezes penetrate even these land-locked recesses of the Upper Harbour, the stretch of deep and open water in the sound at the confluence of the Lane Cove River and the Parramatta River—extending for two miles from Wright's Point eastwards to Long Nose Point—is as pretty a sailing course as the heart of a yachtsman could desire; but, more often than not, the breezes here are fitful. Oarsmen prefer smooth water for speed; yachtsmen like it choppy.

SEE ALSO
PART II THE GLADESVILLE BRIDGE

In the year 1881, work began on a low-level steel bridge with a swing span, crossing the Parramatta River from Five Dock Point to Gladesville. This bridge was completed and opened for traffic in 1884. The construction was carried through by the Department of Public Works, in which the Minister was the Hon. Frank Wright, a brother of William Wright, the owner of Drummoyne. At the same time, work was proceeding on the Iron Cove Bridge, which was opened also in 1884, and on the Fig Tree Bridge, across the Lane Cove River, which was opened in 1885.

The Gladesville Bridge, as the bridge across the Parramatta River, was called, was the first road bridge built across the main stream of Sydney Harbour. It was five miles from the City of Sydney to the North Shore by the route via Pyrmont Bridge, Glebe Island Bridge, Iron Cove Bridge, and the Gladesville Bridge, three miles shorter than the old route via the Parramatta Road and the Great North Road that led to the Bedlam Point ferry. The Fig Tree Bridge across the Lane Cove River was a short cut to the North Shore suburbs from Gladesville.

When the Gladesville Bridge was opened, the Bedlam Point ferry service was discontinued. The "Five Bridges" route between the City of Sydney and the Northern Suburbs remained the shortest way of crossing the Harbour by bridges for forty-seven years thereafter, until the Sydney Harbour Bridge was opened; but even then the "Five Bridges" route continued to be used, as motor traffic increased on the roads, and as population increased in the western suburbs on the northern side of the Harbour.

The Gladesville Bridge was the vital link, for it crossed the main Harbour, whereas the other four bridges crossed arms of the Harbour as short cuts that saved time and distance, but were not essential. With seven spans, supported on concrete piles, the Gladesville Bridge was 1,000 ft long from bank to bank, the water in the channel there being thirty feet deep.

To enable ferries, cargo-steamers, and cargo-carrying sailing vessels (in tow) to navigate in the upper reaches of the Parramatta River, the Gladesville Bridge had a swing span that provided openings of 60 feet on one side and 57 feet on the other side of the central massive stanchion. This bridge remained in operation for eighty years, as one of the minor wonders of Sydney Harbour, but much cursed both by road-users and by masters of vessels on the waterway, for the inevitable delays.

As traffic increased on both the road and on the waterway, the need for a new, high-level, bridge there became more urgent. In the Harbour reaches upstream from the Gladesville Bridge there were many industries along the shores, depending on water-borne transportation, especially of coal and timber, but also of other materials conveyed in steamers that could pass through the swing-span opening of the bridge, but only by delaying the increasing procession of motor-vehicles using the "Five Bridges" route which had been planned for horse-drawn traffic.

The need to "save time" being a modern obsession, without regard to what is done with the time saved, the decision was taken to build a high-level bridge to replace the old swing-span low-level bridge. Work began early in 1960. When the new Gladesville Bridge was opened, on 2nd October, 1964, by Her Royal Highness Princess Marina (then on a visit to Australia), it was the biggest single-span concrete-arch bridge in the world. Sydney Harbour had thus achieved a double claim to world fame in the arch bridges that strode across it.

The new Gladesville Bridge crosses the Parramatta River 400 yards downstream from the old Gladesville Bridge, and four miles upstream from the Sydney Harbour Bridge. Its span is 1,000 feet from bank to bank. The underside of the arch soars to 134 ft above high-tide level, with a gentle curve that allows headroom of 120 feet clear for a width of 200 feet in the middle. That is more than enough clearance for most modern ocean-going vessels, and certainly for those that would be likely to require passage to and from the reaches of the Parramatta River to the westward of this bridge, where the depth of water, though ample for cargo vessels of medium size, such as colliers, for three miles beyond the bridge, would scarcely be enough, in some parts of the channel, for larger vessels, with a draught of more than 18 ft, which would perhaps require a headroom of 120 ft to pass beneath the arch; yet who knows what future industrial developments of the upper reaches of the Harbour, or contingencies of war or peace, or modified designs of ships restoring high mastage for signalling or other technical reasons, might require as a sufficient clearance for a high-level bridge across Sydney Harbour?

The basic consideration in all bridge-building across the Harbour and its arms is that a bridge should not be an obstruction to navigation. In the windjammer era, when masts were often 180 ft tall, low-level bridges with one moveable span permitted transits; but nowadays that system is considered by impatient motorists to cause too much delay to road traffic. The problem of spanning Sydney Harbour with high-level bridges has been partly solved by the building of the two biggest single-arch bridges in the world. There will almost certainly be more of them, if the population of Sydney and suburbs increases, as is expected, to four million by the year 2000, with the Harbour as a gigantic serrated fissure between that urban and suburban sprawl.

The sandstone bedrock of Sydney provides the chief reason why colossal single-span arch bridges are feasible and preferred for Harbour crossings. The immense weight of an arch is borne by concrete "thrust-blocks" embedded in excavations in the sandstone on each side of the stretch of water to be spanned. The sandstone supporting the thrust-blocks provides a large additional measure of stability, and so of safety, in the foundations on which the arch rests. Any failure in the foundations would be calamitous in a concrete-arch bridge of such an immense size; but the experience gained in the Sydney Harbour Bridge and the Gladesville Bridge has fully confirmed the careful calculations of the engineers who knew that single-arch bridges would be more suitable than any other kind, and chose that design accordingly. There may be very few other harbours or rivers in the world where the geological and other conditions are as convenient for the construction of colossal single-arch concrete bridges as in the bed and on the banks of Sydney Harbour.

The cost of the Gladesville Bridge was £4½ million. Its design and building, under the control of the Department of Main Roads of New South Wales, was of technical interest to engineers throughout the world, and of spectacular interest to the people of Sydney—especially to residents of the suburbs on the shores of the Upper Harbour—who watched the work take shape.

The arch was built in four "ribs" of concrete hollow-box units, tied together by "diaphragms" of solid concrete. To support each rib until the arch was joined and could support itself, a scaffolding or "falsework" of tubular steel was erected on steel piles driven into the bed of the river, then removed after the arch was joined. The concrete box-units, each weighing fifty tons, were cast and pre-stressed at a depot three miles downstream, brought by lighters to the bridge site, and hoisted into position by a gigantic floating crane.

The total weight of concrete in the bridge is 78,000 tons. The deck, 84 feet wide, has six lanes of vehicular traffic, and footpaths six feet wide at each side. The deck is carried on concrete beams, resting on concrete headstocks supported by slender but very strong concrete columns which rise gracefully above the arch. The footpaths have hand-rails of steel rods with an elegant filigree effect. The simplicity and nice proportions of the design of the bridge make it a work of art as well as a triumph of engineering. This is in conformity with a statement by the Commissioner for Main Roads, Mr John Shaw, to the effect that road-builders should be "mindful of aesthetics," and that the character of a highway should be of "ordered beauty".

Archaeologists at some remotely future period may describe

the present era as the Age of Concrete, rather than as the Age of Steel, as is often supposed; for steel will corrode and disappear, but concrete may endure as long as the materials of earth of which it is composed. If, as is possible, the Gladesville Bridge is to be only the first of several huge concrete-arch bridges across Sydney Harbour, the time may come when the Harbour will be increasingly world-renowned, not only for its waterways, but for the bridges spanning them.

CHISWICK AND FIVE DOCK BAY

Proceeding westwards along the south bank of the Parramatta River, past the site of the old Gladesville Bridge at Five Dock Point, within Drummoyne Municipality, we see Five Dock Bay, an inlet extending three-quarters of a mile to the southward and averaging 400 yds wide, with waters shelving from 20 ft to 6 ft in the middle, and muddy marges which were originally mangrove swamps. The inlets along this southern shore, being in less ridgy country than the coves along the northern shore, are in general shallower than the main channel of the Parramatta River, and were fringed originally by tidal swamps which nurtured mangroves, some of which remain today. A geological "warp line" gives the country to the southward of the Parramatta River a quality different from that of the sandstone ridges: there are level stretches, with clays and shales, which become eroded and deposit mud, not sand, in those large shallow inlets.

On the western side of Five Dock Bay is the suburb which, during the reign of Queen Victoria, was given the name of "Chiswick," evidently in colonial imitation of the name of the village of Chiswick, on the River Thames, west of London. At about the same time, other names of vicinities on the banks of the Thames were officially applied to districts on the banks of the Parramatta River, among them "Greenwich," "Woolwich," "Henley," "Putney," and "Mortlake"; but whether this was sentimental nostalgia of exiles, imperialistic propaganda, or an example of the Australian sense of humour—after Ted Trickett won the World's Sculling Championship on the Thames—has not been ascertained.

Some restraint was exercised in not renaming the Parramatta River the Thames, or the New Thames; but it was Governor Phillip who had insisted on applying the Aboriginal name to that stream, or at least to the town that he founded at its head of navigation. With that and two other exceptions (Cabarita and Yaralla), all the place-names along the shores of the Upper Harbour, like those of the Lower Harbour (exceptions, Kirribilli Bennelong, Woolloomooloo, Woollahra), have English-language or British Islands reference, and there is one American reference (Concord) and three French-Canadian references (to be noticed presently).

For whatever reason it was so named, Chiswick on the Parramatta River has very little resemblance to Chiswick on the Thames River: the attempt to create "a new Britannia in another world," by nomenclature alone, was not enough.

On the western side of Five Dock Bay, near Blackwall Point (so named from Blackwall on the Thames in London), is a large   195 box-factory and a timber-wharf and timber-bond, where logs and flitches of imported timber are unloaded from overseas vessels and distributed by lighters or by rafting to sawmills along the shores, or taken from the wharf by timber-jinkers elsewhere.

ABBOTSFORD

Westward of Chiswick is Abbotsford Bay and the suburb of Abbotsford, so named from a village near Melrose Abbey, on the Tweed River in Southern Scotland, where Sir Walter Scott was living while he wrote the *Waverley Novels*. He became heavily in debt there, through the failure of a firm in which he held a non-limited share, and ruined his health writing novels to pay off that debt. He died at Abbotsford in 1832. Ninety years later, at the Sydney Harbourside suburb of Abbotsford, Henry Lawson, one of the best-known Australian poets and story-writers, but an habitual drunkard, rented a cottage in the Great North Road, lived there alone for the last eight months of his life, and died there, aged 55, on 2nd September, 1922. The Henry Lawson Park and a Henry Lawson Avenue, named in Abbotsford in 1938 by the Drummoyne Municipal Council, are reminders of Lawson's ruined life and lonely end. He died while he was writing an article cryptically entitled *Deadly in Earnest and Casually Australian,* but his manuscript was unfinished when he walked out of his cottage and casually died beneath the stars, in a suburban back yard, with his boots on.

Abbotsford Bay is the belly of a curve in the Parramatta River rather than an estuarine inlet of the southern shore. It has a width of 1,000 yards between its enclosing promontories, but bulges only 400 yards in its wide curve along the river's shore. At the head of the bay is a large and old-established factory in which wire and wire-netting are manufactured, and adjacent to it a chocolate-factory: these are the two principal industries of Abbotsford and Five Dock.

SEARLE'S MONUMENT

Opposite Abbotsford Bay, on the northern shore of the river, is a promontory named Henley, adjacent to the park-like grounds of the Gladesville Asylum. Off the tip of that promontory, 100 yards offshore, are two almost submerged rocks, at the edge of the deepwater channel. Such rocks, a possible danger to navigation, being extremely rare in Sydney Harbour, were a well-known landmark in the Parramatta River, and were named "the Brothers."

In the heyday of professional sculling, challenge races and national and world championship races were held over a course of three miles on the Parramatta River, from Shepherd's Point (near present-day Ryde Bridge) to the Brothers. Despite the many headlands and indentations on both sides of the river, a perfectly straight course could be steered there for the entire distance. The first recorded challenge match on that course, between Dick Green and Jim Candlish, for £400 stakes, was rowed in January 1858, and won by Dick Green. Thereafter, the course was frequently used, not only by the professional scullers, but also (after 1874) by amateur eight-oar racing crews in inter-club and intercolonial challenges; and then (after 1893) for the Schools' Annual Head-of-the-River eight-oar races, and (after 1896) for the Australian Amateur Sculling Championship.

In 1888, a phenomenal sculler, Henry Ernest Searle, aged twenty-two, from the Clarence River, arrived in Sydney. "The Clarence Comet" (as he was called) had previously rowed only in watermen's skiffs. He quickly became used to outriggers and a sliding seat, and in June of that year broke all records pre-viously set on the Parramatta River course (including world championship times) by winning a challenge match against Wulf, one of the best of the professionals. In the following months he had easy wins over Stanbury, Neilson, and Hughes, in rapid succession, each for a £100 stake, and in September he beat Peter Kemp, holder of the World Championship, for a stake of £500.

In 1889 Searle accepted a challenge from the American Champion, W. J. O'Connor, to defend his World Championship title in a match on the Thames in England, over the classic Putney to Mortlake course (4¼ miles). The race was rowed there on 9th September, 1889 for a stake of £1,000. Intense interest was taken in this match, and large sums were wagered on it by sportsmen in Australia, England, and America. When the news was flashed to Sydney by cable that Searle had won, prepara-tions were made to give him a hero's welcome home. It was not only his rowing prowess that had made him so popular, but his cheerful personality and modest demeanour too.

On board a passenger liner returning home to Australia, Searle became seriously ill from enteric fever, caused by an infection, presumably, at a port of call. When the ship berthed at Mel-bourne, he was rushed to hospital, but died there, of peritonitis, on 10th December, 1889, aged twenty-three years. This news reached Sydney with the effect of a national calamity. It was estimated that a quarter of a million people thronged the streets to see the coffin conveyed from the Sydney Railway Station (at Redfern) to be embarked in the Clarence River steamer.

Searle was buried on Esk Island in the Clarence River. By public subscription a memorial to him was erected, in the form of a broken marble column, on the Brothers Rocks in the Parra-matta River. There it stands, at the finishing-point of the course on which he first made his great renown, now known as the "Ryde Bridge to Searle's Monument" course, 3 miles 176 yards. All the reaches of the Parramatta River on that course—or in general between the Ryde and Gladesville Bridges—are rich in historical memories of professional and amateur boat racing. Throughout the greater part of the nineteenth century, and certainly from the 1830s to the 1880s, rowing was the most popular sport at Sydney, attracting far greater crowds of spectators than football, cricket, or horse-racing; and, though professional row-ing, with its big stakes and its widespread wagering on results, has nowadays gone almost entirely out of fashion, the sport con-tinues to be maintained at a high level of public interest by the amateur clubs, including the Schools clubs, and by the contests for Australian representation at Olympic Games.

THE SYDNEY ROWING CLUB

A hundred yards westwards of the old Bedlam Point punt-wharf at Abbotsford Point, where the shore trends to the southward at the entrance to Hen and Chicken Bay, is the boatshed of the Sydney Rowing Club, the oldest and biggest of the amateur rowing clubs in New South Wales. Within sight of it, 500 yards distant on the same shore, is the Newington College boatshed. On the opposite side of the Parramatta River, at Gladesville, is the boatshed of the Sydney Grammar School, and on the opposite side of Hen and Chicken Bay the boatshed of the King's School, Parramatta. In this vicinity also are the boatbuilding sheds of George Towns & Sons at Gladesville, and of Sanders Brothers at Cabarita Point. That reach of the river, and the large sheltered inlet of Hen and Chicken Bay, may therefore be described as the habitat of a cluster of oarsmen and their racing boats, more closely congregated here than in any other reach of Sydney Harbour and its arms.

Although there had been "gentlemen's races" (i.e., for competitors who were not professional watermen) in the Anniversary Regattas and at other aquatic carnivals from 1832 onwards, the gentlemen competed for prizemoney, stakes, and side-bets, and therefore would have been disqualified as amateurs under definitions that were adopted in later years. On 9th March, 1859 the first strictly amateur boat club at Sydney, the Australian Subscription Rowing Club, was formed with its shed at Woolloomooloo Bay. A week later, at the St Patrick's Day regatta at Balmain, this club conducted an amateur sculling race (in skiffs with fixed seats and thole-pins), which was won by a young Sydney businessman, Q. L. Deloitte.

In the following year, 1860, a sculling race under strictly amateur rules was included in the Anniversary Regatta. Thereafter several amateur rowing clubs were formed. On 7th March, 1870, the Sydney Rowing Club was formed, as a successor to the Australian Subscription Rowing Club, Deloitte being the first President. At the Anniversary Regatta in 1873, four-oar races for amateurs were introduced. The winning crew consisted of W. Deloitte, Q. L. Deloitte, H. H. Bligh, and E. Chisholm, who defeated a crew of four brothers, William, Henry, Fred, and Grantley Fitzhardinge, with a fifth brother, M. A. H. Fitzhardinge, as cox.

The Deloittes and the Fitzhardinges remained for many years prominent in amateur rowing, as also in the business and professional life of Sydney; but many other young men of wealthy or otherwise influential families entered with zest into rowing as a sport, and also into yacht racing, on an amateur basis. The first intercolonial amateur boat race (in four-oar gigs) was rowed on the Parramatta River course in February 1863, between crews representing New South Wales and Victoria. The first inter-university boat race in Australia (four-oared) was rowed on the Parramatta River course in December 1870, between Sydney and Melbourne University crews.

In 1874 the Sydney Rowing Club imported the first eight-oared racing boat to Sydney, and in that same year opened its boatshed at Abbotsford. The boat was rowed from the Club's boatshed at Woolloomooloo Bay to the new boatshed at Abbotsford by a crew which included M. A. H. Fitzhardinge and Q. L. Deloitte. Other "eights" were soon imported or built locally. The first intercolonial eight-oared race (between Victoria and New South Wales) was rowed on the Yarra in 1878, and thereafter in alternate years on the Parramatta River, until other colonies (later States) joined, and the venue rotated among the States.

The first Australian inter-university eight-oared race (between Melbourne, Adelaide, and Sydney Universities) was rowed in 1888 on the Yarra, and then regularly by rotation at Port Adelaide, and on the Parramatta River, and on the Yarra.

The Sydney Schools Annual Regatta was held on the Parramatta River from 1893 to 1935. It included the "head-of-the-river" eight-oared boat race, which attracted immense crowds of spectators along the shores of the course, and in chartered ferries and launches lining the course, to such an extent that it was one of the major aquatic festivals and social occasions of the year at Sydney. The course was from Ryde Bridge to Searle's monument, but, as more schools entered until there were nine boats in the race, it was decided in 1936 to transfer the regatta to the Nepean River, near Penrith, 34 miles westward of Sydney, where there is a wide straight stretch of water for a three-mile course, with ample leg-room for spectators and picnic parties along the banks.

Though the race is held on the Nepean, the schools continue to do their training on the Parramatta River. The adult Sydney clubs of the New South Wales Rowing Association also do most of their training there, and row important matches on the Parramatta River course. The President of the New South Wales Rowing Association from 1902 to 1929 was Q. L. Deloitte, who had seventy years of close association with the sport, as oarsman, coach, and administrator.

II

CONCORD

THE LORE OF THE WATERFRONT MUNICIPALITIES OF CONCORD AND Auburn, in the western reaches of the Harbour on its southern shore, as of Ryde opposite them on the northern shore, and of the City of Parramatta at the head of the Harbour, is not as well known to the general public as it used to be before the steam-ferry service from Sydney to Parramatta was discontinued in 1928.

The Parramatta ferry terminal was at Redbank, 2½ miles by road from the centre of Parramatta City, the journey there from the ferry-wharf at Redbank being by a tramway; but between Redbank and Sydney Cove the ferry called at many wharves, on both sides of the river, giving the residents of those western suburbs, and of Parramatta, the pleasures of travelling along a waterway in which vistas of interest and scenic beauty opened at every bend, curve, or turn in the course. The ferry service was discontinued because, in itself, it was unprofitable in competition with government-owned railroad and tram services, and with the increasing use of the roads by privately owned motor-vehicles; but it was a public utility which, incidentally, had a lively attraction for visitors to Sydney who knew that the best way to see the full extent of the world-famed Harbour was by ferry trips.

There seemed a possibility, in the mid-1960s, that, after being in abeyance for nearly forty years, the Parramatta River ferry service might be restored, with "hydrofoil" vessels or other speedy motor-launches, for travellers who wished to get to a destination quickly, but perhaps also that it would be restored with steamers or other sedate vessels having decks open to the sky and the air, for travellers who consider that the pleasures of a voyage are not only in the destination. It was urged that in forty years the populations of the western municipalities and of Parramatta City had increased so greatly that a restoration of ferry services would do something to relieve congestion on the roads and railways; that the decision to close the Parramatta River ferry service had been taken at the onset of the Economic Depression of that period, which had passed; and that a public transport utility is not expected to be profitable on every route, but that profitable routes should subsidize the less profitable or unprofitable routes.

Above all, it was urged, the "tourist trade" in the 1960s had at last become recognized as an important source of Sydney's prosperity. The slogan was "See Sydney and *live!*" but what visitors chiefly remembered of Sydney was the Harbour—the superb waterway and its ferries. How could the authorities be so obtuse as to disregard the scenic beauties and interest of the

Upper Harbour? Was the recommendation of the accountants of 1928 to remain as a ukase unalterable for ever, or could it be reviewed after forty years?

There was another argument, with some humour in it, that Parramatta City has nowadays expanded so far and so fast that it includes Sydney among its suburbs! The time was when it used to be said of a confirmed city-dweller at Sydney that he had never been further out into the bush than Parramatta; but now it is claimed that Parramatta and Sydney have merged, or at least have met at Concord and Auburn on the southern shore, and at Ryde on the northern shore. This is thinking in terms of roads and railways rather than of the waterway. As measured along the highway, Concord is half-way between Sydney and Parramatta, and would be similarly placed in measurements of the waterway; but, since the ferry service was discontinued, the "merging" of the two cities at Concord depends on landlubbers' ideas of transport rather than on those of seafarers.

It is possible to go by road or rail from Sydney to Parramatta, 14 miles, along the southern shore of the Harbour all the way, without even one glimpse of the water! This is because the Great Western Highway (the original Parramatta Road) keeps a mile or more to the southward of the limits of the shoreline, to avoid swamps, originally at the head of the big bays, which have since been drained and reclaimed and built on. The people who live in those harbour-side suburbs are well aware of the shores so near to their homes; but the stranger who whizzes past on wheels might never know that fish and people are swimming, boats are sailing and being rowed, and ships of the mercantile marine are lying at berths, or proceeding on their lawful occasions, on the broad and beautiful waterway that is hidden, at only a little distance, from his sight.

HEN AND CHICKEN BAY

No one knows, nowadays, how Hen and Chicken Bay got its name. It is surmised that Captain Hunter's chart-making boat party in February 1788 gave it that name as an interim identification, because two sandstone boulders, prominent on shore near its entrance, had a fancied resemblance to the shape of a hen and a chicken. This would be by analogy with the naming of the Sow and Pigs Reef in the Lower Harbour. Either Hunter, or one of his officers, had a lively imagination; but, if Hunter kept logs of his surveying expeditions, those documents have been lost. It was not his prerogative to bestow place-names. Though his chart of the Harbour showed the outline of the shores, and soundings of the channel and in many of the bays, it had very few names on it when it was sent to England, and those names, evidently, had been bestowed, or approved, by Governor Phillip.

The bay that became known as Hen and Chicken Bay had no name on Hunter's chart as published. We are left then with a surmise that, like Long Nose Point, it was named for identification by a landmark; but the other surmise, that Hunter and his party saw an emu and her chick on the shore there, and were so greatly surprised at such an apparition that they named the bay in her honour, is also feasible, and at least a pretty piece of lore-making.

Though Captain Hunter supervised the survey, some of the detailed information was collected by boat parties under the charge of Lieutenant Bradley, and by other parties under Lieutenant Ball. On some occasions, Governor Phillip himself went with boat parties to inspect the Harbour, and made landings at various places, exploring on foot. It is not known which of these parties discovered and named Hen and Chicken Bay. Captain Hunter in person went "up the Harbour" on 30th January, 1788, but we do not know how far he proceeded, or what coves he then explored. He probably made a running survey, and subsequently sent his officers to fill in the details.

Hen and Chicken Bay is one of the three big estuarine inlets on the southern shore of the Upper Harbour. (The other two are Iron Cove and Homebush Bay.) All these were originally swamps at the mouths of small freshwater streams draining northwards into the Harbour from a peneplain in which shales and clays in places overlaid sandstone beds. The swamps were scoured by rainwater floods and by tides to form large, shallow basins with muddy marges, in which mangroves grew. Such bays were described, in nautical terminology, as "flats."

Hen and Chicken Bay is a mile and a half long from north to south, and averages half a mile wide from east to west, but on its western shore there are three bights that increase the width of water there to three-quarters of a mile. The depth of the water is between 6 feet and 12 feet at low water, and shallower at the edges. It gives sufficient floatage for barges and lighters which can lie alongside the jetties at several large factories on the western shore; but on the eastern side, inshore, is a mud flat too shallow for barges, and fringed with mangroves.

Being completely landlocked, the bay, like Iron Cove, is a favourite practising course for the crews of the rowing clubs in their racing eights, fours, pairs, sculls, and beginners' skiffs. The eastern shore of Hen and Chicken Bay is in the municipality of Drummoyne; the industrialized western shore is in the municipality of Concord. The boundary between the two municipalities is at the head of the bay.

The municipality of Concord has a lengthy shoreline, indented by many bays, side by side and separated by promontories that are not bluff headlands, but low and flat ridges. In a large sense the municipality is a peninsula, bounded on the east by Hen and Chicken Bay, on the north by the Parramatta River, and on the west by Homebush Bay; but on this shoreline (of approximately eight miles) there are bays within bays, and harbours within the Harbour, with snug anchorages and berths in profusion. The southern boundary of the municipality is the Great Western Highway, or Parramatta Road, which heads Hen and Chicken Bay and Homebush Bay with a good half mile of clearance of the original mangrove swamps that have now been substantially drained and reclaimed.

At Strathfield, midway between Sydney and Parramatta, the Main Northern Trunk Line railroad diverges from the Main Western Trunk Line, to run northward through Concord and cross the Harbour by the Ryde Railway Bridge. Likewise, the Concord Road to the north branches from the Great Western Highway at Strathfield, and crosses by the Ryde Road Bridge.

The municipality of Concord thus has many facilities of transportation by sea, by rail, and by road, and for this reason it has developed into one of the most highly industrialized of all the municipalities on Sydney Harbour's shore.

THE ORIGINS OF CONCORD

When Governor Phillip established a settlement at Parramatta in November 1788, he expected that its communication with Sydney would be by the waterway. It was three years before a rough foot-track was opened, skirting the southern shore of the Harbour, to connect the two settlements. That track became known as the Parramatta Road. The distance, fourteen miles, being too great to be covered conveniently in one day by parties of convicts on foot, escorted by soldiers, a log stockade was built, half-way along the track, to serve as an overnight guardhouse and staging depot.

That stockade was at a place named The Long Bottom—the word "bottom" there having its old English meaning of low-lying land or swamp, applied to the drainage basin at the head of Hen and Chicken Bay, in the vicinity of present-day Strathfield. An area of 936 acres was reserved, in the surroundings of the stockade, as a government farm, but no sustained effort was made to cultivate it.

When Governor Phillip left Sydney in December 1792, to return to England, his successor in charge of the administration of the Colony was Major Francis Grose, who was the commanding officer of the military garrison. Two months later, in February 1793, the first free settlers (not convicts, troops, or civil servants) to arrive in Australia as migrants landed at Sydney from the ship *Bellona*. These were five men (one of them with a wife and four children) who had been farm labourers in England. They brought with them instructions from the British Government that they were to be given grants of land.

Lieutenant-Governor Grose gave them their grants near the Long Bottom stockade, in a stretch of country (between present-day Strathfield and Bankstown) which became known as Liberty Plains. Some grants of land had previously been made by Governor Phillip to ex-convicts, ex-sailors, and ex-marines, but the grants made at Liberty Plains were the first made to immigrants who had arrived as free men, in civilian status. Soon afterwards, Major Grose began making land grants also to military officers and officials of the government service, assigning convict servants to them as unpaid labourers to clear and cultivate.

In accordance with this policy, Major Grose, on Christmas Eve, 1793, signed ten land grants, averaging 25 acres each. Six of these grants were to non-commissioned officers of the New

203

South Wales Corps, and four others to free settlers. According to the narrative of David Collins, it was Major Grose who, when conferring these grants, gave the district the name of Concord. As Grose had served as a junior officer in the British forces during the American War of Independence in 1776, he had presumably some pleasant memory of the town of Concord in Massachusetts, which caused him to confer its name on that district half-way between Sydney and Parramatta. (There are five other places in the U.S.A. named Concord, the name having been used by the Quakers to mean "brotherly love.")

David Collins stated that the land grants made by Major Grose "extended inland from the water's side, within two miles of the district named Liberty Plains." The grants were located along the shore of Homebush Bay, on the western side of the present-day municipality of Concord. The settlers thus had access by both water and land to Parramatta and to Sydney, and they would have easy boat-communication across the river to soldier-settlements established there at the Field of Mars and the "Eastern Hills" (of Parramatta) in present-day Ryde municipality.

Some Australian historians, over-emphasizing the Convict System, have neglected the "success-stories" of the pioneer free settlers at Liberty Plains, Concord, the Field of Mars, and elsewhere near Sydney and Parramatta; but it was those free settlers, rather than the "government men," who chiefly developed the spirit of enterprise and of self-reliance that became characteristic of pioneering in Australia. Even though some of the free settlers were ex-convicts, their stories are more typical than those of the incorrigibles who were "colonially reconvicted" and banished to Norfolk Island or elsewhere, far from Sydney.

In 1797 Governor Hunter granted 50 acres of land at Concord to Isaac Nichols, an ex-convict who had served his term of seven years' transportation for a petty offence. On that land (near Major's Bay), Nichols established an excellent orchard of citrus and stone fruits. He increased his holding to 100 acres by purchasing adjoining properties. A man of energy and ability, he left overseers in charge of his Concord farm, and built a schooner, the *Governor Hunter*, in which he traded along the coast and to Norfolk Island. He also acquired property in Sydney, and, in 1809, was appointed Australia's first postmaster. He died in 1819. His estate at Concord was sold by his heirs in 1840 to Thomas Walker, who built "Yaralla" mansion on part of it.

THE CANADIAN EXILES

In 1837, there were rebellions against Britain's rule in Upper Canada (Ontario) and Lower Canada (Quebec). The rebels in Upper Canada were mainly of British descent, and in Lower Canada of French descent. The rebellions were crushed by British military forces under command of Sir George Arthur, a former Governor of Van Diemen's Land. A large number of prisoners were taken. Of these, 29 were executed. A special commissioner sent from Britain, Lord Durham, sentenced 149 of the rebels to be transported for life to the Australian colonies. They became known as the Canadian Exiles. Those who were of British descent (including some citizens of the U.S.A. who had been caught helping the rebels) were sent to Van Diemen's Land. The 58 French-Canadian *patriotes* were sent to Sydney, where they arrived on 25th February, 1840.

The arrival of such a large number of political prisoners was an embarrassment to the Governor of New South Wales, Sir George Gipps, at a time when the British Government, under the pressures of public opinion, had decided to discontinue sending convicts to New South Wales. To deal with this difficult situation, Gipps segregated the Canadians under military guard in the Long Bottom Stockade, at Hen and Chicken Bay. Treated as though they were prisoners of war, rather than as criminals, they were required to work at stone-quarrying, but had a certain amount of liberty to wander along the shore of Hen and Chicken Bay, where the three bights on the western shore became known unofficially (and later officially) as Canada Bay, Exile Bay, and France Bay, in commemoration of one of the most remarkable incidents in the history of freedom in Australia.

After two years the Exiles were given tickets-of-leave, which meant that they could work for wages in private employment, and two years later, in 1844, most of them received free pardons and returned to Canada. Of the original fifty-eight French-Canadian Exiles who were sent to Sydney, two died, one married an Australian girl and settled at Dapto, in the Illawarra district, and the other fifty-five returned to Canada. Those of British descent who were sent to Van Diemen's Land were more harshly treated. Twelve of them died, but the others were eventually pardoned, and most of them returned to Canada.

The granting of what was called "Responsible Self-Government" to the Australian Colonies in the 1850s was a direct result of the Canadian Rebellion of 1838. The British Commissioner to Canada Lord Durham, recommended in 1839 that responsible self-government should be granted to a Union of Upper and Lower Canada. This was done, and the same principle was later applied in Australia, New Zealand, and South Africa, thus establishing the idea of a British Empire based on willing co-operation rather than on coercion.

In that sense it was the Canadian Exiles who should chiefly have been given the credit for establishing Parliamentary Democracy in Australia. The rebellion at Eureka hastened a process which they had begun in Canada; and it was those Canadians that gave the name of Concord a special meaning for Australians who seek what is significant, and discard what is irrelevant or merely capricious, in the foundations of history in Australia.

ALONG THE CONCORD SHORE

A cruise along the shores of the Concord Peninsula, beginning at Canada Bay, reveals an alternation of parks and playing-fields, boatsheds and swimming-baths, with factories of many kinds, and important public works and institutions, indicating the wide variety of interests, in work and in recreation, developed in this part of the Upper Harbour, twelve miles from the Heads: a long way from the ocean, it seems; yet the salt tides ebb and flow, and ocean-going ships, though not those of the largest size, berth at wharves and jetties, even here; and strings of barges and lighters, in tow, frequently pass up and down the main river-channel, and into and out of the bays, with plenty of sea-room in this traffic for the pleasure-craft, powered launches, some sailing yachts, and the racing boats of the rowing clubs: the life of the Harbour, here as elsewhere, that is ever-changing, never stilled.

At Canada Bay is a large and old-established tannery, and a copper and aluminium foundry. On the promontory next to it is a public park with a sea-bathing enclosure, municipally owned, admission free. Next, on the shore of Exile Bay, is a large timber yard and sawmill, and a packing-factory of tea-and-coffee merchants; then a public golf course, on land that was formerly mangrove swamp, now drained, filled in, and so "reclaimed" (in the sense in which that word is used by civil engineers) by the Concord Municipal Council. Such reclamations, winning dry land from swamps or tidal flats, have been made, to a greater or less extent, on the foreshores at the head of almost every cove and bay in Sydney Harbour, to provide parks behind sea-walls which halt the tides, as King Cnut did in the English fens, nearly a thousand years ago.

In most of the coves of Sydney Harbour, on the northern shores and in the Lower Harbour, the reclamations have been limited to a few acres of tidal marsh in which reeds grew, at the outlet of small freshwater streams that drained from closed sandstone vales; but in the big and shallow bays along the south-western shore of the Upper Harbour, where mangrove forests grew in the mud-flats, more extensive reclamations have been possible; and there the sea has been, and will continue to be, pushed back, and many acres of dry land won from its grip.

Beyond the golf course, on the shore of Exile Bay, is a paint-factory, and then, on the headland, a picnic park; then, in France Bay, a chemical factory, and a factory that makes tinned cans. At the head of France Bay there are streets of pleasant suburban residences, and the boatshed of the King's School, Parramatta; beyond it, in large grounds, another and very big paint-factory. Most of the factories along this shore have their own jetties.

CABARITA

The suburb of Concord on the north-western shore of Hen and Chicken Bay is named Cabarita, an Aboriginal word fortuitously preserved here, though its meaning is unknown (as may be said of most of the world's place-names). There are some reasons for believing that the names of Cabarita and Yaralla were officially preserved at Concord by Major T. L. Mitchell, who was Surveyor-General of New South Wales from 1828 until his death in 1855. It was his stated policy to preserve Aboriginal place-names, even though as an explorer he did not always follow that policy.

Another theory is that the name of Cabarita was put on the map by a suggestion from the Australian-born poet, Henry Kendall, who was a clerk in the Surveyor-General's office at Sydney from 1863 to 1866. This idea is supported by the fact that a bay on the western side of Cabarita is named Kendall Bay; but it is possible that the bay was named for the poet's uncle, Captain Joseph Kendall, who was a whaling-master.

Cabarita Point projects into the main channel of the Parramatta River, on the western side of the entrance to Hen and Chicken Bay. It is a landmark in the navigation of the river, with a jetty and a (disused) ferry-wharf at its tip, a well-designed public park and public swimming-baths, and a boat-building shed and a "marina" near by. These amenities make Cabarita Park a favourite picnic ground; and on many occasions, for more than a hundred years, big crowds have gathered there to watch boat races: it is as good a point of vantage as any on the classic Parramatta River course.

An obelisk in Cabarita Park, erected in 1938, commemorates the prowess of William Beach, who, as the monument's inscription correctly states, was "the undefeated champion sculler of the world." Born in 1850, Bill Beach learnt to row on Lake Illawarra, where he was a fisherman. When he was thirty years of age, he came to Sydney as a "dark horse" and won an all-comers' skiff race from Woolloomooloo Bay, round Pinchgut and return, on a course of 2½ miles. (This was in fixed-seat skiffs.)

In 1880, a Canadian, Ted Hanlan, beat the Australian holder of the world's championship, Ted Trickett, in a match on the Thames. Hanlan was challenged by another Australian, Elias Laycock, in 1881, and won again, on the Thames. In 1882, Hanlan beat Trickett for the second time on the Thames. In 1884, Hanlan came to Australia, looking for matches. He beat Laycock on the Nepean River course. In April of that year, Bill Beach came up to Sydney again from Dapto, and beat Ted Trickett in a challenge match on the Parramatta River course, both men being thirty-four years old.

This victory gave Beach the right to challenge Hanlan for the World's Championship. The race was rowed on the Parramatta River course on 16th August, 1884. It was estimated that 100,000 people assembled on the headlands along the course, to watch the race, which, amidst great excitement, was won by Beach, after Hanlan had taken a lead of two lengths at the end of the first mile.

In the following year Beach won a return match against Hanlan, again on the Parramatta River course. A press report stated that there were "gala scenes" when Beach won, "every pier and headland being black with people, and multitudes crowding into every available boat and steamer on the river."

In that same year (1885), Bill Beach defended his title against two Australian challengers, T. Clifford and N. Matterson, winning easily. He then went to England in 1886, and, within three weeks, defeated five of the world's best oarsmen in matches on the Thames. He returned to Australia, and, in 1887, aged thirty-seven years, beat Hanlan in their third match, this time on the Nepean.

Beach then announced his retirement, and, as a formality, forfeited to a challenge by another Australian, Peter Kemp, who beat Hanlan twice on the Parramatta course in 1888, and then was beaten by H. E. Searle.

Retired to his home at Dapto, on Lake Illawarra, Bill Beach, undefeated champion sculler of the world, resumed his occupation as a fisherman, and lived to the age of 85 years. The monument at Cabarita was erected by subscription of his "friends and admirers" (as the inscription states), fifty-four years after his first great win against Hanlan. In the modern age, interest in professional sculling has waned; but in their heyday, the Australian champions made not only their own names, but the name of the Parramatta River, known to sportsmen throughout the world.

Another memorial in Cabarita Park, not of such special local interest as the monument to Bill Beach, but of some political historic interest, is an ornate pavilion which, on the initiative of the Concord Municipal Council, was removed in 1951 from its original position in Centennial Park, Randwick, and re-erected at Cabarita. In that pavilion, on 1st January, 1901—the first day of the twentieth century—the federation of the Australian Colonies under the British Crown was officially proclaimed by the first Governor-General, the Earl of Hopetoun, the representative of Queen Victoria. It was one of the last important events of Queen Victoria's reign. She died three weeks later.

It is fitting that Australia's Declaration of Dependence (on Britain) should be commemorated at Concord, where the Canadian Exiles were held as prisoners in a concentration camp sixty years previously. The political constitution of the Australian federation, and the freedoms that it allows (under the Crown) were a direct result of concessions won in Canada, at the beginning of Queen Victoria's reign, in 1838. So the wheel had gone full circle; and in politics one thing leads to another.

SEE ALSO PART II   MORTLAKE

The northern shore of Concord, extending along the Parramatta River, is indented by a series of inlets separated by promontories. The four biggest inlets are, in sequence from east to west, Kendall Bay, Major's Bay, Yaralla Bay, and Bray's Bay. The promontory between Kendall Bay and Major's Bay is named Mortlake. Its frontage on the river extends in a crescent curve for 1,000 yards between Breakfast Point and Mortlake Point. On this shore, near Breakfast Point, are the coal-unloading jetties of the Australian Gas Light Company, one of the biggest coal-gas companies in the world: its works, with five huge gas-holders, and many other buildings housing the retorts and other treatment-plant, occupy a site of 100 acres on Mortlake Peninsula, making a landmark visible from afar.

Breakfast Point was one of the few names marked on Captain Hunter's chart of the Harbour. It was named on 5th February,

1788 by Captain Hunter and Lieutenant Bradley who, engaged in the survey of the Upper Harbour with a boat party, after camping overnight at Cockatoo Island (which they named Dawes Island) got away to an early start and landed to cook their breakfast at a convenient point on the southern shore. Seeing some natives on the opposite shore, the explorers "made signs to them to come over, and waved green boughs." Seven of the natives, in two canoes, crossed the river, left their spears in the canoes, landed, and accepted presents of beads from the trespassers on their terrain.

On 15th February, Governor Phillip, "with three boats manned and armed," and taking Lieutenant Bradley with him as guide, went on a tour of inspection of the Upper Harbour and "stopped at a neck of land to breakfast," presumably the same place where Hunter and Bradley had breakfasted ten days previously.

The Australian Gas Light Company, which opened its first gas-works at Darling Harbour, in 1841, acquired sixty acres of land at Breakfast Point in the early 1880s, and began gas-making there, to supply the western and southern suburbs, on 23rd May, 1886. The installations at Mortlake (it has not been ascertained when or by whom that name was conferred) were steadily increased in scope, but the Darling Harbour works were not closed until 1922, when the Company's entire gas-making operations were brought together at Mortlake.

In all the huge Sydney metropolitan area there are only two Gas Companies, dividing the territory between the Australian Gas Light Company's supply from Mortlake, and the North Shore Gas Company's works at Waverton, North Sydney.

The Australian Gas Light Company supplies gas to 350,000 customers in an area of 300 square miles, including all the districts on the southern side of the Harbour from the South Head to Parramatta and beyond, westward to the town of St Mary's, and some districts in north-western parts of the metropolis, on the north side of the Upper Harbour. The total length of its gas-mains (pipes of four inches diameter and up to 12 inches) is 3,500 miles. In addition, there are 3,300 miles of "service pipe" laid from the mains to the customers' meters.

The Company uses 450,000 tons of coal a year. This is brought to Sydney from Felton Bank colliery at Maitland, in the Hunter Valley, and loaded at Hexham (up river in the port of Newcastle-upon-Hunter) into a fleet of three colliers, each of which makes, on an average, two voyages per week from Hexham to Mortlake, returning empty (i.e., in water-ballast).

The colliers plying on the route between Newcastle and Sydney are known as "Sixty Milers," it being sixty nautical miles from Sydney Heads to the Nobby's Light at the entrance to the port of Newcastle; although, as Hexham and Mortlake are both up-river wharfages, the distance between those two points is 87 miles. Of the three colliers in service on that route, the S.S. *Felton Bank* and S.S. *Mortlake Bank*, each of 1,371 registered tonnage, were built in Britain in 1924; the M.V. *Hexham Bank*, 1,616 tons, was built in Brisbane in 1953.

These are three of the fleet of fifteen colliers owned by various shipping companies that ply regularly between Newcastle and Sydney, bringing a million and a half tons of coal a year to destinations in Sydney Harbour. On an average, five colliers leave Sydney Harbour every day of the working week, including Saturdays, and five enter it. The Masters and Mates' of the "Sixty Milers" hold Pilotage Exemption Certificates for the ports of Sydney and Newcastle, and in practice they navigate mostly by landmarks along the coast, having no need of sextant and compass. Though the colliers are designed for use rather than beauty, they add much to the life and movement of the Harbour; at almost any hours of the day a "Sixty Miler" is in sight, proceeding up-harbour or clearing out: they are almost as typical of the Harbour-scene as are the ferries. Their crews, like those of the much bigger freighters that ply with iron ore and coal on the Australian interstate trade, are an important component of the Australian Merchant Navy. The crews of coasters are ocean-going seamen, who need as much skill in their work as any others, and have much more experience at docking and undocking than is accumulated in many years by the crews of ocean-crossing vessels. Who will sing the Song of the Sixty Milers, that yet remains to be sung?

YARALLA

The district on the northern side of the Parramatta River, opposite Mortlake, is named Putney. Far away on the other side of the world, the distance between Putney and Mortlake on the Thames is four and a quarter miles, but here the two points are only a quarter of a mile apart. A vehicular punt-ferry crosses the Parramatta River there, by means of a wire cable and steam winch. This is the only vehicular punt remaining on Sydney Harbour crossings. It was established by the Main Roads Department in 1926, to provide a supplementary route to and from the "Great North" which has always beckoned across the Harbour.

On the western side of Mortlake is a bay with two arms, Major's Bay and Yaralla Bay, separated by a peninsula on which stands, in beautiful grounds, the mansion named Yaralla, now one of a group of three large hospitals adjacent to one another, on 306 acres of harbour frontage land that was formerly the estate of Thomas Walker, philanthropist, who died in 1886, and of his daughter and heiress, Eadith Walker, who died in 1937. The father and the daughter were two of the most splendidly generous public benefactors in Australia's history.

Born at Leith, Scotland, in 1804, Thomas Walker immigrated to Sydney at the age of eighteen, to join a firm of merchants in which his uncle was the senior partner. That business prospered, and eventually Thomas Walker became one of the principals. In the 1840s and 1850s, he invested largely and wisely in landed properties, in Melbourne and Sydney, and also in pastoral stations and ships. He accumulated a fortune, and was for many years President of the Bank of New South Wales.

One of his investments was to purchase the large block of

waterfront land at Concord, partly from the estate of Isaac Nichols (in 1840). There the mansion, Yaralla, was built in the 1860s. It was, as it remains today, one of the finest buildings on the shores of Sydney Harbour. Ten miles from Sydney by the Parramatta Road and the Concord Road, and eight miles by the waterway, Yaralla was frequently the setting for dinner-parties and balls attended by the most select of Sydney's leaders of fashion and society; but Thomas Walker did not consider that the enjoyment of wealth depends on a display of it: he made frequent large donations, anonymously, to charitable institutions, and also appointed agents to distribute his largesse to poor and deserving families, widows and orphans.

He died in September 1886, aged eighty-two, leaving his mansion and most of his fortune to his daughter, Eadith, then aged twenty-one, but his will also established a trust fund of £100,000 to build and maintain a convalescent home to be known as the Thomas Walker Convalescent Hospital. The building was duly erected at the tip of a promontory stretching into the Parramatta River on the western side of Yaralla Bay, in ample grounds which had been part of the Yaralla Estate. This hospital in its first twenty years received 18,000 patients (non-paying) and continues its good work to the present day.

Eadith Walker's fortune, managed under her father's will by trustees, continued to accumulate. She lived at Yaralla, and upheld the traditions of hospitality there; but she remained unmarried, and, as time went by, she followed her father's example and made frequent and large gifts to charitable institutions, and personal gifts to the needy or distressed.

In 1917, during the Great European War, when she was fifty-two years of age, she made part of the grounds of Yaralla available as a "camp" for returned soldiers suffering from pulmonary tuberculosis, and also made large gifts to the Red Cross and Comforts Funds. On part of the grounds of Yaralla, in 1918, the Australian Federal Government established a hospital for returned soldiers which, in the name of the Concord Repatriation Hospital, eventually became the biggest military general hospital in Australia. Eadith Walker made many gifts to this hospital in its early years, but as a military hospital it is maintained by government funds, expended through the Department of Repatriation, and is reserved for the care and treatment only of active and discharged members of the defence forces.

When Eadith Walker died, aged seventy-two, in 1937, the residue of her father's estate and of her own estate was made available, by his and her bequests, for the upkeep of the Thomas Walker Convalescent Hospital, and to establish also a convalescent hospital in Yaralla homestead in memory of Eadith Walker. Other bequests were to the Returned Servicemen's League and to the Red Cross. There were bequests also to other charities and to friends, relatives, and employees. The total benefactions of Thomas and Eadith Walker to philanthropic purposes amounted to more than one million pounds, but the capital funds invested as charitable trusts in perpetuity will continue to add to their benefactions, to make their names resound for years to come.

There are thus three distinct and large infirmaries, each within spacious grounds, side by side along the Parramatta River, occupying the two peninsulas between the three bays—Major's Bay, Yaralla Bay, and Bray's Bay—in what was previously the 306 acres of Thomas Walker's land. At the head of Major's Bay the Concord Municipal Council is carrying through a large reclamation of the tidal mudflats and mangrove swamp, to build a recreational park and nine-hole golf course. This will give the residents of Cabarita (many of whom are employed at the gasworks), and of Concord generally, an additional waterfront access, alongside the beautiful grounds of the old Yaralla mansion.

Major's Bay was probably so named in honour of Major Grose, who made the land grants to the ten pioneer settlers there in 1793; or it may have been named in honour of Major Mitchell, Surveyor-General, who presumably fixed the boundaries of the various land-holdings there after 1828; or in honour of a family of pioneer settlers whose surname was Major. A suggestion has been made that the bay was named by Isaac Nichol, in honour of his father, who was a Major. No one knows for sure; and, if some aspects of Australia's origins are becoming hazy within less than two hundred years, conjectures will eventually supply explanations where documentary proofs are lacking.

SEE ALSO PART II   THE RYDE BRIDGES

Fourteen miles up-harbour from the ocean entrance, the two bridges from Concord across the Parramatta River to Ryde—a railway bridge and a road bridge—mark the head of navigation for large vessels. The road bridge is 600 yards downstream from the railway bridge; but, though the road bridge has a lift-span which is occasionally opened to allow fairly large vessels with cargoes of timber to pass through to the timber-mills on the Concord shore between the two bridges, the railway bridge has no moveable span. It has a head-room of 38 ft above mean highwater level, which was enough to enable the Parramatta River ferry-steamers to pass beneath it; but to any vessels with a top-hamper higher than that, the Ryde Railway Bridge was and is an obstacle to further progress.

The Ryde Railway Bridge was built in 1886, as part of a grand plan that had been maturing for thirty years, to connect Sydney by rail with Newcastle and the Great North, which had already its independent railway system since the 1850s. That joining of the two systems required bridges across Sydney Harbour and across the Hawkesbury River, each being a major enterprise in terms of the engineering techniques of the period, and of the need not to impede navigation by vessels with high masts. As railway bridges could not properly be built with moveable spans, high-level bridges were required; but, for reasons of expense, a head-room of 38 feet was considered enough to permit up-river navigation, on both the Parramatta River and the Hawkesbury River, for vessels of restricted masthead height.

212

The building of that Great Northern Line, from its junction with the Great Western Line at Strathfield, to run through Concord and Ryde, and so to Hornsby and the Hawkesbury River Bridge, was a stretching out of a tentacle of the Octopus of Sydney to reach Newcastle, the Hunter River, and all the Northern Rivers and Northern Tablelands of New South Wales. Its effect was to destroy, gradually, most of the coastal shipping that had formerly carried passengers, mails, and general cargoes to and from the northern "outports": the sea-route was too slow for people in a hurry. Another effect was to add to the centralizing of trade and industry, and so of population and political power, at Sydney. The Ryde Railway Bridge—which is nowadays known also as the Meadowbank Bridge, that being the name of the immediate vicinity on shore at its northern end—is 10½ miles by rail-distance from Sydney Central Station to the Concord end of the bridge. The river is 300 yards wide where the bridge crosses it. One effect of the building of the bridge was to develop the western suburbs on the north side of the Harbour as residential areas. By that route the distance from Sydney Central to Hornsby is 21 miles. Suburbs, including those with "colonial" names such as Epping and Cheltenham, were developed between the Ryde Bridge and Hornsby as residential districts for people who travelled (and still travel) daily to and from work in Sydney by rail.

The Ryde Road Bridge was built in 1935, to replace a vehicular punt-ferry that formerly crossed the river (there 400 yards wide) from Uhr's Point to Ryde. That route to the Great North is a continuation of the Concord Road, which branches from the Great Western Highway at Strathfield; and the railway runs parallel with it and near to it all the way to the two bridges. Uhr's Point was named in honour of George Richard Uhr, Sheriff of Sydney, who built a prominent house there in the 1840s.

The two bridges have their southern abutments on the rivershore to the westward of Bray's Bay, named in memory of John Bray, who lived there and built the first house in Concord. He was one of the original ten settlers who were granted land in 1793 by Major Grose. On the western shore of Bray's Bay is a factory making electronic apparatus.

On the river frontage at Uhr's Point, next to the abutments of the road bridge, are the boatsheds of the Concord and Ryde Open Sailing Club, and of the Yaralla Sea Scouts. So, even here, fourteen miles up-harbour from the ocean entrance, white sails are to be seen; not of the large deep-keel decked yachts of the Lower Harbour, but of sailing dinghies, in which youthful enthusiasts of aquatic sport seek and find enjoyment and adventure afloat, and acquire skill in one of the healthiest of all recreations and sports: the instinct and heritage of a seafaring folk, practised more extensively on Sydney Harbour, from its one end to the other, for a longer season in each year, and by a greater number of crewmen and recreational sailing craft than could be found in any other harbour in the world.

RHODES

On the western side of Concord is Homebush Bay. The boundary of the municipality of Concord follows its shore to the stream flowing into the head of the bay, Powell's Creek, to the westward of which is the municipality of Auburn, adjacent to the city of Parramatta.

The north-western suburb of Concord is named Rhodes. Before the Main Northern Railway and Ryde Bridge were built, a mansion named Rhodes stood there, owned by a resident named Walker, who was not a relative of the Walkers of Yaralla. Along that shore nowadays are two chemical factories, a stock-feed factory, a paint factory, and a factory making building materials, where once upon a time wild ducks, black swans, and pelicans built their nests in the mangroves on the muddy marge that has been reclaimed from the wash of the tides, here at the Harbour's head.

12

AUBURN AND PARRAMATTA

THE MUNICIPALITY OF AUBURN AND THE CITY OF PARRAMATTA together form a continuous industrial, commercial, and residential district at the western extremity of Sydney Harbour. Auburn was so named in 1878 by an estate agent who subdivided landed properties there for suburban development, from Oliver Goldsmith's poem, "Auburn, loveliest village of the plain." The older and more romantic name of Liberty Plains thus disappeared, except as the designation of a church parish; but in that old name there was an indication of the true history of Australia, a land in which men freed themselves, mentally and physically, from the shackles of European servility, and sought a new way of life.

The village of Auburn—nowadays a densely populated business centre—is twelve miles by road or rail from Sydney. It sits astride the Great Western Highway (the Parramatta Road) and the Western Main Line railway, only two miles from the centre of Parramatta City, and one mile from its boundary with that city at Duck River. The municipality of Auburn is entirely on the southern side of the Parramatta River; but the City of Parramatta extends on both sides of that river at its tidal headwaters. As industry, commerce, and transport take little notice of the boundaries of municipal administration, the whole region there, at the western end of Sydney Harbour, is viewed as one place, with its own special quality, where, on mangrove-lined foreshores and reclaimed tidal flats, some large industries flourish, and . . .

Far back, through creeks and inlets making,
Comes silent, flooding in, the main.

There, too, where, as local pride insists, "Sydney ends and Australia begins," the oldest farms in Australia have been developed into suburban streets, parks, playing-fields, a racecourse, hospitals, schools, cemeteries, abattoirs, oil refineries, and modern factories of many kinds; but some of the old farmhouses, churches, and other buildings of the early colonial period remain as a reminder, and as a proof if need be, that civilization in Australia was cradled here.

HOMEBUSH BAY

One of the largest, but also the shallowest of the inlets of Sydney Harbour is Homebush Bay, on the southern shore, between Concord and Auburn. It is the tidally flooded swamp or "flat" at the junction of two short freshwater streams, Powell's Creek and Haslem's Creek, which flow northwards from a low ridge in the Liberty Plains to join the Parramatta River at what

215

is virtually the head of the Harbour, marked by the Ryde Railway Bridge, beyond which large vessels cannot pass; but any vessel with head-room less than 38 feet can go under that bridge and into Homebush Bay or the upper reaches of the Parramatta River. Lighters, barges, and boats can, and do, work upstream, especially on the rising tide, even as far as Parramatta; but the many industrial undertakings in Auburn and Parramatta rely chiefly on road transport and rail transport. They use the waterway only occasionally, or for part of their transport needs. There are visionaries who predict that, eventually, the head-reaches of the Parramatta River's tidewaters will be dredged and formed into a grand canal, with retaining-walls, like those of Holland, for barge traffic and ferry traffic; but at present that channel is fringed in many of its reaches with mud and mangroves, and its bed is silted with the topsoil washed into it for many years from Australia's oldest farmlands.

Approximately a mile and a half long and half a mile wide, Homebush Bay has a navigable channel, with depths of from 10 feet to 17 feet along its western shore, but elsewhere it shoals in mudbanks and shallows with as little depth as two feet, and has large flats exposed at low tide. The bay was charted, but not named, in February 1788, by Captain Hunter and his officers in boat parties from H.M.S. *Sirius*, as recorded (on 5th February) by Lieutenant Bradley: "At noon, we were far enough to see the termination of the harbour as far as navigable for ships, being all flats above us, with narrow passages that we supposed might run a considerable distance, but very shoal."

Ten days later (15th February, 1788), Governor Phillip accompanied the boat parties to the head of the harbour, as Bradley records:

> We proceeded up to the beginning of the flats, where we landed and went 2 or 3 miles into the country. Found the trees a considerable distance apart, and the soil in general good—grass very long and no underwood.

It is a reasonable surmise that the boat party landed on the western side of Homebush Bay, and explored to the south-westward as far as the vicinity of present-day Granville, in Parramatta. If that surmise is correct, it was on this expedition that the good farmland of Parramatta was first sighted by Governor Phillip, and not, as some historians have assumed, on his expedition of 22nd to 28th April, which was his second and more thorough exploration.

Bradley's account of the boat party of 15th February continues:

> After dinner went in the smallest boat over the flats past a mangrove island and followed a creek some distance to the westward, when it branched away to the N.W. and S.W. which last we followed 4 miles as near as we could judge. The lake or drain is very shoal, and where we stopt was entirely filled with fallen trees from both sides; the water falling fast, we had barely time to get down boats, which, when we joined, returned to the ship.

From that description, it appears likely that the Governor's boat party, after a midday dinner, proceeded up the narrowing Parramatta River from Homebush Bay, to the junction of Duck River, and then followed that stream up as far as they could go in the smallest boat. They would then have again reached the vicinity of present-day Granville, to which they had walked in the morning.

Ten weeks later, on 22nd April, 1788, Governor Phillip personally led an exploring party, which, according to the journal of Surgeon White (a member of the party), "landed at the head of the harbour, with an intention of penetrating into the country westward, as far as seven days provisions would admit of."

It appears from White's narrative that this party left the boats near the junction of Duck River and the Parramatta River, and proceeded on foot to the westward along the northern side of the Parramatta River. On 24th April, they came to a place where "the tide ceased to flow," and progress for boats would be stopped "by a flat space of large broad stones, over which a freshwater stream ran."

Three months had gone by since Governor Phillip's discovery of the Harbour at its entrance; and now he had discovered its head, at the ultimate reach of the tide and of boats. A hill near by was named by Phillip "Rose Hill," in honour of George Rose, a Secretary at the Admiralty who had been helpful in organizing the great adventure of colonizing New Holland; but, when a farm settlement and town were eventually established there, Phillip named the place Parramatta, which, he ascertained, was the Aborigines' name for the head of the tidewater. That was the first time, in the history of British settlement in Australia, that an Aboriginal place-name was ascertained, adopted, and put on the map.

THE WENTWORTHS OF HOMEBUSH

The somewhat enigmatic name of Home Bush was conferred by Surgeon D'Arcy Wentworth on an estate of 920 acres which was granted to him by Governor King, in 1806, on the western side of the bay which now bears that name. If it means, as seems evident, "A Home in the Bush," this was one of the first occasions on which the word "bush" (or, more precisely, "the Bush") was applied to untilled or virgin forested country in the distinctive Australian usage, perhaps abbreviated from "bushland" as a variant of the English word "woodland." (Another possibility is that the expression "the Bush" was developed from "the Brush," meaning "the underbrush," an English term applicable to some of the scrubby country near Sydney.)

In course of time, "the Bush" came to mean every part of the country outside Sydney. Though the word "bush" literally means "shrub," and is thus a diminutive, it was applied in Australia to mountain forests of immense trees, and also to grassy plains on which trees were sparsely scattered; and to this day there is a saying still current, that originated with the pioneers—"Sydney or the Bush"—implying that there are those two contrasted ways

217

of life in Australia.

Why D'Arcy Wentworth named his estate Home Bush (instead of Bush Home) is anybody's guess. There was some whimsy in it, as in John Harris's naming of Five Dock. If no better explanation is forthcoming, we may assume that it was a vernacular shortening of an intended full name: *Home in the Bush.*

D'Arcy Wentworth was born in Ireland in 1764. He was a collateral descendant of the Minister of State of Charles I, the Earl of Strafford, who was executed in 1641 by Bill of Attainder and impeachment in the House of Commons: the first move of the Puritans which culminated in civil war and the execution of the King eight years later. The branch of the Wentworth family in Ireland had been established there, in County Down, for two centuries before D'Arcy Wentworth was born. Though of English origin, they were "more Irish than the Irish themselves."

Having served his time as apprentice to a surgeon in Ireland in 1785, D'Arcy Wentworth, aged twenty-one, went to London to continue his studies. He had powerful friends there, but also, for reasons not now known, powerful enemies. It was presumably by the influence of his enemies that he was twice arrested and charged with highway robbery under arms, allegedly on roads near London, and by the influence of his friends that he was on each occasion acquitted through lack of evidence to identify him as the culprit. He was nevertheless referred to in London newspapers as "the notorious highwayman." To get him out of further trouble, his friends arranged for him to be appointed as surgeon in the convict transport *Neptune*, of the Second Fleet, which arrived at Sydney Cove on 28th June, 1790.

He was not a convict, and could have returned to England in the *Neptune* if he wished. Instead, he applied to Governor Phillip for appointment as a surgeon (government medical officer), and was appointed to serve in that position on Norfolk Island. There he remained for nearly six years. In conformity with the custom of the time and place, he took as his "wife"—without benefit of clergy, for there was no clergyman on Norfolk Island—a young female convict, Catherine Crowley, who bore him three sons. The oldest of these, William Charles Wentworth, was born on Norfolk Island in October 1790, and thus had been begotten at sea on board the transport *Neptune*. His father proudly acknowledged his three illegitimate sons, and brought them and their mother with him to Sydney when he returned there from Norfolk Island in 1796. The stigma, if it were such, on his birth, did not prevent William Charles Wentworth from becoming one of the greatest of Australians.

After returning from Norfolk Island, D'Arcy Wentworth was stationed at Parramatta as resident medical officer. His Catherine died there in January 1800. At that time her eldest son, William Charles, was nine years of age. It is likely that he had received some schooling at Norfolk Island, where Thomas McQueen was the schoolmaster, and that he attended also a Dame's School at Parramatta, conducted by Mary Johnson. There are gaps in the records, but it is evident that W. C. Wentworth spent some impressionable years of his boyhood, presumably from his sixth to his thirteenth year, at Parramatta.

In 1803, when he was thirteen years of age, his father sent him to a boarding-school in England, at Bexhill, in Sussex. There he received a thorough classical and literary education. He was absent from his homeland for seven years, returning in March, 1810, when he was nineteen years of age. During his absence his father had prospered, and had built a fine homestead on his estate, Homebush, which he had been granted in 1806. D'Arcy Wentworth had now married Anne Lawes, who bore him several children.

While developing his estate, D'Arcy Wentworth continued in practice as government medical officer at Parramatta, and was appointed also as a stipendiary magistrate. He rode daily on horseback from Homebush to Parramatta and home again, and to and from Sydney whenever official or private business required. He imported thoroughbred horses from India and South Africa, and established at Homebush the first, or one of the first, racing studs in Australia. Seven months after William Charles returned home, he rode one of his father's horses to win a race in the first officially recorded race meeting held in Australia, at Hyde Park, Sydney, in October 1810. This was one of the many remarkable achievements of William Charles Wentworth.

A neighbour of D'Arcy Wentworth was John Blaxland. He, and his younger brother, Gregory Blaxland, had immigrated to New South Wales as free settlers with a large capital, in 1805. They came from Newington, in Kent. John was granted two square miles of land on the south bank of the Parramatta River, adjoining D'Arcy Wentworth's Homebush on its western boundary. This estate, which they named Newington, was regarded by the Blaxlands as their headquarters. They had extensive grants of land elsewhere, but built their residence at Newington, where also they established salt-pans for evaporating the tidewater, and a slaughterhouse; they salted the beef to sell to shipmasters at Sydney, and to the government stores as rations for soldiers and convicts.

William Charles Wentworth became friendly with Gregory Blaxland, and also with a former army officer, William Lawson, who had a farm at Prospect, near Parramatta. On 11th May, 1813, these three, with four convict stockmen, set out on horseback from one of the Blaxlands' properties, at South Creek, beyond Parramatta, determined to find a way through the Blue Mountains, which, for twenty-five years of British pioneering settlement, had frustrated the many attempts that had been made to cross them. At this time W. C. Wentworth was twenty-two years of age, Gregory Blaxland thirty-five, and William Lawson thirty-nine. There was no officially appointed "leader," the three sharing equally in the expenses and in the glory and reward of success. Each was granted 1,000 acres of land by Governor Macquarie for their great feat.

The success of that expedition was due to its mobility on

horseback. The opening of the Great West, like the opening of the Great South by another Australian-born explorer, Hamilton Hume, in 1814 and subsequent years, marked the beginning of the era of horsemanship in Australian outback history. In that development, the two large pastoral stations, Homebush and Newington, at the head of Sydney Harbour, were starting-points of the immense inland venturing of Australian pioneers on horseback. An Arab stallion named Hector, imported from India in 1803, who remained in service at Homebush for nearly twenty years, provided the basic strain not only of Australian racehorses, but also of the stockhorses that developed to a special breed, the Walers (i.e., horses from New South Wales).

D'Arcy Wentworth was appointed by Governor Macquarie as Superintendent of Police, and in that office established the police force in New South Wales, the first in Australia. He died at Homebush, aged sixty-three, in 1827, leaving his estates, there and elsewhere, to his numerous descendants.

SEE ALSO PART II   THE ABATTOIRS

In 1832, William Charles Wentworth was elected President of the Sydney Turf Club, which, pending the clearing of a racecourse at Randwick, held its meetings at Parramatta. In 1840 a new racecourse was built at Homebush, occupying most of the Wentworth family's land there, on cleared and level ground. The Australian Jockey Club (A.J.C.), founded in 1842, held its meetings at Homebush for seventeen years, until 1859. During that period the Homebush racecourse, with large training-stables and paddocks, was the headquarters of horseracing in Australia. Spectators from Sydney could travel to Homebush by paddle-wheel steam-ferries, or by road on horseback and in horsedrawn vehicles, and, after 1855, by rail.

The A.J.C. transferred its headquarters from Homebush to Randwick Racecourse in 1860. Thereafter the Homebush course became chiefly a training-track, stud, and spelling-paddocks. In 1906 the New South Wales Government acquired the land, which then comprised 850 acres at the head of Homebush Bay (between Powell's Creek and Haslem's Creek) as site for an immense establishment, the State Abattoirs, where cattle, sheep, and pigs, brought from country districts by rail, could be slaughtered and the carcases dressed, not only for Sydney metropolitan consumption, but also—frozen—for export.

Previously, there had been several slaughterhouses, at various places in and near Sydney, including one at the head of Rozelle Bay, from which blood and offal or scraps drained into the Harbour, creating hazards to public health, and incidentally attracting swarms of sharks. The State Abattoirs at Homebush offered slaughterhouse facilities which were leased to wholesale butchers (also known as "carcase butchers"), who bought beasts on the hoof at the saleyards built at Flemington railway siding, adjacent to the abattoirs.

In course of time the Homebush Abattoirs became one of the biggest in the world. Since 1937, the Metropolitan Meat Industry

Board controls the operations of slaughtering beasts (mostly bought at the adjacent saleyards) which are delivered alive by carcase butchering firms. The dressed carcases are then delivered chilled to the carcase butchers for distribution to retailers in Sydney, or to be frozen or otherwise treated for export at canning-works. The immense scale of these operations is startling to the imagination.

In 1964, a typical year, animals slaughtered at Homebush Abattoirs numbered 179,361 cattle, 113,593 calves, 123,139 pigs, and 2,390,780 sheep.

Apart from the flesh and edible organs marketed as food, the hides and skins are sold to tanners and fellmongers, the fats boiled down to tallow, the scraps and trimmings converted into poultry feed, the blood and bone into fertilizer; practically everything in a slaughtered beast has use and value in the market and in industry. There is no pollution of the Harbour by effluent from the Homebush Abattoirs: floor-washings and minor waste material are carried away in the metropolitan sewerage system, as happens with the effluents of many other industries, to outfalls in the open ocean.

On an average, more than 10,000 animals a day, or 50,000 each working week, are slaughtered and converted into chilled carcases and by-products at Homebush. Some 2,000 workpeople are employed at the abattoirs as stockmen, slaughtermen, packers, engineers, truck-drivers, and clerical staff. Looped railway-lines run from the main western line to sidings in the abattoirs saleyards, where acres of post-and-rail stockyards form an intricate system of pens. In the paddocks near by, cattle and sheep, after lengthy train-journeys from the pastoral districts of the interior, may take a short walk and have their last feed and drink before meeting the fate for which they have been predestined.

The immense activity of the saleyards and abattoirs at Homebush, only ten miles west of Sydney, is perhaps not noticed by the two and a half million inhabitants of the metropolis, who buy their cuts of beef, veal, mutton, and pork in butchers' shops or food stores, without thinking of the work and organization required to maintain that supply; for, even though the Homebush Abattoirs are among the biggest in the world, they do not proclaim their identity in any obtrusive manner: they are almost ideally situated for their purpose, on a large flat pocket of land, near the Great Western Highway and railway, yet separated from residential districts, surrounded by water and by paddocks, and visited, doubtless, only by those who have business or work to do there.

The administration offices stand on the site of D'Arcy Wentworth's old homestead, of which only some rubble now remains. Gone, too, are all traces of the Homebush Racecourse. The estuary of Haslem's Creek, formerly known as Wentworth Bay (a bight on the western side of Homebush Bay), became the site of a great land reclamation project, undertaken by the Maritime Services Board in the 1960s, on a ten-year plan. This, and the building of a sea-wall and the dredging of a channel, are intended to provide space for timber wharves, enabling the sawmills at Rozelle Bay to be moved to Homebush Bay. (Such a move would free Rozelle Bay for overseas shipping of general merchandise and coal.)

In 1910, when the first Labor Government was formed in New South Wales, it applied socialistic ideas to the establishment of a "State Brickworks," owned and managed as a government enterprise, adjacent to the Abattoirs at Homebush, with a water frontage. The brickworks were leased later to private enterprise, but were taken over again by the State Government in the 1940s, and have flourished during the post-war building boom of the 1950s and 1960s. The brickworks have their own railway siding, connected to the Abattoirs loop-line. They obtain most of their clay and coal-fuel by rail and road, and deliver the bricks to customers in the Sydney metropolitan districts by motor-trucks. It is considered likely that when the new wharfage and dredging of Homebush Bay is completed, some use may be made of water transport to and from the brickworks.

NEWINGTON

The two square miles of water frontage along the upper Parramatta River granted to John Blaxland in 1806, to the westward of Homebush Bay and Haslem's Creek, bounded on the western side by the Duck River, and on the south by the Parramatta Road, remained in the possession of the Blaxland family until 1863, and thereafter were gradually subdivided and sold.

The homestead, a fine colonial mansion of stone, with veranda pillars of Pyrmont sandstone 12 feet long and 12 inches in diameter, was completed in 1832. John Blaxland died, aged seventy-six, in 1845, and Gregory Blaxland died, aged seventy-five, in 1853.

When the Newington estate was subdivided in 1863, the homestead and its immediate grounds were bought by the Methodist Church, which established a boys' boarding-school named Newington College. This became one of the great public schools of Sydney. In 1880, the school was moved to new premises at Stanmore, only four miles from Sydney, but retained the name of Newington. The Blaxlands' homestead on the Parramatta River was then acquired by the New South Wales Government and used as a home for aged women. It continues to be maintained today as the Newington State Hospital and Home. The colonial-built mansion, still in a good state of preservation, is one of the buildings classified by the National Trust to be preserved in perpetuity. It has an atmosphere of spacious days and gracious living; stone craftsmanship and cedar fittings such as are seen here have vanished from the architectural conceptions of today.

The eastern part of the Blaxland estate, with frontages on Homebush Bay, Haslem's Creek, and the Parramatta River, were acquired in 1906 by the Australian Federal Government for defence establishments. These are principally ammunition dumps and stores, accessible by water transport, and handy also to road and rail communications.

SILVERWATER

Westward of the Newington Hospital is the modern suburb of Silverwater, with a frontage along Duck River and the Parramatta River. A road bridge, opened in 1962, crosses the Parramatta River on the Sydney side of the junction of those two streams. Of reinforced concrete, it has five spans and a total length of 657 feet, the river being at this point approximately 150 yards wide. Known as the Silverwater Bridge, this crossing of the main stream of the upper reach of Sydney Harbour is two and a half miles upstream from the Ryde Road Bridge. Carrying four lanes of vehicular traffic and two footways, it was an important addition to the harbour-crossing routes in the western suburbs, enabling motorists to avoid the increasingly congested routes of the Sydney Harbour Bridge, the Gladesville Bridge, and the Ryde Road Bridge.

In its course of three miles upstream from the Silverwater Bridge to the head of tidewater at Parramatta, the narrowing Parramatta River is crossed by four more road bridges—at Thackeray Street, Aston Street, Macarthur Street, and Church Street—and by one railway bridge, at Camellia. Those four road bridges are all within the boundaries of the City of Parramatta, and are intended for local rather than highway traffic. The railway bridge, which is on the branch line to Carlingford, is not a trunkline bridge.

From the Ocean Heads to Parramatta, the main stream of Sydney Harbour is thus crossed by a total of seven road bridges and two railway bridges, *plus* the Sydney Harbour Bridge, which carries both road and rail traffic. Thus, viewing the Harbour as a water-filled cleft, nineteen miles long, separating the "North Side" districts of the Sydney Metropolitan area from its "South Side" districts, that fissure is spanned by ten bridges; but five of these are within Parramatta City, in the upper reaches, where the stream is less than a hundred yards wide. There, the bridges are of rigid low-level design and construction, but with enough clearance through the spans and headway beneath them to permit navigation by barges, lighters, boats, small powered vessels, and small yachts. The lowest headway is beneath the Camellia railway bridge, 19 feet at high tide. That obstacle, a mile and a quarter from the limit of the tidal waters, would prevent any vessels requiring much headroom from reaching the heart of Parramatta City at Church Street; but the real reason why the waterway, in those upper reaches, has fallen into disuse is the siltation of the river-bed, creating mudbanks that in places now have depths of water of little more than 12 inches at low tide. That channel could—if public opinion at Parramatta insisted on the rights of the waterway, as well as on those of the roads and railways—be dredged to an ample navigable depth for small powered vessels, lighters, barges, boats, yachts, and even passenger vessels.

Four miles in length, the Duck River rises near Bankstown, and flows northwards through level country between Auburn and Parramatta (Granville), to join the Parramatta River at Silverwater, two miles upstream from Homebush Bay. This is the biggest stream flowing into Sydney Harbour on the South Side. Tidally flooded for two miles from its junction, it is navigable by boats and other vessels of small draft for a mile and a half. At its head of navigation, it narrows to 20 yards, and is crossed there by a culvert bridge on the Great Western Highway (the Parramatta Road), thirteen miles from Sydney.

A tributary, Duck Creek, flows into the Duck River from the western side, half a mile below the Highway crossing. The tributary creek, which is tidally flooded, is navigable for a short distance. It drains the eastern side of Parramatta City, flowing between the Rosehill Racecourse and the Granville Showground.

The Duck River and the Duck Creek, in their tidal reaches, comprise an estuarine arm of Sydney Harbour, similar in essentials to the Lane Cove River and Middle Harbour arms on the north side, but smaller.

In the primeval state of the country, as Governor Phillip saw it on his boat exploration on 15th February, 1788, it appeared that Duck River, branching, as Lieutenant Bradley noted, to the south-west, was larger than the Parramatta River, branching to the north-west. Both streams were heavily fringed with mangroves. Phillip explored Duck River to its head of navigation, and thus discovered the good farming country of Parramatta in the vicinity of present-day Granville.

Duck River was so named on Captain Hunter's chart of 1788. The origin of the name is indicated in an entry in the *Journal* of Surgeon-General John White, who accompanied Governor Phillip's exploring party at the head of the Harbour. The party had proceeded on foot, camping out in tents, along the northern side of the upper reaches of the Parramatta River to its headwaters, and then had climbed Prospect Hill on 26th April, 1788.

Returning then by a blazed track, which they had made on their outward journey, White noted on 27th April:

> When we got as far back as the arm or branch of the sea which forms the upper part of Port Jackson Harbour, we saw many ducks, but could not get within shot of any of them.

At that time Governor Phillip and his officers believed, as on their previous exploration of 15th February, that the inlet, which thereafter was named the Duck River, was the Head of the Harbour.

In a practical sense, the junction of the Duck River and the Parramatta River became the head of navigation in the 1890s, when the steam-ferry terminal of the Sydney-Parramatta service was established at a wharf on the south bank of the Parramatta River, 200 yards above the Duck River junction. Connection from that wharf to Parramatta, two miles by tramway, was along

Luna Park, beside Sydney Harbour Bridge, began life in Adelaide and was moved to Sydney in 1935. Although the face originally wore a scowl, it was made jovial by Arthur Brown, who remodelled the face in 1950.

In 1908, these flats at Waruda Street, North Sydney were considered to offer the latest in living styles from America. They were built by the owner of Carbine, the racehorse.

Admiralty House, the Sydney residence of the Governor-General, is so called because it was used as the official residence for the Commander-in-Chief of the British Naval Squadron stationed in Sydney between 1885 and 1913.

The Royal Sydney Yacht Squadron, established 1862. A feature of the grounds is the archway made from the jawbones of a whale.

The submarine base HMAS *Platypus*, at Neutral Bay.

The house, Once Upon a Time, was demolished and moved by barge across the harbour from Garden Island, during the second World War, and rebuilt beside Kurraba wharf.

Mosman Boy Scouts occupy the old stone storehouse of Archibald Mosman, who set up a whaling industry in the bay in 1830.

The renovated front entrance of Taronga Zoo.

The old cannons at Bradleys Head are now classified as part of the National Heritage.

The mast of HMAS *Sydney* at Bradleys Head is a well-known landmark on Sydney Harbour. The warship sank the German cruiser *Emden* at Cocos Island in 1914.

Three houseboats at Pearl Bay are the sole survivors from the Hong Kong type of colony which existed in the 1930s. The oldest boat has been built on a ferry that transported vehicles across the harbour before the Spit Bridge was built.

Innisfallen Castle, in Cherry Place, Castle Cove, was built as a farmhouse between 1903-05 when the only access was by bullock track or by water.

Marineland at Manly, Australia's first oceanarium. One of its attractions lies in watching divers feed the sharks.

The slogan of the now defunct Port Jackson and Manly Steamship Company still greets ferry travellers to the Manly Fun Pier.

The Manly Shark Aquarium was built on an old cargo wharf in the 1930s after the coming of the Sydney Harbour Bridge had put harbour cargo vessels out of business.

A feature of the foreshore seen by Manly ferry passengers is Kilburn Towers at Manly Point. This circular block of home units was considered strikingly modern when it was built in 1959.

The Police Academy at Quarantine Head overlooks the bay where Governor Phillip was speared by Aborigines.

North Head, while it still has its military lookouts, is now part of Sydney Harbour National Park.

The *New Endeavour*, a three-masted schooner launched in Denmark in 1919, has been restored as a sail-training ship for use on the Sydney Harbour.

Sydney Cove from the North Shore, about 1825 *(Photo: Mitchell Library)*.

Sydney Cove, 1802 *(Photo: Mitchell Library).*

Circular Quay about the end of the nineteenth century.

HMS *Formidable* passes Garden Island returning from Tarakan on 6 December 1945 *(Photo: Austarlian War Memorial No. 119963).*

A view of Sydney in about 1800.

Part of a panorama drawn in 1808 to accompany *Mann's Present Picture of New South Wales* published in 1810.

An aerial view of Captain Cook Graving Dock, opened 24 March 1945 *(Photo: Australian War Memorial No. 41218).*

The old ferry Kuttabul, used as a depot ship, was damaged by a torpedo from a Japanese midget submarine during a raid on 31 May 1942 *(Photo: Australian War Memorial No. 43033).*

HMAS *Perth* arrives in Sydney on 31 March 1940 *(Photo: Australian War Memorial No. 1222).*

A drawing of Sydney published in 1823.

A direct north view of Sydney Cove by Thomas Watling, 1794.

a road name Grand Avenue. If the river had been dredged, the ferries could have berthed in the heart of Parramatta, near Church Street, as they did in the 1840s and until the river silted in the 1880s.

THE MERINO PIONEERS SEE ALSO PART II

To the pastoralists of Australia, the stretch of country, approximately 850 acres, with a frontage of two miles on the south bank of the Parramatta River between Duck River and Macarthur Street, Parramatta, bounded on the east by the Duck River and on the south by Duck Creek, is, or ought to be, holy ground; for that was John Macarthur's property, where he—and in his absence his wife Elizabeth—substantially laid the foundations of the Australian Merino sheep-raising industry.

Australia's sheep-population of 150 million (thirteen times greater than the human population) comprises at least 100 million Merinos. Although John Macarthur was not the first to introduce Merino sheep to Australia, he introduced some of that breed, and bred them with others; and he was the first to organize the export of fine wool fleeces from Australia to England, thereby providing English textile factories with the means of a great expansion in output and prosperity. If Australians became, and have substantially remained, "a nation of shepherds," that status was first developed on the banks of the Parramatta River, at the Head of Sydney Harbour.

The sheep brought to Sydney in the First Fleet in 1788 were of an Indian breed, obtained in South Africa. They had hair, rather than wool, and were bred for mutton, not for their fleeces. Some of that strain of goatlike sheep were bred by a military officer, Joseph Foveaux, on his farms at Petersham, on the Parramatta Road, and Toongabbie, four miles west of Parramatta, and by other settlers, including Edward Elliott, of The Ponds, near Toongabbie. The descendants of those hairy sheep, through cross-breeding, contributed one of the many strains in the evolution of the distinctive Australian Merino, an animal with much longer and finer wool, and very much heavier fleeces, than the original Spanish Merinos and Saxon Merinos.

The first Merinos in Australia were brought to Sydney from Monterey, California, in April 1793, in H.M.S. *Daedalus*, a naval storeship. Of the six rams and twelve ewes that were shipped at Monterey, in December 1792, only one ram and three ewes survived the passage. These were degenerate Spanish Merinos, descended from stock that had been shipped from Spain to Mexico perhaps two hundred years previously. They were acquired by Captain Thomas Rowley, a military officer who had a farm at Camperdown, on the Parramatta Road, three miles west of Sydney. The pioneer of the Merino in Australia, he built a flock from them, twelve years before John Macarthur imported Merinos from the royal stud in England in 1805. (Little or no research has been done by historians of the Australian wool industry in reference to the *Daedalus* sheep and Thomas Rowley's part in their acclimatization.)

John Macarthur, a lieutenant in the British garrison forces stationed in New South Wales, arrived at Sydney, aged twenty-three, with his wife (maiden name Elizabeth Veale), aged twenty-one, in June 1790. In 1791 he was posted to Parramatta, and in 1793 was granted 100 acres of land on the eastern side of the town, and the labour of ten convicts to work it. He named that estate Elizabeth Farm, in honour of his wife, who, the daughter of a Devonshire yeoman, managed the farm during her husband's absences on military duties. A stone homestead was built on the farm. It still stands today, in Alice Street, Parramatta, the oldest house extant in Australia.

In 1794, after clearing and cultivating 50 acres of his land, Macarthur was granted an additional 100 acres adjoining it. He also purchased 50 acres, and thus increased the area of Elizabeth Farm to a total of 250 acres. Until then he had owned no sheep, but he then, in 1794, bought sixty Indian sheep, probably from Joseph Foveaux's flock, and began breeding them for mutton. Their fleeces were of no value.

In 1797, Captain Henry Waterhouse, R.N., in command of H.M.S. *Reliance,* brought to Sydney, from South Africa, seven or eight pure Merinos, including rams and ewes, which he had bought as a private investment. They were from a Saxon Merino stud, descended from stock imported to South Africa from Holland. Captain Waterhouse was granted 25 acres of land at the junction of the Duck River and the Parramatta River (later the site of Blaxlands' Newington homestead), and presumably landed his Merinos there. These were the first pure Merinos in Australia. (The Spanish or "Mission" Merinos from California, owned by Rowley, were probably crossbreds, or had degenerated through neglect.) As a serving naval officer, Captain Waterhouse could not spend much time ashore. He delegated the management of his Merino stud to Thomas Rowley, and bought a farm of 140 acres on the north side of the Parramatta River (Subiaco Creek) from the pioneer settler there, a German named Phillip Schaeffer.

From that stud, managed by Rowley for Waterhouse, and almost certainly containing strains of the Californian Spanish and Cape Saxon Merinos, fine-woolled rams and ewes were sold to various landowners, including John Macarthur, the Reverend Samuel Marsden, and William Cox. In 1800, when Waterhouse returned to England, he sold his pure merinos, 99 in all, to William Cox, a newly arrived military officer who had purchased land near Parramatta and on the Hawkesbury River.

At that time, John Macarthur, who had purchased, in 1798, four ewes and two rams from Waterhouse, was building up a Merino flock at Elizabeth Farm, keeping the strain pure, but the flock that Cox had acquired from Waterhouse and Rowley was much bigger, and therefore increased more rapidly, than Macarthur's flock. In 1801 Macarthur, going to England to face a court martial for having fought a duel, took with him some

Merino fleeces from the sheep (or their progeny) he had bought from Waterhouse. He showed those fleeces to woolbrokers and woollen manufacturers in England, and so convinced them that New South Wales could become a source of supply of fine wools, which, at that time (because of the Napoleonic Wars), were difficult or impossible to obtain from Spain and Germany. In that sense John Macarthur's duel and Napoleon's counter-blockade of Britain combined to establish the export of raw wool from Australia.

After an absence of three and a half years—during which his wife managed his farm and superintended the further building-up of his Merino stud—John Macarthur returned to Sydney in June 1805, in a ship romantically named *Argo*, bringing with him five Merino rams and one Merino ewe that he had been allowed to purchase from the King's flock at Kew. These were Spanish Merinos, from a stud imported to England from Spain as an experiment in 1790. Those sheep, conjoined with the descendants of the Merinos that Macarthur had bought in 1798 from Waterhouse, were used to build up Macarthur's stud at Elizabeth Farm. So Macarthur's Merinos became one of the most important of the early strains—but they were not the first of the many strains which, then and subsequently, in the Australian climate and on superb pastures, developed to 100 million Australian Merinos, the world's best.

John Macarthur had to go to England again in 1809, to face charges arising from his part in the "rebellion" against Governor Bligh at Sydney in 1808. Official inquiries into that incident were so prolonged that Macarthur was not allowed to return to New South Wales until 1817. During his absence of eight years, his farm and its ever-increasing Merino flock were managed by his wife, who had thus been the flock mistress at Elizabeth Farm for almost twelve of the first nineteen years of the Macarthur Merino stud.

In 1816, while John Macarthur was absent in England, Governor Macquarie granted him, through his wife as proxy, an additional 600 acres of land adjoining Elizabeth Farm on its eastern side, thus extending its boundaries to the Duck River. In the meantime William Cox, and others, had moved part of their Merino flocks across the Blue Mountains to the western districts, where Merinos thrived better than on the coastal plain. In 1820, Macarthur moved his Merinos from Elizabeth Farm to Camden, where he died in 1834, aged sixty-seven. His widow lived at Elizabeth Farm until her death, aged eighty-one, in 1850. She had lived for sixty years in New South Wales. She had eight children—five sons and three daughters. Her name must remain forever bright among those of the pioneer women of Australia.

Although John Macarthur was chiefly responsible for organizing the export of raw wool from Australia to be fabricated into textiles in England, an Australian woollen textile industry had been established as early as 1801 at Parramatta, where female prisoners were put to work spinning and weaving woollen cloth in their barracks, which became known as "the Female Factory." That industry was founded on fleeces from the Merino flocks bred from the *Daedalus* and Waterhouse strains. It was well established before Macarthur's Merinos arrived in 1805. The Female Factory continued in operation until the 1840s; but, after 1815, its tweed cloth was dressed and dyed in a mill established by Simeon Lord on the shore of Botany Bay. Known as "Parramatta Cloth," that tweed was of such good quality that Bradford manufacturers in England imitated it, and put on the market a tweed which to the present day continues to be known as Parramatta Cloth.

The Blaxlands at Newington also had a woollen mill in operation in 1815. Several other woollen textile factories were established, including one at Blackwattle Bay in 1838. In the 1840s, there were seven woollen mills operating in New South Wales, but the system of exporting raw wool, instead of textiles, has predominated to the present day, tending to prevent Australia's population from rapidly expanding by industrial enterprise in that field. Whatever may be the future trend, Parramatta was the cradle of the Australian wool-growing, wool-exporting, and wool-textile industries. The first in anything must remain forever the first: and for that reason the achievements of pioneers in any field can never be dimmed by those who follow tracks that they blaze.

THE HEAD OF THE HARBOUR

Beyond dispute, the Head of Sydney Harbour is at the weir, 50 yards upstream from Lennox Bridge, Parramatta, where tidewater ends and fresh water spills down, nineteen miles from the entrance of the salt tides at the Harbour's ocean gate. It was there, on 24th April, 1788, that Governor Phillip's party found the place (described by Surgeon White) where "the tide ceased to flow; and all further progress for boats was stopped by a flat space of large broad stones, over which a freshwater stream ran."

Over those stones, as the Aborigines knew, young eels jumped up, on their way from their birthplace as elvers far out in the ocean, making for the quiet freshwater pools of the river above that barrier, and of its tributaries draining the plains of Toongabbie and the undulating grassed uplands that were to be so strangely named the Baulkham Hills. That natural weir was known to the Aborigines as Parramatta—the place where eels jump up. Governor Phillip named the park-like knoll adjacent to the weir Rose Hill, and decided that there, at the limit of boat navigation, would be the site for his capital city, in good farming country, and beyond the reach of enemy naval bombardment.

Surgeon-General White mentioned, on the following day, 25th April, 1788:

The trees around us were immensely large, and the tops of them filled with loraquets and paroquets of exquisite beauty, which chattered to such a degree that we could scarcely hear each other speak. We fired several times at them, but the trees were so very high that we killed but few.

Those "loraquets and paroquets" became known to the pioneer settlers as "Rose-Hillers" (Rose Hill parrots), a name later transformed to Rosella parrots.

As he had many other matters to attend to at Sydney Cove, it took Governor Phillip six months to make the arrangements for a settlement at Rose Hill. Then, on 2nd November, the Governor, accompanied by the Surveyor-General, Baron Augustus Alt, a German, with eleven marines and ten convicts—all conveyed in boats manned by naval seamen—disembarked at the tidal headwaters and made camp. The site for a redoubt and the main streets of a town were marked out, and clearing and cultivation of the soil began.

As there was no track for land communication between Sydney and Rose Hill until a year later, all the pioneering communication was by the waterway. In October 1789, the first waterborne vessel built in Australia was launched at Sydney Cove. She was a flat-bottomed lighter with a mast and sails, known in nautical terminology as a hoy, intended, as Lieutenant Bradley mentioned, "for carrying stores and provisions over the flats to Rose Hill." Being a very slow sailer, especially in the mangrove arcades of the upper reaches of the river, where the dense foliage on the banks shut out the breezes, she was propelled by sweeps, sometimes taking several days to make the passage. She was humorously named the *Rose Hill Packet*, and *The Lump*, but, in the history of shipbuilding in Australia, her immortal renown can never be diminished, for she was the first. . . .

Progress at building huts and clearing the ground for cultivation, with hoes and spades only, was slow, but by the end of two years, 200 acres had been cleared. Of these, 55 acres carried crops of wheat, barley, and oats, and 30 acres were planted with maize. This was the first successful cultivation of cereal crops in Australia. At that time, November 1790, the town was taking shape, with thirty-two huts of wattle and daub for male convicts, and nine for female convicts, each hut accommodating from ten to twelve people. Besides—as Captain Watkin Tench of the Marines noted—there were "several small huts where convict families of good character are allowed to reside."

A brick kiln was in operation, employing fifty-two people, producing 25,000 bricks weekly. A large brick storehouse, roofed with tiles, was nearly completed, and work was proceeding on barracks for the garrison troops, and houses for the officers. There was also a house of "lath-and-plaister" for the Governor, who evidently made frequent visits to the head-of-the-harbour settlement. A garden was planted around the Governor's house, which was on the south bank of the freshwater stream, immediately above the natural weir. In that garden, grapes were harvested in January 1791, perhaps the first in Australia.

In March, 1791, a land grant was made by Governor Phillip to James Ruse, an industrious ex-convict, who thereby became the first private land owner in Australia. His grant, of 30 acres, was officially registered in February 1792. It was named Experiment Farm. Its site is within the present-day City of Parramatta, bounded by Harris Street, Brisbane Street, Good Street, and Beckett's Creek (a drain).

In June 1791, the name of the settlement was changed from Rose Hill to Parramatta. A year later, its population had increased to 1,970, as compared with 1,170 at Sydney; but gradually Parramatta became recognized as a farming settlement, and Sydney developed as the seaport, commercial emporium, and capital city. When, in 1794, the Parramatta Road—previously only a foot track—was cleared and graded for wheeled vehicles, wagons drawn by bullocks or horses increased the road traffic, and so diminished the use of the waterway, between the farming districts and Sydney. It was from Parramatta that roads branched to the Hawkesbury and to the Northern settlements; and from Parramatta also roads were eventually built, after 1814, to the Great West and the Great South.

Thus the town at the Head of the Harbour became, as Governor Phillip had anticipated, a hub of rural production; but its distance from Sydney by road, fourteen miles, was a convenient stage, on horseback or in light horse-drawn vehicles, for one day's travelling. So Parramatta became an overnight stop for squatters from "up the country" on their way to and from Sydney.

HISTORIC PARRAMATTA

Though Parramatta is the second oldest centre of civilized settlement in Australia, it was not municipally incorporated as a town until 1861, and was not raised officially to the dignity of a city until 1938. Its city boundaries were enlarged in 1948 to include the adjacent municipalities of Granville, Dundas, and Rydalmere. The present-day City of Parramatta, with a population of 100,000, thus extends on both sides of the upper reaches of the Parramatta River, for three miles eastward of the old town along the south bank, and four miles on the north bank. Within the city boundaries are many modern industrial estab lishments in residential suburbs from which the old town, developing rapidly as a shopping centre, derives most of its modern prosperity.

In that sense, Parramatta is certainly not a suburb of Sydney, but a sister city, or, more precisely, one of a series of contiguous cities—loosely termed "satellite cities"—developing in the Sydney peneplain. In that sense, because of the congestion of traffic on the roads, and inadequate railway transport, many districts classified as "suburbs," but not yet proclaimed municipally as "cities," are tending to become autonomous as shopping and civic centres, and are cities in all but name.

Parramatta is not like the suburbs of recent or mushroom growth; it is as redolent of Australian history as the City of

Sydney, of which it is not a daughter but a sister. In Parramatta is the oldest extant building in Australia, Elizabeth Farm homestead, erected in 1793. (The oldest building extant in Sydney is Cadman's Cottage, built in 1813.)

The Anglican Church at Parramatta, St John's, began as a chapel in a hut, or with open air services conducted by the Chaplain of the First Fleet, the Reverend Richard Johnson, who from 1788 to 1791 was the only clergyman in New South Wales. He divided his time between Sydney and Parramatta, and also was an energetic pioneer vegetable grower, fruit grower, and eventually, general farmer.

He built the first church in Australia, on a site at the corner of present-day Castlereagh Street and Hunter Street, Sydney. Of wattle and daub, it was opened in August 1793. In the meantime, after the arrival of the New South Wales Corps in June 1790, its regimental chaplain, James Bain, was stationed at Parramatta in September 1791, and presumably continued to hold regular church services in a hut or at church parades in the open air. His duties at Parramatta were taken over in December 1794 by the Reverend Samuel Marsden, an outstanding personality in the pioneering history of Australia and of New Zealand, but especially so in the history of Parramatta, where he continued to be not only the parish priest, but stipendiary magistrate and a large land owner for forty-four years.

Marsden built a wooden church at Parramatta in 1796, three years after Johnson's wattle and daub church was built at Sydney. In 1797 Marsden began the building of a stone church at Parramatta, opened for worship on Easter Day, 10th April, 1803. St John's was the first stone-built church completed in Australia. Twin towers were added to it in 1820, and it was substantially rebuilt in its present form in the 1850s. If a church does not change its identity when it is rebuilt on the same site, it becomes the oldest church extant. (Johnson's wattle and daub church at Sydney was burnt down in 1798; it was replaced, belatedly, by St Phillip's on Church Hill, opened in 1809.)

The first Roman Catholic Church service in Australia, of which there is documentary record, was held at Parramatta on 15th May, 1803, by the Reverend James Dixon, an Irish priest who had been transported to Sydney as a political exile after the Irish Rising of 1798. He had arrived in Sydney in 1800, accompanied, or followed soon afterwards, by two other priests, Reverend P. O'Neill and Reverend J. Harold. They were not allowed to conduct public services until the Reverend J. Dixon was given that permission at Parramatta in 1803. (It is considered likely that the priests had held private services in Sydney before then; and it is practically certain that a requiem mass and funeral service had been held at Botany Bay, where a French priest, Père le Receveur, died in February 1788 during the visit of the ships of La Pérouse, which carried a second chaplain, Abbé Monges; but documentary evidence of those services is lacking.)

St Patrick's Church, Parramatta, rebuilt in 1936, stands on the site of the first Roman Catholic Church building in Australia, opened for worship there in 1822. At that time St Mary's Chapel, on the site of the present-day Cathedral at Sydney, was under construction, but not completed.

As St John's set a fine example architecturally, all the churches of the various denominations at Parramatta are built of stone, and in classic Gothic style, and are prominent in the central part of the City. These and other public and private buildings in classical styles at Parramatta, not yet overtopped by glass house twentieth century styles—as has been the case in some of the older parts of Sydney—give the Head-of-the-Harbour City its atmosphere as a living image of Australian pioneering traditions: the first Inland Town in Australia—if its situation nineteen miles inland, at the head of tidewaters, qualifies it for that description.

The original Government House of lath and plaster, built in 1789 or 1790, was replaced during Governor Macquarie's term of office (1810-21) by a stone building. It continued to be used by the Governors of New South Wales as a "country residence" until 1847, when Lady Mary Fitzroy, wife of the then Governor, was accidentally killed when her carriage overturned in the park surrounding the residence. At that time, the turreted Government House in the Domain at Sydney had been newly built, replacing a ramshackle old building that stood at the corner of Bridge Street and Phillip Street. The residence at Parramatta then fell into disuse. It was acquired and renovated in 1910 by the King's School, for use as a Junior House. It remains today, surrounded by the lawns, gardens, and non-Australian trees of Parramatta Park, as a reminder of the era of Macquarie.

On the north bank of the Parramatta River, adjacent to the weir and opposite the old Government House, is the King's School, conducted by the Anglican Church since 1832 as a boarding-school and day-school. It is the oldest extant school in Australia. Some of its buildings, erected in 1836, remain in use, though much enlarged by annexes and a War Memorial chapel.

The most notable stonework at Parramatta is the Lennox Bridge, a single-arch bridge spanning the river at Church Street, immediately below the weir. This was built, 1836-39, to the design and under the direction of David Lennox, a Scottish stonemason who had immigrated to New South Wales in 1832, and had previously built bridges over the Nepean River, on the Great Western Highway, and Prospect Creek, the gateway to the Great South Road. His bridges, though repaired or strengthened as required from time to time, remain in use to the present day, carrying heavy modern highway traffic.

The Lennox Bridge, spanning the salt water at the head of the tidal reach of Sydney Harbour, was the first, and remains by far the oldest, of the Sydney Harbour Bridges. It was originally—before vehicular ferries were introduced and other bridges built—the only crossing of Sydney Harbour for horsemen, vehicles, and livestock on the hoof. Travellers by road had to come fifteen miles from Sydney to cross by Lennox Bridge.

From that bridge, roads branched eastwards by devious routes on the north side to Lane Cove and North Sydney; northwards to Wiseman's Ferry across the Hawkesbury, and so to the Hunter Valley and beyond; and north-westward to Windsor and Richmond and other farming settlements on the Upper Hawkesbury (which the white Australian natives of that region called the Oxborough).

From Parramatta, the Great Western Highway led to the Blue Mountains and the beyondlands of the West; and from Parramatta also the first road to the Great South was built, heading the George's River with Lennox's bridge across Prospect Creek after 1833 and before then by the Old Liverpool Road through present-day Fairfield.

The Romulus and Remus of Melbourne—Hamilton Hume, who found the way overland to Port Phillip, in 1824, and John Batman, who, on Hume's advice, formed the first settlement there in 1835—were both white natives of Parramatta, who had learnt much of their bushcraft from the darker natives.

Throughout a century of horse and bullock traction, Parramatta was the hub of Australia's overland and inland road system. It remains so, to a considerable extent, even in the motor age. Much of the north-south long-distance road traffic by-passing Sydney, takes the route through Parramatta, and across Lennox Bridge. The Great Western Highway crosses that route, at Parramatta, half a mile on the southern side of the head of Sydney Harbour; this is the oldest intersection of highways in the continent of Australia, remaining to this day the place where North, South, East, and West meet: the turning-point of destiny for those far-farers who, for 150 years and more, have had to decide—"Sydney or the Bush."

NORTH-SIDE PARRAMATTA

Church Street leads across Lennox Bridge to the northern side of the Parramatta River, and to the suburbs known as Parramatta North, Dundas, and Rydalmere. The river in its freshwater reaches flows in from the north and curves to the eastwards in Parramatta Park, between the old Government House and the King's School. On that river-frontage, beyond the King's School, are three public institutions of renown. The Industrial School for Girls, which was established in 1801 as "the Female Factory," was the first woollen textile mill in Australia: it was a women's prison and woollen mill until the 1850s; its buildings are now renovations of the original edifices. Next is the Parramatta Mental Hospital, with nearly 2,000 patients and spacious grounds, established on this site in 1849, transferred from an earlier site at Castle Hill (five miles northward). Next is the Parramatta Gaol, on the site of the original town prison in which "colonially reconvicted" Imperial convicts were confined: nowadays it is one of the principal penitentiaries for long-term prisoners in New South Wales.

Three hundred yards beyond Lennox Bridge, on the north side, the highway to the eastward along that side of the Harbour crosses Church Street. Originally known as the Eastern Hills Road, or Kissing Point Road, it was eventually extended to Gladesville, and so to the Gladesville Bridge. This provided an alternative route to Sydney, officially named in the 1870s Victoria Road. It extends in that name for twelve miles from Parramatta North to the boundary of the City of Sydney at Glebe Island Bridge. It follows the north side (or Left Bank) of the Harbour for nine miles through Rydalmere, Ryde, and Gladesville to Gladesville Bridge. There it crosses the Harbour to the south side (or Right Bank), and proceeds through Drummoyne, across the Iron Cove Bridge, and through Balmain to Sydney. This is an increasingly used alternative route between Sydney and Parramatta, especially since the building of the new Gladesville Bridge.

SEE ALSO PART II RYDALMERE AND DUNDAS

The suburb of Rydalmere, which stretches eastwards from North Parramatta for three miles along the left bank of the Parramatta River, was given that name in 1886 by a land speculator who bought farming blocks there and subdivided them into residential lots. The fanciful name he chose for the subdivided estate was that of a village and lake in Cumberland, England. That strip of country along the left bank of the Parramatta River is a river flat, which rises to low hills a mile from the waterfront.

The higher ground, known to the pioneer settlers of Parramatta as "the Eastern Hills," was officially designated as the District of Dundas, presumably in honour of Henry Dundas, Lord Melville, who was Britain's Secretary of State for the Home Department from 1791 to 1794. Rydalmere and Dundas, which were separate municipalities, were both incorporated into the City of Parramatta in 1948.

The original road eastwards from Parramatta, on that northern side of the river, followed higher ground in the Dundas Hills. It was known as the Kissing Point Road, because it led from Parramatta to a farming settlement at Kissing Point, on the Harbour front, seven miles by that route. Parramatta was the market town for all that country on the north side of Sydney Harbour, variously known as the Eastern Hills, Kissing Point, and the Field of Mars, comprised in the present-day municipality of Ryde.

Before the Lennox Bridge was opened at Parramatta in 1839, the stream was crossed in its freshwater reaches (above the weir) by fords or log bridges, establishing communication for vehicles and livestock to and from those north-side settlements. The Kissing Point Road followed the higher ground of the Dundas Hills to avoid the boggy country of the river flats, and to avoid fording two short streams that flowed from the hills across the flats.

In April 1791, Governor Phillip granted 40 acres of land

watered by one of those creeks, to Philip Schaeffer, a German ex-soldier, who, having fought in the British forces against the Americans in the War of American Independence, arrived in New South Wales as a free settler in the Second Fleet in July 1790. Schaeffer, naming his farm The Vineyard, proceeded to plant grape vines there, for winemaking: the first vineyard in Australia. The creek that watered his farm retains the name Vineyard Creek to the present day.

In February 1792 Governor Phillip made land grants "on the Parramatta River" to a corporal and eight privates of the marines. Phillip jocularly named that settlement the Field of Mars. Those farms were presumably along the river flats of present-day Rydalmere, near Schaeffer's Vineyard; but confusion arose two years later, when Governor Phillip's successor, Major Grose, established a soldiers' settlement near present-day Artarmon, and named it also the field of Mars. Thereafter, a large tract of the North Shore, from Parramatta eastwards to North Sydney, was loosely termed the Field of Mars, or alternately the Eastern Hills.

Half a mile eastwards of the Vineyard Creek, another and larger creek flows from the Dundas Hills into the Parramatta River. This was originally named Bishop's Creek, perhaps because Thomas Bishop, a private in the marines, was given a grant of land there. Schaeffer increased the area of his vineyard estate to 140 acres by purchasing adjoining lots. He then, in 1798, sold it to Captain Henry Waterhouse, R.N., who, in the previous year, had landed his Merino sheep in Australia, and established his stud there, on the opposite side of the river from John Macarthur's Elizabeth Farm.

Captain Waterhouse died in 1812. Next year, the vineyard estate was sold to Hannibal Macarthur, a nephew of John Macarthur. The new owner made a large sheep station of it by purchasing adjoining blocks of land, comprising much of the present-day areas of Rydalmere and Dundas. In 1836 he built a beautiful stone mansion on the Parramatta River frontage, between the Vineyard Creek and Bishop's Creek. His wife, who was a daughter of Captain P. G. King, Governor of New South Wales 1800-1806, bore him five sons and six daughters. In the 1830s and 1840s their homestead was famous for its dinner parties and dances, to which only "the best people" were invited, those from Sydney usually arriving in chartered steam-launches or on private yachts.

Hannibal Macarthur, who was Chairman of the Bank of Australia, lost heavily when that bank failed in 1844, and had to sell his vineyard estate. It was bought for the Roman Catholic Church by Archbishop Polding, who renamed it Subiaco, from the place in Italy where Saint Benedict lived in a cave in the sixth century. The Archbishop sold or leased most of the farmlands on the estate, but kept the homestead and its surrounding grounds for use by nuns of the Order of Saint Benedict as a convent and school. Named as Subiaco House, it was occupied by the Benedictine Sisters for 108 years, until 1957, when they moved to a new and larger building at Pennant Hills. The historic mansion, its site required for the expansion of a factory, was then, to the sorrow of all who value Australian traditions, demolished, leaving nothing but the name of Subiaco Creek—which had replaced the earlier name of Bishop's Creek—as a reminder of pioneering days gone forever; it is doomed perhaps to be banished even from the memory of a nation that values the lore of other countries more than its own.

On the western side of Vineyard Creek, in large grounds, is the Rydalmere Mental Hospital, established in 1888, with accommodation for 1,000 patients. As it is only two miles from the older and bigger Mental Hospital at North Parramatta, the two institutions (both within the boundaries of the City of Parramatta) are able to work in conjunction in some practical aspects of psychiatric treatment. If there are some citizens who ask why Parramatta should be blessed with two lunatic asylums and a gaol, the answer could only be that the peaceful atmosphere of the Head-of-the-Harbour City is more conducive than that of Sydney to the cure of insanity and crime; besides, it takes all sorts to make a world.

SEE ALSO PART II   MODERN PARRAMATTA

The "Cradle City," in which three of Australia's main industries—wool, wheat, and wine, were born and nurtured, had other pioneering industrial achievements emblazoned on its escutcheon; for there the first beer in Australia was brewed, and there the first horse-race meeting in Australia was held: and if those are not Australia's biggest industries, they have grown so hugely that Parramatta's scroll of fame as their Australian birthplace shines with an inextinguishable glitter that any other city in Australia may envy, but cannot surpass.

The beer was brewed in 1800 by James Squire at Kissing Point, which at that time was considered as part of Parramatta. The first race meeting was held on the western outskirts of Parramatta town on 30th April, 1810, six months before the first officially recorded race meeting held at Sydney (in Hyde Park, 16th October, 1810). Incidentally, the first Agricultural Show in Australia was held at Parramatta in 1824. Those are the insignia that she wears; let others claim to be Mother Cities and Queen Cities: she is the Midwife City, the Nurse.

For a century, after railway development, beginning in the 1850s, increasingly reached out to the South, to the West, and to the North, with octopus tentacles, bringing all trade and commerce to the maw of Sydney, the town of Parramatta drowsed like a Sleeping Beauty, awaiting the magical touch of the modern industrial boom, when Sydney, overflowing, stretched westward again, as in the earliest years, seeking wide open spaces at the Harbour's head and beyond it—not for farmlands now, but for factory sites.

The roads to the Great South, the Great West, and the Great North had made Parramatta a hub-town for horseback, horse-drawn, and bullock-drawn traffic, converging on Sydney or dispersing from it. There, travellers coming in from the Outback could stay overnight at the Woolpack Inn, the Red Cow Inn, or the White Horse Inn, and stage-coaches changed horses; but the railways passed through or by Parramatta, and its quality, even as a staging-camp, was lost. Then, as the upper reaches of the river silted—an effect, partly, of damming the freshwater reaches, which prevented normal scouring of silt—even the ferry-steamers from Sydney ceased running to the Queen's Wharf (built 1839) in the town, and made their terminus two and a half miles downstream, at the Duck River junction.

Yet Parramatta's early quality as an industrial centre has never entirely disappeared, and in modern times has become intensified and enlarged. The former grazing-paddocks of John Macarthur are occupied partly by suburban streets of dwellings, but chiefly along their river frontages by some big industrial establishments, including an oil refinery, a tyre factory, and two very large factories producing building-materials (wall-boards and metal ceilings). These factories use water transport, but are served also by railway branch-lines, and by roads.

The oil refinery, one of the biggest and oldest-established in Australia, occupies a site of 235 acres along the western side of the Duck River, in what was John Macarthur's land after Governor Macquarie's grant to him in 1815. This refinery, established in a small way in the early 1920s, and taken over by its present owners in 1927, obtains its crude oil from tankers that discharge their cargo at Gore Bay, on the north side of the Harbour, nine miles downstream from the Duck River. A fleet of twenty-two barges was in service for nearly forty years, conveying the crude oil up-river to the refinery, until a pipeline was built to carry it. More than 1,000 workers are employed at the refinery, which distributes its products throughout New South Wales by means of a large fleet of rail tankers and road tankers. The installations along the shore of the Duck River include more than sixty storage tanks and a formidable array of complicated engineering structures for distilling, cracking, and re-forming the various petroleum products. Nine million gallons of water from the Duck River are pumped through the refinery daily for cooling purposes, and returned to the river.

Adjoining the refinery grounds on their western side is the Rosehill Racecourse, one of the principal Sydney tracks. Controlled by the Sydney Turf Club, this is a comparatively new racecourse, established in the present century, and therefore not identical with the original Parramatta Racecourse, or the original Rose Hill (a knoll on which Government House was built, in what is known as Parramatta Park).

The Rosehill Racecourse is served by a branch railway line, which diverges from the main Western line thirteen miles west of Sydney. Beyond the racecourse, the branch line proceeds to the northward, crossing the Parramatta River by a bridge at a place named by the railway authorities Camellia. Near that bridge, close to the bank of the river, is a well-kept grave, with a modern headstone, engraved, "In this grave lie the remains of

Elinor Magee and her infant child, who were drowned in the Parramatta River January 1793." This is one of the oldest preserved graves in Australia. The burial-places of many who died in the earliest years of settlement have, for various reasons, been unmarked, and so are "lost."

The railway line that crosses the river at Camellia continues northwards to the farming district of Carlingford, to take its products (chiefly orchard fruits) to the Sydney market. On that side of the river—the Left Bank, Rydalmere—is a naval store, which uses water transport to and from what is virtually nowadays the head of navigation in Sydney Harbour. Near Subiaco, also, is a factory making aluminium products.

Large engineering works have been established for many years in Parramatta, at Clyde, on the upper reaches of the Duck River. The city as a commercial centre has gained in the 1950s and 1960s from numerous new factories in its western purlieus, including Blacktown and St Mary's, between Parramatta and Penrith.

Blacktown, originally known as Black's Town, was an Aboriginal settlement, removed by Governor Brisbane in 1823 from Parramatta to a site eleven miles away. Three years later, the first Australian-born poet to have a volume of his poetry published in his native land, Charles Tompson, found the buildings deserted, and wrote one of the first poems ever composed on the theme of the Aborigines:

> *Lost child! Shall we the savage part pursue?*
> *Must all despise thee for thy sable hue?*
> *Will Charity no warm vicegerent [sic] send*
> *To own thee Brother or to call thee Friend?*

The "divide" between the Sydney Harbour basin and the Hawkesbury River basin is a low ridge, known as Seven Hills, six miles westward of Parramatta, curving to the north-eastward in the Baulkham Hills, five miles northward of Parramatta, and then continuing eastwards through Pennant Hills, Kuringai Chase, and French's Forest (heading the Lane Cove River and Middle Harbour), to the ocean shore at Manly.

On the southern side, the Sydney Harbour basin is divided from the George's River and Botany Bay drainage system by a low range that curves eastwards from Seven Hills to May's Hill (originally Maize Hill) a mile south-west of Parramatta; thence to Chester Hill, at the head of Duck River; thence to Dulwich Hill, at the head of Iron Cove Creek; thence to Surry Hills, Darlinghurst, Edgecliff, Bellevue Hill, and Dover Heights to the coast at South Head.

In that full perspective, the Sydney Harbour basin is seen as a drainage area only twenty-four miles from west to east. It is small compared with the 8,000 square miles of the Hawkesbury River system, which is channelled into a main stream 300 miles long (known in its upper reaches by the melodius Aboriginal name of Wollondilly), frequently swollen by floods from the

rain run-off of the Blue Mountains. The Wollondilly or Hawkesbury River is navigable (though seldom navigated nowadays)
for fifty miles from its ocean mouth at Broken Bay; its course
sweeps around the Sydney Harbour basin on the western and
northern sides, thereby preventing the run-off from the Blue
Mountains pouring into Sydney Harbour as effectively as if it
had been designed for that purpose.

With that protection from flooding and silting, Sydney
Harbour receives the rainwater run-off from its comparatively
small drainage area in many little creeks or rills that trickle from
the soakage of short gullies, or pour briefly as stormwater drains
after heavy rain; but, in the strictly geological view, the Harbour
is a tidally flooded inlet of the ocean rather than the estuary of
that small freshwater stream above the weir at Parramatta. It
is a sunken sandstone valley; if it was originally the bed of the
Parramatta River, it may have been deepened by scouring of
the tides following a subsidence of the Continental Shelf of the
ocean (preventing formation of a sandbar at its mouth), or by
an earthquake that happened to make a rift in the sandstone
beds along the line of the watercourse.

How the bed of that little stream widened and deepened into
the large expanse of the Harbour may be surmised rather than
precisely explained: it is a freak of nature. The narrow, shallow,
mangrove-lined upper reaches of the tidewater, for three miles
downstream from Lennox Bridge at Parramatta to the Silverwater Bridge at the Duck River junction, have presumably the
character of the original stream, the bed of which sank, for
sixteen miles eastwards from Silverwater to the Ocean, to form
the fjord-like flooded valley, with its many sheltered arms, bays,
and coves, which, as though it had been designed for that
purpose, became the best and most beautiful harbour in the
world: or, if superlatives are feared, one of the best and most
beautiful.

13

RYDE AND HUNTER'S HILL

EXTENDING FROM PARRAMATTA EASTWARDS, ALONG THE NORTHERN side of the Harbour, the seven contiguous municipalities of Ryde, Hunter's Hill, Lane Cove, North Sydney, Mosman, Willoughby, and Manly are residential districts. They have only a few mercantile wharves; their business activities depend chiefly on the local trade of "dormitory suburbs" from which bread-winners travel daily across the Harbour to and from work on "the Other Side." There are a few enclaves of "high density" flat-dwelling people, especially at North Sydney, but, in the North Side region as a whole, most of the dwellings are brick bungalows with tiled roofs, each standing in its own plot of ground, with gardens, lawns, and trees.

In each of the North Side suburbs, there is easy access to the Main Harbour's northern shore, with its many beautiful coves and promontories, and a plentiful greenery of Australian native trees along the foreshores, especially on some of the bold head-lands, where the original Australian character has been preserved, perhaps fortuitously, but with a striking picturesque effect, as viewed nowadays in contrast with those of the southern shore, where almost all the headlands have been built on; and the dwellers on the North Side have quick access also the riverine reaches of the Harbour's two large tidal arms—the Lane Cove River and Middle Harbour—veining the ridgy terrain in many places with vistas of water and bushland that are sparsely, or as yet not at all, sprinkled with the rash of red-tiled roofs symptomatic of suburban bungaloid growth.

In the pre-Bridge era, that ridgy terrain (making communica-tions by road and rail difficult), and the abundant sufficiency of berths for shipping along the southern shore, saved the North Side from the extensive industrial and commercial development that has virtually abolished "the Bush" on the South Side of the Harbour. It would be impossible to find any place, in any of the North Side municipalities, more than a few minutes' walk from a Harbour view, or at least from a gully that leads to a creek that leads to a cove in the Harbour or one of its arms; and in most of those gullies are gumtrees and ferns and banksia trees and the delicate flowering shrubs of the Sydney Sandstone country; and kookaburras may sometimes be heard chuckling there, or possums seen frolicking, or bluetongue lizards basking on the sunwarmed rocks. . . . Old Australia not yet finally destroyed by the invaders from Europe.

The North Side, then, with its character of an accumulated suburbia set in vistas of Harbour and Bushland, is much less smoke-grimed and more picturesque than the densely commercialized and industrialized dockside districts of the South Side; but the history of the North Side fits into the pattern of the crossings of the water by boats, ferries, and bridges; the livelihood of its inhabitants has depended largely on ways and means of crossing the Harbour, either to go to work or to do business in the City of Sydney, where most of the commerce, professions, and government offices were originally concentrated: and, because of that necessity to make regular or at least frequent crossings of that grand saltwater-filled fissure, the North-siders are, in general, more aware of the Harbour's sparkling life than those who do not have to cross it to the City.

The specialized term, "North Shore"—though applicable in its literal meaning to all the northern side of the Main Harbour, from Parramatta to Manly—is restricted by custom to that part of the northern shore directly opposite the City of Sydney, and to its hinterland in the "North Shore [Railway] Line" that crosses the Sydney Harbour Bridge and proceeds from North Sydney, along the dividing ridge between the Lane Cove River and Middle Harbour, to Hornsby. That restricted usage originated within the first two years of settlement, but it never was, and is not now, an official designation of any district with defined boundaries; its restricted application is a matter of tradition: but because of that tradition the term "North Side" is preferred to "North Shore" when reference is intended to the entire region along the northern drainage slopes of Sydney Harbour, from Parramatta to Manly; and the people who live on those slopes are North-siders.

The country to the westward of the Lane Cove River (incorporated since 1870 in the municipality of Ryde) has fertile soil, of shales and clays, whereas the country to the eastward of the Lane Cove River is chiefly of sandstone ridges, not suitable for cultivation. For that reason most of the North Side remained uninhabited in the earlier years of settlement, except in those regions that were developed as outposts of Parramatta, and were known for that reason as "the Eastern Farms," or "the Eastern Hills" (i.e., to the eastward of Parramatta), but also variously as Kissing Point, the Field of Mars, and Hunter's Hill.

Those names, having various applications, official and unofficial, at various times, have caused some confusion among historians. Legends have arisen from oral traditions, and sometimes from guesswork by dogmatic chroniclers. Here, as often as elsewhere on the shores of Sydney Harbour, and throughout Australia, local lore, as reflected in place-names, has origins almost forgotten.

KISSING POINT

There is a romantic legend that Kissing Point was so named because Governor Hunter (who held office as Governor of New South Wales, 1795-1800) gallantly carried a lady ashore from his boat, to prevent her feet from getting wet, and at the same time bestowed upon her a gubernatorial kiss; but whether she was a convict, a free settler's wife or daughter, or a black gin, the legend leaves to the imagination.

Much more likely "the Kissing Point" was so named by Captain John Hunter or his officers in 1788—seven years before he was appointed as Governor—when they were exploring the Harbour and making a chart of it, with soundings, in conformity with naval routines. "The Kissing Point" was the point near the head of the great estuarine inlet beyond which deepwater vessels could not safely proceed without being grounded on the mudflats. Westward of that point the deepwater channel ended, and the water shoaled to flats with soundings of between one and three fathoms, where the keels of larger vessels would brush or "kiss" the mud.

The word "kiss" was in regular nautical use in the meaning of touching lightly. There is apparently no documentary evidence of the origin of the name of Kissing Point in that meaning, as the end of the deepwater channel of Sydney Harbour, but there is sufficient evidence that the name was in official use in 1794, when land grants were registered as located at Kissing Point. That was one year before Captain John Hunter was appointed Governor of New South Wales. He was then in England, where he had returned early in 1792, to face a formal court martial for losing his ship, H.M.S. *Sirius*, at Norfolk Island, in March 1790.

The promontory which, on the modern charts of the Australian Naval Hydrographic Service, is named Kissing Point, is on the northern shore of the Parramatta River, opposite to the Thomas Walker Convalescent Hospital and the Concord Repatriation Hospital on the southern shore. The river there is only 230 yards wide; the channel has depths of from five to seven fathoms, but beyond that point—which is 500 yards upstream from the Mortlake Gasworks coal-wharves—the water shoals rapidly, and ocean-going vessels of large size cannot safely proceed.

That Kissing Point promontory is three-quarters of a mile downstream from the Ryde Road Bridge, and one mile downstream from the Ryde Railway Bridge; but all that reach of the northern side of the Parramatta River was originally known as "the Kissing Point," where cargo-carrying schooners and brigs, unable to sail across the flats to Parramatta, loaded and unloaded merchandise at wharves and jetties serving the "Eastern Farms" of Parramatta.

The first land grants in the Eastern Farms district were made by Governor Phillip in February 1792 to marines—his Field of Mars. This was not an official designation, but it later acquired official status when a large reserve of Crown Land near the Kissing Point was named the Field of Mars Common. Other land grants were soon made along the waterfront and in the hinterland of good country extending for five miles northwards (to Pennant Hills). The term Kissing Point, which was originally applied to the settlement near the schooner-jetties in the vicinity of the present-day Ryde Bridges, gradually became applied to the whole district, as an alternative to the earlier names of the Eastern Farms, the Eastern Hills and the Field of Mars.

Those earlier names did not fall entirely into disuse, but, during the heyday of the Harbour schooner traffic, for nearly forty years (1795-1835), the Kissing Point wharves and jetties brought into existence a commercial settlement along the waterfront on the northern side at that limit of deepwater navigation. From there timber and farm produce were shipped to Sydney, and also general merchandise was unloaded there, for a thriving community of farmers spread widely over the Wianamatta Shale country of twenty square miles between the Lane Cove River and the Dundas Hills and between the Pennant Hills and the Parramatta River's shore. Not only that waterfront, but also its hinterland, then became known as the Kissing Point District, and the road to that district from Parramatta was named the Kissing Point Road.

To interpret the local historical references, it is necessary to understand that at various times the different names applied to that region were stretched or contracted like elastic to apply to the whole region, or to one part of it, in both popular and official usage.

From the earliest years of settlement, the whole of the northern shore of the harbour was sometimes called Hunter's Hill. That name is lettered on early maps of land grants as far up-river as Meadowbank, at the western end of the Kissing Point schooner-port. From there a road led to Pennant Hills, and beyond to the Hawkesbury River. Today there is a residential district in Kuringai municipality, at the head of the Lane Cove River, near Pennant Hills, five miles inland from the original water frontage of Kissing Point on the Parramatta River; but that inland district is officially named "Kissing Point," and is shown on modern maps, stubbornly clinging to the pioneering name that has been discarded in other parts of that large region which was the hinterland of the original Kissing Point schooner-port.

Similarly the name of "Hunter's Hill" has been localized to one part of the northern shore—the peninsula between the Lane Cove and Parramatta Rivers at their confluence—and the name of the Field of Mars is preserved only in a park and in an old cemetery near the eastern border of Ryde municipality. The name Eastern Farms (or Eastern Hills) is preserved vestigially in the suburb of Eastwood, on the railway, two miles north of the original settlement on the shore of the Parramatta River. That suburb takes its name from the estate of Samuel Terry, "the Botany Bay millionaire," who built a mansion, Eastwood House, there, most probably so named because it was in the Eastern Farms district. Or it may have been named from the village of Eastwood, in Nottinghamshire (the birthplace of D. H. Lawrence).

The commercial centre of the original Kissing Point waterfront settlement was at Church street, to which the present-day Ryde Road Bridge abuts. Anyone with a respect for Australia's early history must regret that this bridge (on the site of the original Kissing Point punt-ferry to Concord) was not named the Kissing

Point Bridge when it was opened in 1935; but the colonial syco-
phantic nomenclature of Ryde was adopted, as though it were
incurable. Different was the spirit of John Dunmore Lang, the
fiery Scottish clergyman who more than a century previously
had protested against unsuitable names for Australian places:

> . . . Had I the reins
> Of government for a fortnight, I would change
> These government appellatives, and give
> The country names that should deserve to live.

If "Kissing Point" seemed a name too flippant for a suburb or
a bridge, there was an alternative which it seems, was never
considered. The aboriginal name of that district which has been
so incongruously renamed Ryde was Wallumetta: a name
euphonious and distinctive, that should "deserve to live," fit to
compare with those preserved along the North Shore Line—
Killara, Turramurra, Warrawee, Wahroonga, Waitara—and in
Kuringai and Warringah eastwards, Parramatta and Toongabbie
westwards, and Yaralla and Cabarita southwards on the other
side of the water. Such names have the true Australian ring,
which Ryde so sadly lacks.

The farming settlement at Kissing Point, and its hinterland,
well established in the 1790s, conterminously with the settlement
at Parramatta, rates as one of the oldest agricultural districts
in Australia. Many land grants, of from 30 to 60 acres each, were
made there to ex-soldiers and other free settlers, and to well-
behaved time-served convicts; but larger grants also were made
to absentee owners, who appointed managers (or "overseers") to
live on the properties and supervise the unpaid labour of
assigned convicts. Among the absentee land owners was the
Reverend Samuel Marsden, of Parramatta, whose estate, Brush
Farm, was on the Kissing Point Road, five miles from Parramatta
and two miles from the schooner wharves. Another absentee land
owner was Surgeon Balmain, who was granted 425 acres at the
Field of Mars, near Meadowbank. In course of time the Blaxlands
of Newington also acquired farm-holdings in that district.

Sheep were grazed on the larger properties, but mixed farming,
with a character of peasant agriculture was practised on the
smaller holdings. In particular, fruit and vegetables were grown
there for the Sydney market. The first commercial citrus orchards
in Australia were established at Kissing Point in the 1790s, from
seedlings supplied by the Reverend Richard Johnson, who had
planted, in his garden in Sydney, in 1788, seeds saved from fruit
he had bought at Rio de Janeiro in 1787 on the passage in the
First Fleet. Those seeds grew to trees which bore fruit, and
their seedlings were planted at Kissing Point. Thereafter, for
more than fifty years, Kissing Point oranges, shipped by schooner
to the Sydney market, were plentiful and cheap, much sought,
not only by the populace of Sydney, but by shipmasters.

One of the first churches in Australia was a chapel built at
Kissing Point by Rowland Hassall, a lay preacher of the London
Missionary Society, who arrived in Sydney in May 1798 from

Tahiti. He acted as an assistant to Samuel Marsden, who gave him a home at Brush Farm, and delegated to him the duties of holding services at Kissing Point, as a catechist. In August 1798, near the waterfront, Hassall built a chapel, which was dedicated as a church in the year 1800. On weekdays he conducted a school —one of the first in Australia—with an enrolment of twenty pupils. The church was rebuilt in 1826, as St Anne's, and stands there today, one of the oldest in Australia.

Among the first settlers at Kissing Point was John Small, who was granted land there in 1793. He and his wife (née Mary Parker) were ex-convicts, who had arrived in the First Fleet and had been domestic servants in Governor Phillip's household. Their daughter Rebecca, born at Sydney in September 1788, was in later years a person of renown, claimed to be the first white child born in Australia.

It is difficult to prove or disprove that claim. Rebecca was born eight months after the First Fleet arrived at Sydney Cove. There are records of several "baptisms" of infants at Sydney before she was born, but these may have been children of the wives of marines or of convicts, or of unmarried convict women, born at sea, or before the Fleet left England. It is undeniable that Rebecca Small was *one of the first* white children born in Australia. When she went with her parents to live at Kissing Point she was five years old. Possibly she was then the oldest *surviving* white child born in Australia, for infant mortality was heavy in the first year of settlement.

All things considered, she deserves an award of high merit in the True Australian Shrine of Memory. Her father became a successful farmer, and afterwards an innkeeper at Kissing Point. Rebecca lived there with her parents until 1807, when, aged nineteen, she married Francis Oakes, a former lay preacher of the London Missionary Society, who had been appointed, in 1805, as Head Constable at Parramatta. She bore him twelve children, and reared ten of them, all of whom married and had large families. Whether she was the first, or only one of the first of the native White Australians, she proved that her native land was a healthy place to live in. She died, aged ninety-five, at Parramatta in 1883. Her direct descendants are a legion. More than forty with the name of Oakes are listed in the Sydney telephone directory; there are others in country towns and in other States; and, on the female side, though the name of Oakes is obscured, the descendants of Rebecca are as numerous as the males. Many of her descendants are now of the sixth generation of the Australian-born. She deserves at least a statue at Kissing Point, or in a niche of the Australian Pantheon, and to become a legend in the land of her birth.

Another celebrity of Kissing Point was James Squire, the first brewer of beer in Australia, who perhaps for that reason deserves a statue. He immigrated as a free settler, at the age of forty, and was granted land at Kissing Point in 1795. He was successful as a farmer, and bought some additional blocks of land, on the waterfront, including the site of the present-day Halvorsens' boatbuilding yards. In 1796 an attempt was made at Sydney by a man named John Boston to brew beer from malted maize, bittered with Cape Gooseberry leaves and stalks. That brew was not "beer" in the ordinary meaning of that word—an alcoholic beverage made from the fermented liquor of malted barley, bittered with hops. It was therefore not surprising that Boston's brew failed to please the customers, and his business soon failed.

James Squire saw the opportunity, and seized it. He was a man of vision, with capital to invest. Presumably he had come from Kent in England, and understood hopgrowing, malting, and brewing. On his farm at Kissing Point he grew barley, and built a malthouse, also buying barley from other farmers. It may be supposed that he imported vats and other brewing utensils from England, and also, at first, dried hops. At the same time he was experimenting with the growing of hops from seeds, or possibly from "sets" (cuttings) imported from England. His brewery was in working order, and produced its first brew, at Kissing Point, in 1800. It was not until 1806 that he succeeded in cutting a crop of hops (the first successful cultivation in Australia). The beer that Squire brewed was true beer. He prospered, and built a fine mansion at Kissing Point, next to the brewery, which flourished until he died in 1822, and thereafter was carried on for some years by his son-in-law, James Farnell.

A picture of Squire's home and brewery is among the engravings in the book, *Views in Australia,* published in London in 1825 from drawings made by Joseph Lycett, an artist who had served a term as a convict in New South Wales from 1810 to 1822. The engraving, showing the view of Kissing Point across the water from Concord, is accompanied by an explanatory note that serves as an eloquent obituary of James Squire:

> His beverage had a general good name throughout the Colony, and he was universally respected and beloved as a friend and protector of the lower class of settlers. Had he been less liberal, he might have died more wealthy, but his [practical] assistance always accompanied his advice to the poor and unfortunate, and his name will long be pronounced with veneration by the grateful objects of his liberality.

Among the "poor and unfortunate" who found in James Squire a "friend and protector" was the renowned Bennelong, a member of the Manly tribe, who had been forcibly captured, in November 1789, on Governor Phillip's orders, and compelled to learn English in order to act as an interpreter. He had lived, at first as a prisoner and later as a willing guest, in Governor Phillip's household, and later again in his own humpy on Bennelong Point (site of the Sydney Opera House). He had accompanied Governor Phillip to England in 1792, and returned home in 1795. He then took to the bush, and, according to some accounts, was "killed in a tribal fight," but the local legend at Kissing Point is emphatic that he eventually sought and found sanctuary at the homestead of James Squire, where he lived in a humpy in the garden, and died and was buried there in 1815. If any registration of his death and burial was made, the documents have apparently been lost. Presumably a headstone was placed on his grave, and remained until the 1860s, and then was removed—as often happened on lonely graves by acts of vandalism, committed by people of no conscience on seeing a good paving-stone, or door-step, going to waste. In 1927 some of the old inhabitants of Kissing Point located the site of Bennelong's grave, from their boy-hood memories, but no note was made of it by any responsible person, with a sense of history; and today the exact site is unknown, although the vicinity—in Waterview Street, Ryde, at the back of Halvorsens' boatshed—may be reasonably surmised.

If the Opera House is not to be considered as Bennelong's monument, this would be a suitable place, at or near the grave of the first Australian Aborginal to be civilized; and on it could appropriately be inscribed a couplet from the poem by E. O. Schlunke, *Bennelong Returns to Heaven*:

> *All the land ruined by that awful invention, the plow—*
> *Hardly one goanna to the acre it is carrying now . . .*

Another celebrity of Kissing Point was James Squire Farnell, a grandson of James Squire, the brewer. Born at Kissing Point in 1827, J. S. Farnell was educated at Parramatta. He was elected Member of Parliament for Parramatta in 1860, and, after serving as Minister for Lands in the Parkes Ministry, 1872-75, he became Prime Minister (as the office was then named) of New South Wales in 1877, but held that office for only one year. His ministry resigned when it was defeated on a Land Bill; but during the twelves months when Farnell held office as Prime Minister, another high office was bestowed on him; he became the first Grand Master of the New South Wales constitution of Free-masons—the first regularly constituted and recognized Grand Lodge of Freemasons in Australia.

Historians of Freemasonry state that the New South Wales Grand Lodge of 1877 was formed by thirteen lodges of the Irish and Scottish constitutions, but lodges of the English constitution did not join them until the United Grand Lodge of New South Wales was formed in 1888. The name of Constitution Road, the main thoroughfare connecting the present-day business centres of Meadowbank and Ryde, is derived not from the political constitution of New South Wales but from the Masonic consti-tution. J. S. Farnell's tenure of dual office as Prime Minister and Grand Master may be unique in political and Masonic annals.

Among the celebrities of Kissing Point there was one whose fame may outlive that of all the others. Maria Ann Smith, wife of Thomas Smith, was the original cultivator, by chance, of the now world-famous Granny Smith apple. Born at Kissing Point in the early years of the nineteenth century, Maria Ann Smith, widowed, was living on a small farm near Eastwood in the 1860s, when one day—according to her recollection some years later—she tipped out, on to the bank of a little creek that was in her property, the contents of a wooden packing-case, including a rotted apple.

One of the seeds from the core of that apple germinated, took root, grew from a seedling into a tree, and, not being in the way, on that sloping creek-bank which was Granny Smith's rubbish dump, was not cut down. In due time it bore fruit. By the one chance in ten million, or perhaps a hundred million, among apple-seeds or any other seeds, that plant had developed a genetic variation that produced a fixed mutation of species. Granny Smith's apple-tree was almost as paradoxical as a platypus. It produced fruit that was green when it was ripe; a cooking-apple that tasted as well uncooked as cooked; and, after being picked from the tree, it would keep in good condition without refrigeration, for eight or ten months, sometimes a year.

The local fame of Granny Smith's apple grew; in 1868 experts examined the tree and the fruit; in the meantime Granny Smith had planted some seeds from the tree. They germinated, and the seedlings grew to trees which produced fruit identical with those from the mother-tree on the creek bank. Friends and neighbours planted out the seedlings, and the local fame of Granny Smith's apple increased. An orchardist, Edward Gallard, planted out a grove of the seedlings. The trees fruited perfectly in the new species, which was therefore proved to be a fixed mutation, and not a hybrid likely to revert to parent or ancestral stocks. The apples were marketed at Sydney, and their reputation gradually spread far and wide.

In 1895, approximately thirty years after the first fruiting of Granny Smith's original tree, large-scale plantings were made at the Government Experimental Station at Bathurst, and the experts decided that Granny Smith's apple was a "sport" or fixed mutation of the French Crab apple, a cooking-apple much grown in Tasmania. Whether the mutation had occurred in a tree in Tasmania, or only in the "freak" tree at Eastwood, it was not possible to say. From the Bathurst plantation, seedlings were distributed widely throughout New South Wales. One hundred years after that first fruiting of Granny Smith's apple, its name and hers were known not only throughout Australia, but in many foreign countries to which Australian apples are exported. The long-keeping qualities of the Granny Smith apple make it a favourite in the home market, and also for export.

In 1950, the Ryde Municipal Council dedicated a small public reserve at Eastwood, near the site of Granny Smith's home, and named it the Granny Smith Memorial Park.

SEE ALSO

PART II   THE MUNICIPALITY OF RYDE

Incorporated in 1870, the Municipality of Ryde was enlarged in 1945 to include Eastwood. It now has an area of eleven square miles and a population of 70,000; it has lost its former character as a district of farms, orchards, and market gardens, and has become chiefly a suburban residential district, with a sprinkling of light industries. Some rural aspects remain, in paddocks not yet built on, especially in the northern parts of the municipality.

In those open spaces the third university of the Sydney metropolitan region, to be named the Macquarie University, is being established.

Changes in the character of the district from rural to suburban have been due almost entirely to increased means of transportation, by road, rail, and harbour-crossing bridges, at first supplementing, and later replacing waterborne traffic to and from Sydney. The two Ryde Bridges, the Gladesville Bridge, and the Sydney Harbour Bridge have all "tapped" that western district of the North Side, which long ago ceased to be an outpost of Parramatta, and became a dependency of Sydney.

The waterfront of Ryde municipality, on the Parramatta River, stretches from Meadowbank (opposite Homebush Bay) eastwards for four miles through the original Kissing Point schooner-port, and then through districts incongruously, and even absurdly, named Putney and Tennyson, to Bedlam Point at Gladesville. There, on its eastern side, it has boundaries with the municipalities of Hunter's Hill, Lane Cove, Willoughby, and Kuringai, part of that boundary being the upper reaches of the Lane Cove River, which are preserved in a National Park.

A rowing-boat ferry service, crossing the Parramatta River between Kissing Point and Concord, in the vicinity of the present-day Ryde Road Bridge, established contact between those two pioneer farm settlements in 1794; this was the first regular cross-Harbour ferry service as such. (The *Rose Hill Packet*, on her passages to and from Parramatta, would call at Kissing Point, and also at Concord, but that was not strictly a cross-Harbour service. The settlements at Kissing Point and Concord were established before grants of land were made on the "North Shore," opposite Sydney Town.)

As settlement extended in the hinterland of Kissing Point, to Eastwood, Pennant Hills, and beyond to the Hawkesbury, a network of roads converged to the schooner-port, from which, beginning at a date not ascertained, but probably in the year 1800, a punt-ferry, capable of carrying livestock and vehicles, plied across the stream to Concord. Traffic could then proceed by the Concord Road and the Parramatta Road, a route of ten miles from the Kissing Point punt-ferry to Sydney. This was much shorter than the detour through Parramatta, which crossed the river there in the freshwater reach above the weir. From Pennant Hills to Sydney via Parramatta, the road distance was twenty miles. The Kissing Point ferry shortened that distance by five miles. The punt-ferry service there remained in operation for 135 years, until the opening of the Ryde Road Bridge in 1935. Then the ferry, which had been such a feature of the Upper Harbour scene for such a long period of time, disappeared like a puff of smoke, as though it had never been, or lingering perhaps like a ghost only in the memory of those, an age-group dwindling in number, to whom it seemed that a romantic relic of the past had gone into the Limbo of the Obsolete, on the ever-accumulating rubbish-tip of Time.

After the transportation of British Imperial Convicts to New South Wales had ceased in 1841, there was a sudden large increase in the number of free immigrants to the Australian colonies, including New South Wales. Among these was one, G. M. Pope, from the town of Ryde, in the Isle of Wight, off the coast of Hampshire, England. He settled in the village of Kissing Point, and opened a shop selling general merchandise there. In sentimental remembrance of his native place, he named his shop "the Ryde Store." (The word "Ryde" means in the Danish language, "a clearing in the forest"; it was bestowed by the Danish conquerors of England on their settlement in the Isle of Wight, a thousand years before G. M. Pope bestowed it on his store at Kissing Point, New South Wales.)

Apparently G. M. Pope, and some of the other residents of the village of Kissing Point, felt that it was beneath their dignity to have letters from England addressed to them at such a strangely named place as Kissing Point. By their influence, the name of the Kissing Point post-office was changed in 1846 to Ryde. Perhaps the churchwardens of St Anne's supported that alteration, feeling that there was some incongruity in the name of the church, "St Anne's, Kissing Point." When the name of the post-office was changed, the name of the village was gradually changed. Nobody had thought of ascertaining the aboriginal name of the place, "Wallumetta." When the municipality was incorporated in 1870, the name of Ryde was extended from the village to its hinterland. Pope Street, near St Anne's Church, commemorates not the Bishop of Rome, but the immigrant from the Isle of Wight who succeeded in obliterating one of the most interesting names in the early history of British settlement in Australia.

One of the first settlers along the north-side shore eastwards of Kissing Point village was John Glade. He was an ex-convict, who had arrived in New South Wales in 1791, and, being a well-behaved man, was given a grant of farmland, a few years later, on the riverfront at a place which became known as Glade's Bay. He prospered, and extended his farm to 140 acres. That land, subdivided for residential settlement in the 1880s, was given the name of "Gladesville," from its proximity to Glade's Bay. Probably the origin of the name of Glade's Bay had by then been forgotten, but it so happened that the name of one of the convict pioneers was perpetuated, prominently, on the map. The Gladesville Bridge and the Gladesville Mental Hospital are outstanding features of that part of the Upper Harbour; they are landmarks known to millions of travellers by road nowadays crossing that bridge between Sydney and the North Side.

In the 1820s, a "lunatic asylum" was established on a headland, which was thereupon named Bedlam Point, near the eastern boundary of John Glade's farm, on the opposite side of the Harbour from John Harris's Five Dock Farm. Lunatics in those days were regarded almost as criminals, and were closely imprisoned and guarded. Under the laws of the time, in England, a proportion of persons convicted of crimes were insane, and some of those were shipped to New South Wales as Imperial Convicts.

The lunatic asylum at Bedlam Point was guarded by a detachment of soldiers. It served also as a military signal station, one of a series of five stations that relayed semaphor signals of military or governmental urgency between Sydney and Parramatta. In 1829 the asylum at Bedlam Point was closed, pending the erection of a new building on a site three-quarters of a mile further east, on the bank of Tarban Creek. It was then that a vehicular punt-ferry service began to ply across the Harbour between Bedlam Point and Abbotsford Point (Five Dock), replacing the skiff-ferry service which had been in operation there for twenty years or more.

The Bedlam Point punt-ferry provided a route to Sydney—via the "Great North Road," which joined the Parramatta Road at the head of Iron Cove—two miles shorter than the Kissing Point punt-ferry route via Concord. On the North Side, roads converged to the Bedlam Point ferry from far and wide. One road from the Hunter Valley crossed the Hawkesbury River at Wiseman's Ferry, and then led through Pennant Hills, with branches to Parramatta, to Kissing Point, and to Bedlam Point; another, from Pittwater, at the mouth of the Hawkesbury River, headed the Middle Harbour and Lane Cove River, then turned southward to Bedlam Point; it was joined by a road from Willoughby and Chatswood that crossed the Lane Cove River at Fuller's Bridge; another came in from the districts north of Parramatta, via Dundas, Eastwood, and Kissing Point village.

The Bedlam Point ferry remained one of the principal gateways to Sydney from the North Side, for vehicles and horseback riders, for fifty-five years. It was replaced in 1884 by the Gladesville Bridge, one mile downstream from Bedlam Point, which shortened the distance to Sydney from the North Side by three miles. Then the Bedlam Point ferry, which had been for so long so significant in cross-Harbour traffic, ceased operating, and it faded gradually from living memory.

The building of the Gladesville Bridge in 1884 was followed almost immediately by the building of the Ryde Railway Bridge in 1886, and the opening of the Great Northern Railway Line from Strathfield, via Concord and Ryde, to Hornsby, *en route* to the Hawkesbury River Bridge (completed in 1889). The two bridges across the Upper Harbour, and the direct access by rail and road from the North Side to Sydney, transformed the municipalities of Ryde and Eastwood. Farms, orchards, and market gardens were subdivided to form suburban residential sites, especially along the railway-line, where suburbs with sentimental English names, such as Epping and Cheltenham, sprang into existence among groves of gum trees.

At this time many of the market gardens in the Ryde, Eastwood, and Gladesville districts were cultivated by Chinese, who had immigrated during the Gold Rushes, or subsequently, before the White Australia policy was given legislative shape. Special rates for "Chinaman with baskets" were charged on the punt-ferries, and on the Gladesville toll-bridge. Many Chinese were to be seen on the roads, jogging to market with a pair of baskets slung on a yoke over their shoulders, and "pigtails" down their backs. Some carried their vegetables all the way to the markets in Sydney; others sold them from door to door in the suburbs on the South Side. With the increase of population, parts of the Crown Reserve, the Field of Mars Common, were subdivided in 1885 and sold as building sites or market garden allotments.

The traffic to Sydney by road and rail across the Harbour killed the schooner trade from Kissing Point to the City; the bridges also adversely affected the ferry-steamers carrying passengers between the City and the more distant reaches of the Upper Harbour. The steamers continued to run, but on reduced schedules; that was an effect to be expected from bridge building across the Harbour; but in the 1890s, and until the opening of the Sydney Harbour Bridge in the 1930s, cross-harbour ferry traffic continued to thrive in all the reaches of the Harbour below Gladesville Bridge.

The Gladesville Bridge was the first of the three main road bridges across Sydney Harbour. It was the only road bridge across the Main Harbour until the Sydney Harbour Bridge was built in 1932. Then the Ryde Road Bridge was built in 1935. When the Gladesville Bridge was rebuilt in 1964, the old bridge had stood for exactly eighty years.

Ryde Municipality today is almost entirely a residential district, with some light industries. Vestiges of the district's former character as a market gardening region are to be found in plant-nurseries—of which there are more at and near Ryde than in any other suburb of the Sydney metropolitan spread—and in the Ryde School of Horticulture, one of the only two institutions in Australia specializing in teaching the art and science of flower-growing. (The other is the Burnley School at Melbourne.)

The district of Meadowbank, on the river front at the northern end of the Ryde Railway Bridge, is said to have been so named by William Bennett, a civil engineer who was prominent in public works in New South Wales from the 1850s to the 1870s, and was the first Commissioner for Roads. It was probably at his suggestion that the site of the Ryde Railway Bridge was chosen, but the name Meadowbank was in use there before William Bennett immigrated to New South Wales in 1854. It may have originated with the first settlers in the 1790s. This was the site of a schooner wharf, and later of a ferry wharf, communicating with Pennant Hills.

In 1945 a technical college was established in Constitution Road, near the Meadowbank railway station. It is attended by students from the western suburbs and Parramatta, including apprentices at the engineering shops and in the various light industries of all the districts on the shores of the Harbour's upper reaches.

Cruising downstream, along the northern shore of the Parramatta River, a sightseer would immediately notice, 500 yards below the Ryde Road Bridge, the large building, and the wharf and slipways of Halvorsens' boatshed, which stands on the site of James Squire's Kissing Point brewery of the early days. Lars Halvorsen, a Norwegian, immigrated to Sydney, with his wife and family of five sons and two young daughters, in 1925. He began boat building at Drummoyne, and then moved to Neutral Bay. He died in 1936, aged forty-nine years, but his sons carried on the business that he had taught them. In 1937 they bought five acres of land on the waterfront at Ryde—which to them, as Norwegians, was a name from the land of their birth. On the outbreak of war in 1939 they received orders from the Australian Government to build ocean-going decked motor-boats for use by the Australian armed services. Of one type of vessel—the "Halvorsen 38"—they built during the war years a total of 147, supplied to the Australian services, and to the Americans and the Dutch. Some of these were used, not only in the Pacific, but in the Mediterranean. Larger vessels—the "Halvorsen 62" and the "Fairmile" 112-ft submarine chaser—also were supplied in considerable numbers to the armed forces, and won wide renown.

After the war, the Halvorsens continued to build motor-cruisers and sailing yachts, to meet the peace-time demand for pleasure craft and commercial craft. In 1961 they were entrusted with the responsibility of building *Gretel*, the first 12-metre sailing yacht built in Australia, in which an Australian crew sailed in the first challenge match between Australia and the U.S.A. for the "America's Cup," in September 1962. *Gretel* was narrowly defeated in some of the closest racing ever seen in matches for that Blue Riband of World Yachting. There will inevitably be more challenges by Australia, in which experience gained in this special kind of yacht racing may be expected to increase the chances of an ultimate success.

Five hundred yards downstream from Halvorsens' boatshed is the promontory to which, in modern times, the name of Kissing Point has been applied. It is one of the headlands of Kissing Point Bay; the other headland, 750 yards to the eastwards, is absurdly named Putney Point (opposite to Mortlake).

The next two indentations eastwards along that shore are typical Sydney Harbour coves, narrow at the mouth and tapering to a head into which a creek flows. These are named Morrison's Bay and Glade's Bay, from two of the original settlers, Morrison and Glade, but the suburb adjacent is incongruously named Tennyson—not so much in honour of the poet, Alfred Lord Tennyson, as of his son, Hallam Lord Tennyson who, after serving as Governor of South Australia from 1899 to 1902, was appointed Governor-General of the Commonwealth of Australia, and held that office for eighteen months, from July 1902 to January 1904.

Six hundred yards eastwards of Glade's Bay is Looking-Glass Point, so named in the earliest months of exploration and settlement as a temporary means of identification that was later adopted unofficially and eventually officially. It was in this vicinity, on 15th February, 1788, that Governor Phillip, and the officers and others with him in a party of three boats, had a demonstration of the powers of observation and reasoning which Australian Aborigines, in their primitive state, had developed to a remarkable extent. The incident was recorded by Lieutenant Bradley:

> We stopped at a neck of land for breakfast. We were soon met there by a native armed. He laid down his spear as soon as he joined us, and had more curiosity than any we had before met with. He examined everything very attentively and went into all our boats from one to the other. . . . The Governor gave this man a hatchet, and a looking-glass, which, when he looked into, he looked immediately behind the glass, to see if any person was there, and then pointed to the glass and the shadows which he saw in the water, signifying they were similar.

No fooling Jacky of the Wallumetta tribe with a looking-glass! It must have been the first time that he had seen such a thing, but he knew that its mirror effect was the same as that of water. His reaction immediately indicated reasoning by analogy, the product of a well-developed logical faculty. Instantaneous deductions of that kind enabled the Aborigines to track animals or men for miles through the bush, from slight indications which white men, untrained in that skill, usually did not notice.

On Looking-Glass Point a schooner wharf was built for the trade from Gladesville to Sydney. This was also a point of call after the 1830s for the ferry-steamers plying on the Parramatta River run. It was only 300 yards upstream from the Bedlam Point punt-ferry crossing. Near the wharf nowadays are the boatsheds of the Scots College and Sydney Grammar School rowing clubs. In the vicinity also is a large factory in which linseed oil and oil-cake are made; it is one of the few big industrial establishments on the North Side of the Upper Harbour.

Between Looking-Glass Point and Bedlam Point is Looking-Glass Bay, a typical V-shaped Sydney Harbour cove. It is 300 yards wide at its mouth and 600 yards in length, a secluded haven for boats, launches, and small yachts, with a jetty. Near by is the boatshed of George Towns and Sons, where most of the racing boats for the rowing clubs of Sydney Harbour (and for clubs in other States) are built. The founder of this firm, George Towns, won the World Sculling Championship in 1901 from J. A. Gaudaur of the United States, who had held the title for five years. The match was rowed on Lake of the Woods, in Ontario, Canada.

Towns defended his title successfully against several challengers, in matches rowed on the Parramatta River and on the Nepean. He was beaten in 1905 by a veteran fellow Australian, J. Stanbury—who had held the world championship title from 1890 to 1896—but Towns beat Stanbury in a return match in 1906. He forfeited his title to his brother Charles in 1907, but Charles was beaten in August of that year by William Webb, a

New Zealander.

Public interest in the World's Professional Sculling Championship was maintained until the 1930s, but thereafter declined, as rowing became more and more a sport for amateurs, fostered by schools and universities, rather than by the old-time watermen, or wherrymen, who became an extinct species when motor-engines were installed in small boats for commercial use.

At Bedlam Point, the Old Punt Road forms the boundary between the municipalities of Ryde and Hunter's Hill. Part of the suburb of Gladesville is in Ryde, part in Hunter's Hill. The large mental hospital known as the Gladesville Asylum, in spacious grounds, and the north-side abutments of the Gladesville Bridge, are within Hunter's Hill municipality, a district, chiefly residential, that is one of the most picturesque, and historically distinctive, of all the Sydney harbourside suburbs.

HUNTER'S HILL   SEE ALSO PART II

The Municipality of Hunter's Hill, incorporated in 1861, is the smallest, and also one of the oldest, suburban municipalities in the Sydney metropolitan region. It comprises the tongue of land, three miles in length from west to east, but on an average only half a mile wide, between the Parramatta River and the Lane Cove River at their confluence. It is girt by sea on three sides, with the Parramatta River as its southern boundary, and the Lane Cove Rive as its eastern and northern boundaries. Only at its base, on its western boundary, is it joined to the land; its boundary there is for two miles along the old Pittwater Road, which ran from the Bedlam Point ferry, along the edge of the Field of Mars Common, to head the Lane Cove River in the vicinity of present-day Pymble, *en route* to the mouth of the Hawkesbury.

Part of that old road, through Gladesville, on the western boundary of Hunter's Hill, is merged nowadays into the Victoria Road, the highway leading from North Parramatta, through Ryde, to the Gladesville Bridge. From the Hunter's Hill Town Hall it is four miles by road to St Anne's, Ryde; ten miles to Parramatta; and seven miles to Sydney via the Gladesville Bridge, by the detour round the head of Tarban Creek (that distance reduced to six miles by the opening of the Tarban Creek Bridge in 1965); but the distance by ferry-steamer from Hunter's Hill to Sydney Cove is only three miles.

It was as a suburb which had a convenient waterway communication with the city that Hunter's Hill was developed, in the 1850s and 1860s, as an elegant residential district, a quality which it retains today; and the fact that it was a compact community, with natural boundaries on its river frontages, led to its incorporation as a municipality only three years after the Municipalities Act of 1858 permitted local government in that form.

Today, with a population of 12,500, Hunter's Hill may proudly claim the distinction of being the smallest municipality—in both area and population—on the shores of Sydney Harbour; and with that claim is implied also a soundly based belief, supported by the experience of more than a hundred years, that Hunter's Hill has an Arcadian quality all of its own, a peaceful and picturesque atmosphere unexcelled among Sydney's harbourside districts; for everything here speaks of a real-estate development in the mid-nineteenth century which was planned by men of good sense and good taste, not to make a quick profit, regardless of natural and architectural beauty, but to create, or to re-create here, a "village" in the spirit of Watteau's pastoral paintings. The extent to which they succeeded in that aim caused Hunter's Hill to be known as "the French Village." The atmosphere they evoked remains.

In a printed *Guide to Old Hunter's Hill,* issued in 1961 by the Hunter's Hill Historical Society, the special quality of the district is well described:

> Much of Hunter's Hill is a peninsula, a fact which had a distinct bearing on the way of life here over one hundred years ago, and still has today. It is somewhat cut off, geographically, from the main streams of suburban growth and alteration, and retains much of the Nineteenth Century in its gracious, well-preserved stone houses and their mellow stone surrounding-walls which still front its footpaths. It is famed for the thousands of lovely trees which grace its streets and private grounds, and the attendant bird life.

The name "Hunter's Hill" has been applied since the incorporation of the municipality in 1861, and is applied today only to that peninsular region between the Parramatta River and the Lane Cove River at their confluence. The Aboriginal name for the vicinity, "Mookaboola" ("the meeting of the waters") has been preserved in the municipality's coat of arms, if not on the map. That name is, geographically, more apt than Hunter's Hill. The peninsula, though ridgy, is not a "hill" in relation to the surrounding country; yet, as Hunter's Hill commemorates Captain John Hunter, who first explored the Upper Harbour, and made the first charts of the entire Harbour and its arms, it is well and worthily named. Unfortunately that ascription has become confused by an historical misconception.

Governor Phillip did not allow his own name, or that of the Lieutenant-Governor, Major Ross, or of the Judge Advocate, Captain David Collins—or any of his staff—to be bestowed on geographical features in the Harbour; but he allowed the names of naval officers who took part in the chart-making—Lieutenant Bradley and Lieutenant Ball—to be bestowed on prominent headlands. It seems unlikely that the officer in command of H.M.S. *Sirius,* Captain Hunter, who supervised and took an active part in the chartmaking, would have had his name attached only to a bay in Middle Harbour (later absurdly renamed "Balmoral Beach").

Many of the names of Harbour features were never officially bestowed, but gradually became fixed in public usage. The whole of the high country on the North Shore (opposite Sydney Cove) was known to the pioneer settlers as "Hunter's Hill," in honour of Captain John Hunter, and not, as is sometimes asserted, because a Scottish convict gave that name whimsically to his farm there.

In February 1794, Lieutenant-Governor Grose established a farm settlement in that district for men of the armed forces, who wished to be discharged from active service in order to become free settlers, or had previously served in the forces. Eighteen grants, each of thirty acres, were made in the vicinity of present-day Chatswood, which Grose named "King's Plains." That settlement was on the eastern side of the upper reaches of the Lane Cove River, communicating with the Field of Mars on the western side of that stream, and so by road with Kissing Point village and with Parramatta. The road crossed the Lane Cove River at Fuller's Bridge, six miles upstream from that river's junction with the Parramatta River. The distance by water from Fuller's Bridge to Sydney Cove was nine miles, whereas the distance by road to Kissing Point village was only five miles. At that time there was no short-cut through the bush from "King's Plains" (Chatswood) to the shore of the Harbour directly opposite Sydney. The high and ridgy country there, with steep gullies and dense scrub, made that route too difficult.

The ex-sailors and ex-soldiers found it hard to make a living on their farms. The soil was unsuitable for farm and garden crops on that side of the Lane Cove River, and the distance from markets in Sydney too great. Most of the settlers soon sold their farms to speculators in Sydney at small prices.

On 3rd October, 1794, Lieutenant-Governor Grose made a grant of thirty acres in that district to Henry Hacking, who had been a seaman in H.M.S. *Sirius,* and, in charge of hunting parties, had proved himself a good bushman: he was the first white man to earn and deserve that description, for at least he could find his way back to the settlement at Sydney Cove after shooting kangaroos, instead of getting lost and perishing in the bush, as many of the newchums did. On one of those excursions he had discovered Port Hacking (to the southward of Botany Bay). In August 1794 he had attempted to cross the Blue Mountains, and had penetrated twenty miles farther inland than any previous explorer. It was in return for those services that Major Grose made the land grant to Henry Hacking on 3rd October, 1794. The official record of that grant is significant in its description of the land as ". . . in the District of Hunter's Hill . . . situated at Lane Cove, on the north side of the Harbour of Port Jackson."

On 25th October, 1794—three weeks after Henry Hacking's land grant "in the District of Hunter's Hill" had been officially recorded—a convict transport ship, the *Surprize,* arrived at Sydney from London, having on board, among other convicts, four Scots who had been convicted of sedition, and were known as the Scottish Martyrs. They were well-educated men, with money of their own, and were treated by Lieutenant-Governor Grose (on instructions from London) with courtesy as political prisoners or exiles, and not as felons. They were not required to live in the convict barracks, or to do any work. They rented two houses in Sydney, near Government House, and settled in there to live as gentlemen of leisure, using funds they had brought with them from Britain. They had complete freedom of movement.

One of these pampered prisoners, Thomas Muir, soon after his arrival, bought a "farm" of thirty acres from one of the ex-soldiers, named Samuel Lightfoot, in the "Hunter's Hill" District (presumably near present-day Chatswood).

By an extraordinary coincidence, Muir's father lived on a farm named Huntershill Farm, near Glasgow, in Scotland. Muir whimsically conferred that name also on the scrub farm that he had bought from Sam Lightfoot. In November (1794) Muir wrote a letter to a friend in Scotland, in which he declared:

> I have a neat little house across the water [which] I have called after my father's home in Glasgow, Huntershill.

On that inadequate evidence, several historians, copying one another, have declared that Hunter's Hill was so named by Thomas Muir! That Scottish martyr, in fact, did not live on the patch of scrub, miles out in the bush, that he had bought from Sam Lightfoot. He lived in a hut on the promontory later named Milson's Point (opposite Sydney Cove). There he had the use of a boat for fishing or crossing the Harbour to the town, and was awaiting and planning an opportunity to escape.

In February 1796, after having lived as a "gentleman convict" in New South Wales for sixteen months, Thomas Muir absconded in an American ship, the *Otter*, which had been sent to Sydney to rescue him. It is unlikely that the people and officials at Sydney would have known of the name that Muir had given privately to the patch of scrub that he had bought from Samuel Lightfoot, and equally unlikely that the fanciful name of one neglected farm in a soldiers' settlement would have been applied in popular or official usage to the whole district extending for many miles around that settlement.

There has been no need to seek such an odd and unconvincing explanation of the name Hunter's Hill, which was in official and popular use, as a well-deserved compliment to Captain John Hunter, of H.M.S. *Sirius*, before Thomas Muir was ever heard of at Sydney. The attempts that have been made to deprive Captain John Hunter's memory of that honour must be rejected as faulty lore-making, especially deplorable because Sydney Harbour was discovered, explored, charted, and developed as a seaport by a sustained naval operation, in which Captain John Hunter took a leading part. Of the four Naval Captains—Phillip, Hunter, King, and Bligh—who were the first four Governors of New South Wales, Hunter is the only one whose name is commemorated in the cartography of that Harbour.

During the term of office of Governor Bourke (1831-37), the large District of Hunter's Hill, extending along the northern shore from Kirribilli to Kissing Point, was divided into two "parishes"—that being a term used for an administrative rather than an ecclesiastical area. The Parish of Willoughby was on the eastern side of the Lane Cove River. The Parish of Hunter's Hill then residually comprised all the land on the western side of the Lane Cove River which had the village of Kissing Point as its market centre. Official maps showing the land grants at Meadowbank, of that period or earlier, are over-lettered with the name "Hunter's Hill."

When Kissing Point was renamed "Ryde," the name of Hunter's Hill remained to be applied only to the peninsula of Mookaboola, which began to be sparsely inhabited in the 1830s, adjacent to John Glade's farm and the Gladesville Lunatic Asylum then being built on the shore of Tarban Creek. So, when the Municipality of Hunter's Hill was incorporated in 1861, it preserved the historic name but defined its own boundaries as an enclave within the larger district which had formerly borne that name.

Tarban Creek is named from the anglicized spelling of an Aboriginal word, meaning "fish," or "fishing-place," which, in local variations—spelled in the orthography of Europeans as "Tarwin" in Gippsland, and "Theebine" in Queensland—was used by many of the Aboriginal tribes of Eastern Australia. The creek with that name on the southern side of Hunter's Hill Peninsula is the estuarine mouth of a short freshwater streamlet, in a typical Sydney Harbour sandstone gully. Its tidally flooded inlet on the Parramatta River's shore extends east and west for half a mile, with a breadth of 200 yards, and depths of from 10 feet to 12 feet—an excellent little boat haven, secluded, like many of the other north-side coves.

The lunatic asylum that had been established in the 1820s at Bedlam Point was described in the 1833 *Directory of Roads* as "now deserted and in ruins." The patients had been transferred to an asylum at Liverpool; but in 1834 Governor Bourke decreed the building of a new asylum on the bank of Tarban Creek, three-quarters of a mile to the eastward of the deserted Bedlam Point asylum. That new building received the patients from Liverpool in 1838; it developed into the present-day Gladesville Mental Hospital, which, with accommodation for 1,500 patients, stands in large buildings in spacious grounds, and forms one of the four big Mental Hospitals (Callan Park, Gladesville, Rydalmere, and Parramatta) on the shores of the Upper Harbour.

The Tarban Creek Asylum was the first large building erected on the peninsula of Mookaboola; but there was a camp of construction workers there which was linked by boat with Sydney.

The first recorded purchase of Crown Land on the peninsula was 42 acres, bought in 1834 by William Morgan, who was known as "Billy the Bull." He was described on the land-title as "a merchant, of Sydney," and apparently bought the land as a speculation. His land was in the vicinity of present-day Ferry Street, centrally situated in the peninsula.

In that same year (1834), a block of land was bought by John Clarke, at the eastern end of the peninsula, in the vicinity then or later incongruously named Woolwich (named from a dockside district on the south bank of the Thames, in the East End of London). Clarke built a home, on the waterfront near present-day Alfred Street, Hunter's Hill. He cleared his land for cultivation, and was the first white settler to build a home on Mookaboola Peninsula.

In December 1834, the renowned Mary Reiby, who was then fifty-seven years of age, bought a block of land on the Lane Cove frontage of the peninsula. When she was a child, only thirteen years old, she had been convicted in Staffordshire, England, of the crime of "stealing a horse," and sentenced to seven years transportation beyond the seas. (She was an orphan, living with her grandmother; it was said that she went for a ride on a cart-horse without the owner's consent.)

Arrived in Sydney, aged fifteen, in 1792, Mary Haydock (her maiden name) was assigned as a nursemaid in the household of the Lieutenant-Governor, Major Grose. Two years later, in September 1794, she married Thomas Reiby, a ship's officer, who became a shipowner and merchant. She bore him three sons and four daughters, and helped him to manage his trading business in Sydney.

Thomas Reiby died in 1811, when Mary was thirty-four. She then took over the sole management of the business he had left to her, and showed outstanding commercial ability, to become one of the most prosperous merchants, shipowners, and land owners in the Colony. The land which she bought at Hunter's Hill in 1834 had a large native fig tree growing on it, and from that landmark was known as "The Fig Tree." In the 1840s, she had a stone house built there, known as Fig Tree House, which (with some later additions) is still extant, in Reiby Street, near the Fig Tree Bridge across Lane Cove River. She owned much property and many houses in Sydney, and lived at the Fig Tree only on her occasional visits there. (She died in Sydney, aged seventy-eight, in 1855.)

In 1836, "Billy the Bull" sold his land at Hunter's Hill to John Tawell, a pharmacist of Sydney Town, who also owned a whaling vessel. Tawell, who professed the religious beliefs of the Quakers, and preached against strong drink, had attracted attention to his doctrines in March 1836 by purchasing 492 gallons of rum and 116 gallons of gin, all of which he then poured into the Harbour at Sydney Cove. In 1838 Tawell returned to his homeland (England), after selling his business in Sydney and his land at Hunter's Hill to Ambrose Foss, one of the foundation members of the Congregational Church in New South Wales. Foss owned the property at Hunter's Hill for eighteen years (until 1860), and built a small cottage on it as a country residence. This was later enlarged, and is extant as Carey Cottage, a name conferred on it in the 1950s when it was renovated and equipped as a "Colonial Cottage Restaurant." (After returning to England in 1838, John Tawell was hanged in 1845 for murder.)

Another Sydney merchant who owned land at Hunter's Hill in the 1830s was Samuel Onions. In 1835 he bought a beautiful building-site at the extreme easterly tip of the Mookaboola Peninsula, at the actual point where the waters of the Lane Cove River and Parramatta River meet. It is unlikely that Samuel

Onions lived there very long, as in July 1836 he was convicted of perjury at Sydney, and was sentenced to seven years' exile on Norfolk Island. (He had sued a man named Raine for assault, and swore falsely that Raine owed him money: the punishment was severe for a crime difficult to prove beyond doubt.) Despite that unfortunate incident, the name of Onions Point continued to be applied to that beautiful headland which is also one of the most significant landmarks in Sydney Harbour, at the very meeting-point of the two upper arms, which conjoin there to form the Harbour's main basin; yet as Samuel Onions was the first white settler there, his name applied to that point has a local historical validity that names such as Ryde, Putney, Mortlake, Henley, Woolwich, and Greenwich lack when they are applied to places on the shores of Sydney Harbour.

The configuration of Onions Point, as a narrow neck of land round which the Lane Cove River flows in a U-bend to join the Parramatta River, provides the most feasible explanation of the origin of the name, "Lane Cove." It is reasonable to suppose that the naval chartmakers in 1788, proceeding westwards up the Parramatta River past Long Nose Point, did not at first sight realize that a river lay hidden behind the neck of land which, forty-eight years later, was to be named Onions Point. Among a multiplicity of coves, this indentation of the shore appeared to be a typical cove, with a small creek apparently at its head (later to be named Gore Creek, flowing down from Gore Hill and Artarmon).

Not until they had rounded the point on that neck of land, in a further boat exploration, could they have become aware that what they had marked at first as a "cove" was in fact a sea-lane leading to a tributary river, 400 yards wide, its channel extending westerly and northerly for several miles. To distinguish that apparent cove from others, they informally named it "the Lane Cove." From that usage, the river that flowed around the U-bend into the Lane Cove became identified as "the Lane Cove River."

As with so many other place-names on the shores of Sydney Harbour, there is no documentary record of the bestowing of these names. The cartographers in 1788 had no means of ascertaining Aboriginal names of places, and presumably felt that it was not their responsibility to bestow English names on such a multiplicity of coves, bays, and headlands. They were concerned only with navigation, taking soundings all over, and looking for hidden rocks. Names which they used among themselves—such as the Lane Cove and the Kissing Point—had practical application, and became fixed in general usage without official procedures.

When the Tarban Creek Asylum was completed, and received its patients in 1838, and, in the following year, when Cockatoo Island became a site of convict labour and soon afterwards was proclaimed as a prison, there was much boat traffic, and a general increase of activity in the vicinity of Hunter's Hill. Those governmental institutions, with their inmates and guards, were

261

consumers of goods and services which, in a commercial sense, stimulated the prosperity of the region. At the same time, improvements in the Parramatta River paddle-wheel ferry-steamers reduced the time of the passage between Sydney Cove and Hunter's Hill to half an hour. It was that convenience of access by the waterway which led to the development of Hunter's Hill as a residential suburb, beginning in the 1840s.

In 1841 an investor, A. H. Huntley, bought nineteen acres of land at Tarban Point (the promontory on the south of Tarban Creek), adjacent to the Asylum. He built a residence there, which (with extensions made in 1880) is named Point House, and still stands in the 1960s. The suburb that developed from the subdivision of Huntley's estate is officially named Huntley's Point. The abutments of the new Gladesville Bridge, and the expressways connected with it, rest upon that promontory and soar through it, bringing the rush and roar of modern motor traffic to a district that was formerly secluded and quiet.

The distinctive character of Hunter's Hill as a residential district, which caused it to be known as "the French Village," was given to it by three Frenchmen—the brothers Jules Joubert and Didier Numa Joubert, and the Count Gabriel de Milhau—investors in the development of real-estate who were inspired, not only by the expectation of profits, but also by visions of practical idealism.

The initiative in this development was taken by Jules Joubert, who was born at Charente, near Bordeaux, in France, in 1824. He arrived in Sydney as a cadet in the French corvette *Héroine* in 1841, at the age of seventeen, and was then transferred to the French Consular service at Sydney. In that year, when the transportation of British convicts to New South Wales had ended, a new era of a great expansion of civilization in Australia had begun. There was a large influx of free immigrants. This had, as Governor Gipps stated in 1844:

> . . . the good effect of adding 50,000 souls to our population, and of changing, in the almost incredibly short space of six years, the whole character of the Colony—of converting it, in fact, from a convict colony to a free one.

In 1837, the population of New South Wales was 85,000, including 32,000 British convicts. Ten years later, in 1847, the population had risen to 205,000, of whom only 6,600 were British convicts. Then came the Gold Rushes of the 1850s and 1860s, which brought an influx of one million free immigrants, reducing the pathetic remnants of the British convict system to 0.4 per cent. (one in 250 persons) of the population. It was with that large influx of free immigrants, many of whom were from non-British countries, that Australian life began to take on a quality different from that of a British penal settlement. The development of Hunter's Hill as "a French village" was an example of those new influences.

In 1847, Jules Joubert had persuaded his brother Didier, and the Count de Milhau, to immigrate to Sydney, bringing with them funds for investment. Instead of investing in pastoral properties, they bought land, and built houses for sale, at Hunter's Hill. D. N. Joubert bought 200 acres of land there, including Mary Reiby's land at the Fig Tree. The French investors then proceeded with an ambitious plan of subdivision and house building. They brought forty stonemasons from Italy, and employed them for several years in building houses and cottages of stone, showing influences of French and Italian architectural designs, combined adroitly with the Australian colonial use of verandas and balconies. The buildings, and the stone garden-walls that surrounded them, were made from sandstone quarried at Hunter's Hill, usually on or near the actual site of construction. This was an admirable use of Sydney Sandstone (called by geologists "Hawkesbury Sandstone") which is one of the best building-stones in the world.

Most of the buildings erected by the enterprise of the Joubert brothers and the Count de Milhau are extant a century and more later. They were sold to professional and business people of Sydney, including some who were French, and others of British descent. When the character of the district was thus established, land was bought and residences of good quality and design—mostly of stone, but some of timber—were built for various individual owners, some of whom employed stonemasons from Ireland and Scotland.

In the 1840s and 1850s, residents of Hunter's Hill travelled to and from Sydney by the Parramatta River paddle-wheel ferry-steamers *Australian* (launched 1836) and *Rapid* (launched 1838), which called at Huntley's Point wharf and at the original Hunter's Hill wharf at the foot of Ferry Street, on the Parramatta River shore of the peninsula. Some of the residents owned sailing yachts which, manned by professional watermen, sailed with small parties to and from the City on business or sociable occasions. There were professional watermen also who carried passengers in skiffs on that, as on all other harbour routes. Jules Joubert owned a steam yacht, the *Ysobel*.

Throughout the 1860s, the Hunter's Hill Regatta, held on New Year's Day, was one of the biggest occasions in aquatic sport on the Harbour. The races started on the Parramatta River side of the peninsula, at Pulpit Point, a promontory so named by the pioneers from a rock formation at its tip.

In 1860, Jules Joubert put the S.Y. *Ysobel* into service as a ferry-steamer on regular runs between the Lane Cove River and Sydney Cove. She provided a more frequent service than the Parramatta River steamers, and called at wharves in the Lane Cove River which the Parramatta steamers by-passed.

When the municipality was incorporated in 1861, its first Mayor was Jules Joubert. The town hall, built in 1866, is one of the oldest and best of the town halls of the Greater Sydney region.

Many people of renown in the life of Sydney made their homes at Hunter's Hill. Among them was Sir George Dibbs, K.G.M.G., who was three times Premier of New South Wales, in the 1880s and 1890s. He had entered Parliament in 1874 as a republican,

263

but was knighted by Queen Victoria in 1892, presumably for his zeal in helping to organize the sending of a contingent of New South Wales soldiers to assist Britain in the Sudan War (1884-85). Families prominent in the legal profession, whose members have included Justices of the Supreme Court (Simpson, Manning, Owens) have made their homes at Hunter's Hill in succeeding generations.

In 1857 an Irishman from Tralee, aged twenty-seven, Robert David FitzGerald—who, after being trained in Ireland as a land surveyor, had an appointment in the New South Wales Surveyor-General's office—went to live at Hunter's Hill, in a house named "Croissy." This was one of four timber houses which, prefabricated in Hamburg, had been exhibited at the Paris Exhibition in 1854, and bought by a Frenchman named Bordier, to be erected at Hunter's Hill.

It was typical of the "New Australian" atmosphere of Hunter's Hill in the mid-nineteenth century that a dwelling designed in Germany, bought in Paris, and erected at Hunter's Hill, was occupied by an Irishman! R. D. FitzGerald was a skilled botanist. He remained in the employ of the Surveyor-General's office for thirty years, but devoted his spare time to the study of orchids. His careful drawings of Australian orchids, published in two volumes (the first in 1875, the second posthumously) have made his name as an orchidologist world-renowned. He died at Hunter's Hill in 1892. His grandson, also named Robert David FitzGerald, born at Hunter's Hill in 1902, is also a land surveyor by profession, and is renowned too—as one of the foremost Australian poets; and he lives at Hunter's Hill.

In the same year (1847) that the Jouberts began their building operations at Hunter's Hill, the missionary priests of the Roman Catholic Society of Mary (known as the Marists) bought a block of land on the southern side of Tarban Creek and built there a stone cottage for use as their priory, or headquarters of their missionary endeavours in Australia and in the isles of Oceania. Most of the Marist Fathers at that time were French. The Society of Mary had been founded at Bordeaux in 1816, and its first missionaries in the Pacific had arrived in Sydney in 1836. It may reasonably be assumed that Jules Joubert, in his capacity as an official of the French Consulate at Sydney, advised the Marist Fathers to build their priory at Hunter's Hill, in proximity to the intended French settlement there.

That decision had far-reaching effects. The original priory is extant, near present-day Salter Street, but now within the Gladesville Mental Hospital grounds. After a few years, the Marist Fathers sold it to Thomas Salter, and moved to a new and larger home, which they had built in Mary Street, on the northern side of Tarban Creek, and had named Villa Maria. In 1857, they began building the Villa Maria Church, to the design of an architect in Sydney, but doing most of the building themselves, assisted by lay brothers of the Marist Order brought from France. The result was, and remains today, one of the most beautiful

Gothic-style churches on all the shores of Sydney Harbour.

In 1872, the first Teaching Brothers of the Marist Order came to Sydney from France. As a special section of the Society of Mary concerned with the general school education of boys, they began their work as teachers in a small day-school connected with St Patrick's Church, in Harrington Street, on Church Hill (near The Rocks) in the City of Sydney; but they quickly realized that the space there was too restricted for the scope which they envisaged, including plans for a large boarding-school, imparting secondary as well as primary education.

Seeking a site for that purpose, the Marist Brothers in 1876 bought twelve acres of timbered land at Hunter's Hill on the northern side of the Villa Maria grounds, and began clearing it and building wooden huts there, with their own labour. This was the beginning of St Joseph's College, the biggest boys' boarding-school in Australia (it has 600 boarders). The College was officially opened in 1881, with fifty-five pupils, transferred from St Patrick's in the City. The Marist Brothers proceeded, mostly with their own labour, to erect a large stone building, which was opened in 1894. The buildings have been much extended since then, and have become the most prominent feature of the Hunter's Hill skyline, as viewed from the Parramatta River side of the peninsula. In its riparian surroundings, St Joseph's College has a special interest in the sport of rowing, and is often "Head of the River."

In the same year (1857) that the Villa Maria Church was built, the Anglican Church, St Mark's, was built in Church Street. It was known as "the Fig Tree Chapel." In the 1960s, it was moved, stone by stone, to a new site in Fig Tree Road, to clear the ground for the Expressway that now cuts a swathe from the New Gladesville Bridge to the New Fig Tree Bridge, across the base of the Hunter's Hill Peninsula.

The opening of the Old Gladesville Bridge in 1884, and of the Iron Cove Bridge in the same year, brought the Hunter's Hill Peninsula into communication with Sydney by road, a distance of five miles from the Gladesville end of the bridge, and seven miles from the Fig Tree, by a detour of two miles around the head of Tarban Creek. In the following year (1885), the Fig Tree Bridge was opened, thus completing the "Five Bridges" route between Sydney and the North Shore.

The Fig Tree Bridge, which crossed the Lane Cove River near Mary Reiby's old home, had nine fixed spans, of which the central span, with a clear opening 46 feet wide and a headway of 19 feet, permitted navigation for small vessels, lighters, barges, yachts, and boats to the upper reaches of the river, which is navigable, at least for boats, to the head of tidewater, five miles upstream from the Fig Tree Bridge. The terminal for ferry-steamers was at the Joubert Street wharf, on the downstream side of the bridge.

The distance from North Sydney to the City of Sydney by the "Five Bridges" route, twelve miles, was three miles shorter than the distance by the roads which, before the building of the

Fig Tree Bridge, had crossed the Lane Cove River at Fuller's Bridge and (further upstream) De Burgh's Bridge. The Five Bridges route, though very much shorter than "heading" the Harbour at Parramatta, was a roundabout way from North Sydney to Sydney, especially in the days of horse-drawn traffic. Before the Sydney Harbour Bridge was built, that problem was partly solved by the vehicular punt-ferries between Blue's Point and Dawes Point, and between Milson's Point and Bennelong Point. The building of the Fig Tree Bridge across the Lane Cove River enabled traffic to flow not only between the North Side and the South side of the Main Harbour, but also along the North Side, between Mosman and Parramatta, and points intermediate. In that sense Hunter's Hill, after 1885, was linked to the road transport system on both sides of the Harbour, as a sort of half-way staging-point; but even that aspect did not alter the character of the district as a desirable residential resort.

A more serious threat to that peaceful and genteel atmosphere had occurred in 1884 when a firm of mechanical engineers, the Atlas Engineering Company, bought a large block of land on the waterfront at the eastern end of the Mookaboola Peninsula, formerly John Clarke's land in the vicinity which then or previously was named Woolwich, near Onions Point, one of the most beautiful vistas of water and shoreline in all Sydney Harbour. There, the Atlas Company cleared the ground, built large, ugly engineering workshops, and, in 1888, imported from England a floating dock for ship repairs and ship cleaning. This industrial enterprise, in proximity to the earlier-established naval dockyard at Cockatoo Island and to Mort's Dry Dock at Balmain, was not successful commercially. In 1898 it was taken over by the Mort's Dock Company. The new owners proceeded to excavate, at Woolwich, a dry dock in the solid sandstone, 850 feet long and 80 feet wide, with a draught of water of 26 feet—by far the biggest graving-dock in Australia at that time, and one of the biggest in the world. It was opened in 1902, and continued in operation until Mort's Dock and Engineering Company went into liquidation in 1959.

The excavation of that large dock in the sandstone at Woolwich, within four years, from 1898 to 1902, provided employment for a large number of "navvies," mostly newly arrived immigrants. A false legend ascribes this work to convicts, ignoring the fact that it was carried through sixty years after the transportation of British convicts to New South Wales had ended, and fifty-five years after the employment of prisoners on works in public view had ceased. (It was the Fitzroy Dock at Cockatoo Island that was excavated by convicts.)

In addition to the dry dock and the floating dock, there were slipways laid down at Woolwich, and some of the Manly ferry-steamers were built there. In the 1960s, the site of the dismantled workshops, shipyards, and dockyards had the appearance, in contrast with its naturally beautiful surroundings, of the Abomination of Desolation—a man-made scar on the landscape, which perhaps time would heal. Temporary use was made of the site by the Main Roads Board, for "pre-casting" and "pre-stress-ing" the concrete used in the Gladesville Bridge arch. The concrete box-units for that arch, each weighing fifty tons, were lightered three miles upstream to the bridge site.

The industrial activity at the Woolwich end of the Hunter's Hill Peninsula scarcely disturbed the Arcadian peace of the suburb. The noise, grime, and ugliness were all at the tip of a peninsula three miles long, and out of sight, except for passengers on the waterway. In the 1960s the suburb's peace was temporarily disturbed by the building of the "North-western Expressway," with three bridges—the New Gladesville Bridge, the Tarban Creek Bridge, and the New Fig Tree Bridge. The Expressway made a scar while it was being built, but when it was completed, motor traffic could roar across the base of the Hunter's Hill Peninsula, at a high level, leaving most of the quiet tree-lined streets of gracious homes and gardens of the now venerable "French Village" to the enjoyment of their civilized solitudes.

14

LANE COVE RIVER STATE RECREATION AREA

Lane Cove River State Recreation Area is perhaps not strictly part of Sydney Harbour, but it is a large recreation area — 400 hectares — and should be mentioned briefly here. Set up originally in 1938, it is owned by the Lands Department and run by a trust. It is a popular picnic area, where people can hire boats, a further attraction being the paddle wheeler which can carry almost 200 people at a time on trips in the upper reaches above the weir.

RIVERVIEW

Across the Lane Cove River from Hunters Hill is St Ignatius College — Riverview. This Roman Catholic college has had a colourful history. It was founded in 1880 by Father Joseph Dalton, S J, who was born at Waterford, Ireland, in 1817, and died at the college in 1905 at the age of eighty-eight.

In the later years of his life Father Dalton wrote his impressions of those pioneering days. The district, he said, was a *terra-incognita,* with many winding inlets, deep gullies, and dense bush. It was the rendezvous of runaway sailors, of deserting soldiers, and all sorts of wild characters wanted by the police. Burns Bay, west of Riverview, was known as Murdering Bay, and the bay on the east got its name of Tambourine Bay from a notorious Sydney character named Tambourine Nell who had retired there for a season to avoid the attentions of the police. After a long search they found her sylvan retreat and took charge of her and her tambourine.

The original owner of the land in the area was Manuel Francis Josephson, who lived in Riverview Cottage for about ten years in the period 1866 to 1876. Before his death he spent considerable sums in planting forest trees, rare shrubs, and numerous varieties of flowers. His wife built a rock garden which remains to this day a monument to her taste and energy. One of the rockery attractions is a concrete crocodile on a plinth hidden by thick bush and adorned with scores of shrubs. It is said that new boys got the fright of their lives when they were lured into the jungle by the older lads and suddenly met a snarling crocodile face to face.

Lane Cove River ferries called as required from the time of the foundation of the college in 1880. The exact date this service began is uncertain. D.N. Joubert probably commenced the service about 1860, although Lise Joubert, in a letter preserved in the Riverview archives, mentions that she believed 1856 was the approximate year the ferries began running.

The first college regatta was held on the Lane Cove River in 1885 and has been held annually ever since. The 1979 regatta attracted almost 1800 competitors in seventy-six events from thirty clubs and schools. Riverview won Head of the River races in 1899, 1901, 1905,

1907, 1958, 1964, 1974 and 1975. Head of the River has now become the annual event of the great public schools and is held on the Nepean River at Penrith.

LONGUEVILLE

According to the Department of Land's 1840 map the area now known as Longueville was owned by Rupert Kirk who had a grant of 150 hectares. Kirk used the land for the refining of oil and sugar and the manufacture of vinegar. He named it Woodford Park. Today's Woodford Bay marks the boundary of his property.

The Lane Cove 12-ft Sailing Skiff Club with 500 members has a clubhouse at Longueville, being founded in its present form in 1916. Earlier records of sailing on the Lane Cove River describe the club in terms of "yachting". The Lane Cove Yacht Regatta Programme of 1895 is framed in the entrance of the clubhouse.

Open boat class racing was initiated by the Sydney Flying Squadron "18-ft" boats in 1880, followed by the "16-footers" at the turn of the century. Development of "12-ft" skiffs in 1916 at Cremorne was quickly taken up in the Lane Cove River. The Lane Cove club spawned other clubs at Greenwich, Drummoyne and The Spit, as well as influencing the development of clubs at Vaucluse, Double Bay and Balmain. The first championship was held in 1921, and since then the club has had an outstanding record in races at local, national and inter-dominion level. Prior to 1940 there were few clubhouses around Sydney Harbour. The Lane Cove Club built a clubhouse-boatshed for $700 in 1937. The club introduced VJs to the register in 1939, the Moth class being added in the 1950s, Sabots in the 1960s and the Flying 11s and Lasers in the 1970s.

NORTHWOOD

The Department of Land's 1840 map shows that the area now known as Northwood was granted to Isaac David Nichols, who also had land on either side of Lane Cove Road at "Kings Plains" — now known as Pacific Highway, Chatswood.

GREENWICH

Greenwich bears the same name as the London suburb on the River Thames, the Sydney suburb taking its name from Greenwich House, built in 1836. It stands on the corner of George Street and St Lawrence Street, sited in land originally granted to George Green, a boat builder, in 1836. In 1840, Captain Gother Kerr Mann resided there with his large family. Mann called the house Willoughby but the family later changed it to Greenwich to avoid confusion with the postal district of Willoughby.

Manns Point, a pleasant picnic spot, is named after the Mann family. There is a tunnel from this point across to Long Nose Point, Birchgrove, built by the Electricity Commission to bring power to Greenwich. The remaining stone wharves at Manns Point were a salt and copra bond store known as the Salt Bond which burned down in 1917.

A prominent foreshore landmark is the ferry wharf. The first ferry to leave Greenwich was on 24 October 1840, when tickets cost 6d.

Along the shore, past the Greenwich Sailing Club, are the Greenwich Baths, the second oldest tidal pool on the harbour, the oldest being at Balmain. Another pool existed nearby, before the present site was chosen, on property belonging to the Mann family. The present baths were part of a large oyster lease. A leaflet published by the Greenwich Memorial Community Centre says they were opened in 1916, but locals have since told the baths manager that the date was, in fact, 1906.

Are Sydney Harbour waters satisfactory for swimming? A commonly accepted indicator of suitability is the density of bacterial organisms. Extensive investigations by the New South Wales State Pollution Control Commission have established that, in dry weather, bacterial densities are generally no higher than natural, or "background", levels.

Raw sewage has never been discharged into the harbour or the Lane Cove and Parramatta rivers, and it is only after prolonged rainfall that harbourside pools may be affected by urban runoff and sewer overflows. The most obvious feature of wet weather is the large quantities of silt carried downstream although, because of the large dilution and tidal flushing afforded by the harbour waters, they are rarely muddied by storm flows. Health authorities consider it prudent to close tidal baths for short periods after heavy rainfall.

GORE COVE

Gore Cove, a sheltered inlet near Greenwich, is a depot for oil tankers. It is named after William Gore (1765-1845), who was one of the early landowners on the North Shore, although his property was at Artarmon, some distance from the harbour. Gore served under Governor Bligh as provost marshal.

After the New South Wales Corps arrested Bligh in the famous Rum Rebellion of 1808, they also arrested Gore. He was sentenced to transportation for several years and sent to the Coal River (Newcastle), where he worked alongside ordinary convicts. In 1810, Governor Macquarie restored Gore to his former office. He was given land on the North Shore and probably named his property Artarmon after his home in Ireland. Gore Hill, where the Australian Broadcasting Commission television studios now stand, is named after him.

On Manns Avenue, on the south side of the Shell depot, is a wall hewn from stone where sailors once guarded the oil works with rifles. Gore Cove has a surprisingly long association with the oil industry. A Scottish-born oil engineer, John Wilson Fell (1862-1955), established the original oil refinery on the Greenwich foreshores of Gore Cove. The Fell family operated oil shale refineries at Newnes and Hartley in New South Wales as well as their own refineries at Gore Cove and Clyde.

The firm suffered from the competition of cheap kerosene imported by the Standard Oil Company (of America) and Shell, and the company closed in 1927. Meanwhile, the Fell family had sold the Gore Cove installation to the British Imperial Oil Company Pty Ltd, which, in turn, sold it to Shell. The first bulk shipment of kerosene arrived at the Gore Bay installation on 14 June 1901, aboard Shell

Transport and Trading Company's S S *Turbo*. The kerosene was brought from the Russian port of Batum on the Black Sea.

BERRY ISLAND

Berry Island is a pleasant bushland park and popular picnic area named after Alexander Berry, one of the pioneer settlers of North Sydney. The island was formerly the property of the Berry Estate.

In 1906, it was vested in the Government to provide revenue for the David Berry Hospital at Berry. Premier Jack Lang dedicated the island as a public park in 1926. It is no longer an island, as Berry himself had a causeway built between it and the mainland. The mud flats were finally filled in during the early 1960s. The Sydney Jazz Club meets there regularly on one Sunday each month and outdoor jazz is freely enjoyed by everyone in this superb setting.

BALLS HEAD

Balls Head and Balls Head Bay are named after Henry Lidgbird Ball (?-1818), a naval officer who commanded HMS *Supply* in the First Fleet and who discovered Lord Howe Island. He became a pioneer explorer of Sydney's North Shore. Soon after the first settlement in 1788, an official party went by boat to North Harbour. Ball, in charge of some members of the group, blazed a trail over to the Middle Harbour, at about the area of present Roseville, then across to the area of present Greenwich and around the bays till they could be seen from the Sydney Cove settlement and rescued.

Balls Head is one of the few Aboriginal archaeological sites near the heart of Sydney. There are a number of Aboriginal rock engravings at several places. At the entrance to the driveway on a ledge above the road is a fenced and outlined group, showing figures which some people see as a man and whale and others claim are a shark and a dingo. A cave contains Aboriginal stencils of small fish, and hands on a rock.

When Balls Head was declared a reserve by Premier Jack Lang in October 1926, it was a rocky area. Some gum trees and other forms of vegetation grew there in the 1920s but after North Sydney Council took it over, many native trees were planted there. A plaque erected in 1967 pays tribute to the work of Mr Ludowici in replanting the area. A track along the eastern cliff leads to a tidal swimming pool. Balls Head shelters the Royal Australian Navy depot, HMAS *Waterhen* which controls the Navy's patrol boats.

The coal depot next door is not one of the beauties of the harbour but it has an interesting history of its own. Its original task was to supply fuel to coal-burning steamers. The coal came at first from the Illawarra but later from the Newcastle area. A cable railway was constructed by Mead Morrison of Chicago in 1920. The old railway was replaced in 1976 with a conveyor belt system. Today, the depot stores export coal and serves barges of harbourside customers.

BERRYS BAY

Berrys Bay is named after Alexander Berry (1781-1873), a Scottish merchant. Berry went into partnership with Edward Wollstonecraft (1783-1832) whose name is remembered in a nearby North Shore suburb. The two men decided to settle in New South Wales in 1819 and conducted a general business. Their store was in George Street but their ships were moored in what is now Berrys Bay. The two men later became brothers-in-law as well as partners, because Berry married Wollstonecraft's sister, Elizabeth, in 1827.

Wollstonecraft obtained a grant of land on the North Shore in 1819, which was made official in 1825, and he built a cottage there which he named Crows Nest. North Sydney Demonstration School now stands on part of what was the old Crows Nest farm.

Berry and Wollstonecraft were granted land in the Shoalhaven district and pioneered the area. When Wollstonecraft died in 1832, Berry then controlled the vast estate. He died at Crows Nest House in 1873, and he and Wollstonecraft are both buried at St Thomas's Park (formerly Cemetery), West Street, Crows Nest.

Berrys Bay today contains an oil depot, shipyards and boiler-makers. The Americas Cup challenger, *Dame Pattie,* was built by a shipyard at Berrys Bay. The quarantine section of the Department of Health has a fumigation depot on the shores of the bay.

In 1979, North Sydney Council, aided by a Government grant, paid nearly $700 000 to buy back harbour foreshore land between French Street and Munro Street at Berrys Bay for public parkland.

McMAHONS POINT

McMahons Point is named after a member of the first North Sydney Council, which was incorporated in 1890. McMahon was a brush and comb manufacturer and land speculator who moved to the point in 1871. The tip of McMahons Point is called Blues Point.

BLUES POINT

Overlooking the harbour and Blues Point is Blues Point Towers, a twenty-six-storey apartment block designed by Harry Seidler and built at McMahons Point in 1961. Blues Point Towers occupies the site of a mansion named Belleview (or Bellview) which was designed by the architect Edmund Blacket. It was bought in 1873, as a newly built house, by Moses Bell of the original Star of Hope Gold Mining Company. The gold mining company syndicate was formed in 1872 by German-born Bernard Otto Holtermann who, after years of failure, struck gold at Hill End near Bathurst. On 19 October 1872, the Star of Hope syndicate uncovered in a reef mine the biggest chunk of gold in the world, which they named the Holtermann nugget.

Holtermann built a mansion on the heights of North Sydney, which was acquired by the Church of England after his death in 1885. This became the famous grammar school, usually known as "Shore".

Billy Blue (?-1834), the man commemorated by the towers and the point, was probably part-Jamaican Negro and became Sydney's first ferryman. He was sentenced to seven years' transportation at the Kent Quarter Sessions in 1796, and he arrived in Sydney in 1801. He became a boatman on Sydney Harbour. In 1805 he married Elizabeth Williams and they had six children. In 1811 he was

appointed a water bailiff, and in 1817 Governor Lachlan Macquarie gave Billy Blue a grant of land on the North Shore. Billy named his property Northampton Farm. In about 1830, he began a rowboat service with his two sons, William, aged twenty-two, and Robert, aged eighteen. For many years the few North Shore residents living on the North Shore had to rely on a rowingboat to transport them over the 700 m between Blues Point and Dawes Point when they wanted to go to town. Blue was given the nickname of the Old Commodore, and was regarded as a local "character".

In 1842, the first paddle punt, the *Princess*, came on the run, serving the small North Shore population who were mainly settled in the Lavender Bay area, but the service ran at a loss and had to be discontinued. In 1845, a paddle-wheel steamer, *Ferry Queen*, began a service for vehicles between Windmill Street, Millers Point, and Blues Point. This service proved profitable and other ferries later joined the run.

LAVENDER BAY

Lavender Bay is named after George J. Lavender, who married Susannah Blue, the daughter of Billy Blue. In 1834, George Lavender became a boatman, ferrying passengers across the harbour and back again. After selling his cottage at Lavender Bay, he went to live at the Commodore Hotel at Blues Point Road where, on 28 February 1851, at the age of sixty-six, he shot himself.

A couple of kilometres uphill from Lavender Bay, in West Street, is St Thomas's Park, a graveyard of pioneers. It is here that George Lavender is buried, with his wife, Susannah, who died 6 February 1861, aged fifty-four. Vandals smashed part of the Lavender tombstone in 1978.

The ferry service helped make Lavender Bay a select area of large homes surrounded by several hectares of land. One of the few homes which have survived is Euroka, a two-storey residence built in the 1850s by a ship owner, Edward Mawney Sayers. After he sold Euroka, it passed to the Dibbs brothers — first George (afterwards Sir George), Premier, and when he became unfinancial, his brother Thomas, a banker, took it on and the name was changed to Graythwaite. During the first World War, Dibbs presented the house to the State as a hospital administered by the Red Cross for the care of wounded soldiers. The house in Edwards Street, North Sydney, is still used by the Health Commission.

Today Lavender Bay has a combination of fairly old houses and high-rise apartment blocks. Visible from the harbour at Lavender Bay today is a 13-m circular white brick Norman tower with a thatched roof. This incongruous structure is attached to a three-storeyed Victorian house inhabited by the painter, Brett Whiteley, who added the tower after he bought the house. Whiteley's studio is in the old Oyster Cove gasworks building, some 3 km west from Lavender Bay, on the harbour foreshore.

A pleasant feature of Lavender Bay today is the fish restaurant called "Sails" which opened in 1977 and enjoys beautiful views of the harbour. In 1979 North Sydney Council proposed planting trees and installing gas barbecues on the foreshore. Some Blues Point residents objected to the trees because they thought they might

273

interfere with their views, and they also opposed the installation of gas barbecues, but a compromise was finally reached.

LAVENDER BAY BATH HOUSE

Lavender Bay had a long history of swimming before the North Sydney Olympic Pool was built. In 1881, "Professor" Fred Cavill, the father of the famous swimming family, took possession of the Lavender Bay pile baths. His youngest son, Richard (Dick), is credited as the inventor of the Australian crawl. North Sydney Council has a copy of Richard Cavill's letter in which he claims he invented the crawl and was world champion.

The bath house in various forms had a chequered career, including being damaged by a gale in 1910. Although in disrepair by 1975, it had acquired a nostalgic charm, but the North Sydney Council finally decided to pull the bath house down, after discussing the pros and cons of demolition for about twenty years. Its last occupants were the Lavender Bay Boy Scouts.

NORTH SYDNEY OLYMPIC POOL

On the other side of the bay is the North Sydney Olympic Pool. Since it was opened in 1936, the Olympic Pool has been one of the most important swimming centres in the world. It was built on land left over from building the Sydney Harbour Bridge. Fresh water was used during the 1938 British Empire Games, but normally water from the harbour — filtered and chlorinated — is used in the pool. Five British Empire records and twenty-four Australian records were set at the games.

The earliest world record set at this pool was by Frank O'Neill in 1953. Between then and 1980, eighty-five world records were set at the pool by the greatest Australian swimmers of their times, from the Konrads Kids and Dawn Fraser to Shane Gould and Stephen Holland and Michelle Ford. The number of records set there is itself a record for any pool in the world.

LUNA PARK

Beside the Olympic Pool is Luna Park. Sydney's Luna Park began life in Glenelg, a suburb of Adelaide in the early 1930s, but it moved to Sydney where queues 50 m long formed from the gates when they opened on 4 October 1935. The park took its name from the original Luna Park built in 1903 at Coney Island, Brooklyn, New York. It was established by Herman F. and Leon Phillips, who had established previous parks in Melbourne (1912) and Glenelg, South Australia (1932), with the Abrahams family. David Atkins, who had previously been involved with a fun park at Manly and the Coogee pier, came from Luna Park, Glenelg, to manage the new Luna Park, Sydney. Ted Hopkins, who had been part of the Glenelg organisation, was promoted to assistant manager.

The Milsons Point site had been used as a construction site by Dorman and Long, the builders of the Sydney Harbour Bridge, which had been completed a few years earlier. Phillips won a tender to develop the area and part of the agreement was to spend $80 000 on the site within six months. Much more than this was spent in considerably less time. Construction took three months; 1 000 000 m of timber and 60 000 bags of cement were used; approximately 800 people were employed; a team of eighty electricians installed all the electrical equipment in six weeks; and the whole 3 hectares were paved in four days.

A ship was chartered to bring the attractions from Glenelg. These included Penny Arcade slot machines, Noah's Ark, the Goofy House, the River Caves and the Big Dipper. The Big Dipper was disassembled log by log in Glenelg, each piece numbered, then rebuilt on its present site. Other original attractions were: Coney Island, Hey Dey, Dodgems, Whip, Whirler, Ghost Train and Tumble Bug. The original entrance fee was 6d and all rides were 6d each, except for the Big Dipper and Coney Island, which were 9d. A year later, the entrance fee was abolished.

During the second World War with the Japanese involvement in the Pacific, there was a "brownout" in Sydney which required the shading of all exterior lighting. At Luna Park all festooning, naked lights and neons were prohibited but the park continued to operate, illuminated only by well-shaded lights. During this time the military wanted to use the park for storage, but came to realise that it filled an important recreational need both for civilians and off-duty military personnel and it remained an amusement park and operated as such right through the war years.

In 1945, David Atkins and Ted Hopkins combined to buy a former Dutch submarine, the K12. It served two purposes: at a time when Sydney was plagued with power shortages it helped to augment other emergency power, generating equipment to keep the park operating; and it provided an additional walk-through attraction, being moored just near Coney Island.

Originally, the front entrance towers were outlined with high intensity neon lights and were, at that time, the largest neon installation in Australia. After not having been used during the war years most neons proved to be faulty when turned on again, and a faulty neon in the tower caused a fire on top of the south-west tower, destroying the shells. That was the end of neons on the towers — they were replaced by incandescent lighting.

A variety of events were held in the park during the 1940s and early 1950s. These included mardi gras, bathing beauty contests, ladies' woodchopping contests, free band concerts, a swaypole act, a diving act, a high wire act, with appearances by Berosini, Don Webb and Dixie Lee.

After the winter of 1950 new additions were made to the park — Davy Jones Locker, the Burmese Temple in the River Caves, the Jack and Jill, the U-Drive, and the Palais de Danse; a large flat pontoon used during the construction of the bridge, which was bought from the Department of Main Roads, modified and redecorated, was added, along with a number of new slot machines.

In 1970 there was a takeover of Luna Park shares by Sydney World Trade Centre Pty Ltd, for the purpose of building a World Trade Centre on the site. This did not eventuate as the State Government said such redevelopment would be unsuitable on the harbour foreshores. Nathan Spatt and Leon Fink bought out the principal shareholder, an American life assurance company, and formed Luna Park (NSW) Ltd and continued to operate the amusement park.

Restoration work was started on the merry-go-round, a hand-crafted masterpiece built in 1910. Horses were repainted, thousands of multi-coloured "jewels" were imported from Europe, and the old steam organ was restored and adapted to work on electricity. At the same time a team of artists, including Martin Sharp, Richard Liney and Leigh Hobbs, were involved with the rejuvenation of the front face and towers, the dodgem building and the Coney Island building.

Rupert Brown originally designed the Sydney and Melbourne Luna Park faces. Melbourne retained the original "scowling" face, but Sydney's face was remodelled in 1950 by Arthur Barton, an Archibald prize-winning artist who gave it a jovial expression. He was also responsible for many of the visual concepts of Luna Park. In 1973 the Arthur Barton face was re-decorated by Martin Sharp as part of the general rejuvenation programme.

In August 1975, a pay-one-price admission policy was introduced and patrons paid $2 admission, which entitled them to fourteen rides. Until 1979, the park had had only one fatality in a history of over forty years. This occurred when a drunken sailor stood up on the Big Dipper before it had stopped. He overbalanced and was thrown against a post. On another occasion, an unthinking youth tried to ride the Big Dipper while hanging from the back of a carriage. He was lucky to escape with shattered kneecaps. Perhaps the luckiest passenger was another sailor who dived from the Spider into the harbour, a dangerous feat.

None of these accidents could be blamed on mechanical faults in the park's equipment. However, in April 1979, thirteen teenagers were hurt in a crash in the Big Dipper. The steel which protected the wooden runners came loose, causing the wheel on the front car to dig into the wood. The car ground to a halt, and there was no time for park operators to stop the second car before it hit the stationary one.

Then on 9 June 1979, tragedy struck Luna Park. One adult and six children were burned to death in a fire when the Ghost Train in which they were riding caught fire. The probable cause was a carelessly discarded match or cigarette. Giving his findings on 3 September after an inquiry, Sydney coroner Keven Anderson criticised the park's owners for what he termed their reluctance to implement safety measures, but he said there was not enough evidence to support a charge of criminal negligence.

After the tragedy the park was closed and remained closed for the rest of the year while negotiations concerning a new lease went on.

MILSONS POINT

James Milson (1783-1872) was one of the first white settlers in North Sydney. He arrived in Sydney in 1806 and was given a grant of land on the North Shore. Here he built what is generally regarded as the first house on the northern side of Port Jackson. It was situated near where the north-east pylon of the Sydney Harbour Bridge now stands and his farm extended to the point where St Aloysius College,

Admiralty House and Kirribilli House now stand. Milson supplied ships in Sydney Cove with fresh milk, meat and other agricultural produce. Milson's first cottage was burned to the ground in a bushfire in 1826, but despite this setback Milson prospered.

A ferry service between Circular Quay and Milsons Point began in 1861 with the establishment of the North Shore Ferry Company which launched the *Kirribilli*. In 1886 a cable tram was put into service between Milsons Point and Ridge Street, North Sydney. This had the effect of drawing the majority of ferry passengers to the Milsons Point terminus.

A railway line built from Hornsby to St Leonards was opened in 1890, and an extension to Milsons Point was opened in 1893. The old Milsons Point Railway Station had to be demolished to make way for the Sydney Harbour Bridge, opened in 1932, as the station was where the bridge pylon now stands.

The building of the Warringah Expressway in the 1960s caused further demolition. Some of the cottages removed were the homes of Sydney's most notorious criminals from whom you could "hire a gun" for a few pounds.

NORTH SYDNEY

During the 1970s the population of North Sydney fell as houses were demolished to make way for high-rise office blocks. At the 1976 census the population was 48 515, compared with the 52 000 in 1965.

Northpoint, 195 m above sea level, became the largest building in North Sydney — or for that matter one of the highest anywhere in Sydney — in the late 1970s. Meanwhile, the people who lived in the area as opposed to those who simply worked there became increasingly concerned about their environment during the 1970s.

15

KIRRIBILLI

Kiarabilli, or Kirribilli, is believed to be the Aboriginal name for this area. It has been suggested that it was adapted from the name of an early Milson family cottage, Carabella, which is understood to be Spanish for "a basket of flowers".

Some of the houses built by the Milson family still remain. It is possible that part of the house which is now Number 54 Willoughby Street, is the old Wia Wia, built in 1834 for James Milson Jr.

Number 6 Winslow Street, was built for John Milson (1822-91), who called it Fern Lodge. It has been restored and is now used as professional offices by Brian Ahearn. Elamang, built by James Milson Jr in 1851, is now part of Loreto Convent, and Carabella is occupied by the Royal Sydney Yacht Squadron. Several books give its date of building as 1824 but it was probably built later. Another building, Carabella Cottage, was built for Milson's daughter, Sophia Shairp, at the (then) head of Careening Cove. It eventually became Number 34 McDougall Street, until it was demolished to make way for a block of flats.

The first block of flats to be built on the North Shore is said to be the building now standing at Number 1 Waruda Street, built in 1908 by Mrs James White, the owner of the famous racehorse, Carbine. At the time, flat living was described as the latest thing from America.

For 31 years the Pastoral Finance Association wool store was a landmark on the shores of Kirribilli, but the seven-storey building was destroyed by a spectacular fire in 1921.

Today, Kirribilli, an area of home units, has several interesting old houses, including Admiralty House and Kirribilli House. The headquarters of the Australian Security Intelligence Organization in Sydney is located in a big house in Kirribilli near Kirribilli House and Admiralty House. It is invisible from the street but can be clearly seen from the harbour.

ADMIRALTY HOUSE

Admiralty House is the Sydney residence of the Governor General. It stands on an area of land granted to Robert Ryan in 1800. In 1806, Robert Campbell, the successful merchant who built Campbell's wharves, acquired Ryan's land. In 1842, Campbell leased the land to Lieutenant Colonel J.G.N. Gibbes, who had a single-storey Georgian house erected in 1843.

In 1856, the Government, fearing an attack from the Russians, resumed the tip of the point for building fortifications. The house has had various owners, including Colonel George Barney, the designer of Fort Denison. In 1869, it was bought by Thomas Cadell. In 1885, Cadell sold Wotonga House, as it was then known, to the Government of New South Wales for use as a residence by the

Commander-in-Chief of the British Naval Squadron stationed in Sydney. So Wotonga became Admiralty House. A number of admirals lived in the house until 1913, when the house was lent to the Federal Government for use as the Sydney residence of the Governor-General. Admiralty House finally became Commonwealth property by a Crown grant in 1948.

KIRRIBILLI HOUSE

Alongside Admiralty House is Kirribilli House, also a house with a history. It is used as the Prime Minister's Sydney residence.

In September 1854, Mr Travers excised a portion of his land, the present Admiralty House property, and sold it to Mr Adolph Feez, who built a small two-storey house of six rooms with twin gables, from which he had a view across Neutral Bay. Over the next sixty five years Kirribilli House was enlarged in stages, by various owners, through the addition of extra rooms at ground and first floor levels.

On 20 June 1919 it was sold at a public auction to Mr Arthur Allen for £10 000. When it was reported a little later that the land was to be subdivided there was public agitation for the house and garden to be preserved. Following this expression of public concern the then Prime Minister, the Rt Hon. W.M. Hughes, gave his approval for purchase or compulsory acquisition. The land was resumed by special Commonwealth gazette on 17 January 1920, and £15 505/19s paid as compensation.

During the Depression Kirribilli House was closed as a vice-regal residence and in 1930 it was leased to Captain A.E. Lungren, CBE, in 1935 to Alfred House, in 1937 to George Henry Deaton, and in 1943 to Commander Karl E. Oom who continued in occupation until October 1953. In 1956 the Commonwealth Government decided to re-furnish and re-decorate Kirribilli House as a residence for official guests of the Commonwealth and it is still being used for this purpose.

ROYAL SYDNEY YACHT SQUADRON

A yacht club was formed in 1862 at the office of the Hon. William Walker, MLC, on 8 July, 1862 by nineteen yachtsmen. The following year the Prince of Wales accepted the office of patron and so Sydney Yacht Squadron became the Royal Sydney Yacht Squadron.

In 1902, it leased Carabella on Wudyong Road with its land fronting Careening Cove. The squadron's ensign was hoisted over its new headquarters on 24 January, 1903. Today, the club has an interesting reminder of the past in its foyer in the form of the bell of Ben Boyd's schooner, *Wanderer*. Another interesting feature is the jawbones of a whale beside the water.

In 1979, Alderman Phyllis King of the North Sydney Council protested at a plan to reconstruct the Royal Sydney Yacht Squadron's facilities. It was the latest in a series of proposals put forward by the squadron since 1969. The squadron claimed that the existing facilities were functionally and aesthetically obsolete and did not provide adequate water and dry storage to service the vessels on the club register. It wanted to provide a calm water basin protected by a floating breakwater to permit the safe handling and servicing of

279

yachts in most weather conditions. The project included a concrete deck for yacht storage extending over the water on steel piles and the installation of crane hoists.

The scheme drew protests from local residents, who objected to noise from cranes, increased traffic in the neighbourhood, and the possible closure of the High Street ferry wharf because the proposed marina would make ferries swing too far out to be able to manoeuvre into the wharf.

CAREENING COVE

Careening Cove, with its sheltered position and deep water frontages, was used, as its name implies, for beaching and careening vessels for cleaning purposes. The beach was subsequently reclaimed and is now Milson Park.

When the *Sirius* of the First Fleet was anchored at Careening Cove in 1788, John Mara, a gunner's mate, landed on the thickly wooded shore to look for water. He was lost for three days at the head of the cove. Careening Cove, like Neutral Harbour and Great and Little Sirius coves, was used in the 1830s by whaling ships. Later, a number of large houses were built there.

The Ensemble Theatre, beside the water at Careening Cove, has one of the best positions on the harbour. Its founder, an American actor and producer, Hayes Gordon, came to Australia in 1952 for the production of *Kiss Me, Kate* and stayed on to start an actors' workshop in North Sydney. When the workshop's premises were closed as a fire hazard in 1959, Hayes Gordon and his enthusiastic youthful helpers converted an old warehouse into the present Ensemble Theatre, which opened in 1960.

Near the theatre is the Sydney Flying Squadron Ltd, Sydney's oldest "18-ft" sailing club. It was founded in 1890.

NEUTRAL BAY

Neutral Bay got its name in 1789 when England was at war with France. Governor Phillip decided that there should be a large bay set aside for neutral ships visiting the harbour. At one time it was a noted fishing area, and oysters were also plentiful, although the fish and oysters disappeared when a gas company erected works on the western side in the 1870s.

During the early days of Neutral Bay, residents had to travel by sail or rowingboat. They used to walk through the bush to Lavender Bay or Milsons Point, where a waterman named Andrews, who lived on Careening Cove at the foot of Willoughby Street, took them over at 6d a head. The North Shore Ferry Company began a service in 1873 with the *Florence*.

Neutral Bay is still served by ferries at Hayes Street wharf and Kurraba wharf and High Street. Hayes Street is named after Patrick Hayes who had a soap and oil factory and brickworks for many years.

The navy's aptly named HMAS *Platypus* — the submarine base — is located in Neutral Bay at the old gasworks site. Oberon class submarines of the First Australian Submarine Squadron operate from the base.

Overlooking Neutral Bay is a town house complex named Southern Cross Gardens, which was opened in 1976. Its name commemorates a flight made from Anderson Park beside the harbour below the complex, when Sir Charles Kingsford Smith and Sir Patrick Gordon Taylor made their historical take-off on 17 July, 1934. In the gardens of the town houses is a propellor from a Lockheed Altair — the same type of aircraft as Smithy's *Lady Southern Cross*, in which he was lost flying in the Bay of Bengal in November 1935. Smithy's widow, who later remarried, was flown out from the United States for the opening of the town houses.

BEN BOYD

Ben Boyd Road in Neutral Bay commemorates Ben Boyd (1796?-1851), a Scottish whaler and businessman who arrived in Sydney in 1842. He established a whaling station at Boyd Town in Twofold Bay near Eden. Wool from his Monaro property was brought to Twofold Bay and shipped to Sydney, where at Neutral Bay he constructed a large store for wool storage and erected dams for wool washing.

Boyd lived in a splendid house called Craignathan from 1844-49. It was built in 1831 by another early settler, James McLaren, after whom McLaren Street in North Sydney is named. Traces of Craignathan's bakers' ovens can still be seen today in the Royal Australian Air Force car park. A plaque commemorating Ben Boyd is set in a brick wall at the corner of Ben Boyd Road and Kurraba Road, where the Customs Department now has offices and a slipway for their boats. On the Customs Department workshop is a plaque on a wooden pump shaft marking the locality of "the residence, dam, wharf, and woolstore". If any of the original Craignathan survives, it is much overbuilt.

Boyd lost the house and everything else, except his yacht *Wanderer*, when his business collapsed. He went off to California in a vain search for gold. He disappeared in the Solomon Islands in 1851.

KURRABA POINT

Kurraba Point was originally known as Thrupps Point after Lieutenant Alfred Thrupp, who received a grant of land there in 1814. Another name for it was Ballast Point, because ballast was obtained from the stone cliffs there for ships returning with insufficient cargo to London or those carrying wool which needed extra weight. Stone for Fort Denison was quarried there.

A view of the harbour from high ground can be seen from Spains Lookout on Kurraba Road. It is named after the alderman who was responsible for securing it for public use. The Spain family lived nearby in Wallaringa from the 1860s.

The partly developed reserve at Kurraba Point is one of the recent acquisitions of public foreshore open space. When the Port Jackson Steamship Company moved its repair yards to Balmain this site was acquired by the State Planning Authority and handed over to North Sydney Council to develop and maintain as parkland.

The pillars of the house named Once Upon a Time at Number 115 Kurraba Road, Neutral Bay, near Kurraba wharf, make it a landmark on the harbour. The house has an intriguing history, being built by a wealthy Mr Crowle after whom the Crowle Home for Subnormal Children at Ryde is named.

Once Upon a Time originally stood on the other side of the harbour in Wylde Street, Potts Point, in the grounds of a larger house Crowle owned called Wyldefel, built by Eliza and Walter Hall, who found the Mount Morgan gold mine. In 1940, the Government took possession of part of Wylde Street for use by the Navy. As they filled in the water between the Crowle house and Garden Island, they puled down Once Upon a Time. The demolished house was brought across the harbour in many barges and in 1941-42 it was re-erected exactly as it had been, using the original bricks, as bricks were impossible to buy at the time.

The columns at the entrance were originally around a big swimming pool which was never furnished, so on Mr Crowle's death his widow turned it into a patio. A boatshed under the house was turned into a flat. The rest of the house was also turned into apartments, with Mrs Crowle retaining the top one.

A stone gargoyle at the entrance was purchased by Mr Crowle in London when stones from the Houses of Parliament, dislodged by the bombing during the war, were offered for sale to raise public funds for restoration. The beautiful wrought-iron gates on the waterfront came from the old home, Wydefel, at Potts Point, and probably came from England at the end of the century. The quotations which hang outside on the ferry steps are from the old Wylde Street gardens and have been put there with permission from North Sydney Council. One is from Goethe saying, "Live peaceably with all — so shalt thou lead a happy life thyself". On the wall outside is a marble plaque with another quotation in German, *"Wenn Jemand eine reise thut fo kann er was verzahlen"*, which roughly translates as "When somebody makes a journey they have a story to tell".

SHELL COVE

Shell Cove was originally known as Hungry Bay because two convicts escaped on a raft from Pinchgut and were recaptured there, exhausted and half-starved. It gets its present name from the fact that oyster shells were once crushed and burned there in lime kilns to make lime for mortar used in building.

CREMORNE POINT

The original owner of the whole of Cremorne was James Robertson, who was granted land there in 1823 in recognition of his work repairing scientific instruments at the Parramatta Observatory. Robertsons Point at the tip of Cremorne Point bears his name.

In 1853 Robertsons Point was sold to James Milson for £4000. Milson then leased a portion of the land to Clarke and Woolcott, two promoters who improved the jetty and ran ferries from Woolloomooloo. They charged the public for use of the pleasure grounds, which they named Cremorne after the famous Cremorne Gardens of London. They offered a quadrille band and a huge dancing stage, and there was a merry-go-round for the children. Other attractions included skittles, archery, rifle shooting, and fireworks at night. The business failed six years later.

In 1891 the owners offered to sell land with water frontages for home sites, but the Crown intervened and contested their right to do so. The court finally decreed that a stretch of water frontage 2 km long by a depth of 30 m from high water was public property. In this way Shell Cove foreshore was saved for the people in perpetuity.

Two years later on 11 November 1893, an important coal discovery at Cremorne was announced, coal being struck at a depth of 1000 m; but because of public opposition, the venture was abandoned.

MOSMAN BAY

The name of the bay and the suburb comes from Archibald Mosman, who set up a whaling station there in 1830. He built a stone wharf, a large residence for himself, and two stone dwellings for ships' officers and crew. One of his two stone storehouses still survives and is used today as a scout hall. Its doorway is flanked by two large whale bones. In 1835, half the income of New South Wales came from whale oil and bone. Mosman sold out in 1839 and moved to the New England district. The whaling industry collapsed in 1841.

Mosman's home was bought in 1859 by Richard Harnett, whose name is remembered by Harnett Park. He opened a quarry which provided sandstone for many Sydney buildings and also for the wall in the Botanic Gardens which runs round Farm Cove. Harnett also began the first ferry service in 1871. The ferry still serves Mosman and an interesting walk from Cremorne Point to Mosman can be combined with a ferry ride. People with tired feet or tired children or both can walk from either direction and make the return journey by ferry.

At the beginning of the century Mosman, with its romantic harbour inlets, became a popular place for artists to live, some of the best-known people who lived there being Julian Ashton, Phil May, Tom Roberts and Arthur Streeton.

LITTLE SIRIUS COVE

Little Sirius Cove is named after the ship *Sirius* which brought supplies from Capetown in 1789 and saved the struggling young colony of Sydney from starvation. The ship was careened at Great Sirius Cove, now called Mosman Bay.

TARONGA PARK

A ferry trip to Taronga Park Zoo is one of the nicest family outings Sydney Harbour can offer. The zoo was well named when it was first established on the slopes of Mosman in 1916 — taronga is the Aboriginal word for "water view". Situated as it is, overlooking Sydney Harbour, the zoo has one of the most spectacular water views in the world. Founded by the Zoological Society of New South Wales in 1881, the zoo was originally situated on 3 hectares of land, known as Billygoat Swamp, in Moore Park, east of Sydney. It was such a success, and the collection of animals grew so large, that it was necessary to find another site.

When the zoo moved across the water in 1916, one of the highlights of the operation was the transportation of Jessie the elephant. Since she arrived in Sydney in 1883, a gift from the King of Siam, Jessie had been a great favourite at the Moore Park site and when she was moved, on 24 September, she caused great excitement as she shuffled along beside her keeper to Circular Quay. She caused no trouble during her half-hour punt crossing to Taronga and showed great interest in her new surroundings. From then until 1938, Jessie remained one of the major attractions of the new zoo, continuing to give rides to thousands of children.

Sir Edward Hallstrom (1886-1970) a Sydney manufacturer and philanthropist, served as chairman of the Taronga Zoological Park Trust for many years and donated hundreds of birds and animals to the zoo. By the 1960s the zoo was looking rather shabby, so in 1967 a redevelopment plan was drawn up with the help of the Government architect's branch of the New South Wales Public Works Department.

By 1980 a number of projects had been completed. They included a new walk-through aviary, a new platypus house, a veterinary quarantine station, a nocturnal house, and a koala house. The best features of the old zoo, such as the main gates and the elephant house, were kept and renovated, but many of the concrete "uglies" which housed the animals were demolished.

That first stage of the redevelopment was accomplished by the combined efforts of a truly multi-disciplinary team. Architects, landscape architects, engineers and graphic designers from the Government architect's branch produced the overall plans and the detail designs, and much of the construction and planting was carried out by zoo staff. In 1979, the zoo's new director, Jack Throp, announced that a restaurant with harbour views was to be built above the old aquarium.

ASHTON PARK AND BRADLEYS HEAD

Taronga Park was orignally part of Ashton Park, named after one of Sydney's leading citizens, the Hon. James Ashton, MLC. At the tip of this magnificent bird and animal sanctuary, is Bradleys Head. William Bradley was a lieutenant on HMS *Sirius*, the flagship of the First Fleet. The Aboriginal name for Bradleys Head is "Burrogy".

In 1841 it was decided by the military to turn Bradleys Head into a fortress, and a gun-pit surrounded by a stone wall was built. The fort was then forgotten for thirty years until 1871 when three gun-pits, a powder magazine, and a stone gallery were constructed. Much of Bradleys Head was acquired by the Crown, until over 50 hectares were proclaimed as Ashton Park and reserved for public use. Ashton Park and its guns are now part of Sydney Harbour National Park. As well as its military relics, this area offers several interesting foreshore walks with beautiful views of the harbour.

In 1978, the Australian Heritage Commission gazetted the Bradleys Head fortifications as part of the National Estate. The fortifications included the 1840-42 gun-pit and firing wall, the 1871 gallery for riflemen and its associated stone wharf and sea retaining wall. Also on Bradleys Head is the fighting top of HMAS *Sydney*. A solitary stone pillar marks "the measured mile", that is, one nautical mile (1.8 km) from the Fort Denison tower (Pinchgut) used for testing the speed of all vessels launched at Sydney.

ATHOL BAY

The navy has permanent dolphin moorings at Athol Bay beside Taronga Park. It uses the moorings for oil lighters and as a staging post for old ships which have been put out of commission and are awaiting disposal.

During the second World War the giant *Queen Mary* and *Queen Elizabeth* were used as troopships and they were moored at this safe deepwater anchorage.

TAYLORS BAY

Taylors Bay, between Chowder Head and Bradleys Head, is named after Lieutenant James Taylor, a member of the 73rd Regiment based in Sydney in 1810.

Taylors Bay was the scene of a tragedy in 1889. At nine o'clock in the evening of 23 August 1889, the *Centennial*, an iron screw steamer of 600 tonnes, left her wharf in Darling Harbour on a voyage to New Zealand, loaded to the Plimsoll mark with coal, together with eighty passengers and crew. The night was dark and clear.

A few minutes later, after rounding Bradleys Head, she collided with the collier *Kanahooka*, 240 tonnes, which was struck on the starboard side. The *Centennial* leaked so badly that an unsuccessful attempt was made to beach her in Taylors Bay. She sank three minutes later in 26 m of water. The chief cook was drowned, but the others on board were rescued by the aid of boats from the *Kanahooka* and the pilot boat. The *Kanahooka,* also loaded with coal, inward bound from Wollongong, fortunately stayed afloat and nobody was hurt.

CHOWDER BAY

The name Chowder Bay was bestowed by Americans who anchored there in whaling ships over a century ago. The sailors made "clam" chowder from rock oysters that were plentiful on the rocky shores of the bays and coves in Sydney Harbour. The whalers anchored below the farm of Captain Cliffe. Today, only the stone pillars and iron gates at the entrance to what is now a block of town houses remain from Cliffe's estate.

A recreation reserve with saltwater baths, known as Clifton Gardens, at the head of Chowder Bay, has been a favourite picnic spot for many years. It was once a popular place for ferry excursions from Circular Quay in the days when the only access was by water.

When private motor cars were much less numerous than today, ferry trips were popular as family outings. The route which had its first call at Athol Gardens proceeded to Clifton Gardens in Chowder Bay. Here the attractions included a swimming enclosure and dance hall. The ferry then proceeded to Balmoral, another popular picnic spot with baths and levelled grass areas where itinerant showmen often set up merry-go-rounds. The final port of call was The Spit, where there was a wharf on the eastern side.

For many years the Clifton Gardens Hotel was a feature of Clifton Gardens. The Mosman Council bought the hotel in 1969 and added the area to the Clifton Gardens Reserve.

GEORGES HEAD

Georges Head is named after George III. Governor King had a battery installed in 1801 and the area was used for defence purposes until 1979 when 13 hectares of land at Georges Heights were handed over by the military for inclusion in the Sydney Harbour National Park.

In 1978 the Australian Heritage Commission gazetted the battery of five guns and the WRAAC officers' mess as part of the National Estate.

OBELISK BAY

The two white obelisks from which Obelisk Bay gets its name can be lined up to give ships a clear passage through this part of the harbour.

MIDDLE HEAD

Middle Head is opposite the North and South Head entrances to the harbour. In 1978, the Australian Heritage Commission gazetted the fortifications known as the Old Fort at Middle Head as part of the National Estate. In 1979, 38 hectares of land at Middle Head were transferred by the military authorities to Sydney Harbour National Park.

On 4 April 1891 there was a terrible explosion at Middle Head due to the premature explosion of a mine. Four men were killed.

BALMORAL BEACH

Balmoral was named after the royal castle of Queen Victoria, built in 1853 at a cost of £100 000 at Braemar, Aberdeenshire.

In 1924 an amphitheatre was completed at Balmoral, Sydney, by a body of people called the Order of the Star of the East. This was a world-wide organisation comprised of people of numerous religious beliefs who had one idea in common — that a great religious teacher would appear. The amphitheatre was erected as a lecture hall for the expected teacher, and for other purposes such as drama, ballet, and religious pageants.

Following a custom which was adopted in the building of the Albert Hall, London, seats were sold in order to help raise funds for the erection of the amphitheatre, estimated to cost £20 000. Later the Order of the Star of the East was dissolved, and in 1939 the amphitheatre passed into other hands, and a block of home units has since been built on the site.

Part of Balmoral Beach and its surroundings was classified by the National Trust in 1978 and by the Australian Heritage Commission in 1979. The Commission said the character of the Balmoral Beach conservation area could be described as having an atmosphere of controlled 1930s civic design superimposed on to an important landscape setting of high quality. The landscape setting is the long curving beach.

Enjoying beautiful views of the harbour, Mischa's, one of Sydney's best fish restaurants, was established in part of the old beach pavillion beside the netted swimming pool in December 1970.

HMAS *Penguin* at Balmoral is mainly used as the Royal Australian Naval Hospital. It includes a section devoted to underwater medicine which has a decompression chamber for divers.

Hunters Bay, in which Balmoral Beach is located, is named after Captain John Hunter of the *Sirius* and the second Governor of New South Wales. The next beach to Balmoral is called Edwards Beach. Captain Edwards, a retired whaler who lived on a 10-hectare property at Balmoral, was one of the first people to sight the *Dunbar's* wreckage when the ship broke up on South Head in 1857.

BALMORAL SAILING CLUB

Balmoral Sailing Club organises Heron sailing dinghy races on Sundays. These family sailing dinghies usually carry Dad or Mum at the helm with son or daughter as crew, although junior skippers are now quite numerous. The 3.4 m dinghies, originally designed by an Englishman, Jack Holt, have grown to form the most numerous class in Australia, with more than 4500 having been built since 1958. There are about 1600 registered Herons sailing throughout the country. Other Sydney Harbour sailing clubs which organise Heron races are at Concord-Ryde, Double Bay, Middle Harbour and the Dobroyd Athletic Club. Other clubs also organise Heron races at Botany Bay, Narrabeen Lakes, Port Hacking and Pittwater.

CHINAMANS BEACH

Shell Cove between Parriwi (meaning "spit") and Wy-ar-gine Point includes Chinamans Beach. One explanation of this name is that the beach has long slender shellfish like extended fingernails that are called Chinaman's Nails. A more likely explanation is that it gets its name from the Chinese market gardens which once existed behind it.

Sand's New South Wales Directory of 1890 lists Ah Sue, a market gardener, as one of the five residents in Spit Road. He was possibly the first of the Chinese to work vegetable gardens in the area behind the foreshore that became Chinamans Beach.

THE SPIT

The Aborigines called the sand spit which gives The Spit its name, Parriwi or Burra-bra which also means "spit". A spit is, of course, a small point of land running into the sea. The Spit Bridge can be raised and lowered to allow ships to pass through the narrow channel, causing considerable traffic jams, especially at weekends. However, it is a vast improvement on the old punt which Peter Ellery started in 1850. Peter Ellery ran the punt until 1888, when he made over to the Government both the punt and the road which ran through his property. Steam punts replaced the old Government hand-operated punts in 1889 and continued to carry vehicles and passengers until 1924, when a timber toll bridge was opened. Meanwhile, a tram service from The Spit to Manly began operation in 1911 and continued until 1939. The old wooden drawbridge was replaced by the present bridge in 1958.

Not all crossings of Middle Harbour have been by boat or bridge. In 1877, on four separate occasions, Henry L'Estrange, described as an "adventurous gymnast", walked a tight-rope stretched across Middle Harbour from north-east to south-west. He was no doubt emulating the Frenchman, Charles Blondin, who four times crossed Niagara Falls in this way between 1858 and 1860. Although we do not know the exact location of these exploits, it was about one hour by ferry from the Quay, and can't have been far from the site of the present Spit Bridge.

On The Spit are several sailing clubs — the Middle Harbour Amateur Sailing Club, the Middle Harbour Yacht Club, and the 16-ft. Skiff Sailing Club. The Royal Volunteer Coastal Patrol is also located here. Appropriately enough, The Spit has two excellent fish restaurants.

The Middle Harbour Yacht Club, founded in 1939, is the largest keel yacht club in the Southern Hemisphere. It organises four ocean races. Like the famous Sydney to Hobart race, the South Solitary Island yacht race, over 760 km, also starts on Boxing Day, yachts leaving Middle Harbour at 3 pm. The course is round South Solitary Island, off Coffs Harbour, and back to cross the finishing line at Pittwater. The Sydney-Brisbane yacht race, over about 900 km, starts on the Wednesday week prior to Easter. The Montague Island yacht race, over 630 km, starts on the six-hour-day weekend in October. The course is around Montague Island off Narooma. The club also organises the Sydney to Suva yacht race every two years. The inaugural race, over a distance of 3120 km, started in Sydney Harbour on 30 May 1976.

Middle Harbour Skiff Club, founded 1904, has won more Australian and State titles than any other club in the country. It holds races on Saturdays for "16-ft" skiffs, 505s, and B-class boats of about 3 m known as Flying Ants. On Sundays it holds races for Hobie Cats - catamarans 4.3 - 4.9 m long.

ROYAL VOLUNTEER COASTAL PATROL

The idea for the Royal Volunteer Coastal Patrol was born in 1937. Commander Long of Naval Intelligence felt that it would not be long before Australia was at war. He felt an organisation was needed to assist the under-strength Navy in the defence of Sydney Harbour and other ports. Commander Long approached Harold Nobbs, a well-known Sydney yachtsman, to form a unit among the boating fraternity. The result was that the Volunteer Coastal Patrol came into being with an inaugural meeting in March 1938, comprised of twelve private vessels and a number of personnel.

After the outbreak of war in September 1939, the patrol quickly built up to 5000 men and 500 boats, all privately owned. Their base, *Seahorse*, was close to where the submarine base at Neutral Bay is today. Their main wartime role was the protection of ships, wharves, and oil installations in Sydney Harbour and to guard against sabotage attempts on the Sydney Harbour Bridge and so on.

At the end of the war the Volunteer Coastal Patrol decided to carry on, but in a search and rescue and educational role. The membership fell away drastically to a peacetime level and it gradually built up to today's strength of 600 men and 160 boats. It operates duty bases from Coffs Harbour to Port Phillip Bay in

Victoria, with its headquarters at The Spit, Mosman, on Sydney's Middle Harbour. The patrol works today as an auxilliary to the water police and assists the Maritime Services Board. It answers about 1300 calls for assistance annually, and provides help with harbour security and crowd control for such events as the start of the Sydney to Hobart yacht race.

By far the biggest operation of recent years was the opening of the Opera House in 1973 when the patrol fielded 146 boats. A fierce westerly gale resulted in many injured spectators needing medical and hospital attention. The patrol had six doctors and several ambulance people afloat that day. After the Opera House opening, the Queen bestowed the royal title on the patrol and it became the Royal Volunteer Coastal Patrol. A couple of years previously, its then commanding officer, Harold Nobbs, had been given an MBE.

MIDDLE HARBOUR

Middle Harbour is a major branch of Sydney Harbour. Much of its foreshore is still natural bush as it was when the first white explorers, lead by Captain Arthur Phillip, made their way to the head of Middle Harbour at Bungaroo, St Ives, on 16 April 1788, during the first European land exploration of the north shore of Sydney Harbour.

One of Captain Hunter's first duties after the arrival of the First Fleet was to survey Port Jackson. After the initial exploration, when land near the waters of Middle Harbour were seen to be of little use to agriculture, this section of the harbour was largely ignored by the settlers. Even today — thanks largely to Government land claims for various purposes, there are large areas of bush around Middle Harbour.

PEARL BAY

The Maritime Services Board will not allow people to live permanently in boats on Sydney Harbour. The exceptions are the four licensed houseboats beside The Spit which all have special mooring and houseboat licences. One houseboat on the Manly side has a telephone but no access except by water; the other three are at Pearl Bay on the Mosman side in Middle Harbour.

There used to be many licensed and unlicensed houseboats in the harbour. During the Depression, numbers of people lived on boats and even in caves around Pearl Bay and other parts of Sydney Harbour. Today the three remaining houseboats at Pearl Bay are highly elaborate affairs with their own jetties, telephones, television, and all modern conveniences — even roof gardens. After many battles, they have been accepted by the local council and the owners are on friendly terms with the Maritime Services Board.

The oldest, *Spec*, belonged originally to Harry and Annie Ryan, who lived there from 1910 to 1960. It was the third houseboat ever to be registered with the Maritime Services Board and still carries the proud number HB3 of Sydney Harbour. The house was built on an old barge which locals say was once a vehicle ferry used at The Spit before the bridge was built there. Harry and Annie settled in the shelter of the corner of Pearl Bay nearest Beauty Point. They had the pick of the sites in the harbour in those days.

Harry was an old sailor who set up a slipway and boat-building business on the shore alongside his floating home. After his death, Annie was unable to carry on without him and sold her home to a local resident, A.R. Lhuede, a real estate agent who, in the 1930s, had bought most of the land around Pearl Bay. He wanted to get rid of *Spec.* The Maritime Services Board would have allowed the old boat to be towed past the Heads and up the main harbour to an area beyond the Gladesville Bridge. However, it was doubtful if the hull would have been able to stand such a trip. So he gave it to his daughter for a birthday present. Valerie Lhuede, an architect, had fallen in love with it and with local children set about the task of restoring it. She owned it for seventeen years and installed amenities, living on it for some years herself.

In 1965, the foreshore was reclaimed by council with rock taken from the Spit Road and the residents lost their tiny beach. After a battle, the area was re-designed by a well-known landscape architect, Russell Smith, and the beach artificially restored. Native plants replaced the foreshore weeds and the houseboats and the public now have a beautiful land setting as well as water views. Finally Valerie also decided reluctantly to sell *Spec.* It fetched $12 000 but changed hands again in 1975 for $45 000.

According to the owner of the houseboat next door, Mr Thistlewayte, his much larger home, *Lodestar,* would be worth at least $150 000, but in 1980 it was not for sale. It was a derelict shell on the mud flats when he bought it and began renovating it in 1960. Today it is a beautiful boat. Its large lounge undoubtedly commands one of the finest views in Sydney. The houseboat next door, *Tanderra,* has changed hands several times and its latest owner, Ron Pile, hired interior designer Kaye MacKenzie to redecorate it for him in 1979.

BEAUTY POINT

Beauty Point was the name given to the headland when an estate there was subdivided. It used to be called Billy Goat Point. The original developer, Fitzpatrick, went bankrupt in the Depression and A.R. Lhuede, a local real estate agent, took over the land. When he offered waterfront land at Pearl Bay in 1936, he did not receive a single bid. He finally persuaded somebody to buy at £400. When land at Beauty Point reached $1000 in 1939, a well-known real estate agent said "We have reached the peak". In 1980, the Lhuede family had for sale the last remaining blocks of land overlooking Pearl Bay: some were selling for over $100 000 each.

LONG BAY

Long Bay contains a number of smaller inlets including the picturesquely titled Quakers Hat Bay which is named for its shape. It contains a number of luxurious homes. Overlooking the bay is Joel's boatshed, bought by Charles Joel in 1928 from Harold Holloway. Tom Joel took over the boatshed when he returned from New Guinea where he had been in the Navy.

Mosman is full of "castles" but perhaps none is more elaborate than that of Vivian James Chalwin, who arrived from England in

1951 and built Chalwin Castle at the rim of Quakers Hat Bay. It has a Roman-type swimming pool and a private theatre where local musical groups regularly give concerts.

Folly Point in Long Bay is supposed to have got its name because an early builder who erected a cottage there mixed his mortar with saltwater. The house collapsed. He re-erected the building using the same materials — with the same result.

NORTHBRIDGE

Northbridge gets its name from the suspension bridge across the gorge of Middle Harbour which leads to the suburb. The bridge's arches have been gazetted as part of the National Estate. The original bridge was built in 1891 to carry a tramline which the company hoped would open up land on the other side where they had plans for a township and a port at Middle Harbour. It was an engineering marvel of its time. But when the bridge was completed the syndicate that owned the land was unable to pay for the bridge. The contractor installed a system of tolls. The bridge was later taken over by the Government and trams ran across it. In 1936 the bridge was considered unsafe and it was closed during the construction of a modern reinforced concrete bridge. The modern bridge is no longer suspended but the imposing sandstone arches have been retained from the original bridge.

Salt Pan Cove, below Northbridge Park, is said to have got its name because the early settlers evaporated saltwater in shallow salt pans to obtain salt there.

Northbridge Sailing Club was formed in 1949 as a VJ and VS club sailing from Clive Park. Of the boats which presently sail the Tasar, NS 14, Laser, Flying Ant and Northbridge Junior fleets are the most active. The Northbridge Junior and the NS 14 were developed at this club by Frank Bethwaite and the Tasar is a development from the NS 14, which he also designed.

The current membership is in the vicinity of 555, which is very largely made up of family groups. An extremely active training programme is conducted by Mr Don McKenzie and attracts between thirty and fifty youngsters each training day.

CASTLE COVE

The original land grant in this area was made to H.G. Alleyne in 1858. In the 1870s, H.C. Press acquired 6 hectares of land at Castle Cove and turned it into picnic grounds. Press was already famous throughout Sydney for building and racing "18-ft" dinghies. The Press family also owned several other picnic grounds around Sydney Harbour.

On Sundays, ferries and boats would bring the merchant princes of Sydney living in mansions at Mosman on picnics. Family parties of thirty or more were common — complete with their retinue of nannies, cooks, and butlers. When the era passed and people no longer picnicked, the Press family closed the grounds and chose Castle Cove as their home.

Standing on a superb vantage point, overlooking Middle Harbour, is Innisfallen Castle, named, presumably, after the castle of the same name in Ireland. It is a Gothic style building complete with ramparts, tower, and stout stone walls. It was built from sandstone quarried on the site between 1903 and 1905 for the father of a former Mayor of Willoughby, Dr Hastings Willis. There are four bedrooms, staff quarters, a ballroom, dining room and a large reception room. Before the house was built, the Willis family had a weekend cottage on the land when most of the district was almost virgin territory. The Willis family ran their estate as a farm, storing corn, oats, potatoes, and salted eggs in winter in the castle basement. A governess, cook, housemaids and farmhands were employed.

Settlement was slow at first because the area could only be reached by rough bullock track or by water, and at this time rowingboats had to be used. The introduction of the motor boat made it possible to come from as far away as The Spit — the terminus of the electric tram.

A twenty-minute water-taxi service in the launch *Dreadnought* from the boatshed at The Spit cost 3s in those days. Miss Calliope Willis, one of the last of the Willis family still living in the castle in 1980, spent seventy years there and went to school by water.

The Willis family sold off the land bit by bit as Willoughby grew. By the 1970s, the castle was Number 14 Cherry Place, Castle Cove, surrounded by suburban houses. Willoughby Council bought the last few lots of land around the castle for public parkland. The Council wanted to buy the castle itself when Miss Willis and her sister tried to auction it in 1975 to pay for death duties. The council could not raise the money and the house itself was passed in at auction when it failed to reach the reserve. The castle was still on the market in 1980.

CASTLECRAG

The earliest grants around Castlecrag were made in 1856-57 to J.W. Bligh, who later became the first chairman or Mayor of Willoughby. Whether he was related to Captain Bligh of the mutiny of the *Bounty* has never been established. The name Castlecrag was given to the locality originally because of a large rocky outcrop on the peak of Edinburgh Road above the tower reserve. On early maps it was marked as Edinburgh Castle.

The American architect, Walter Burley Griffin, designed the present suburb. He named the streets and reserves after parts of a medieval castle — The Battlement, Sortie Point, The Bastion, The Barbican, The Parapet, The Barbette and The Bulwark are a few of the narrow winding streets which Griffin designed to follow the natural terraces.

Walter Burley Griffin (1876-1937) was a colleague of the even more famous American architect, Frank Lloyd Wright. In 1912, Griffin won a worldwide competition for the design of the new Australian capital of Canberra, and in 1913 he came to Australia. After endless frustrations forced him to resign from the Canberra project, he came to Sydney and then planned the suburb of Castlecrag, where he and his wife, Marion, lived for twelve years prior to his death in India in 1937.

In 1920, backed by a group of Melbourne businessmen, Griffin formed the Greater Sydney Development Association to develop the Castlecrag estate.

Griffin's houses — first of stone and later of concrete blocks — had flat roofs and were designed to blend with the landscape. They had several unusual features for the 1920s. For a start, Griffin insisted on no fences. He tried but failed to get underground wiring. He did succeed with his own houses in avoiding obvious drainpipes — these were concealed with columns, sometimes inside the house! There were double sinks and plate drying racks — startling innovations at the time. The kitchens faced the street, a fact which caused much consternation in Willoughby Council in the 1920s. The local community built an open-air theatre named the New Haven — a scenic theatre where the Griffins cajoled and bullied their neighbours to brave the mosquitoes to perform and attend Greek dramas and medieval morality plays, lit by magnesium flares.

Griffin's plans did not go well. The roofs leaked, although this was due to poor workmanship rather than design. White ants attacked the floors. But, worst of all, his ideas were years ahead of his time and were not acceptable to the Australian house buyers and bank managers, who refrained from purchasing and financing Griffin's houses in large numbers. Then the Depression of the 1930s affected all building in Sydney. When Griffin left for India in 1936 to design a library at the University of Lucknow, fewer than twenty of his houses had been built.

Some idea of what the suburb could have looked like can be gained from studying the original Griffin houses which, today, despite their subdued grey stone, shine like diamonds among the surrounding mainly ugly Australian suburban homes. The houses are fairly small because they were built for average families at a time when money was short, but they are beautiful houses nevertheless. Number 8 The Parapet, built around 1922, was Griffin's own home from 1924. It has been sympathetically restored and extended. Other Griffin houses include Number 14 The Parapet (1924), Number 2 The Barbette (1930), and Number 4 The Barbette (1929).

SUGARLOAF BAY

Sugarloaf Bay is named from the shape of the inlet's middle cape. In the early days of sugar refining, sugar was compressed into cone-shaped blocks called loaves.

The hill and the point were first seen by white men from the water during Governor Phillip's exploration of Middle Harbour in April 1788. A map of 1880 shows the area as being granted to J.B. Wilson and G.S. Cairns. The name Sugarloaf first appears in the New South Wales *Gazetteer* of 1886.

In 1904, Sugarloaf Bay was still an area of primeval wilderness, although an article on Willoughby in the *Evening News* said that it was "of equal beauty to the admired Willoughby waterfall". At this time, about 50 hectares were reserved at Long Bay for docks, 10 hectares at Sugarloaf for defence purposes, and 20 for recreation.

One of the pioneering industries north of the main harbour was a tannery run by J.S. Forsyth at Sugarloaf Bay. The Forsyth family provided Willoughby with three generations of mayors after the municipality was formed in 1865; at that time only 400 people lived in the area.

DAVIDSON PARK

At the head of Middle Harbour an area was set aside as a public reserve in 1923. It was named Davidson Park in memory of Sir Walter Edward Davidson, a former Governor of New South Wales. During the 1970s, the foreshore area was extensively exploited by a sand-mining company for building material. The area above Roseville Bridge was the subject of extensive restoration work in 1979 and 1980 in an effort to return the foreshore to parkland.

ROSEVILLE BRIDGE

The first Roseville Bridge across Middle Harbour was opened on 20 September 1924. The present bridge was constructed in 1965. Beyond Roseville Bridge only shallow draught vessels can sail.

BANTRY BAY

The name of Bantry Bay, like that of its neighbour, Killarney Point, has obvious Irish derivations. The Aborigines who lived around Bantry Bay made good use of the flat sandstone rock for their carvings. These were connected with their spiritual and everyday life, and are found in several places scattered throughout the reserve. Many tool-sharpening grooves are also found near creek beds and rock shelters which the Aborigines occupied.

One of the most extensive groups of carvings in the whole of the Sydney region is found near Bantry Bay Road. According the archaeologist, F.D. McCarthy, it consists of almost eighty figures, among which are men, fish, wallabies, a dingo, unusually large shields, a bark canoe, basket and bag, boomerangs, circles, stone axes, clubs, snakes, an echidna, and a fine whale. One composition shows two men, one of whom is carrying two bark canoes. Figures in groups of this kind were probably added to the series from time to time and many of them are unrelated. There is one huge figure of a spiritual ancestor that has now almost eroded away. Anthropologists believe these rock engravings are not surpassed by any other similar carvings anywhere else in the world.

In 1856, James Harris French, after whom Frenchs Forest was named, acquired land in the forest and developed a timber industry with two sawmills. The large-sized trees were cut and split by hand and then hauled along Bantry Bay Road and down to Bantry Bay by bullocks. From a wharf in Bantry Bay, the timber was shipped to various parts of the harbour shores, where settlers used it for building and fencing. Traces of the old bullock road, closed in 1908, can still be found in the bush. Nevertheless, the early settlers did little damage to the bay area.

In 1917, Bantry Bay became an explosives storage area for the Department of Mines, which had the effect of keeping both the public and the land developers out of the area which has remained largely virgin bushland. By the 1970s the Department of Mines no longer required the area for the storage of explosives and conservationists urged that the area should be set aside as parkland.

294

The old brick buildings used for storing explosives at Bantry Bay have been classified by the National Trust. Because of the fact that public access was denied for so many years, the whole area is in a remarkably pristine state. For this reason, conservationists believe it should be added to the Sydney Harbour National Park, and one proposal has been put forward for using the buildings for a field study centre as part of the National Parks and Wildlife Service education programme.

SEAFORTH

Seaforth's name has Scottish associations in Loch Seaforth and Seaforth Island. The area now known as Seaforth was subdivided into numerous allotments by its owner, Henry F. Halloran. The first auction sales were held on 10 and 11 November 1906. Houses built there subsequently have some of the best harbour views in Sydney. A peculiarity of the Seaforth estate is that most of the streets have names beginning with the same letter: Allan Avenue, Edgecliffe Esplanade, Battle Boulevarde, and so on.

Adjoining the Seaforth estate is the Bluff estate which was sold by auction on 6 February, 1909. This auction was unique because it was held aboard the steamer *Lady Rawson* which stopped opposite each lot as it was offered for sale. The auctioneers provided a band and a trip around Middle Harbour as an extra bonus to attract buyers who all paid 3d for the trip.

Pickering Point, a headland of North Seaforth, opposite Sugarloaf, was frequently used as a camp site by three sailing enthusiasts, William, Harry and Fred Pickering.

POWDER HULKS BAY

Powder Hulks Bay got its name because of the hulks full of gun powder that were once moored there. The explosives lighter, *Pride of England* was acquired by the Explosives Department of New South Wales in 1882 for use in Middle Harbour and was anchored in this bay.

The powder hulk, *Behring,* built in the United States in 1850, was acquired in 1878. It was dismantled and sold in 1919. In 1925 the hull was towed to Sailors Bay where it was set on fire and burned to the water's edge.

CLONTARF

Clontarf is thought to be named after the pleasure resort on the Bay of Dublin. Clontarf was known to the Aborigines as Warringa — a name now used in Warringah Shire. In the middle of the beach between Grotto Point and Clontarf Point is Castle Rock, so named because it is thought to look like a castle. Clontarf made world headlines on 12 March 1868, when an Irishman named Henry James O'Farrell, a supporter of the anti-royalist Fenian Society, tried to shoot the twenty-three-year-old Prince Alfred, Duke of Edinburgh, who was visiting Australia during a world tour on HMS *Galatea.* The prince staggered and fell crying, "Good God, I am shot; my back is broken". O'Farrell was seized before he could fire again. He was executed at Darlinghurst Gaol on 21 April 1868. The prince made a good recovery and continued on his journey.

GROTTO POINT

Grotto Point Recreation Reserve was dedicated as a public reserve in 1912. It is now part of Sydney Harbour National park. Grotto Point was first named for the caves there by the exploratory expedition which Captain Arthur Phillip sent to investigate Port Jackson before the First Fleet moved north from Botany Bay in January 1788. Also in January 1788, when Phillip made his famous landing at Manly, he noted that Aborigines were living in caves in what is now Wellings Reserve. The National Parks and Wildlife Service lists a number of sites in the area in its Aboriginal Sites Register. They include two sets of engravings on flat rock shelves above Washaway Beach, near Grotto Point.

Grotto Point has a trail down the peninsula to a closed lighthouse. There is a lookout at the end of Cutler Road. The Sydney Harbour National Park will eventually include a track which will lead from Castle Rock Beach around Grotto Point to Dobroyd Head and around to Reef Beach. It will join up with the track which runs from Forty Baskets Beach to the North Harbour Reserve.

CRATER VALLEY

Visible from Dobroyd Head Scenic Drive are seven driftwood and stone huts built by squatters who live there growing their own vegetables and enjoying one of the most beautiful views of Sydney Harbour. The huts were still occupied in 1980 but as the area has become part of the Sydney Harbour National Park their future is in some doubt.

The earliest hut built at Crater Valley was erected by Bob Cadwell in 1923. A second hut was built about 1929 by Fred Williams. Fred is said to be the first person to "body surf" at Manly. He swam regularly at the Crater and "cracked" the waves in the Bombora off Dobroyd Head during the 1930s. He died at the Crater after fighting a bushfire, and a plaque at the spot reads, "In memory of Fredk. Chas. Williams, Honorary Ranger, who died here 28th. April, 1940".

DOBROYD HEAD

Dobroyd Head — not Dobroyd Point — is now part of the Sydney Harbour National Park. The Geographical Names Board now officially give the name Dobroyd Head to the main headland and the name Dobroyd Point applies to a small area within the municipality of Ashfield. Most of Dobroyd Head belonged to the Commonwealth Defence Department until it was handed over to the State Government for inclusion in the Sydney Harbour National Park in the late 1970s.

During the 1940s, the Army constructed two concrete observation posts, one at what is now Tania Park and one on the ridge overlooking Washaway Beach. These posts were never manned permanently, and the Army made little impact on the area. A monument has been erected beside Dobroyd Head Scenic Drive to Commander John Thomas Gowland. He and a companion were drowned by the reef wave call a "bombora" in the water below on 11 August 1874. Gowland was working on a survey of Port Jackson.

Dobroyd Scenic Drive was constructed before 1947. The road and its lookouts command spectacular views of the harbour, the heads, Manly, and the ocean, and it is an excellent place to view the start of the Sydney to Hobart yacht race. There are a number of walking tracks — an offshoot from the track which goes from Beatty Street to the crater leads to Warrior Lookout where two inscriptions have been carved.

REEF BEACH

Nude bathing has been popular at Reef Beach on the north side of Dobroyd Head for many years. Before the announcement on 19 October 1976, that nude bathing would be permitted on a trial basis at Reef and Lady Bay beaches there had been considerable harassment by police of illegal nude bathers at both beaches. In December 1975, two men and one woman appeared in Manly Court following the last major raid at Reef Beach by police early in the swimming season. The nudists had been visited by the police during 1975 more than in any other previous years.

The Liberal State Government at the time set up a Cabinet sub-committee after a District Criminal Appeals Court judge upheld an appeal by a man against his conviction of indecent exposure at Lady Bay. At the time, thirty five men and five women were arrested for obscene exposure and there were 200 bathers on the beach. This was the first real indication of a wider social acceptance in the community of nude bathing as a legitimate form of recreation. As a result of popular demand for legalised nude bathing beaches, the Government made Reef Beach and Lady Bay Beach the two official nude bathing beaches in 1976.

The local residents in general were not happy about the nudists. Protest and vigilante groups were formed and included television sports commentator, Rex Mossop, who created headlines by performing a "citizen's arrest" on one unfortunate nudist as he tried to get into his car. Perhaps because of the residents' opposition, the nudists created something of a club-like atmosphere on the beach — one of their number, wearing only a beach inspector's hat, used to greet newcomers. The nudists arranged social events at venues away from the beach to raise money for national parks.

FORTY BASKETS BEACH

The picturesquely named Forty Baskets Beach is said to have got its name from forty baskets of fish once caught there. There are Aboriginal hand stencils in a rock shelter near Forty Baskets Beach; the engravings include a kangaroo, emu, shark, fishes, and boomerangs, and are fairly well preserved. The first Balgowlah Progress Association constructed a walking track from North Harbour to Reef Beach in about 1918 and, as a result of this, the foreshores became popular for picnics and "gypsy teas". Forty Baskets Beach and Reef Beach were favourite anchorages for private pleasure craft, especially during the 1930s. One yacht, which became somewhat of a local legend, was the schooner *Boomerang* (originally named *Bona* and built in 1903), bought in 1933 by Frank Albert, the music publisher. Albert had a private buoy off Reef

Beach and the schooner was frequently moored there, where guests were served tea by formally dressed waiters.

The Bible from the wrecked ship, the *Dunbar*, was washed up on Forty Baskets Beach.

NORTH HARBOUR

On 15 April 1788, Governor Phillip set out from Manly to explore an overland route to Pittwater. It is thought his starting point was at the head of North Harbour near the present foot of Boyle Street. The Manly Historical Society erected a commemorative tablet there in 1939 to record the event. Phillip's party found Narrabeen Lake. From the coast they turned inland and made their way to the upper reaches of Middle Harbour. The party then moved far enough west to see the Blue Mountains before coming back and making their way down to Middle Harbour to waiting boats.

One of the popular "fun and fitness tracks" which have resulted from the Goverment's "Life, Be In It" campaign has been established along the northern foreshores of North Harbour in Esplanade Park. The length of the track is 4350 m and there are fourteen stations for exercises along the way.

FAIRLIGHT BEACH

In 1853, Henry Gilbert Smith (1802-86) bought land north-west of the Corso and built the original stone Fairlight House. It was demolished in 1939 and a block of flats was built in its place. It is remembered by the name Fairlight, now an area of Manly.

Smith was a remarkable individual who probably deserves the title of "the father of Manly". Struck by the prospects of Manly as a seaside resort, he built cottages, a hotel, a church, a school, and swimming baths. He started a ferry service linking Manly and Sydney in 1854. As a further attraction, he had a stone kangaroo erected overlooking Manly in 1856. The statue, in Kangaroo Street, is now listed as part of the National Estate. Opinion is divided as to the name of the sculptor. Smith is also credited with having some of Manly's famous Norfolk Island pines planted on the ocean front as well as the Moreton Bay figs in the Corso.

MARINELAND

Australia's first oceanarium, Marineland, beside the harbour at Manly, opened in 1963. It is a circular tank where divers handfeed sharks, turtles, and other fish, while spectators watch the performance through the windows. The sharks are caught locally — out of the harbour nearby or out to sea. The job of feeding the sharks may look easy enough, and Marineland advertises from time to time for girls to take on the job, but divers have been attacked. Fortunately, all have escaped with only minor injuries so far.

Marineland has had other problems in the twenty-odd years of its operation. In 1965 a faulty valve allowed water to escape from the tank overnight and the manager, Geoff Goadby, arrived at work next morning to find the tank almost empty. Manly fire brigade used pumps to refill the tank and managed to save the turtles and some of the fish.

One visitor turned up with his fishing tackle and expected to be allowed to fish in the tank after paying his entrance fee. For three years between 1967 and 1970 a daring poacher scaled the wall of Marineland at night to do some midnight fishing. Once he even landed a whaler shark which proved too heavy so he left it behind on the rocks. In 1973, a mysterious disease affected a number of sharks. The mystery disease which killed eleven Australian kingfish, a wobbegong shark, a Port Jackson shark and two boxfish was eventually traced to a minute parasite. At the time, one of the divers went down to smear medicated jelly over the grey nurse sharks in an attempt to save them.

MANLY ART GALLERY

The Manly Art Gallery, near Marineland at the far end of West Esplanade in Manly Cove, was opened by Sir Phillip Street, Chief Justice of New South Wales, on 14 June 1930.

Near the Art Gallery is the Manly Pier Seafood Restaurant which overlooks the harbour. This was originally opened as a restaurant by the Port Jackson and Manly Ferry Company. Later it was rented to several different proprietors, including the Doyle family of Watsons Bay, who sold out because it was too far from their home base for them to run it effectively.

MANLY COVE

A memorial unveiled in 1929 commemorates the January 1788 landing of Governor Phillip. The cairn stands between West Esplanade and the beach of Manly Cove, but nobody is sure exactly where Phillip actually stepped ashore.

By tradition Little Manly is the place where Phillip was impressed by the "confidence and manly behaviour" of about twenty natives who waded out to his boats. However Captain Hunter's first chart of the harbour shows Manly Cove at what we now call North Harbour. The name Manly Cove seems to have been applied to this whole northern section of the harbour. Phillip also recorded, "The same people afterwards joined us when we dined", and that because of "their lively curiosity" he had to draw a circle and indicate to them to stay outside it. The long sweep of harbourside beach near which the monument is placed is thought to be the most likely spot for this landing.

Perhaps as one of fate's little ironies, the suburb named for the manliness of its inhabitants found itself nearly 200 years later — in 1980 — with a female Mayor, Joan Thorburn, and a female Deputy Mayor, Judy Mellows.

The Corso, Manly's main street, leads from the ferry wharf to the ocean front. Its name is said to derive from the Italian word "corso" which designates a place to race horses or the principal street of a town where horse-drawn carriages used to parade and festivals were held in the larger towns of Italy. The best-known of these is the Corso in Rome. A $400 000 pedestrian mall was built in the Corso in the late 1970s.

At the other end of the Corso beside the ocean, Manly's famous pines have been slowly dying since the 1950s. The death of the trees at Manly and at other places along the harbour shore from Bradleys Head to Mosman has been attributed to a fine spray of saltwater and household detergent carried along a natural wind tunnel. Sea spray laden with chemicals from Sydney's coastal sewer outlets is another culprit, according to a scientific study made in the mid-1970s. The plight of coastal trees was investigated by a research team led by Professor M.G. Pitman, president of the Australian Museum Trust and head of the School of Biological Sciences at Sydney University.

The team's findings, published in the museum's journal, *Australian Natural History*, showed that the leaves of Norfolk Island pines were protected from excessive salt spray by a thick, waxy covering. But commercial detergents released from sewerage outlets became concentrated on the surface layer of seawater and, as spray, dissolved the protective covering. Leaves, and ultimately trees, were then killed by excessive salt. Modern detergents started to be used in quantity about the time the problem first appeared, during the 1950s , the committee reported.

MANLY FERRIES

The old Port Jackson and Manly Steamship Company slogan, "Seven miles from Sydney and a thousand miles from care" still greets ferry passengers at the Manly wharf. But now in these metric days Sydney is 11.2 km away. The Port Jackson and Manly Steamship Company is no more. Brambles took over their ferries in 1972 and the company in turn sold them to the State Government in 1974.

Latest research disproves the claim that the first Manly ferry ran in 1847. Till Henry Gilbert Smith began his development, there was no call for a ferry. Today it is believed that Smith used to charter ferries in 1854 to bring people across for holiday occasions when extensive entertainment was provided. In 1855, he built a wharf at Manly and gave the right of access to a ferry operator, who used vessels from the Parramatta run. By 1857, a daily service had begun. After a war between rival ferry companies in the early 1890s the two companies amalgamated in 1896 to form the Port Jackson Co-operative Steamship Company Ltd.

The swimming pool, built by the Port Jackson and Manly Steamship Company in 1933, was destroyed by a violent storm in May 1974. A small netted enclosure has replaced the large pile baths. Also destroyed in the storm were the Municipal Swimming Baths round past East Esplanade near the foot of Stuart Street. "Boy" Charlton and other swimming "greats" of his era used to swim there.

Manly has had a long history of swimming. It was there that Tommy Tanna from the New Hebrides introduced surfing to the youths of Manly in the 1890s.

An Act of 1833 prohibited bathing between 6 a.m. and 8 p.m.; the morning hours were later altered to 7 a.m.; later they stood at 8 a.m. in 1902, when W.H. Gocher, proprietor of a Manly newspaper, announced that he intended to defy the law against daylight bathing. He sallied forth in his neck-to-knee swimming costume and waited to be arrested. But no beach inspector came.

Gocher also defied the law on day-time surfing, doing this three times in 1902. He continued his campaign in the paper, *Manly and*

North Sydney News, of which he was proprietor. The by-law to allow day-time bathing was not passed till 2 November 1903.

MANLY FUN PIER AND SHARK AQUARIUM

Beside the ferry wharf is the Manly Fun Pier and Shark Aquarium. The fun pier opened in 1931 and the shark pool in 1939. Both were scheduled for renovating and rebuilding in 1980. The jetty where they stand dates originally from about 1890. It was a cargo wharf where barges and small cargo vessels brought goods from Sydney to the Manly-Warringah area. The opening of the Sydney Harbour Bridge ended this trade because goods could then be delivered by road.

Manly has a long history of amusement parks. There was a huge water chute at Manly in about 1904. David Atkins, one of the founders of Luna Park, had a Luna Park area in Manly where the Far West Children's Home now stands. He moved to Adelaide and returned to found the Milsons Point fun fair in 1935. He obtained permission to use the name Luna Park from the proprietors of the Manly amusement park, and both operated together for some time.

As with the fun fairs, there is also a tradition of aquariums at various parts of Manly. One stood in the Corso in the 1880s, but it did not contain sharks. Opened in 1885, it is said to have contained an octopus tank, fish tanks, a seal cavern and a pond, together with ferns and plants.

MANLY YACHT CLUB

Manly Yacht Club is a family sailing club with 200 members on the eastern shore of Manly Cove. It was formed in 1949 by some disenchanted skiff sailors led by Harry Pollard, a West Australian "14-ft" dinghy sailor. It was then known as the Manly 14-ft Sailing Club. The name was changed in 1964. Boats were housed in Farrell's boatshed at Little Manly, and the races were started from a rowingboat by Bill Edgely, who later became the club's first president. The club bought premises at Manly Cove in 1954. In 1980, the club was preparing to move into new premises at the old baths building. The junior trainer or the Manly Junior (MJ) was designed by Ralph Tobias, an enthusiastic "14-ft" yachtsman. This small boat became so popular that the club formed two divisions of this class which raced under international rules. Later, an intermediate craft, the Manly Graduate, evolved and various multi-hulled classes were included.

MANLY 16-FT SKIFF SAILING CLUB

The Manly 16-ft Skiff Sailing Club has its clubhouse at East Esplanade, Manly. The club was founded in 1921. It has a membership of 700 with twenty four "16-ft" skiffs on its register and also a junior fleet of fifteen Flying 11s.

MANLY POINT

A prominent feature of Manly Point is Kilburn Towers, a circular building of sixty two home units built in 1959 with magnificent harbour views. Designed by a local Manly architect, it was considered strikingly modern at the time, but the passing of the years has left it looking rather dated.

LITTLE MANLY

In the past, Sydney has had a habit of building gasworks on its harbour foreshore. Fortunately, these have been disappearing in recent years with the coming of natural gas. The gasworks at Little Manly were pulled down in 1971 to make way for a park. This is another example of a recent acquisition by the State Government of harbour foreshore land for public parkland.

COLLINS BEACH

Collins Beach is named after Captain David Collins, Judge Advocate on Governor Phillip's staff. Collins Beach is thought to be the place where Governor Phillip was speared by a local Aboriginal, one of a group who were feasting on a whale caught in the harbour in September 1790.

Among the group feasting on the beach was Bennelong, who had been captured by Governor Phillip in November, and who had remained at Government House until he escaped in May. Phillip was anxious to see him again and approached the group. To show his good intentions he threw his knife aside. This action may have been misinterpreted. In any case, an Aboriginal called Wilee-ma-rin speared Phillip through the shoulder. In the confusion that followed, Bennelong disappeared. Lieutenant Waterhouse managed to break off the barb which was sticking out of Phillip's back. The Governor was then rowed back to Sydney Cove where the spear was removed. A plaque unveiled at Collins Beach in 1933 records the incident. There is also an Aboriginal rock carving in the area where the society has erected the monument. Bennelong later returned to Sydney and Phillip built him a small house at what is now called Bennelong Point where the Sydney Opera House now stands.

QUARANTINE HEAD

Quarantine Head gets its name from the quarantine station there. The area was first set aside for a quarantine station in 1832 and first used in 1837. Carvings on the sandstone cliffs of the headland are an interesting record of the station's history. Some of the carvings and gravestones recall ships like the *William Rodger*, which entered Port Jackson in 1838 after six adults and ten children died on their way to the colony. Another twenty nine died after the ship reached the quarantine station.

Six months before the *William Rodger* moored at Spring Cove, the typhus-ridden ship, *Minerva*, had already unloaded its dead and dying. Aboard the *Minerva* was Peter McNeill whose headstone tells how he died within sight of his goal — Sydney Town.

The quarantine station has also served as a base for troops of three wars. Military insignia from the Boer War and the first and second World Wars have been chiselled into the sandstone. While the British chose to work on the rocks near Spring Cove beach, Japanese and Chinese seamen did the carving on high rocks overlooking a vast stretch of ocean and harbour. More recently, after Cyclone Tracey flattened Darwin on Christmas Eve, 1974, 750 people were evacuated to the quarantine station. They too have left their marks carved in sandstone.

In 1979, it was announced that the quarantine station area would eventually be handed over to Sydney Harbour National Park, but the authorities expected that it would be some years before this finally took place.

PARKHILL RESERVE

Parkhill Reserve, beside Manly Hospital at the entrance to North Head, was set apart as a recreation area in 1933. It was formally opened on 3 June 1933 by the Postmaster-General, Sir Archdale Parkhill, after whom it is named.

NORTH HEAD

A total of 157.6 hectares of land at North Head was handed over to the State Government by the Army in 1979, and now forms part of the Sydney Harbour National Park.

A lone pillbox midway down the 90-m cliff on North Head is a reminder of the second World War. During the war it was connected by a tunnel cut through the sandstone. Huge guns able to hit targets as far away as the mouth of the Hawkesbury River were positioned in the scrub ready to repulse invaders. The Army's presence in peacetime has helped preserve the head almost as a wilderness area.

An area of marshland near the barren cliff edge is home for scores of wild ducks and other birdlife. It is also the refuge for hundreds of rabbits. The area has been so little used in the past that in 1978 the Army discovered a shallow cave in the hillside containing the skeleton of a man who died there some thirty years before. Remnants of the man's few possessions, including a rusting typewriter, provided no clues to his identity. His name as well as his reason for being in the cave are likely to remain a mystery.

Next door to the newly founded Sydney Harbour National Park area on North Head, the Metropolitan Water, Sewerage, and Drainage Board was doing its bit for the environment in quite a different way in 1979. The board was gouging out large holes in the sandstone for a waste water treatment plant. This, together with a projected $100 million extension to the major sewer outfalls at Malabar, Bondi, and Manly, 2 km into 100-m-deep water where offshore currents would deal with grease and other unsightly matter, was expected to improve the look of Sydney's ocean beaches in the 1980s.

THE NEW ENDEAVOUR

The story of the *New Endeavour* seems to symbolise the accent on conservation and restoration that Sydney Harbour enthusiasts had during the 1970s.

The *New Endeavour* was laid down by R. Ring Anderson at Svenburg, Denmark, in 1918 and launched as a three-masted schooner in 1919. She sailed from Ramsgate in England in 1965 to Sydney and then ran cruises in Sydney Harbour. She ran into a reef and was badly holed in 1966. In 1969 she was used by a television film production company in the Great Barrier Reef in Queensland. In 1977, a group of Sydney ship lovers formed an association to restore the old sailing ship for adventure cruises.

By 1979, the Australian Sail Training Association had restored the *New Endeavour* to the extent that the old barquentine could once more become a familiar sight under sail on Sydney Harbour at weekends. The association hopes to use the ship in Australia's bicentenary celebrations in 1988.

Part II After 1966.

(Read in conjunction with Part I.)

I

THE GENERAL VIEW

P.R. Stephensen's classic description of Sydney Harbour has dated surprisingly little in the period of time that has elapsed since it was first published in 1966. In a few areas, recent research has supplied historical details which were not available when Stephensen died in 1965, and many of the descriptive sections have themselves become history since that time. The aim of this section of the book is to try to chronicle some of the changes which have affected the harbour.

The most important technical change to have affected Sydney Harbour since 1966 has been the introduction of container shipping. It has changed the look of the ships in the harbour and the work of the Sydney wharfies.

Perhaps the most exciting development in the 1970s was the establishment of the Sydney Harbour National Park on several islands, headlands, and other parts of the harbour foreshore. This harbour national park at the centre of a city of three million people is probably unique in the world.

Other changes have taken place in the society that lives around Sydney Harbour. Anybody old enough to remember when Bondi beach inspectors used to prosecute girls for wearing what now seem fairly modest bikinis will still find it surprising that not only does Bondi now allow topless bathing, but there are even a couple of beaches around the harbour where nude bathing is legally permitted.

In 1966 the Sydney Opera House was still under construction. Other buildings around the shoreline have also changed since 1966. In fact, the city indulged in an orgy of demolition and rebuilding throughout the 1960s and early 1970s. At the same time, a growing number of people began to stress the need for preserving something of the city's history before it disappeared completely.

An important factor in this move towards conservation has been the formation of many infuential resident action groups such as the Paddington Society, the Balmain Association, and the North Sydney Society. These groups have resulted from changes in the social structure where middleclass professionals have moved into traditional workingclass areas.

2

THE SIGNAL STATION

Signal Hill, Vaucluse, was transferred to the State Government in 1979. The northernmost area was transferred immediately with the understanding that the rest of the 1.9-hectare area would also be taken over by the State Government when it was vacated by the Commonwealth. The area adjoins the signal station and enjoys magnificent views along the coastline.

HMAS *WATSON*

The elevated terrain provides HMAS *Watson* with extensive views of Sydney Harbour and to the seaward.

The first Action Information Training Centre (now demolished) was completed in 1952. It was, at the time, the most modern in the Southern Hemisphere and was used to train ships' operation teams. The building in which it was housed provides a story in itself, the building being an exact replica of one at HMS *Dryad* in England. This planned replication made good sense, except that the English building was a converted barn, complete with hay loft, which somewhat disguised its military importance. The Australian copy, however, was made of fibro on a wooden frame and was situated on the top of a seaside cliff.

In 1971 excavation started on the site for the Tactical Trainer building which is situated mostly below ground level. The Tactical Trainer was completed in 1975 and it now houses the Action Information Organisation Tactical Trainer, the Submarine Command Team Trainer, and the RAN Tactical School. The Action Information Trainer and the Submarine Command Team Trainer can be linked for training or can run as separate units.

THE MIDGET SUBMARINES

In 1978 a diver with the Department of Fisheries, Steven Carruthers, found what he thought was the wreck of a Japanese midget submarine, the I-24 that was lost after the attack on Sydney Harbour in 1942.

He found the object half burried in mud at a depth of 12 m. It was about 50 m off Grotto Point, Middle Harbour. However, it later turned out to be a buoy.

Another group claimed to have found it in 1980, but this proved to be a hoax designed to promote the opening of a new restaurant at Manly on April Fools' Day.

3

ABORIGINAL NAMES

The Geographical Names Board of New South Wales has reviewed a number of names in the Sydney area since Stephensen's book appeared in 1966. The following information comes from Mr D.C. Miller, the board's secretary.

In general, the board's policy is to drop apostrophes in all names. In particular, the names Outer North Head, Inner North Head, Outer South Head, and Inner South Head have been changed to North Head, Quarantine Head, Dunbar Head, and South Head, respectively.

Bishops Creek is now officially Subiaco Creek. The Brothers are now the Three Brothers Rocks. Dobroyd Point is reserved for the area in the municipality of Ashfield. The correct name for the area near Manly is Dobroyd Head. The Hornby Light is the Hornby Lighthouse. Tarban Point is now Huntleys Point. Vaucluse Point has become Bottle and Glass Point. Waterview Bay is now Mort Bay. Clarke Island is officially spelled with an "e".

The board's policy is to encourage the use of names of Aboriginal origin. However, it prefers not to change long established place names. Again, where names have been changed or corrupted by long established local usage, the board has assigned those names currently in local usage. It did consider a request received some years ago for the reintroduction of certain Aboriginal names, such as Boambilli in place of Shark Island. The board agreed, however, that as the anglicised names were so well established, no attempt should be made to assign Aboriginal names to the features.

LADY BAY

This little bay near Camp Cove in the lee of South Head received a great deal of publicity in the 1970s as a popular nude bathing beach. For some reason or other, newspapers and the public in general referred to it wrongly as Lady Jane beach.

A number of nudists were prosecuted before the State Government finally gave in and made it legal to swim nude at Lady Bay and at Reef Beach on the northern side of the harbour, near Manly, in 1976.

WATSONS BAY

In 1978 the Australian Heritage Commission gazetted the Hornby Lighthouse and former fishermen's cottage groups in Cove Street and Cliff Street, Watsons Bay.

The Doyle family, who pioneered outdoor restaurants in Sydney, now operate two harbourside restaurants at Watsons Bay and one on the pier at Rose Bay.

Sitting at an outside table on a fine day, looking out over the water, drinking a bottle of Wolf Blass Rhine Riesling and eating fish at Doyles on the Beach Restaurant, is one of the most pleasant experiences that Sydney Harbour has to offer.

Mrs Alice Doyle can trace her family's involvement back to the 1800s, when her great-great-grandfather was a fisherman at Watsons Bay. Her grandparents opened tea rooms on the site of the present restaurant in the late 1880s. The Ozone Cafe was built on the site in 1908. It closed during the Great Depression and opened again in 1948. Part of the original building is still used in the restaurant on the beach today.

Mrs Doyle drew on her experience to write a fish cook book, which was published in 1979.

NIELSEN PARK

The National Parks and Wildlife Service uses Greycliffe House in Nielsen Park as the headquarters of the Sydney Harbour National Park. The mansion was built in 1850 by John Reeve, who married Fanny Catherine Wentworth, a daughter of William Charles Wentworth, the early Australian explorer and politician. She left for England in 1850 and apparently never lived in the house. A colonel J. Gibbs lived in the house until 1859. In the late 1870s, it was occupied by a Mr Joseph Willis and later by the writer Nesta Griffith.

The whole Wentworth property, including Vaucluse House nearby, was neglected and allowed to deteriorate after 1900. In the early part of the century an action group, known as the Foreshore Vigilance Committee, urged the State Government to return private lands surrounding Sydney Harbour foreshores to the public estate. As a result, the Government resumed the Wentworth estate in 1912. Greycliffe House became the Lady Edeline Hospital for Babies. The National Parks and Wildlife Service took over the old mansion and began restoring it in 1976.

The choice of Nielsen Park as the headquarters of Sydney Harbour National Park was particularly appropriate. Nielsen Park is named in honour of Neil Rasmus Wilson Nielsen, one of the strongest supporters of the Foreshore Vigilance Committee. Nielsen was an Australian Workers Union official, who became the first New South Wales Labor Minister for Lands in the McGowan Government of 1910-13. He was a far-sighted advocate of harbourside reservations, urging preservation of a public reserve all around the harbour. Writing in the *Sydney Morning Herald* in 1911 about a walk around Ashton Park, he even used the term "national park".

This dream did not become a reality in Nielsen's lifetime and, in fact, Sydney has the armed services rather than Nielsen to thank for the foreshore land that makes up most of the city's unique national park. The military took over the headlands in stages during the 1800s. Fortifications were constructed on Bradleys Head for Britain's struggle against Russia in the Crimean War and on South Head and Middle Head about the time of the Civil War in America in the 1860s. In 1871, the headlands were declared reserve. Fortifications were strengthened and modernised at South Head during the first World War and the second World War. The historical fortifications are now a feature of the national park.

The original proposal to return the harbour foreshores to the State of New South Wales can be dated by Lands Department records going back to 1928. But at that time it still made sense to have the headlands reserved for defence. Coastal guns were fired at a Japanese submarine off Sydney in 1942 during the second World War.

However, developments in the post-war era made the defence arrangements at North and South Head seem rather archaic. A few guns pointing hopefully out to sea seemed rather an anachronism in an era of atomic bombs and supersonic jet fighters. In fact, the main role of the military proved to be its defence of the foreshores from the developers who might otherwise have got hold of the land. Although the armed services were often criticised for their occupancy during peacetime, conservationists have every reason to be grateful to them. Most of the area they occupied was left looking much as it did when the First Fleet sailed into Sydney Harbour.

The Sydney Harbour National Park evolved slowly as part of a general movement by the New South Wales Government, which began buying foreshore land through the State Planning Authority in 1965. In 1968, the National Trust suggested the establishment of a Sydney Harbour National Park. In 1969, Tom Lewis, who was then Minister for Lands, announced a master plan for the harbour: the Commonwealth would sell its harbour lands to the State Government, and, in return, the State would sell the Commonwealth land at Holsworthy and at Beecroft Peninsula near Nowra.

However, legal and other complications held up the birth of the national park for several more years. The Sydney Harbour National Park was finally gazetted on 4 April, 1975. This park comprised about 73 hectares of State-owned foreshores and Clarke and Shark islands. About 21 hectares (Nielsen Park) were added in 1978.

The official designation of the Sydney Harbour National Park finally took place in April 1979, to coincide with the one-hundredth anniversary of the founding of the Royal National Park, south of Sydney. The official transfer of the headlands from the Commonwealth to the State also began in 1979 — ten years after the idea had first been revived, and fifty years after it had been first suggested.

In 1979, five parcels of land were handed over for inclusion in the Sydney Harbour National Park. They were 157 hectares at North Head, 6 hectares at South Head, 13 hectares at Georges Heights, 38 hectares at Middle Head and 38 hectares at Dobroyd Head. Further transfers of land were expected at that time to eventually bring the total size of the park to 463 hectares.

The Federal Minister for Administration Services, Mr McLeay, said at the time that the remainder of the Sydney Harbour defence lands would be handed back progressively to the State Government as Commonwealth authorities transferred military and other establishments. But he expected it might be some years before the quarantine station, the artillery school, and the police academy on

North Head were available for transfer. Not included in the land handed over for Sydney Harbour National Park was the Garden Island Naval Base and a large area at Bantry Bay, formerly used by the State Government Lands Department as an explosives storage depot. Access to the various parts of the park at present is by car, foot, and boat. Perhaps, in the future, a ferry service will enable people to visit the widely separated areas on the one day.

Pockets of typical sandstone vegetation manage to exist on the exposed headlands. The barren soil supports a surprisingly hardy vegetation, stunted by the salt sea winds, while in the protected gullies of Dobroyd Head and Bradleys Head, miniature forests have developed. Despite the poor soil, the various areas of the park are surprisingly rich in flowering plants and shrubs. Besides bottle-brush, she-oaks, and wattle, there are a number of species of spider flowers and yellow pea flowers. Needlebrush, tea trees, irises, trigger plants, and native orchids can also be found.

There is also a great deal of introduced vegetation such as coral trees, and less welcome plants classed as weeds such as lantana, kikuyu grass, crofton weed, and morning glory. The larger marsupials, such as kangaroos and wallabies, have long since disappeared, but there are still a number of possums and marsupial mice as well as fruit bats and gliders, and a number of snakes and lizards. Birds include honeyeaters, wattle birds, ravens, white-faced herons, the albatross, fork-tailed swifts, white-breasted sea eagles, pied currawongs, silver gulls, cormorants, brown scrub wrens and kookaburras.

The littoral zone has oysters, periwinkles, limpets, chitons, tubeworms, barnacles, cunjevoi, kelp, sea lettuce and hormosira. Aboriginal rock engravings on sandstone and Aboriginal middens still exist on the foreshores of the park.

SHARK ATTACKS

In 1975, skindivers reported finding large holes in the 50 m net guarding Parsley Bay, Vaucluse. The harbour is still full of sharks and many people swim in areas that are not even netted. Nevertheless Sydney remained relatively free of shark attacks between 1963 and 1980.

In January 1963 a young actress, Marcia Hathaway, bathing in shallow water, was attacked in Sugarloaf Bay in Middle Harbour. Her fiance fought the shark with his bare hands as it twisted in the bloodstained water, but the girl died in twenty minutes from terrible injuries and shock. The shark had almost torn off her right leg.

Two skindivers had a lucky escape in 1972 when swimming in deep water off Waverton Park in Berrys Bay, when a 3-m tiger shark mauled them both savagely. One diver had his arm ripped open and the other had a piece taken out of his leg. It seems that the most dangerous place for sharks is Marineland at Manly where divers feeding sharks and turtles in the exhibition tank have been attacked on a number of occasions, although to date all have escaped with only minor injuries.

ROSE BAY

Ansett Sunderland flying boats ceased flying from Rose Bay in 1974. The old hangar was taken apart and re-erected at Tamworth, and the whole area was then returned to parkland. Ansett Airways had taken over the base in 1953, flying to Hobart, Grafton, Southport, Brisbane, the Barrier Reef, and Cairns. In 1955, it was Australia's main international airport with seaplanes flying to London. But by the time it closed in 1974, it was only serving Lord Howe Island.

In 1978, David Hooker began a Cessna float plane charter service and operated scenic flights from Rose Bay. The company, Water Wings, flies as far as Forster in the north, and Batemans Bay in the south. It used the Point Piper marina as a base while waiting for its own dock to be built. Company employees and volunteer pilots undertake rescue work for the Seaplane Operation Search (SOS).

Rose Bay has two restaurants that take special advantage of the harbour. Flanagan's Afloat Restaurant is located on a specially built boat moored at the corner of Lyne Park and New South Head Road, while the Doyle family has a fish restaurant on the Rose Bay pier with beautiful views of the harbour.

In 1971 the Royal Prince Alfred Yacht Club's Rowe Street property was sold and an arrangement was made with the Sydney Club to accept the total membership of the "Alfreds" as yachting members of the Sydney Club, thus maintaining a meeting place for yachtsmen in Rowe Street. The sale of the Rowe Street property allowed the Pittwater premises to be developed considerably. In 1980, the Royal Prince Alfred Yacht Club has a total membership of 1850 members and 616 yachts on the register.

SHARK ISLAND

Shark Island is now part of the Sydney Harbour National Park. It has gently rolling grass slopes and can accommodate up to 500 picknickers, although a maximum of fifteen people per group is imposed. There is a pleasant foreshore walk, a number of majestic pine trees, and a gazebo at the top of the island. Parties must book into Shark Island and pay a fee not less than one week in advance.

DOUBLE BAY

Resisting all attempts at metrication, the New South Wales 18-ft Sailing Club Ltd has retained its title and still has its headquarters at Bay Street, Double Bay. The other 18-ft club is not at Balmain, but at Kirribilli. The boats are sailed by a three-man crew who all swing off the boats on trapeze wires. Sail area is unlimited and can easily exceed 4000 sq m.

CLARKE ISLAND

Clarke Island is slightly smaller and more rugged than Shark Island, the other Sydney Harbour National Park island. There has been extensive landscaping carried out with native plants by the landscape architect, Bruce Mackenzie. Both islands have water and toilet facilities. Gas barbecues are permitted. Access to both of them is by chartered ferries or private craft which can be tied up at the wharf. Small boats with outboard motors suitable for families can be hired from the nearby marina at Lavender Bay.

Anybody can visit Clarke Island provided the number in any party is not more than fifteen. The hours are from 9 a.m. to 5 p.m. No fee is charged.

RUSHCUTTERS BAY

In 1979, it was announced that a 0.59-hectare area occupied by the Rushcutters Bay Naval Reserve was to be transferred from the Commonwealth to the State Government. The area accommodated a slipway, a naval research laboratory, the Command sailing pool, and the RAN Sailing Association. the land was to be transferred immediately and leased back, at nominal rental, to the Commonwealth, pending relocation of the naval facilities. A lease of the area occupied by these facilities was to be granted to the RAN Sailing Association when the Commonwealth lease was terminated.

The stadium which once saw world heavyweight boxing championships was demolished to make way for the Eastern Suburbs Railway during the early 1970s. (The Eastern Suburbs Railway, which opened in 1979, took 100 years from the first plans for it to the opening, but that's another story). The last boxing promotion took place at the stadium on 9 June, 1970. The large sea-bathing pool on the eastern shore mentioned by Stephensen has also been removed.

The Cruising Yacht Club of Australia was founded in 1945, the year of the first Sydney to Hobart race. The club still organises this annual event which always starts on Boxing Day in Sydney Harbour. The race has established itself as one of three of the world's ocean racing classics and covers a distance of 630 nautical miles.

The Southern Cross Cup is a biennial event held during the same year as the Admiral's Cup in England. The series comprises two thirty nautical mile offshore races, a 180 nautical mile race and, finally, the Sydney to Hobart yacht race. The series attracts a large number of overseas competitors and, in recent years, the Cruising Yacht Club of Australia has conducted a race for maxi yachts. In 1979, John Kahlbetzer's 23.2-m maxi yacht, *Bumblebee 4*, won the coveted title "Cock o' the World".

Another famous race conducted by the Cruising Yacht Club is the Sydney to Nouméa yacht race, the first Australian international race to be held. This biennial event held in association with the Cercle Nautique Caledonien in Nouméa covers a distance of 1944 km. A record for the race was set by the famous ocean racing yacht, *Helsal*, in 1977.

As an indication of the importance placed on this race, the French Navy provides an escort vessel for the fleet, and the French Air Force, aerial cover. In 1979, Sydney was treated to a "French Week" by the French Chamber of Commerce during the week preceding the race, while in Nouméa the Australian Trade Commission held an "Australian Week".

313

4

ELIZABETH BAY

Elizabeth Bay House is now run by the State Government. It was opened to the public for the first time in March 1977.

NAVAL HEADQUARTERS

A modern tower block rises above one of the more unusual items listed in the register of the National Estate — a gazebo in the grounds of HMAS *Kuttabul* at Potts Point. The modern glass and concrete structure throws into contrast the splendid masonry of the gazebo, and the fantasy of another era. The National Trust describes the gazebo, situated on a rock ledge overlooking Garden Island and the harbour, as neo-classic in style. Two open bay windows have wrought iron grilles with stone seats below. A carved frieze decorates the entrance doorway leading inside to an area with a floor of patterned black and white marble and shallow-domed stone roof. It is believed to have been built around 1850.

GARDEN ISLAND NAVAL DEPOT

In 1979, the Department of Defence proposed taking over much of Woolloomooloo Bay for a $180-million scheme to modernise the Garden Island Naval Base. The Minister for Planning and Environment, Mr Paul Landa, felt that Garden Island should be given back to the State for open space. But as a navy spokesman pointed out, a move to Jervis Bay would cost anywhere up to $2 billion.

Dr Geoff Mosley, Director of the Australian Conservation Foundation, also pointed out that Jervis Bay was still a predominantly unspoiled natural coastal environment — a valuable nature reserve and scenic landscape. Because of this, he stated it was too valuable a resource for the establishment of a naval base at Jervis Bay even to be considered.

Landscape architect, Allan Correy, claims that the warships and waterside industry of Garden Island add contrast and variety in visual terms to the harbour landscape, in that Navy Day displays in Woolloomooloo Bay have become a vital part of the Sydney social scene.

WOOLLOOMOOLOO BAY

Woolloomooloo has seen some changes since 1965 when a third of the passengers entering Sydney Harbour came through the Woolloomooloo terminal. The advent of the jumbo jet has reduced the number of passenger ships visiting Sydney Harbour to a few cruise ships and Woolloomooloo is used as a passenger terminal only occasionally.

On shore, Tilly Devine, the mink-coated bejewelled "Queen of the Loo", died at Concord Repatriation Hospital in 1975. But the Loo she knew — the centre of the Sydney sly-grog trade — had already vanished. At the Tradesman's Arms in Palmer Street there were smoothly tailored young men drinking at the bar once famous as a haunt of standover men.

Woolloomooloo in 1980 was in a rather battered state. The Eastern Suburbs Railway's elevated line had carved a route through its old terrace houses. Elsewhere, boarded-up buildings and spray-can slogans remained as evidence of the war that raged in the 1970s between developers and those opposed to them.

In 1969, the State Government's plan saw the area as an extension of the central business district. In 1972, a developer, Sid Londish, announced plans for "a city within a city" which would become one of the "show places of Sydney". The proposals included complexes of office buildings, shopping centres, tourist facilities, hotels, motels, transport terminals and entertainment facilities. The plans were never realised.

Residents, conservation groups and the communist-led Builders Labourers Federation joined together to oppose the developers with "green bans" and protest rallies as they did in the Victoria Street district up the hill at Kings Cross. In 1975, most of Woolloomooloo was re-zoned from high rise to residential. This finally torpedoed the Londish project. Those facing large losses from the cancellation of the project included, ironically, the Moscow Narodny Bank.

The New South Wales Housing Commission resumed parts of Woolloomooloo from the developers in 1975 and set about re-designing the lower part of the suburb as a residential area. During the 1970s the population of Woolloomooloo had dwindled to fewer than 500. The Housing Commission plans envisaged a new Woolloomooloo with 770 homes accommodating 3 000 people in new or rehabilitated houses.

Meanwhile the Sydney City Council negotiated an agreement with the Maritime Services Board to open public access to Woolloomooloo Bay beside the wharves.

FISH OF SYDNEY

The Australian Museum's study of fishes in Sydney Harbour, directed by Dr John Paxton, the Curator of Fishes at the museum, ran from 1971-76. As very little work had previously been done on fishes in the harbour, it was a very significant study. About 550 species of fishes were taken. This total is more than the number of all the known fish species in the waters of the United Kingdom or Europe. Included in the total are eighteen species new to science and a number of these have yet to be described or named.

It is illegal to gather shellfish from Sydney Harbour. However, the authorities have found it difficult to police the regulations, and migrant groups in particular spend their weekends gathering shellfish. One of the problems is that nobody has jurisdiction over the inter-tidal zone. In any case, eating oysters which pump in large amounts of Sydney Harbour water each day is not recommended for health reasons. No oysters are grown commercially in the harbour.

In 1978 there was a major scare over the "Sydney rock oysters" grown commercially in the adjacent Hawkesbury and Georges rivers, when several people became sick after eating them. The oysters are now treated in purifying plants.

5

THE BOTANIC GARDENS

In 1978, the Australian Heritage Commission gazetted the garden gates and a number of the buildings and statues of the Royal Botanic Gardens and National Herbarium. In general, the gardens have changed very little since 1965. One striking new feature is the large pyramid-shaped glasshouse built in the early 1970s, while in the late 1970s the kiosk burned down and had to be rebuilt. Other new features of the gardens include educational beds to cater for school visits. The beds illustrate plant classification, plant growth forms, economic plants such as vegetables etc, characteristic species of major plant communities and Australian Aboriginal food plants.

The location of the gardens has proved rather restricting to the work of the botanists employed there, with the result that, in the late 1960s, the gardens acquired a magnificent site for a mountain annexe at Mount Tomah in the Blue Mountains.

THE DOMAIN

An integral part of the Domain is the popular Andrew (Boy) Charlton pool. In 1963 the Maritime Services Board accepted the City Council's offer to rebuild the old Domain Baths — the cradle of Australian swimming. The old baths were demolished and the new pool, constructed in 1966, was called after the swimmer who had made the Domain Baths famous — Andrew "Boy" Charlton (1908-75). The Domain Baths were opened in October 1908 — on the site of the old George Farmer's Baths and Robinson's Hot and Cold Sea Water Baths — the largest and finest of their kind in Australia.

All-time greats who made swimming history there included the Cavills, Alick Wickham (pioneer of the Australian crawl stroke), Fred Lane (Australia's first Olympic champion at Paris in 1900), Harold Hardwick, Billy Longworth, Frank Beaurepaire, Barney Kieran, "Boy" Charlton, Arne Borg (Sweden) and the Hawaiian Duke Kahanamoku.

When the site was first used for swimming over 100 years ago, the long limbs of the huge Moreton Bay fig trees provided natural springboards for the divers. Men bathed in the nude at first but, as swimming gained popularity, they wore trunks. Segregation for the women was ensured by the hulk *Ben Bolt* which was moored between the two baths. Its decks were divided into cubicles and the deck house fitted for serving coffee, biscuits, brandy snaps and Chester cakes. A galvanised iron roof was installed over the women's baths, to "give the ladies protection from the lascivious eyes of the males". Many squatters visiting Sydney first went to the Domain Baths to cool off and wash away the dust. Even horses were taken to the baths for swimming exercises.

When the famous old Natatorium in Pitt Street was closed at the turn of the century, and Dave Pike had ceased to pump water from Woolloomooloo Bay, it was natural that the attention of the swimming stars should turn to the Domain Baths. One of the brightest was Barney Kieran who joined the training ship *Sabraon*, not for disciplinary purposes but to learn carpentry. In 1904-05 he was acknowledged the greatest swimmer in the world.

Alick Wickham swam what was then the 100 yards breaststroke in 1 min 17 4/5 sec there to set a new world record. At the Domain Baths his underwater swimming, amazing diving and feats with a water polo ball were legendary. Old-time boxing champions, West Indian Peter Jackson, Cornishman Bob Fitzsimmons and Australia's own Albert "Griffo" Griffiths, of The Rocks, were regular customers at the baths. Women who swam there on special occasions included Fanny Durack, Annette Kellerman, Mina Wylie and Bonnie Mealing — all winners of swimming fame.

Bobbie Pearce, Olympic sculling champion, broke tradition with a sculling exhibition in the baths. Eyewitnesses said in awed tones that he pulled just once at the sculls and was at the other end of the pool. The Norddeutscher Lloyd steamer *Elsass*, in her haste to put to sea when the first World War broke out, crashed bows foremost into the baths, the damage not being paid for until nine years later. In 1926 a giant stingray occupied the pool for several days.

The early baths were demolished in 1907 to make way for the new. That wonderful day in January 1924, when Andrew "Boy" Charlton, of Manly, beat Swedish star Arne Borg, will be forever remembered. Charlton's youth — he was only sixteen — coupled with his modesty, had made him the public swimming idol. Although Borg swam desperately Charlton won by almost 20 m. The officials announced to the hushed, expectant crowd that Charlton's time was 5 min 11 4/5 sec, equalling Arne Borg's world record. The applause was deafening and people in city streets a kilometre away guessed who had won.

THE SYDNEY OPERA HOUSE

The Sydney Opera House, perhaps the only Australian building known outside Australia, may well be the twentieth century's finest piece of architectural sculpture. It may well be also the biggest architectural adventure of our times, for the design with which Joern Utzon won that competition long ago in 1957 needed roof vaults for the building so big and difficult in shape that there were serious doubts in engineering circles as to whether they could be built at all. In the end, the roofs were built only after collaboration between architect, structural consultant, and general contractor, a collaboration in which existing technology was stretched to its limits.

Today the result stands in all its glittering splendour on Bennelong Point — the Sydney Opera House, a complex of theatres for the performing arts, congresses and exhibitions which can contain   317 about 7 000 spectators, artists, staff, and diners at one time.

The Opera House, open for public use in 1973 after sixteen years of planning and fourteen of building, remains, in its appearance, unique. The outline of the roof shells soon became a new Australian symbol abroad and the building became one of the biggest single tourist attractions within Australia. Over 180 000 visitors go on guided tours each year.

Most importantly, the Opera House is a tremendous addition to the whole cultural life of Australia. And it is not just "culture" with a capital C. Artists as diverse in their interests as Joan Sutherland and John Denver have sung there. The name "Opera House" is, in fact, rather inappropriate. It is true that opera seasons are presented there, but the Opera House also presents performances of orchestral and chamber music, ballet, drama, choral works, jazz, pop, and folk concerts, recitals, films, and variety shows. Each of the halls is fitted with facilities for conventions.

The huge complex contains nearly 1000 rooms, ranging from the majestic concert hall down to a humble concrete chamber in which stands simply one piece of machinery.

There are four architectural elements in the Opera House — a podium, or base, with an area of about 1.82 hectares, and three sets of roof shells; one set of four shells, placed on top of the western side of the podium, covering the roof and the walls of the concert hall; another set of four shells on the eastern side of the podium covering the opera theatre; and a third set consisting of two much smaller shells housing the main Bennelong restaurant; other halls and operating areas lie within the podium.

The highest point of the podium is about 20 m above mean sea level, and the tip of the biggest shell above mean sea level (about the height of a twenty-two storey office building) is 66 m — almost 9 m higher than the centre of the roadway of the Sydney Harbour Bridge.

The building had its genesis in 1957 when a set of architectural sketches by Joern Utzon, a young thirty-eight-year-old Danish architect, won an international competition for an opera house promoted by the Government of New South Wales. Utzon was commissioned to develop his plans and supervise the construction of the building. Ove Arup and Partners of London were appointed as structural consultants. During the building, the ribs were covered with the famous white tiles which give the Opera House its waterproof exterior skin, all tiles being imported from Sweden where they were made at Utzon's request.

The last pre-cast segment of the roof system was lowered into place on 17 January 1967, three years and two months after roof construction started. In the meantime, a most dramatic event had occurred. Joern Utzon, creator of the Opera House, had resigned on 28 February 1966 and the State Government had appointed a team of four Australian architects: the Government architect, E. H. Farmer, Peter Hall, Lionel Todd, and David Littlemore, who completed the huge, daunting building.

This stage of the building of the Sydney Opera House offered many extremely difficult constructional problems. The laying of about 10 000 slabs of paving and cladding went ahead virtually as

Utzon had planned it; these were concrete slabs veneered with reconstituted granite quarried at Tarana in the Blue Mountains; they were steadily laid until 1973. But otherwise the early days of this period were a time of nerve-testing changes in planning.

For one thing, Hall, Todd, and Littlemore realised that there was no hope of achieving Utzon's dream of a principal auditorium which would be acoustically excellent for both symphony music and opera. In their 'Review of Programme' approved by State Cabinet in 1967, Hall, Todd and Littlemore announced a plan to turn the principal auditorium into a straight concert hall, which later involved removing the stage tower, the proscenium arch and the machinery beneath the stage. In this machinery space a large rehearsal/recording studio, the recording hall, was built and there were other changes of function in other parts of the building as well.

It has been said that the Sydney Opera House is the most accurately constructed building ever erected. Engineering mathematics and their handmaiden, the computer, played an essential role. The plywood ceiling panels in the concert hall and opera theatre had to be fabricated in a great variety of sizes and shapes. A computer was programmed and it printed out the exact dimensions of each panel. The panels were then prefabricated to the stated sizes, hoisted and attached to hangers suspended from the concrete. For this, the erection crews used a traditional but very large birdcage scaffolding.

The glass walls presented the same worries, but on an even larger scale. The northernmost and southernmost shells of the three roof systems of the Opera House were enclosed with glass, in what must surely be the most complicated glazing job ever undertaken in Australia. There is more than 0.5 hectares of laminated glass in the Opera House, almost all of which arrived from France by sea in wooden crates. However, the glazing was not completed without its nervous moments; with glass costing $1 500 a blank pane, nobody wanted to drop any. The total breakage during wall erection was two panes.

The first performance in the Opera House, presented in the Opera Theatre on 28 September 1973, was the Australian Opera Company's production of Prokofiev's 'War and Peace'. The complex was officially opened by Her Majesty Queen Elizabeth II in the presence of HRH the Duke of Edinburgh, on 20 October 1973.

The Opera House cost $102 million to build. An appeal fund raised about $900 000 of this cost and the remainder was raised from the profits of the Opera House lottery. The final payment for the complex was made in January 1974.

The Australian artist, John Coburn, was commissioned by the New South Wales Government in November 1969 to design tapestry stage curtains. Made from Australian wool, the curtains were dyed and woven by Pinton Frères, of Felletin, near Aubusson in France. The Curtain of the Sun in the opera theatre is 8 m high and 16 m wide. Its abstract shapes, dominated by an heraldic sun, represent the elements of fire, earth, air and water. It is made predominantly in reds, yellows, pinks, and browns. Gold thread is interwoven with yellow wool to emphasise the featured sun.

319

The Curtain of the Moon in the drama theatre is 5 m high and 20 m wide. Featuring a crescent moon and abstract shapes which represent plant forms, its predominating colours are green, blue and brown. The crescent moon is woven in off-white wool and silver thread.

The new grand organ was designed and built by Sydney-born Ronald Sharp. He was assisted by a small personal staff and, during the final months of construction, by the Austrian organ-building firm of Gregor Hradetzky. The instrument was built under the supervision of the New South Wales Department of Public Works, with construction costs amounting to $1.2 million. The organ was officially handed over to the trust by the Deputy Premier and Minister for Public Works, Mr Jack Ferguson, on 31 May 1979, and the first recital was given a week later on 7 June by Australian organist, Douglas Lawrence.

Various national schools of organ-building have influenced the design of the Opera House organ, including French, Italian and north German. It has five manuals and pedal and contains approximately 10 500 pipes, of which 109 are visible from the auditorium. There are 205 ranks of pipes grouped into 127 speaking stops, with twenty-eight couplers, the front showpipes being of 95 percent tin, 5 percent lead and burnished to a mirror-like finish. There is a glockenspiel of seventy-three bronze hand bells, twenty-four of which are visible, and a carillon of twenty-four small bronze hand bells. The tympanon operates a soft bass drum roll and there is an imitation cuckoo and a nightingale.

6

SYDNEY COVE

The view from the water in Sydney Cove has been changed dramatically by the building boom of the late 1960s and 1970s. Until the 1960s the AWA tower, built in 1939, was the tallest structure in Sydney, and was a feature of tourist postcards.

Now it is hard to believe that the twenty-nine-storey AMP building, only 114 m high, completed in 1961, was the tallest building in Sydney in the early 1960s. Goldfields House went up to balance it at the other end of Alfred Street facing Circular Quay in 1967. Meanwhile, the 73-m IBM building in Kent Street with its distinctive sun hoods joined them in 1964. Further back from the water, but dominating the city skyline as viewed from the harbour, Harry Seidler's much-admired circular building, Australia Square tower (170 m), was begun in 1961 and completed in 1968. It, in turn, was passed by two new buildings completed in the 1970s. The new 198-m AMP centre in Bridge Street was completed in 1976, and Harry Seidler's 244-m MLC centre opened on 12 September 1978. Centrepoint, also constructed for the AMP Society, passed the MLC centre in 1978 and kept on climbing to its final height of 304.8 m, opening in 1980.

In 1978, one of the world's leading professional journals, London's *Architectural Review,* produced an issue devoted to Australian cities and buildings. The two editors, who spent five weeks looking at buildings in Australia, were ecstatic about the unique style of Sydney's architecture, and paid tribute not only to internationally known architects like Harry Seidler and John Andrews, but also mentioned lesser known local architects such as McConnel, Smith and Johnson, Don Gazzard, Phillip Cox and Ancher, Mortlock and Woolley. They wrote:

Sydney is superb, an exhilarating conjunction of sea, landscape and buildings with nature and master sculptor. Its centre, a silhouette of gleaming office towers, rises Cavilia-like from the blue waters of the finest harbour in the world — mini New York but in a far more glamorous setting. Its image is unforgettable — created by the great arc of the Sydney Harbour Bridge rising behind the delicate glistening shells of Utzon's Opera House. Seemingly afloat, the latter is a sight to make the spirits soar — a triumph inside and out . . .

SEMI-CIRCULAR QUAY

In 1979, work began on a Sydney City Council scheme to decorate and landscape Circular Quay at a cost of $2.4 million. The scheme included planting trees and installing lighting and outdoor seating. Plans for a nineteen-level building overlooking Circular Quay and the Royal Botanic Gardens, containing twenty-five home units, were announced in 1979. This spectacular project involved demolishing an old paper store to construct a $3-million building virtually two doors from the Opera House on Circular Quay East. The building was designed to be the same height as the adjoining Unilever House. The top eight floors were to have one unit each, while others were to have two units each; the bottom two were for parking. The building was also to have a rooftop swimming pool, sauna and barbecue area. Living on a shore of the cove near where the British flag was unfurled in 1788, residents would have views of the Harbour Bridge and The Rocks on one side, and the Royal Botanic Gardens on the other.

THE FERRIES

Government ferries are available for charter and many organisations hire them for picnics, dances, and moonlight cruises. There are regular harbour cruises every Wednesday, Saturday, and Sunday.

As well, a number of private companies operate on the harbour, with one company even catering for wedding parties. Captain Cook Cruises operates from Circular Quay and offers a coffee cruise and a lunch cruise; Australian Cruising Services operates the *Bennelong* from Rushcutters Bay and also offers lunch cruises; and the *John Cadman* offers a four-hour dinner cruise. In addition, many small boats are available for hire at a number of places around the harbour.

In 1980, there were ferries running to Manly and Taronga Zoo, and to the various wharves around Neutral Bay, Milsons Point, Cremorne, Greenwich, Balmain and Hunters Hill areas. In addition, there were weekend cruises up Parramatta River as far as Ryde Bridge and also up the Lane Cove River and Middle Harbour.

An attempt by Stannard Brothers Launch Services to operate services to Meadowbank and Rose Bay in the 1960s failed through lack of patronage and there was an understandable reluctance to revive "historical" services to places such as Clifton Gardens and up the Parramatta River where a tram once met ferry passengers at Redbank near Silverwater Bridge.

When looking at a map of Sydney Harbour the logic of ferry travel seems obvious. However, despite the fact that it has become fashionable to want other people to travel by public transport, the logic of ferry travel still escapes most motorists and the Government still loses money on its ferry service. However, the soaring oil prices and petrol shortages predicted for the 1980s may change all that.

Writing in the early 1960s, P. R. Stephensen was forecasting that "a time must come when the fleet of coal-burning, oil-burning, double-ended steamers will become obsolete to be replaced perhaps by hydrofoil craft or hovercraft or by motor driven speeders or by helicopters or by more bridges across the harbour or by tunnels beneath it". Some of these predictions have come true. There is now a helicopter pad at Darling Harbour, although helicopters have not replaced the ferries. Nor has anybody yet built a tunnel or another bridge, although both have been suggested at various times. There are, however, hydrofoils.

The first hydrofoil, the seventy-two-seat *Manly*, was introduced in January 1965, but it was soon replaced by larger hydrofoils carrying up to 140 people. The new hydrofoils are more expensive to travel on than the ferries but they can cover the 11 km between Manly and Circular Quay in fifteen minutes, against thirty-five minutes taken by the old ferries. By 1980 there were five hydrofoils on the harbour.

There were still fifteen ferries in service in 1980, but most of them belonged to the new, smaller "Lady" class era, ushered in by the *Lady Cutler* in 1968. The *Baragoola*, built in 1922, was scheduled for replacement in 1981 by a new $8.5-million 1100-passenger ferry designed to cut the crossing time from thirty-three minutes on average to twenty-two minutes. The 1268-passenger *North Head*, built in 1913, was still on the run in 1980 but obviously its days were numbered.

The last coal-fired ferry, the SS *Balgowlah*, made its final trip back on 27 February 1951. One by one most of the other old ferries have also travelled into oblivion. The *Curl Curl* was taken out of service in 1961 and in 1969 it was taken out of Sydney Harbour, where the plug was unceremoniously pulled to send her to the bottom. Her sister ship, the *Dee Why*, came off the run in 1968 and went to a deep sea grave to make an extension of Long Reef in 1976, and in 1971 the *Lady Chelmsford*, aged sixty-one, sailed to Adelaide to become a floating restaurant, making the 1600-km voyage without incident.

The *South Steyne* was launched at Leith in Scotland in 1938. At that time it was the biggest and fastest ferry in the world, 1227 tonnes gross and able to carry nearly 1800 passengers. Fire seriously damaged it after what proved to be its final public trip on 23 August 1974. The owners, the Port Jackson and Manly Steamship Company

Ltd, decided it was not economic to restore it, so it was then bought by a private interest. Next it was bought by a group of enthusiasts who formed the Save the *South Steyne* Preservation Society which aimed at restoring the old queen of the ferries, and in 1976 the National Trust gave it an A1 classification — the first such classification to be given a boat by the National Trust. The ferry was then acquired by the South Steyne Steamship Club Ltd.

In 1980 both young and old ferries gathered for Sydney's first official Great Ferry Boat Race. Line honours went to the younger *Lady Woodward* with the elderly *Kanangra* in second place.

7

THE ROCKS

No part of the Sydney Harbour foreshore reflects the change in attitude towards Sydney's historical buildings since 1965 as much as The Rocks. P.R. Stephensen lamented that "it is proposed that in the late 1960s whatever then remains of the old-style buildings in the vicinity will be demolished and replaced by a gigantic planned development Tower of Babel architecture in which tiers of apartments serried in glass, steel, and concrete honeycombs will once again make The Rocks a high density residential district as it was in those early years when it was a crowded dockside slum".

Fortunately, the plan was never put into effect. In the 1960s and 1970s Sydney began to change its attitude to old buildings. As a result, many of the historical buildings of The Rocks were saved from demolition and restored. Many of them are now used as arts and crafts shops and as restaurants, and the whole Rocks area is a popular tourist centre, with the old historic buildings as its main attraction.

In 1966, Sir John Overall, of the Commonwealth Government Development Commission, at the request of the New South Wales Government, considered The Rocks area at Sydney Cove and recommended that an authority be set up to revitalise that area. Following his report, in December 1969, the State Government announced the establishment of the Sydney Cove Redevelopment Authority. Former army brigadier, Owen Magee, was appointed as director and also acted as deputy chairman of the authority. He was an army engineer, and had worked on loan on many civil projects, including the Snowy Mountains Hydro-Electric Authority.

Plans for the $5-million Sydney Cove Redevelopment Scheme were released in February 1971. The authority had also proceeded to purchase the 1 hectare which it did not already own. This brought the area to its present size of 25 hectares. The authority went through a difficult period in gaining vacant possession of many buildings which had virtually been a haven for many merchants, one disputed example concerned the lease of 3 000 sq m for a total sum of $3.96 a year, the incumbent of which fought an unsuccessful court case to try to maintain his right to stay there at that price.

The plan of the authority from the very beginning was two-pronged. It planned redevelopment, either in conjunction with others or by itself, and it also planned the restoration of all worthwhile and historical buildings in the area. The "green bans", led by communist activist Jack Mundey, of the Builders Labourers Federation, meant deferment of the redevelopment section of the scheme, and managed to put the total project almost two years behind schedule, but the authority maintains the bans did not in any way cause it to place any greater emphasis on the original priorities of restoration.

CIRCULAR QUAY WEST

The twelve-storey Housing Commission apartments aroused a storm of controversy when they rose above the Harbour Bridge road level in 1979. They were built to house people displaced by the re-development of The Rocks, offering low income earners million-dollar harbour views for $20 to $30 rents. The controversy, however, was not about the rents but the aesthetics of the building itself, which occupied such a prominent position.

In 1979, the Premier, Mr Neville Wran, announced plans for a new thirty-storey international hotel with 600 rooms to be built near Circular Quay in George Street near Harrington Street and the Cahill Expressway. Building was expected to take three years and to cost $40 million.

DAWES POINT

Bligh House in Lower Fort Street, Dawes Point, is worth mentioning here. This Georgian mansion, built in 1833, is the only remaining major townhouse from the colonial period still remaining in the city. The Royal Australian College of General Practitioners has used the house for offices since 1961.

The Rocks is now used appropriately as the main centre for the Australia Day celebrations in January. A salute is fired by the army from guns at Dawes Point.

FORT PHILLIP

The National Trust took over the old Fort Street Girls School and opened the S.H. Ervin Museum and Art Gallery in 1978.

Richmond Villa, originally built behind Parliament House, and for many years a residence for Country Party members of parliament, has been reconstructed on a site in Kent Street, adjacent to the National Trust headquarters. Built in 1849, it was designed by the Colonial Architect, Mortimer Lewis, as his own residence. It is now the home of the Society of Genealogists. It was moved to the Rocks site to make way for the new Parliament House extensions overlooking the Domain.

SYDNEY OBSERVATORY

The Sydney Observatory continues to drop its time ball — although almost from the beginning it has been dropped at 1 p.m., and not at noon, as P.R. Stephensen's original text said.

WALSH BAY

In 1979, the Maritime Services Board accepted a tender for a restaurant and shopping complex to be built at the picturesque Walsh Bay's Number One wharf, one of the many built between 1907 and 1920, offering a fine view of the harbour. The Rocks had taken a further step towards the eventual aim of creating a centre to rival San Francisco's famous Fishermen's Wharf area.

SAILORS' TAVERNS

A number of old pubs in the area around The Rocks have been restored, including the Orient and the Australian Steam Navigation Hotel.

There are two hotels in The Rocks that have rival claims to being the oldest hotel in Sydney. The Hero of Waterloo occupies the oldest building, being built as a soldiers' garrison in 1796. The name was changed from the Little Princess to The Hero of Waterloo to commemorate the famous battle. The Lord Nelson, built as a house in 1834, claims to be the oldest hotel in Sydney because it holds the oldest licence — beating the Hero of Waterloo by a few months in this respect. It was established as a hotel on 6 June, 1842.

THE ARGYLE CUT

For many people, the focal point of the The Rocks is now the Argyle Arts Centre, where pottery and other craft shops are housed in the old Argyle Stores, built in 1829. It was here that Mary Reiby (1777-1855), a former convict, ran her various businesses, accompanied by her servant, a giant Fijian woman named Feefoo.

The McMahon family leased the stores about 1926, and Sam McMahon, brother of the former Prime Minister, Sir William McMahon, converted the cellar into a restaurant in the late 1960s. With its pioneer style, with people sitting at long wooden benches and singing convict songs, the Argyle Cellars became the first of many unique restaurants established in The Rocks. The brisk trade enjoyed by all of these restaurants is indicative of the appeal of The Rocks to the general public. The rest of the Argyle Stores has been converted into an arts centre which opened in 1970.

THE MARITIME SERVICES BOARD

There are many claimants for having the best view of Sydney Harbour. But nobody could have a better view, in fact, than the operators looking out over the shipping in Sydney Harbour from the Port Operations and Communications Centre at Millers Point. The odd-shaped tower that they work in, completed in August 1974, rises 87 m above sea level, and from the centre, operators have a view of the critical waterways outside the marked channels, and most of the port's commercial wharves.

The centre is manned round the clock, throughout the year. Each watch is under the control of a port operations officer — a qualified master mariner who is assisted by two communications attendants. It is the port operations officer who controls the port traffic management system, maintaining constant watch on vessel movements and giving approval for ships to enter the port or leave a berth.

The purpose of the centre is to see that shipping movements take place safely and efficiently. It keeps watch over the port area so that prompt action can be taken to deal with incidents such as oil spillages, smoke pollution, fires on wharves or ships breaking adrift in high winds, and so on. It provides information required by pilots and ship masters for safe navigation inside port limits, giving traffic information, the state of the tide and weather forecasts.

One of the less pleasant tasks performed by the Maritime Services Board is cleaning up the rubbish people drop in the harbour. Six boats are employed full-time in this job. Among the 6000 tonnes of rubbish removed from the harbour each year are paper cups, tree cuttings, dead dogs and cats, and even the odd dead kangaroo. People can be fined up to $400 for dumping refuse in the harbour but catching offenders is difficult.

Even stiffer penalties — up to $50 000 — can be imposed for oil spillage (up to thirty minor oil leakages occur each year). The biggest oil spill to have occurred to date was in 1973, when between 350 tonnes and 700 tonnes of oil leaked from the British Petroleum tanks at Berrys Bay. Another bad spill occurred in 1977, when about 10 tonnes of oil spilled over Sydney Harbour from Mort Bay to the Heads after a British tanker released oil while it was discharging at Ballast Point in Mort Bay. The company concerned was fined $10 000.

GEORGE STREET NORTH

The Morgue moved to new premises in Glebe in 1971, and the building was taken over by The Rocks Visitors Centre.

The main Seamen's Mission building, the Rawson Institute, named after a former Governor of New South Wales, was opened in 1909. It was built around the original chapel designed by the architect, John Bipp, in 1857 for the religious group, the Sydney Bethel Union. The chapel, which still forms part of the building, became the Seamen's Chapel.

Also adjacent to the Visitors Centre is another interesting old structure erected by the Australian Steamship Navigation Company. A large solid brick establishment, it is to be re-established as a craft centre.

One of the most famous pubs in the area, Jim Buckley's Newcastle in George Street, was demolished in the 1970s. It was once the gathering place for Germaine Greer and other members of the group of libertarians and Sydney University lecturers known as The Push.

In 1979 the Governor's Pleasure Tavern complex opened. A special "Newcastle Bar" was set aside for Jim Buckley to hold court. The tavern complex occupies one end of the historic Campbell's storehouse, restored at a cost of over $1 million. Restoration had to be extensive because the building is so close to the sea. As there was no damp course, the lower levels were constantly damp, causing much of the sandstone to deteriorate. The technique used to overcome the problems was a sophistication of the original method used in the Temple of Dawn in Thailand. Later in the same year The Waterfront, a seafood restaurant, opened at the other end of the Campbell's storehouse, leaving the centre area available to house cultural activities.

Like so many buildings in The Rocks, Campbell's storehouse was a product of several building phases. The two lower storeys were built by the Campbell family from 1838 onward, while the upper storey was added around 1895.

Among the restaurants opened in The Rocks in the 1970s is the Old Spaghetti Factory in George Street North, a fun place for family lunch. The interior decorators have gone mad with old stained-glass windows, and have even installed an old Bondi tram. There is also a pancake house that never closes. Altogether, there are more than 2000 restaurant seats in The Rocks, employing nearly 400 people.

Another attraction for The Rocks was provided by the Department of Sport and Recreation, which opened a Hall of Champions at Sports House in Gloucester Street in 1979. The hall commemorates the achievements of the sporting champions of New South Wales. Another Government office — the State Archives — found an appropriate home in 1979 in Harrington Street in The Rocks behind a ninety-year-old stone archway off George Street North. The arch acts as an entrance to the Archives, which were designed and built by the Sydney Cove Redevelopment Authority.

The arch is the entrance to an old carriageway beside the former George Street North police station (1882-1976), itself erected on the site of the colony's first hospital, a canvas structure used between 1788 and 1816. This passage runs to the rear of the police station building, once the hospital gardens. Here, in front of the Archives office, the Sydney Cove Redevelopment Authority constructed a new pedestrian lane known as Nurses Walk. The walk connects Globe Street at the southern end of the block with Harrington Place and the Suez Canal passageway near the northern end. The Suez Canal, which runs beside Phillip's Foote restaurant, was known by that name in the *New South Wales Government Gazette* as early as 1860. The name is thought by Redevelopment Authority historians to derive from the days when stormwater drained down its slope into George Street (the Suez Canal, on which construction began in 1859, was big news in that period). The small plaza at the entrance has been named Surgeons Court.

A public right-of-way from the Suez Canal passageway across the rear yard of the restaurant leads to Greenway Lane and into Argyle Street. This restored lane is named after the convict architect Francis Greenway, who lived for some years in the Surgeons House on the corner of George and Argyle streets early last century.

These historic precincts surround the modern, $7-million Archives office below Harrington Street. The office is known as the building with the "wriggly roof" because its copper roofs have been staggered at different levels and its Harrington Street facade given five different designs to harmonise with the old terrace houses of The Rocks. The New South Wales Archives Authority packed its collection of priceless Australian historical records for transport to its new headquarters in 1978; it was formerly housed in the State

Library, Macquarie Street.

Even demolition in The Rocks area provided interesting finds. In 1979 the Sydney University archaeological dig near Essex Street was confirmed as the site of Sydney's first jail, built in 1797. The archaeologists discovered a convict leg-iron which contained the locking device and the link to which a chain would have been attached.

CADMAN'S COTTAGE

A good deal of additional information on Cadman's Cottage has become available since P.R. Stephensen's book first appeared in 1966. The cottage itself — the oldest dwelling still standing in the city of Sydney — has been restored by the Sydney Cove Redevelopment Authority.

The old house was in an advanced "state of decay" in 1966. The Sydney Sailors' Home, in whose trust it remained, had closed it off and surrounded it with a high corrugated iron fence. In 1971, plans were made to retain and restore the cottage on its original site as part of the Sydney Cove Redevelopment Scheme, and work on restoring the cottage began in October 1972. Tests made on samples of mortar from the upper and lower walls of the cottage backed up evidence from sketches that the central part of the cottage was originally built as a two-storeyed structure in 1815-16.

Woodwork throughout the building had to be replaced. The cottage was rebuilt internally, refloored, and rewindowed. External structures, including two wooden verandahs added over the years, were removed. The entire restoration cost more than $75 000. When the corrugated iron was removed from the roof, the original decayed shingles were uncovered and authentically replaced by the authority. Various layers of plaster were removed to show off the fine stone facade — chipped by masons at the time of Governor Macquarie under the supervision of the famous convict-architect Francis Greenway.

The cottage was declared an historic site under the control of the National Parks and Wildlife Service. With restoration completed, it was opened in October 1973.

A full account is published in an excellent booklet *The Coxswain's Barrack Known as Cadman's Cottage (The History of Sydney's Oldest Dwelling)* by J.S. Provis and K.A. Johnson, written to commemorate the restoration and opening of the cottage. Provis and Johnson had been commissioned to research the history of the cottage and contribute to the restoration.

Keith Johnson has kindly suggested the following corrections to Stephensen's original text: the cottage was most probably erected in 1816 rather than 1813; and it was the front door rather than the back which was "eight feet from the water's edge", as the cottage faced the water.

Johnson and Provis have this to say about the man who lived in the cottage:

John Cadman was arrested in Bewdley, in the County of Worcester, England, while leading a horse along the tow-path beside the River Severn. On the 11th March, 1797, he was tried at

Worcester on a charge of stealing a horse, was found guilty and sentenced to death; this was commuted to transportation for life to New South Wales. Together with 195 other male prisoners, he sailed from Portsmouth on the Barwell and arrived at Port Jackson on the 18th May, 1798.

John Cadman was an assistant coxswain before becoming superintendent of Government boats. He was seventy six, not seventy, when he retired in 1846. Stephensen says Cadman retired to the Hunter River district where he died, but Johnson says he went in fact to live at his Steampacket Hotel in George Street, Parramatta, and died there in 1848.

THE SYDNEY HARBOUR BRIDGE

In 1979, $11.8 milllion was still owing on the original loan. In theory, this amount could be paid off by 1995. But the bridge will probably never be fully paid off because toll payments go to pay for maintenance and improvements to the bridge and the construction of freeways around the bridge.

The construction of expressways and freeways at both ends of the bridge has speeded up traffic flow. The Cahill Expressway reached the Conservatorium in 1951, and was extended to Woolloomooloo in 1962; the first section of the Warringah Freeway on the north side opened in 1968; and extensions to Willoughby Road opened in 1978.

On the south-west side, the Western Distributor was still under construction in 1980. The first section over Darling Harbour was opened in 1980 and the rest was due for completion in 1983, but the project's final plan to replace the low level Glebe Island Bridge was not expected to become a reality before the year 2000.

In 1977 the Australian Heritage Commission listed the Sydney Harbour Bridge on the register of the National Estate. Meanwhile, proposals for a second harbour crossing continued to be made off and on as they had done for many years. Some people favoured another bridge, others urged the building of a tunnel. In 1978 Premier Neville Wran came out with yet another proposal for a $400-million harbour tunnel, but because of the long history of tunnel proposals nobody was holding his breath, for from as far back as 1896 plans for a tunnel under Sydney Harbour have been proposed, considered and rejected.

The *Sydney Mail* of 30 May 1896 published a full-page article including diagrams, describing proposals for a railway tunnel to be built at a cost of about £350 000 between King Street, City and Milsons Point. A separate tunnel for vehicles was to be built between Circular Quay and Milsons Point for about £250 000. The articles said the scheme, which was before the New South Wales Parliament, offered one solution to the pressing need for "a better means of passing vehicular traffic over or under the harbour than the present punt service affords".

In September 1954, the Labor member for Dulwich Hill, Mr H.C. Mallam, proposed a tunnel with two entrances in the city — one near the Haymarket and the other at the lower end of William Street — emerging on the North Shore near St Leonards Park. By November

1955, the Town and Country Planning Advisory Committee, which had been asked to investigate Mr Mallam's proposal, had rejected the idea as impracticable.

In May 1958, the State Government rejected a proposal from a Darling Point engineer, Mr D. R. Carter, for a prefabricated tunnel to lie on the harbour bed. The estimated cost of the project was £20 million, and the Government said the money would be better spent on arterial roads. In March 1960, the then Minister for Local Government, Mr Hills, rejected three schemes submitted by an international firm of civil engineers for a tunnel under the harbour.

In July 1964, Mr Askin, Leader of the Opposition, said that if the Liberal Party was elected it would start building a new bridge or a tunnel under the harbour in its first term. By July 1970 Mr Askin was Premier and was reported as saying that it seemed out of the question for the State Government to build another Sydney Harbour crossing because of financial circumstances. In March 1975, the then Minister for Transport and Highways, Mr Fife, rejected a proposal by the Australian Transport Study Group for a road-rail tunnel to be built from the Spit Bridge to the Cahill Expressway.

No route was suggested for the tunnel proposed in 1978 but southern approaches for the tunnel under Darlinghurst were mentioned. Many factors were expected to govern the choice of an exit on the north side, if the project did in fact ever go ahead.

Various sites have been suggested for the new crossing. In 1973 Maurice Neitous, a senior lecturer in Engineering at Sydney Technical College, designed a bridge that would have dwarfed the present bridge. He suggested a crossing between Mrs Macquarie Point on the south side of Farm Cove opposite the Opera House to Kirribilli Point.

8

WHARVES PUBLIC AND PRIVATE

Coal, wheat and sugar were already bulk-handled in 1966 when P.R. Stephensen's book first appeared. But, since then, container shipping has revolutionised the look of most of the large vessels sailing up Sydney Harbour.

While the container revolution was changing the appearance of the vessels on the water, the Maritime Services Board carried out an ambitious ten-year redevelopment plan that changed the look of the harbour itself. By the late 1970s, twenty-two new or reconstructed wharves had been brought into service. The scheme was virtually completed by 1980, although Number 3 berth in Darling Harbour was still under construction.

In Darling Harbour, the original area of water was reduced by about one quarter when the Maritime Services Board finally completed its redevelopment. The eastern side was aligned out to the end of the old wooden wharves, and south of the Pyrmont Bridge the scheme added to the large area reclaimed by the railways between the wars.

Around Balmain, hundreds of tonnes of rubble went into making long straight wharves and wide handling aprons for container ships. Glebe Island was resculpted and capped with silos and bulk-loading facilities. Along the northern side of Rozelle Bay the timber industry was given sizeable new installations. At the same time, the Maritime Services Board began working on plans to develop Botany Bay as a major port, complementary to Sydney, dealing mainly with the larger bulk cargoes. A new container terminal leased to Australian National Lines was opened at Port Botany in 1979.

Passengers continue to use terminals at Sydney Cove and Pyrmont, but they land at Woolloomooloo only occasionally. Under the ten-year plan, Woolloomooloo and Walsh Bay were set aside for general cargo and some bulk loads. Darling Harbour also handles general cargo, particularly heavier items.

Special facilities were built to handle roll-on, roll-off shipping. The Pyrmont foreshore was altered comparatively little, but areas of Glebe Island and White Bay were heavily rebuilt to take the new container terminals. People living in the area did not welcome the noise and potential danger introduced by the huge vehicles used to carry containers to and from the new terminals; in fact, in the early days of container operation, local residents pelted waterside workers' cars with rubbish and dead cats. The board responded by offering to buy out at previous values residents in areas affected by noise from the container wharves. Oddly enough, when the offers were accepted, the board generally ended up reselling the houses at a profit to people anxious to move into the area.

New timber-loading dolphins at Snails Bay were finished in the early years of the scheme. A number of private facilities, most notably the Australian National Line Terminal at Mort Bay, were enlarged; others, such as the CSR berth near Glebe Island Bridge, and the Caltex depot at Ballast Point, between Mort Bay and Snails Bay, continued much as they were.

Today, Sydney Harbour handles more than 2800 ships a year, about 31.7 million tonnes of cargo, with more than 80 000 passengers arriving and about the same number departing. The gross tonnage of ships using the harbour amounts to 35 million tonnes. About 16 km of commercial wharfage is available, most of it situated within 6 to 8 km of the sea and within 2 km of the heart of the city.

GLEBE ISLAND

In the late 1970s a number of groups began campaigns for more waterfront parks and greater public access to harbour foreshores in their areas. Prominent among them were the Glebe Society, the Annandale Association and the 4-Shores Committee.

The Glebe Society pointed out that Glebe, with a population of 14 000, had only 45 per cent of the minimum amount of open space regarded as desirable for urban areas. Of the 21.7 km of harbour foreshore between Sydney Harbour Bridge and Iron Cove Bridge, only 1.1 km was accessible to the public. Glebe had less than 80 m of accessible foreshore. The society wanted a series of waterfront parks linked by walkways — on the waterfront where possible — from Johnstons Canal to Pyrmont Bridge Road near Wentworth Park. The parks would have a total area of 1.6 hectares.

In 1979, the Annandale Association asked the Minister for Works, Mr Ferguson, to meet a delegation to discuss public access to foreshores controlled by the Maritime Services Board on Rozelle Bay at Annandale and Glebe. The association said Annandale, which had a population of 7787, had only 15.6 per cent of the minimum desirable amount of open space. The 4-Shores Committee wanted waterfront parks and walkways on the eastern side of Blackwattle Bay, Pyrmont, a waterfront park at the foot of Darling Harbour, Ultimo, and a waterfront walkway linking the new Blackwattle Bay Park, Glebe to Wentworth Park.

The 4-Shores Committee report supported the proposals of the Glebe Society and the Annandale Association. "The people of Annandale have no access to the Harbour foreshores in their suburb", their report said. "Their access is being blocked at present by the unnecessary and inefficient use of their foreshores by the Maritime Services Board".

Representatives of harbourside environmental groups met on 14 March 1979, and formed a committee called the Sydney Harbour Trust Steering Committee. Its brief was to investigate the need for a permanent group which could present a comprehensive plan for the harbour to the State Government, making the case for high priority to be given to the ecological and visual aspects of the harbour environment. Approximately twenty-five groups were involved.

On July 18, the steering committee reported to the membership, recommending that an organisation be formed to investigate and make submissions to the Federal and State Governments, on the many matters which were arising, such as public versus private use of the foreshores and bays, the boundaries of the Sydney Harbour National Park and other parks and reserves, expansion of the Garden Island naval complex, oil spills and their treatment, bushland regeneration, dredging and its effects, tree screens for waterfront industry, and so on. The Sydney Harbour and Foreshores Committee was formed, and in 1980 was developing policies while responding as much as possible on crises as they arose.

One of the many people interested in Sydney Harbour foreshores is landscape architect Allan Correy. Although he is a concerned conservationist, he takes the view that it is impossible to return all the foreshores to the condition that Captain Phillip saw. He also feels it is probably undesirable. For him, the interest of Sydney Harbour is in its variety and contrast — whether it is bushland, the Opera House, or boatbuilders' yards. Since he believes that neither landscape architects and conservationists nor companies and councils have any right to impose their wishes on the people, Allan has worked out a system to try to evaluate people's reactions to the harbourside environment and to assess how they feel about changes to the harbour foreshores.

On 9 October 1976, Sir James Cardinal Freeman, Catholic

Archbishop of Sydney, officially renamed the reserve bounded by Glebe Point and Federal roads and the foreshores of Blackwattle Bay, "Pope Paul VI Reserve". The reserve was previously known as Marine Reserve. The object of renaming the reserve was to commemorate the historic occasion when on Wednesday, 2 December 1970, Pope Paul VI was conveyed by the launch *Supply* across the harbour to Glebe Point; there the Holy Father alighted *en route* to the Royal Alexandra Hospital for Children, Camperdown.

BLACKWATTLE BAY

In 1978 residents battled against a plan to build units at Blackwattle Bay. The owners, Parkes Development Pty Ltd and Burns Philp and Company Ltd, wanted to build 105 units. Residents wanted the foreshore land preserved for public use and said that a 100-m-wide strip along the 160-m water-frontage set aside for this purpose was not enough. The result was a compromise. The developers gave up some of the land in return for permission to build the block of units higher.

PEACOCK POINT

One of the first areas of industrial foreshore land to be turned into public parkland is the area now known as Illoura Reserve. Considered by some to be a conscience-salving exercise by the Maritime Services Board for the development of the container terminal in Balmain, it is, nevertheless, a valuable piece of waterside open space. It is also a good example of the current trend of establishing native vegetation around the harbour.

SIMMONS POINT

Not far from Peacock Point, on the north-western end of the Balmain Peninsula, is another recently developed foreshore park. Although small in area and not easily accessible, it is a very important park for local residents. It gives visitors some interesting and unexpected views across to Goat Island.

9

GOAT ISLAND

Nobody — except a caretaker — lives on Goat Island anymore, but the island is still used for boat building and maintenance by the Maritime Services Board.

BALMAIN PENINSULA

Balmain has changed since 1965. Many writers, journalists, artists, architects and so on have moved into this traditionally workingclass suburb. Dramatist David Williamson, novelist Frank Moorehouse, radio personality Bob Hudson and many others have moved to Balmain which has acquired a "trendy" image. A lot of the old houses have been renovated, thereby changing the spirit of the suburb and giving it a charm of a different kind.

The newcomers have been concerned about "the environment", with the result that one of the most interesting proposals put to the State Government in the late 1970s came from the 4-Shore Committee, asking the Government to purchase or transfer from the Maritime Services Board, vacant and derelict harbourfront land to provide greater public access to the foreshores between the Sydney Harbour Bridge and the Iron Cove Bridge. They wanted a waterfront park on Blackwattle Bay and a waterfront park on Rozelle Bay, and suggested building a waterfront walkway between these two parks and a series of parks linked by waterfront walkways on Mort Bay, Darling Harbour and Johnstons Bay. They also asked for a buffer zone park at White Bay. They urged the Government to plan for the future public use of the ANL terminal at Mort Bay and the Caltex oil depot on Ballast Point, and pointed out that of the 21.7 km of foreshore between the Sydney Harbour Bridge and the Iron Cove Bridge only 1.1 km was public open space.

Land formerly used for waterfront industrial purposes was either vacant or derelict in the late 1970s and the group felt this offered a unique opportunity for the Government to return some of this land to the people — otherwise, they said, the land would be built on and the public would be excluded from it forever. The cost was estimated at about $1.2 million.

Part of the Dickson Primer site which the group wanted the Government to acquire included the stone mansion Ewenton, built in the 1850s, a building that was in a state of disrepair despite its National Trust listing. The building dates back to 1854 when a Georgian stone mansion, Blake Vale, was constructed but was sold in 1856 to Ewan Wallace Cameron (who changed the name to Ewenton), as part of a choice property fronting Jubilee Bay, with uninterrupted water views and absolute water access. The property changed hands in 1886 and from 1911 to 1951 was owned by the Swan family (both father and son holding at different times the position of Mayor of Balmain). In 1951, Ewenton and its grounds, together with the Wallscourt Lodge site, became the property of Dickson Primer. Wallscourt Lodge was demolished and Ewenton became derelict.

In 1978 the Australian Heritage Commission gazetted a number of foreshore areas in the Callan Park Conservation Area. The commission included in the National Estate the Thames Street ferry wharf and shelter at the foot of Thames Street, Balmain, on the shore of Mort Bay

BALMAIN AQUATIC SPORTS

The Dawn Fraser Swimming Pool at Elkington Park used to be called the Elkington Park Baths until the name was changed in 1964 to honour the famous swimmer, who was born in Balmain. Dawn Fraser won three successive gold medals in the woman's 100-m freestyle race at the Olympic Games. She won this event in the games held in Melbourne in 1956, in Rome in 1960, and in Tokyo in 1964. She is now the licensee of the mock-Tudor Riverview Hotel in Birchgrove Road, Balmain — just a few doors from where she was born, and not far from the pool which is now named after her. The pool itself is the oldest in the harbour, dating back to 1881. Admittance used to be 2d per adult bather; youths were charged 1d.

In 1980 the Liechhardt Council engineers had further proposals for the old baths. They wanted to demolish them and return the area to being a natural harbourside beach.

Elkington Park was named after Albert Elkington, who was Mayor of the Borough of Balmain in 1880.

LONG NOSE POINT

One of the best examples of the current policy of returning harbour foreshores to the public is at Long Nose Point, Birchgrove. The site was formerly owned by Morrison and Sinclair Pty Ltd, who built there a range of fine wooden ships, including many Sydney Harbour ferries as well as trading vessels and yachts. The site was acquired by the State Planning Authority in 1972, and the landscape design was prepared by Bruce Mackenzie Associates. An attempt has been made to use, as far as possible, only plant material which is indigenous to the area.

COCKATOO ISLAND

In 1978, the Australian Heritage Committee gazetted a number of buildings on Cockatoo Island. They included Biloela House, the prison barracks, and underground grain silos on the island.

IRON COVE

Rodd Island, in Iron Cove, is Crown land administered by a private trust. There was a certain amount of controversy in July 1975, when some publicity was given to the fact that the trust had granted a ten-year lease to a private company which, in turn, was charging $250 a day to hire the island.

A Lands Department official rushed into print the next day to assure Sydneysiders that there was nothing to stop members of the public from landing on the island. However, if they used facilities for which there was a fee, they might have to pay. The island has a large hall and an enterprising theatrical company staged a production of Treasure Island on Rodd Island as part of the City of Sydney Festival in 1977.

On Rodd Point, in Iron Cove, a large stone cross marks the original mausoleum of the Rodd family of Drummoyne. The family was buried in a mausoleum carved out of a huge rock on the point, and the cross was cut from a single piece of sandstone by convicts. It was removed to Rookwood Cemetery in 1903, but was returned to its original site in 1975 by Five Dock Rotary Club.

IO

DRUMMOYNE

A feature of the waterfront is Drummoyne Olympic Pool, originally cut out of solid rock about 1904, with a concrete wall built on the bayside with valves to let the harbour water in. Extensions were made about ten years later, but the transition from a tidal pool to today's full Olympic Pool was gradual, the pool not being finally complete until 1957.

Drummoyne Council began a programme of erecting historical markers around its municipality in the late 1970s. It decided to put a metal plaque to mark the site of Drummoyne House after which the suburb was named. William Wright's mansion itself had gone under developers' hammers to make way for a block of white-brick units. The remains of Wright's steps, the river landing point for Drummoyne House, still survive and the council decided to mark them with a plaque.

The council also decided to mark some of the other historic places and houses of the district. One of the most interesting marks Five Docks: "The original five natural crevices (two of which remain) situated on this headland were known as the Five Docks from which the suburban name was derived". Yet another records Abbotsford House, Abbotsford Bay, the home of Sir Arthur Renwick, medical practitioner, politician, administrator, and philanthropist. This fine building has been carefully restored and is now the office of the Nestle Company (Australia) Ltd.

Perhaps the most elegant building of the district is Erina House, in Erina Street, Five Dock. This was the home built by Peter Faucett (1814-94), an outstanding legal and political figure of early Sydney. Born in Dublin, Faucett arrived in Sydney in 1852 and was New South Wales Solicitor-General from 1863-65. Erina House originally was surrounded by a vineyard.

BIRKENHEAD POINT

On the waterfront north of Iron Cove Bridge, DJ's Properties Ltd has restored the old Dunlop rubber factory at Birkenhead Point as a shopping and marina centre.

The Birkenhead shopping complex began trading on 26 July 1979, providing a major retail market, open shopping malls, specialty shops, restaurants and a tavern. The marina in Iron Cove provides facilities for more than 375 craft. Plans for the complex included a car museum, a fishing museum, and one of the largest maritime museums in the world.

The model for Birkenhead Point was San Francisco's Cannery where old buildings were also stripped back, cleaned up, replumbed, and replanned with plazas, malls, trees, pot plants, and outdoor seats. In giving Birkenhead Point's Dunlop factory the same treatment, the architects Jackson, Teece, Chesterman and Willis removed the shoddiness and applied litres of refreshing paint over the old iron roofs, balconies, and windows. They re-used buildings with enormous timber columns and hefty beams, replacing damaged sections where appropriate. There was no real cost saving by keeping the old buildings, but they did represent an economy because these recycled spaces have high ceilings and cute details that could not be easily — or cheaply — reconstructed.

Perhaps the most exciting part of the Birkenhead project is that it combines the shopping complex with a maritime museum. The Sydney Cove Maritime Museum had been the dream of a dedicated group of nautical enthusiasts since 1965. DJ's Properties Ltd enabled the dream to come true when it formed a joint company with the Sydney Cove Maritime Museum, offering it a ninety-nine year lease in return for a 12 per cent return on invested funds. The commercial arrangement gave the museum a permanent home and provided the capital needed to develop the wharf and shore buildings.

The centrepiece of the museum, the square-rigged barque *James Craig*, was built in 1870. It was raised from Recherche Bay in southern Tasmania in 1973, and towed to Hobart, where it underwent a $1-million restoration and was prepared for towing to Sydney.

The museum also owns a number of other vessels. They include the old VIP steam yacht, *Lady Hopetoun*, which was handed over by the Maritime Services Board in 1965. The only remaining vessel of her kind in the world, the *Lady Hopetoun* is fully restored, and can be seen steaming around the harbour on most weekends. The *Lady Hopetoun* was built in 1902, and seven years earlier, in 1895, another of the the museum's relics — the steam tug *Waratah* — left the slipway of her builder in England and sailed to Australia under her own power.

The *John Oxley*, another, was built in Scotland in 1927, and served as a pilot vessel, maintaining navigational buoys along the Queensland coast until 1968. It served with the RAN during the second World War and is one of the last remaining examples of coastal steamers in Australia.

The museum has several smaller vessels, among them the *Swan*, which was built around 1894 and is said to have the oldest petrol marine engine in the world. The *Swan* was used for missionary work on inland rivers. Another vessel, the little ferry *Wenonah*, was built in 1912 and was used on the Mosman run. A steam-powered launch called the *Sundowner*, built along vintage lines by a member of the museum a few years ago, a rowing skiff made in 1900, and an old speedboat called the *Kookaburra*, plus an old "18-footer", the *Yendys*, are also owned by the museum.

In preparation for the opening of the museum, 300 volunteers worked to restore the ships at a temporary dry dock at the old ash hoppers at Blackwattle Bay where barges used to be filled with ash from the Pyrmont Power Station for dumping at sea. Most of the $1.2 million needed to establish the museum complex was provided by DJ's Properties Ltd, but $100 000 was raised each year by the museum through art unions.

In addition to the old ships it has restored, the museum has working models of ships, old pieces of equipment from the days of sail, paintings, and other artifacts. A replica of the bottom end of Sydney's Pitt Street with ships' chandlers, ships, and so on, was designed to show visitors what this part of Sydney looked like at the turn of the century. The museum built its own boilers to enable it to power steam vessels without their leaving their moorings, to allow people to see the pistons rotating and machinery going.

THE GLADESVILLE BRIDGE

In 1979 the Gladesville Bridge was outstripped as the world's longest concrete arch bridge by a 390-m bridge in Yugoslavia, which is 90 m longer.

II

MORTLAKE

The gas industry has changed dramatically since 1965. During the 1970s the Australian Gas Light Company obtained a substantial holding in North Shore Gas and planned to merge it into its company during the 1980s, leaving only one gas company serving Sydney.

Meanwhile, the coming of natural gas during the 1970s led to a technical revolution. The old "60-milers" hauling coal from Newcastle to Sydney were no longer needed. One by one the old gasometers around Sydney Harbour were either demolished or scheduled for eventual demolition. Plans were drawn up in the late 1970s to redevelop the Australian Gas Light Company's property on the harbour at Mortlake. Under the new scheme, the old gasometers and retorts were to be demolished.

The company ceased making gas from coal and oil at Mortlake in December 1976, when natural gas arrived in Sydney. Natural gas is piped from Moomba, in Central Australia, through an 86-cm-diameter main. The pressure is reduced at the outskirts of the metropolitan area and the gas is reticulated throughout Sydney. A considerable percentage of this natural gas is brought to Mortlake and distributed from there.

THE RYDE BRIDGES

A $10-million five-span railway bridge, opened in 1980 over the Parramatta River at Meadowbank, replaced the existing rail bridge built in 1886. Work first began on this bridge in 1947. At that time it was proposed to build two parallel double-track bridges. When work on this project was halted during the 1954 financial recession, the piers and northern abutment were almost completed for the first of these bridges.

In 1975, when work on the bridge was resumed Public Transport Commission design engineers were faced with the problem of utilising the piers built over two decades ago. Their solution was to modify the piers and abutment to accommodate four rail tracks.

12

THE ABATTOIRS

In 1968 the Homebush abattoir and saleyards became the largest meat complex of its kind in the world. The metropolitan Meat Industry Board was replaced by the Homebush Abattoir Corporation in 1979, with meat processing facilities available to satisfy the metropolitan demand for fresh, clean, quality meat. Homebush holds licences to export anywhere in the world, and it is so highly regarded overseas that it is the first inspection point for all meat-industry observers visiting Australia.

With 15 hectares of concreted saleyards, the abattoir can handle 4000 head of cattle, 35 000 sheep and lambs, and 3500 calves and pigs daily. The by-products derived from non-edible offal at Homebush contribute over $A1 million annually, with over 4000 tonnes of tallow being derived from offal and fat trimmings to meet ready local and overseas markets. One of the main sources of protein in the stock feeds manufactured' at Homebush is meat trimmings and blood and bone. Fertiliser, too, is made from blood and bone. Waste material is no longer put into the metropolitan sewerage system, as it once was.

Homebush leads Australia in the size of its meat refrigeration storages. It has three beef chiller rooms, each with 700-carcass capacity, two lamb carcass chillers, each of 7000 capacity, and a combined pork (3000) and veal (600) capacity. It has over 10 000 tonnes cold storage capacity, and blast freezers each capable of handling 132 tonnes a day complement the output of the boning rooms which service the demands of the pre-packaged meat trade. About 3000 people work there.

During the 1970s investigations were carried out by the State Government to find a site suitable for development as a major international sports centre capable of providing facilities for holding the Olympic Games. Areas under investigation were the Homebush Bay and Silverwater regions. However, as Homebush Bay is a significant wetland area for water birds, environmental conflicts have arisen. In 1978, a student study at Macquarie University suggested a compromise solution and proposed a bicentennial park for Sydney at Homebush Bay, including both recreation and wildlife areas. A proposal from the report, supported by Concord, Auburn, and Strathfield councils, is for parkland adjacent to the wetlands to be incorporated with the preserved wetlands into a bicentennial park to be opened in 1988.

RYDALMERE AND DUNDAS

One of the more unusual items named by the Australian Heritage Commission in 1977 was an old boatshed in the grounds of the Rydalmere Hospital. It was built around 1930 on the site of an earlier boatshed. The boatshed was not listed for itself but because it formed part of the Female Orphan School which the Commission was anxious to see preserved. The precinct was named after its original use which was as a school for female orphans. The foundation stone was laid by Macquarie in 1813 and the building, now part of Rydalmere Hospital, was completed in 1818. The Reverend Samuel Marsden was treasurer of the orphan fund before and during construction and actively supervised the work. Other parts of the precinct to be listed include the former chief attendant's cottage, the dispensary (once a mortuary), and the hostel which is now a ward. The architect is unknown.

THE MERINO PIONEERS

The Elizabeth Farm Trust was formed in 1968. Its aim was to restore Elizabeth Farm House with the help of New South Wales State Government funds.

MODERN PARRAMATTA

In 1977, there was a row between the Australian Heritage Commission and the National Trust on the one hand, and Parramatta Council on the other, over the building of an amphitheatre beside Old Government House in Parramatta Park. The National Trust said that archaeological evidence of Australia's first settlers had been lost forever because of earthworks undertaken to prepare the amphitheatre. The park is the site where Governor Phillip landed from the Parramatta River to establish the settlement of Parramatta on 2 November 1788, and the area selected for the amphitheatre was the place where Australia's first successful wheat farm had been established in 1789.

In an attempt to prevent such conflicts in future, a Plan of Management was prepared by consultants for the whole of Parramatta Park.

PARRAMATTA RIVER

In 1976 the National Trust commissioned an environmental study of the entire Parramatta River. This study identified siginificant landscape values and also suggested guidelines for management which have been taken up by several of the local municipalities along the river.

One of the big success stories of Sydney in the 1970s was the way pollution in the Parramatta River was brought under control. Storms can still cause sewers to overflow there, as in other parts of the harbour, but in general the improvement has been dramatic.

In the 1950s it was already evident that industrial growth was causing serious pollution of the Parramatta River. The Clean Waters Act of 1970 was introduced to reduce and prevent pollution of all New South Wales waters. In the Parramatta River it was found that the most significant pollution was caused by discharges of organic compounds and oily residues into the river by two large organisations — the Shell refinery one and the Petroleum and Chemical Corporation (PACCAL) the other. Both companies discharged their wastes close to the meeting place of the Duck River and the Parramatta River at Silverwater.

The problems arising from the two largest discharges were solved in different ways. Shell constructed a recirculating freshwater system with biological treatment facilities to provide cooling. Polluted process wastes were diverted into the sewers and all discharges to the river ceased. This was accomplished at a cost of $5 million in a plant commissioned in 1975. PACCAL's establishment was eventually abandoned for a number of economic reasons, not the least being the cost of proper air and water pollution control. All discharges ceased in 1975 and the site has since been cleared.

As an indication of the reduction in pollution levels from industry as a result of the Clean Waters Act, and policing by the State Pollution Control Commission, Dr John Paxton, of the Australian Museum, who made a study of fish in the harbour between 1971 and 1976, said, "In 1971, not a single species of fish was taken in Duck River, and only two freshwater species (both dead) were found below the weir at Parramatta. By 1976, twelve species of fishes had returned to this part of the upper Parramatta River and are now present in reasonable numbers". The result was not quite as dramatic as the sixty species which have returned to the Thames over about a ten-year period, but it was a step in the right direction.

13

THE MUNICIPALITY OF RYDE

The Ryde Council protested to the Minister for the Environment in 1979 when the navy bought 1.5 hectares of land from Lars Halvorsen Pty Ltd for craft repair facilities. The council had wanted the land for foreshore park extensions.

HUNTERS HILL

The Hunters Hill Peninsula was declared a conservation area by the Australian Heritage Commission in 1978. The municipality is so rich in historic houses that the Hunters Hill Trust has published a whole book giving details of the beautiful old homes in this harbourside area.

Built in 1866 and enlarged in 1902, the Town Hall was one of the oldest and best known in the greater Sydney region. It was further altered in 1937 and 1967 to add a council chamber and historical museum. The building was destroyed by fire on Sunday morning, 8 January 1978; the rebuilding of the Town Hall and Civic Centre was completed early in 1980. The entire front wall of the building, containing the original 1866 stone-gabled entrance, has been repaired and retained as the focal point of the structure. An unusual architectural feature is that the capping stones on the original pediment actually slope outwards towards the street.

In 1978, Hunters Hill Council began planting trees and developing Clarkes Point at the western point of Sydney Harbour as a park. The waterfront reserve is at the mouths of the Parramatta and Lane Cove rivers. It commands superb views of the Sydney Harbour Bridge and the Sydney skyline.

The site, covering 3.5 hectares, was formerly part of the industrial land owned by the old Morts Dock and Engineering Company. After lengthy legal proceedings the site was resumed in 1973 by the State Government for open space. In 1976 it was vested in the council for use as a public park. It adjoins the old spectacular dry dock hewn out of sandstone by the Morts Dock Company in the last century, which is now occupied by the Army's .35 Water Transport Squadron.

In the late 1960s and early 1970s residents battled developers for foreshore land in an area of Hunters Hill called Kellys Bush. Part of an early grant to John Clarke, Kellys Bush derives its name from T.H. Kelly who owned the land (about 8 hectares) between Woolwich Road and the Parramatta River in 1892, when a smelting works was first established on the foreshore. Apart from some slag deposits, the bush was allowed to remain in its natural state as a buffer between the industrial site and the residential area on top of the hill.

When the County of Cumberland Planning Scheme was introduced in 1951, the land was zoned waterfront industrial (about 2 hectares) and living area (about 0.5 hectares) with the remainder (about 7 hectares) reserved for open space purposes. In 1956, the Hunters Hill Council, assisted by the then Cumberland County Council, purchased from the Sydney Smelting Company almost 4 hectares of the "reserved" land and named it Weil Park. In 1966, the council unsuccessfully asked the State Planning Authority to acquire the remainder of the "reserved" land as open space.

The Smelting Company moved its industrial activity to another suburb, and in May 1968, A.V. Jennings Industries (Australia) Ltd, which held a conditional contract, made application to the council to build 147 home units, including three buildings, each eight storeys high. The council opposed the development and once more asked the State Government to buy the whole area for parkland.

Finally, in 1976, the State Government bought about 2 hectares of the land and the developers kept 3 hectares. Barely a week after the revival of the Kellys Bush story, Hunters Hill again made headlines over the discovery by the Health Commission of high level radiation in Nelson Parade and in the old smelting works. In 1980, Kellys Bush Foreshore Reserve on the site of the old smelting works had still not been landscaped by the developers as promised under their agreement with the Government. There were several reasons for this. First, the Builders Labourers Federation "green ban" was still in force, preventing the developers from building on their land. Secondly, the discovery of radioactive material created doubts about the advisability of using the land for building or recreation unless radioactive soil was first removed.

The Hunters Hill Historical Society has made the following observations on the original text:

The present text infers that Hunters Hill was described as "the French Village" because some influential early citizens endeavoured to recreate a "village in the spirit of Watteau's pastoral paintings". This seems incorrect. Jules Joubert, one of the earliest major developers in the district, purchased land and built houses there solely as an astute business speculation. In fact, in his *Shavings and Scrapes from Many Parts* he states, "I made up my mind to settle down. In order to do so I looked about for some land having a prospective value".

It was called the "French Village" because some of its leading citizens were French: for instance, Jules and Didier Numa Joubert, Count Gabriel de Milhau, Louis Francois Sentis, the Consul for France, as well as some of the French Marist priests who built a school and church there; these particular people also had an impact on the community.

There is no proof that the ship *Otter* had been sent from America by George Washington to rescue Muir. It would be more correct, if a reference has to be made to the rumour, to state "...the *Otter*, which some sources (without any reliable evidence) believe had been sent from America to rescue him".

Governor Hunter, in his despatch of 30 April 1796, mentions that "an America ship named the *Otter,* commanded by Ebenezer Dorr and belonging to Boston, carried off several people for whose embarkation he had not obtained permission and amongst the number, Mr. Thomas Muir".

The origin of the name "Lane Cove" given here is debatable. It is more likely, but only likely, that it was so named by Governor Phillip in the early days of the colony in honour of his great friend, John Lane, a well-to-do London merchant. However, there is no proof whatsoever as to the correct origin of the name "Lane Cove".

The following paragraph is misleading: "In 1847, Jules Joubert had persuaded his brother Didier and the Count de Milhau to immigrate to Sydney, bringing with them funds for investment. Instead of investing in pastoral property, they bought land and built houses for sale at Hunter's Hill". Actually, de Milhau had no reason to come to Australia in 1847, as he was not exiled from France until 1848. He then went to England where he formed a partnership with another Frenchman, Chauffert, and a Swiss, Etienne Bordier-Rowan, for the purpose of migrating to New South Wales and arrived here in 1849. In 1850, they took over a property, Ramornie, on the Clarence River. In 1852, because of the lack of labour following the discovery of gold, they disposed of Ramornie and de Milhau eventually purchased land at Hunters Hill. (This information comes from two articles in the *Daily Examiner* (Grafton) for August 1965, written by Dennis Rowe of the Clarence River Historical Society). Joubert may have influenced de Milhau to go to Hunters Hill after 1862, but not in 1847 as Stephensen says. He did not even influence his brother to come as Didier was here two years before Jules's arrival in 1839. The following sentence needs clarification: "They *(Jules and Didier Joubert and de Milhau)* brought forty stonemasons from Italy". Jules Joubert did bring out a number of tradesmen. In *Shavings and Scrapes from Many Parts* he states: "I sent home to Lombardy for some artisans under special contract". A few lines on he writes, "... when my operations at Hunter's Hill came to an end the assistance of these seventy odd tradesmen enabled me to take contracts in an around Sydney for large buildings, wharves, etc." The paragraph commencing "The Lunatic Asylum that had been established in the 1820s at Bedlam Point" ... seems incorrect. The following extract from the *Journal of the Royal Australian Historical Society* (vol xxxi, No. 6, 1945, pp. 396-7), is more likely correct: "Bedlam Point — This point was not named after the mental hospital which is adjacent. In 1820, James Squire warned the public against trespassing his property, 'as such Farms and Lands', the notice continued, 'are well known ... being situate from Mr. Glade's Bethlem Point'. In passing, it might be noted that a large mental hospital in England was originally called Bethlehem Hospital and this was corrupted to Bedlam Hospital. One W.C. Dyer wrote a letter in May, 1822, and stated that he lived at 'Bedlam'. It was stated in 1827 that the 'house occupied by the Signal Man at Bedlam is in a very dilapidated state'. In the Itinerary of Roads in 1834, the following description occurs: '9½ miles from Sydney — On the right, Bedlam, a lunatic asylum, now deserted and in ruins. There is a signal staff here named the Bedlam Telegraph ...'

"Despite this statement however, there is no evidence that an asylum existed at this point prior to the erection of a building in 1837-38 which was used as a mental hospital. In 1810, Governor Macquarie converted a building at Castle Hill into an asylum, and it was used for this purpose until 1827 or 1828, when the patients were removed to Liverpool. It is probable that the writer of the Itinerary referred to above concluded that the old building used by the signal man had been an asylum."

The Geographical Names Board of New South Wales, in a letter to an enquirer dated 18 May 1978, also uses the arguments set out in the Royal Australian Historical Society's journal.

The Anglican chapel built in Church Street in 1857 was known as the "Old Chapel" or "All Saints Chapel" or the "Fig Tree Chapel", but not as "St Marks' " until 1962 when it was moved stone by stone to Fig Tree Road.

The old Gladesville Bridge was opened in 1881, not 1884. The states: "The Gladesville Bridge. The Bridge over the Parramatta River between Five Dock and Gladesville was opened for public traffic on Tuesday, February 1 by Mr. Bennett, Commissioner and Engineer-in-Chief for Roads". The Iron Cove Bridge was opened in 1882.

INDEX

346